CHRISTIAN ECONOMIC ETHICS

CHRISTIAN ECONOMIC ETHICS

HISTORY AND IMPLICATIONS

DANIEL K. FINN

To Fiona —
a co-worker in the vineyard

Fortress Press
Minneapolis

CHRISTIAN ECONOMIC ETHICS

History and Implications

Cover image © iStockphoto.com / tomograf

Cover design: Justin Korhonen

Library of Congress Cataloging-in-Publication Data

Print ISBN: 978-0-8006-9961-1

eBook ISBN: 978-1-4514-5228-0

The paper used in this publication meets the minimum requirements of American National Standard for Information Sciences — Permanence of Paper for Printed Library Materials, ANSI Z329.48-1984.

Manufactured in the U.S.A.

This book was produced using PressBooks.com, and PDF rendering was done by PrinceXML.

To Paul Caron,
Polymath and Friend

CONTENTS

Part V. Coming to Conclusions

Acknowledgments

In writing this book, I have incurred significant debts to many people who have helped me improve both the substance and presentation of the ideas included here. Colleagues who have attended exceptionally carefully to the manuscript and have provided extensive critical advice include Sylvester Theisen, Patrick Henry, David Cloutier, Albino Barrera, O.P., Mary Hirschfeld, Thomas Massaro, S.J., and Andrew Yuengert. I am indebted to many who took time from their days to provide careful advice on particular parts of the book, including Brian Matz, Jon Gunnemann, Joseph Friedrich, John Erb, Christine Firer Hinze, James Childs, Karen Bloomquist, and Bronwen McShea.

My colleagues in the economics department at the College of St. Benedict and St. John's University provided helpful feedback on Chapter 13. The theologians at New Wine, New Wineskins provided really helpful input on several chapters. And numerous colleagues at the Society of Christian Ethics, the Catholic Theological Society of America, and the Association for Social Economics have improved my thinking about the issues underlying this book over the past three and a half decades. I have likewise been assisted over the years by a number of able and generous student research assistants at St. John's, including James Foley, Tylor Klein, Natalie Landwehr, Richard DeVine, Shafak Samsheer, and Adam Liske.

I am particularly grateful for the generous help of editors at Fortress Press, particularly Will Bergkamp, Esther Diley, Lisa Gruenisen, and Marissa Wold.

I am deeply grateful to St. John's University, where, since 1977, I have been a member of the Department of Economics, the Department of Theology, and the School of Theology, and where since 1984 I have held the William E. and Virginia Clemens Chair in Economics and the Liberal Arts. Many people at St. John's and St. Ben's have helped me in a myriad of ways over the years. Of all those who contributed directly or indirectly to this book, I owe the greatest debt of gratitude to Judy Shank, who has painstakingly typed and made a multitude of changes—and changes of the changes—in each page of this book. Her patience and care have made this final version possible.

PART I

Introduction

Introduction: Well Water Deep Down

It's easier to see what we are already expecting.

They have an undying
tremor and draw,
like well water far down.[1]

In the poem "Out of This World," the Irish poet Seamus Heaney describes a man who has lost his faith as a Christian but whose heart still resonates when he recalls the words *host* and *thanksgiving* and *communion bread*. Even after years of absence from any church, he finds that these "have an undying tremor and draw, like well water far down."

Few citizens of the industrialized world think much about well water, as most get their water from a large water-distribution system. Even if the system originally drew that water from a well, the liquid has typically been filtered, treated with chlorine to kill bacteria and fluoride to improve health, and has flowed through miles of pipes to get to the end user. The tap at the kitchen sink has a sort of technological predictability about it, and that drink of water on a hot day occurs at a great psychic distance from any well.

But those of us who depend on the well in the yard for that gulp of refreshment on a steamy July afternoon think about wells more frequently—and differently. The well is not only a necessity of life, but depending on the geology of the area it often bears a significant fragility, as it can fail to produce that life-giving liquid when it's overused or if the drought lasts long enough. There's an increased connection to that water lying far below ground, partly because it is so far down there—inaccessible to eye and ear but compelling, more powerful in life for its importance and the frailty of our access to it.

This seems to be the sense Heaney appeals to when he says the man recalls former religious beliefs that still have a hold on him—the way well water deep down has a hold on those who are conscious of their dependence on it every day.

This book aims to answer an important question: What does the history of Christian views of economic life mean for our economic life in the twenty-first century? Over its pages we will review a large number of texts in that history, from the Bible to the writings of the early church, the Middle Ages, the Protestant Reformation, and much that has been said about all this in the last century.

Very few Christians today know about most of these texts, which are like well water deep down. They lie in wait to provide refreshment, guidance, and even relief to believers today caught up in an economic system—and often in a job—that they think of as a kind of inevitable necessity, an arid fact of life, the unquestioned way the world works. Yet by investing the proper time and attention, we can experience these ancient texts in their persuasive insight, their call to meaning, their "tremor and draw"—and they can help us reflect critically on much that we may have unconsciously assumed about our economic life in the twenty-first century.

DISPARATE VOICES IN CHRISTIAN ECONOMIC ETHICS

Our engagement with ancient Christian texts on economic life must be part of the conversation about the economy today. Yet as soon as we turn to this contemporary task, we find that debates about economic life within the Christian churches in our era exhibit a range of opinions almost as wide as within secular society itself. This is something of a surprise, since it would seem that the moral doctrines of Christianity ought to operate as limits on the range of views that can actually be warranted by the Christian tradition. However, it is a fact of life that both Christian socialists and Christian libertarians believe their views are supported by Christian faith. Thus it will be helpful to start with a close view of how one representative of each approaches the issues. As we will see, each includes a view of the person and community, but the character and relationship of these two differ significantly.

A CHRISTIAN SOCIALIST CRITIQUE

Consider the views of Franz Hinkelammert, a Central American economist who criticizes capitalist business culture for holding to a kind of "metaphysics" or set of unproved assumptions. The quotations in this section are taken from his essay, "The Economic Roots of Idolatry: Entrepreneurial Metaphysics."[2]

Entrepreneurial metaphysics
At first glance, it must surely be surprising that mention is made of entrepreneurial metaphysics. Although there is such a metaphysics, and it has spread to all parts of our bourgeois world, it is very seldom perceived for what it is. It often appears as nothing more than a candid description of reality, or it takes on the appearances of a set of widely accepted slogans. . . . Capitalist entrepreneurs are devotees of this metaphysics, treating it as the framework of their religion. . . . Thus, all the values, guidelines, and conditions of entrepreneurial behavior are converted into "laws of nature" that cannot be broken. Entrepreneurial metaphysics turns the "behavioral logic" of the market into a law of nature. . . . Except from the view of entrepreneurial metaphysics itself, it is quite clear that such metaphysics is idolatry, in the very sense in which this term is used in the biblical tradition.

Hinkelammert urges his readers to step back and think about the belief system underlying capitalism as a sort of metaphysics that has not been proven but is such a basic part of public consciousness, particularly business consciousness, that it goes without challenge in the normal course of life. His point, of course, is that this set of beliefs is deeply wrong and, employing biblical language, makes an idol—a false god—out of the market.

The religion of economics
Entrepreneurs do not view themselves as the prime movers. From their standpoint, the business firm is the prime mover; they are nothing but the leading employee of the business firm. . . . The business firm is converted

into an entity with a personality of its own, which operates independently from the concrete lives of concrete persons. . . . Entrepreneurs (great captains; nay, generals) sense the dynamism of commodities, and know how to accept their challenge. As great captains, they steer their ships that are driven by a far greater force than they—namely, the market, the great object of devotion. Entrepreneurs obey this great force, and it is this obedience that makes them *great* entrepreneurs. Hence, the conviction of entrepreneurs that they are ideally humble and truly exemplary persons. The maximizing of profits appears to them as an act in the public service they render, and it gives them compensation commensurate with their devotion. Even if they are not churchgoers, entrepreneurs are deeply religious persons, who preach to the entire world the good news of subjugation to the anonymous machinery of the markets, wherein a Supreme Being issues them challenges.

Hinkelammert understands business people, entrepreneurs, as not only sharing in the metaphysical illusions mentioned above, but seeing themselves as great leaders because they can harness the force of the market. They are looked up to by many as the most influential figures in a commercial society and yet they don't see themselves as powerful, since most decisions they make are clearly indicated, with market forces not leaving them much room for discretion.

Freedom and death
In entrepreneurial metaphysics, this freedom of commodities is basic and, in the final analysis, the only freedom. Human rights, for example, are purely incidental. With commodities free, business firms are free; therefore, entrepreneurs are free, and the entire society is free. . . . When food is scarce, according to the law, prices should increase. This means that some will be left without food, and consequently will die. According to entrepreneurial metaphysics, they die as a result of a dictate of nature. If, on the contrary, prices and distribution of food are controlled, everyone would survive. But, according to entrepreneurial metaphysics, that would be an act against nature: the law of nature calls for increased prices. Price control is an unnatural, depraved act, breaking the social contract, and, in the end, an act against humankind. Freedom is lost, and what is life worth without freedom?

In this entrepreneurial metaphysics, the only true freedom is that of the market, with other human values and human rights being less important, or actually defined in terms of market freedom. Thus the law of supply and demand in the market is understood as "natural," and any attempt to alter its outcomes is seen as misguided human interference in natural processes. Thus when the prices of necessities rise, the poor go without. There is no one really to blame, since this is a "natural" result.

Wealth and justice
In this nature, it is a law that business firms accrue profits, although human beings have no right to live. To live or not is a matter of "values," not natural laws. The entrepreneurial metaphysician views the business firm as a Creator of employment, and overlooks the fact that employment is the requisite for the creation of wealth on the part of the business firm. It is claimed, on the contrary, that investment creates wealth and employment. Therefore, it is presented as a path to social justice, the only kind of social justice that the entrepreneurial metaphysician understands: the kind that does not break the law of profitability.

Hinkelammert thus understands the outcomes of the capitalist market as ideologically supported by this erroneous metaphysics broadly held in commercial society. That misunderstanding goes so far as to think that the wealthy create wealth by their investment and completely overlooks the role of ordinary workers in that process. Thus in a long history of socialist critique of capitalism, Hinkelammert appeals to his readers to understand the misplaced confidence in markets and in the profit-seeking of firms, and instead recommends, out of an appeal to the fundamental Christian concern for the neighbor, that believers should work to transform the economy to a more just (and socialist) economic system.

A CHRISTIAN LIBERTARIAN VIEW

Consider now the views of George Gilder, an American philosopher who came to prominence in the public sphere with his broad endorsement of capitalism as the only reasonable economic system for the modern world. The text below comes from an interview he gave in which he addresses his convictions about the relation of capitalism and Christianity.[3]

The primacy of faith
Like every other human activity, capitalism can succeed to the extent that it accords with the deeper principles that inspire religion. God comes first,

> obviously. Capitalism comes second. But when churches abandon God through various secular fads and enthusiasms, they are betraying God. When they maintain there's something inherently antagonistic between Christianity and capitalism, they're being obtuse. In other words, the church is perfectly capable of betraying God, and when it does, it betrays its deepest purpose in the world. . . . Capitalism is dependent on the church for the moral values that redeem it, so clearly the church has to stand in judgment. But it should not imagine that there is some other social system that partakes of Christianity in a better way than capitalism itself.

Some secular scholars have endorsed capitalism in complete separation from any religious belief, but not George Gilder. He urges his readers to understand the close relationship that Christianity and capitalism have and argues that only the misguided Christian will see socialism as a better fit for Christian belief than capitalism.

> *Helping the poor*
> The World Council of Churches and the National Council of Churches routinely accept a lot of socialist propositions and try to infuse them with a kind of holy light they don't deserve—helping the poor, for example. This is a practical problem, not something that can be done through good intentions alone. But the liberal policies some churches have endorsed have hurt the poor in America. . . . The fundamental and paramount role of the church is to transmit moral, inspirational teachings to the poor. There is nothing more important that can be done for the poor. When the church goes to the poor, it tells them that the source of their difficulties lies in some conspiracy by others and in the conditions of the society rather than in their own relationship to God.

Just as Hinkelammert criticizes those who put their faith in capitalism, so Gilder criticizes those Christians who endorse policies associated with socialism. His fundamental claim is not simply religious but also empirical: that the policies endorsed by the churches have actually hurt the poor by offering them a security that leads to their dependence on the welfare system. Only when all able-bodied workers are responsible for providing for themselves and their families will the poor pull out of such dependency and into a life of freedom and independence.

> *Moral capital*
> Yet in every material way, the American poor today are better off than most in the history of the human race. Their fundamental problem is spiritual. For the church to continue its preoccupation with material problems while denying the centrality of the spiritual estrangement is to betray the poor. The middle class and wealthy, although they are often not more virtuous, depend on the accumulated moral capital of their culture and society to live productive lives. This moral capital has been destroyed in many poor communities.

Quite basic in Gilder's argument is what has come to be called the "culture of poverty" argument broadly held among conservative Americans: that the fundamental problem of the poor is not the lack of money but the lack of the right attitudes, habits, skills, and cultural support that lead them to an independent life.[4]

Gilder does not describe the middle class and wealthy as more virtuous people than the poor; rather, that they have accumulated "moral capital" to rely on. What he has in mind here are the everyday habits of life that successful people exhibit. These include the ability to get up when the alarm clock sounds every morning, to follow through on workplace commitments, to resolve interpersonal conflicts without violence, and a host of others. Gilder's claim is that these attitudes and skills are missing among the poor and that no government program will ever put them there again. Only parents and communities can provide such training for children, and only the necessity of coping with life without reliance on government will press the adult poor to develop the moral capital they and their children need.

> *Welfare programs*
> I reject the idea that it's good for the poor to destroy their motivation, to destroy their families, and to destroy their moral integrity. These social programs that are allegedly charitable are in fact profoundly destructive. . . . A welfare system is indispensable to capitalism, because capitalism is based on freedom, on voluntary response to the needs of others. A society that's based on forcing people to work under the pain of starvation is just as coercive as one that forces them to work at the point of a gun. Welfare is indispensable to capitalism, and capitalist societies generate welfare systems. However, when the benefits of the welfare state far exceed the needs of subsistence or the possible earnings of an employee at an entry-level job, then it becomes destructive. . . . Where a social insurance system,

> or welfare, offers benefits far more valuable than work, the welfare state causes poverty. That's what we're doing now: we're causing poverty by paying for it.

Gilder's fundamental critique of the welfare system is that it offers the poor benefits that are more attractive than those of an entry-level job, thus turning their incentives upside down. The welfare system, he argues, leads a rational poor person to stay on welfare rather than look for a job. Thus while he insists there must be a welfare system to prevent the basic violation of freedom, he wants that support to be extremely low so that it will not be a tempting refuge for the poor. The welfare reform of the mid-1990s imposed a five-year lifetime limit on federally funded cash assistance, and average monthly benefits that are less than 25 percent of what a minimum-wage job pays, but conservatives such as Gilder remain concerned about the problem of dependency. Employing the metaphor from acrobatics, we might say that Gilder wants no more than a loose social safety net—it should be tight enough to prevent a person from dying when they fall off the high wire but loose enough that when they fall, they will hit the floor when the net stretches. Walking away bruised is the goal—to create an incentive not to fall off again.

> *Dependence on God*
>
> It's interesting that almost anybody who does achieve something really stunning and amazing, whether he is a boxer or a scientist, always claims that in some sense he wasn't the one who did it. In some way there was external help. If he is explicitly religious, he refers to God. If he's not, he refers to some mystical transcendence that made possible his achievement. . . . Intellectual creativity—any breakthrough of human achievement—is a willingness to give up yourself to others and to God. It's that essential principle that infuses Christian teaching and that also pervades all human life. Most psychological and sociological analyses say you should be much more self-conscious and rational and introspective and that through these means you can achieve a kind of autonomous mental health. But mental health comes from giving yourself up to others and to God, having faith in others and in the divine truth.

Fundamental to the conservative understanding of economic growth is the role of intellectual creativity. In his perspective as a Christian, Gilder cites the awareness that so many successful individuals have reported that they received help from outside themselves; religious people understand this to come from

God. Thus like Hinkelammert, Gilder differs from those individualists who claim that economic success is their own doing. But unlike Hinkelammert, who points to the ordinary workers who make the entrepreneur wealthy, Gilder points to a spiritual relationship with God as the underlying outside assistance that successful inventors and entrepreneurs rely on.

WHAT SHOULD WE HOPE FOR?

The views of Franz Hinkelammert and George Gilder are so divergent that it might seem impossible for them to agree on any way forward, and perhaps even impossible for them to agree on what success for the poor would look like.

The problems facing the poor of the world are overwhelming. Approximately one and one-half billion people on the planet live in dire poverty, defined as living on less than $1.25 a day. This is an immense problem with no quick solutions. Nonetheless, in recent decades certain regions of the world have experienced success in this fight against poverty. Thirty years ago, China had more than one-third of the world's poor people, but by the year 2005 that share had dropped to 15 percent. There are other areas, however, where poverty has gotten much worse, particularly in sub-Saharan Africa, where during that same time period, the number of people in dire poverty rose from about 300 million to nearly 400 million.[5]

Much more could be said in detail about the extent and characteristics of poverty and any potential reduction in poverty around the world, yet it is helpful to consider not just the statistics but the lives of individual people who make the transition from abject poverty and hopelessness to an important degree of self-sufficiency.

A very helpful collection of reports of hopeful economic change in the lives of the poor is provided by Jeffry Korgen in *Solidarity Will Transform the World: Stories of Hope from Catholic Relief Services*.[6] In one of those case studies, Korgen describes the situation of Sharmila Marandi, who lives with her husband, Premprakash, and their daughter, Anita, in a small rural village outside of Kolkata (Calcutta), India.

Sharmila and her husband used to try to support their family by producing homemade alcohol to supplement a dollar-a-day income. The alcohol did provide some extra cash for food and supplies, but had two significant problems. The first was that it often was used by individuals who were addicted to it and thus contributed to social problems in the region. The second was that Sharmila and her husband both drank too much of their own product and often argued, with Premprakash frequently beating her.

Help for this family, and for many others, came in the form of a social development program sponsored by the Roman Catholic diocese of Dumka, with expert assistance from the U.S. organization, Catholic Relief Services (CRS).

Sharmila first came in contact with a CRS self-help group in her village. She noticed that the women in the group were able to save a little bit each week from their businesses, establish credit with a micro-lending agency, and borrow small amounts of money (typically loans ranging from $5 to $30) to purchase livestock and seeds.[7] Sharmila was impressed with this and when the opportunity came to join a second self-help group in the region, she and nineteen other women attended the workshops on social development to learn about group process, recordkeeping, and basic literacy.

Sharmila reported that it was hard to save money at first, but the women from the original group helped, suggesting that she take a measure of rice from each day's allotted food and set it apart in a special bag to be sold for cash at the market when the bag was full. Joining with other members of her group, she cultivated various vegetables in the village garden and was able to profit from the group's savings.

The most important development came when the women decided there was a need in the village for good-quality bricks. They sought technical assistance as well as a loan from a local bank to purchase and construct a brick kiln. Because the bank saw the record of savings of this group of women—they had saved about 5000 rupees, about $100—it was willing to make the loan of 25,000 rupees. The group members purchased a kiln and made thousands of bricks, selling them on the market at a profit, which allowed them to pay back the loan quickly and divide up a portion of the profits to each of the member families.

The effects of this development project in this Indian village extend far beyond an improvement in the family's economic well-being. Sharmila and Premprakash no longer argue in drunkenness, and her own economic success has greatly increased his respect for her. And the life prospects for their daughter, Anita, are now considerably improved.

MAKING SENSE OF THE DIFFERENCES

Let us now return to our two commentators, Hinkelammert and Gilder, and ask what each would think of this success story. Here we find reason for some optimism in resolving at least some of the differences between the left and right on the political spectrum. Because Sharmila's group is operating in the market economy, selling their bricks and vegetables, George Gilder will be happy that they have come to self-sufficiency. He might be surprised that a church organization was responsible for getting poor people involved productively in the market, but he would praise the creation of "moral capital" within Sharmila's group and the increase in virtuous activity in her family.

At the same time, because the group has achieved this success through a kind of economic cooperative employing interdependence and common goal setting, Franz Hinkelammert will be appreciative of what is possible without dependence on large corporations and a greedy business class. He would likely be worried about the long-term prospects of Sharmila's brick-making enterprise in a capitalist business system, but he would celebrate what poor people can accomplish when they work together.

Sharmila's group is one of 50,000 women's self-help groups supported by CRS in India.[8] In a nation of more than one billion people, this is still a small number, but it represents a remarkable step in the right direction. Commentators on both the left and the right do indeed share a vision for what is best for the poor of the world: that ordinary people have the skills and opportunity to support themselves and their families through their daily work.

There is a realistic hope for assisting people to move out of dire poverty into a self-respecting capacity to support themselves. But micro-financing is no panacea.[9] While it can reduce dire poverty, it will not produce a basic prosperity for many. And it does not address the systemic barriers that keep so many in poverty, whether government bureaucracy and corruption, or corporate power and greed. Most of the economic decisions to be made in the world, whether in private business or in government, stand a long distance from these tiny self-help groups, in spite of their importance. Thus while hope is real, we need nonetheless to sort through the differences in the analysis of economic life that so often prevent communities and nations from a common concerted effort to help meet the needs of all.

As we step back and consider such divergent interpretations of what Christianity requires of our economic lives today, we have to be struck with the powerful effect that perspective has on people's perceptions. Coming from quite different perspectives, Franz Hinkelammert and George Gilder highlight very different elements in the Christian tradition and recommend quite different policies because of them. Here we come up against a significant intellectual problem that requires not just an inquiry into economic life but an understanding of how the human intellect works.

Put quite simply, we are most likely to see what we are already expecting.

The so-called "magic eye picture" at the beginning of this chapter may appear to be simply an interesting pattern of shapes, but if we know to look for something within it, we might, after considerable effort, see the image there. (For those unfamiliar with such computer-generated images, it helps to hold the center of the printed image right up to your nose. It should be blurry. Focus as though you are looking beyond the image into the distance. Very slowly move the image away from your face, keeping your eyes focused behind the page, not on it. An image "inside" the picture should appear.)

A similar thing happens when we ask, "Does our economy treat everyone justly?" Or even a more technical question, such as "Is the economy heading into a recession or out of one?" We are most likely to see what we're already expecting. It is difficult to perceive "what is actually happening" simply because there is so much complexity in the world that it takes some sort of conceptual framework to make sense of it. Ideally, this is the role that science plays, and we are indeed reliant upon economics as a social science to describe the economy as it is. However, as we will see in more detail in Chapter 13, we find even among economists significant differences in how they describe our world. Thus it will be helpful to step back from the immediate debates about capitalism and socialism in economic life in this chapter and consider several insights arising from the sociology of knowledge.

THE SOCIAL CONSTRUCTION OF REALITY

Sociologists Peter Berger and Thomas Luckmann wrote a now classic book entitled the *Social Construction of Reality*.[10] In it, the authors describe how what we presume to be "just the way things are" has often been actually constructed by humans long before us and passed down to us as an obvious fact.

Berger and Luckmann use the example of two people from different cultures who meet and must come to understand each other.[11] We might make that more concrete and think of two people on two different ships in the South Seas, both of whom are shipwrecked in a severe storm and washed up on the same deserted island. Neither can speak a word of the other's language and yet they meet on the beach the next morning and have to begin working out a life together.

They need food. So person A walks over to a bush, digs around it and tears out one of its roots. After brushing the dirt off, A begins to chew on the root. Only then does person B realize that this is food for A; in B's culture no one eats roots like this. Person B instead notices the trees nearby and climbs up to pick several coconuts. Opening one of them with a rock, B begins to drink the milk and eat the flesh. Again, only after B begins chewing does A realize that this is food, since there are no coconuts in A's world. Over the long run, however, they quickly depend far more on coconuts than on roots, as they are tastier and more nutritious.

Similarly, when it comes time to start a fire, Person B makes a small pile of dead leaves and rubs two sticks together, to the puzzlement of Person A. After ten minutes, B gets a small fire going. Only at that point does his companion realize what B has been trying to do all along: start a fire. We can imagine person B's surprise when A gathers a small pile of dried leaves and, picking up two stones found on the edge of the beach, strikes them together to create a spark. In a few seconds A starts a fire. B is amazed since there is no flint in his culture and B soon abandons his traditional method for starting fires in favor of the far better method he learned from A.

With no ship to rescue them, we can imagine the two living for years together and over time they rarely eat roots and never use sticks for lighting fires. Perhaps over enough years they may forget about rubbing sticks together. On that first morning the two had a vivid awareness of a decision about what constitutes fire starting. Eventually that decision becomes less transparent, a bit murky in the memory—their shared world "thickens" and "hardens"—after a decade or two of using flint without having to *decide* to use it.

If A and B are of different sexes and they have children together, we can easily imagine that the children are taught only the more efficient way to start fires, though perhaps for the first generation or two the parents teach the old method as a sort of cultural remembrance. However, we might expect that after several generations the very memory of sticks to start fires may be lost. What began as a perfectly transparent decision ("this is how we've decided to start fires") became translucent, in the sense that "this is how we start fires." After a longer time the translucence moved to opacity. Subsequent generations hear only "this is how fires are started." The sense that the use of flint was a decision becomes lost in history. The world as our ancestors created it becomes "just the way things are."

Berger and Luckmann employ this example to remind the reader that much of what we do in daily life appears to us as simply the natural way to do things but in fact arose from prior human decisions and actions and was socially constructed.

For many of us, our first vivid awareness of this fact of life comes with travel to another country. Our experience of life there often brings about an intense awareness that the way we do things at home is not the only way they can be done. The undeniable proof is that people in that other country do them quite differently.

For example, it is surprising to most North Americans to discover the lively meanings of things considered insignificant or harmless at home.[12] Gift giving is popular in Asia, and the gift should be wrapped attractively, but the wrapping paper must not be white, as that is the color of mourning at death. And in most of Asia, to write the name of the recipient of the gift in red ink will end the relationship, not enhance it; it's like putting a curse on the person you intend to honor by the gift. Manners are very important in Japan, but to slurp your noodles at dinner is quite acceptable, as it is believed to make them taste better.

Asians do much less touching (handshakes, hugs, etc.) than North Americans, but Latin Americans do much more. In the U.S., people stand two to three feet away from each other when talking, but in much of Latin America the distance is twelve to eighteen inches. And, oh yes, what North Americans associate with Friday the 13th, Latinos link to Tuesday the 13th. Even compliments can be tricky in many places. If you speak too appreciatively of a beautiful item in the home of your Japanese friend, he may feel obliged to give it to you, an idea that would never cross the mind of your friends at home.

Examples abound where cultural misunderstandings have caused disasters. Speakers of English who are not used to the difference between intimate and formal modes of address to another person (as exist in French, German, and Spanish, for example) often make the mistake of addressing a much older individual (who merits the formal mode of speech) with an intimate second-person form. While it may seem to the Anglophone as simply a grammatical mistake, those in the actual situation see it as an unthinkable cultural violation, something like calling the elderly lady living next door "babe" or "hey you."

Corporations also make cultural mistakes. One Japanese traveler tells the story of being given a white carnation by a smiling U.S. stewardess upon boarding an international flight home. He wondered whether the whole plane was going to a funeral, since in Japan white carnations are closely associated with grieving someone's death. The airline had no idea. Revlon made a similar mistake by introducing a new carnation-scented perfume in Brazil without knowing that, as in Japan, carnations are associated with funerals there. Not so good for sales. Some corporations even misunderstand U.S. culture. The Swedish vacuum cleaner manufacturer, Electrolux, misfired in the U.S. when its marketers tried the slogan: "Nothing sucks like an Electrolux."[13]

Thus one of the primary lessons to learn from this insight into the social construction of reality is that we can come to understand our own views better through personal experience in a different cultural setting, where "they" don't think like "we" do. Without that experience of contrast, we will probably just assume that our ways of acting and thinking are "natural."

THE TRADITION OF CHRISTIAN SOCIAL THOUGHT

This volume will look back at the views of economic life in the Christian tradition, views that date back three thousand years into the Hebrew Scriptures. With a history as old as the Judeo-Christian tradition, simply traveling back in time to read how our spiritual ancestors thought about economic life is very much like traveling to a foreign country. Presumptions about culture and faith, family and individual, society and nation—as well as economic life—in those eras were significantly different from ours and thus operate as a helpful critique of any blinders that we may be wearing today.

OUTLINE OF THE BOOK

Part I of the book includes the current chapter and Chapter 2, which will look at how a living tradition develops and generates contextually relevant implications for each new era.

Part II contains the bulk of the book, which will take a close look at texts about economic life written in various periods from the Scriptures (Chapters 3 and 4) to the early church (Chapters 5, 6, and 7) to the Middle Ages (Chapters 8 and 9) and the Reformation (Chapter 10).

Part III begins with Chapter 11, which will look at issues of the development of teaching on economic issues (for example, slavery, usury, and human rights) within the Christian tradition—since such developments help us understand how this tradition does and doesn't change as the world situation changes over time. Chapter 12 provides four ways to sort out modern disputes about economic life. Chapter 13 provides a brief treatment of what we should and should not learn from the discipline of economics today.

Part IV, comprising Chapters 14, 15, 16, and 17, will examine the teaching on economic life represented by the encyclicals of the modern popes on economic life and by denominational statements of Protestant churches.

Part V, Chapters 18, 19, and 20, will then propose from the perspective of Catholic social thought what this history should mean for making decisions about economic life today. This will include both general principles and implications, as well as applications to several critical social processes in the twenty-first century. Although many of the elements contained in these chapters are also affirmed within contemporary Protestant thought on economic life, they do rely on a Catholic conceptual framework and worldview that Protestants would understand differently. Thus while the hope is that these concluding chapters will be helpful to Protestant readers, there is no claim here to speak for Protestant Christianity.

If all goes well, by the end the reader will be well prepared to develop his or her own answer to the basic question of this volume: What does the history of Christian views of economic life mean for our economic life in the twenty-first century?

Notes

1. Seamus Heaney, "Out of This World," *District and Circle* (New York: Farrar, Straus & Giroux, 2006). Used with permission.

2. Franz Hinkelammert, "The Economic Roots of Idolatry: Entrepreneurial Metaphysics," in *The Idols of Death and the God of Life*, ed. Pablo Richard (Maryknoll, NY: Orbis, 1983). Used with permission.

3. George Gilder, "Where Capitalism and Christianity Meet," chapter 50 in *Border Regions of Faith: An Anthology of Religion and Social Change,* ed. Kenneth Aman (Maryknoll, NY: Orbis, 1987). Used with permission.

4. See, for example, Oscar Lewis, "The Culture of Poverty," *Society* 35, no. 2 (Jan./Feb. 1998): 7–9.

5. See http://databank.worldbank.org/data/views/variableSelection/selectvariables.aspx?source=world-development-indicators. Accessed January 29, 2012.

6. Jeffry Odell Korgen, *Solidarity Will Transform the World: Stories of Hope from Catholic Relief Services* (Maryknoll, NY: Orbis, 2010).

7. For further discussion of the role of micro-finance in economic development, see Muhammad Yunus and Alan Jolis, *Banker to the Poor: Micro-lending and the Battle against World Poverty*, (New York: Public Affairs, 1999) and Dörte Weidig, "Three Myths about SME Finance," World Bank Publications, http://www.cgap.org/blog/three-myths-about-sme-finance. Accessed January 31, 2013.

8. Korgen, *Solidarity*, 58.

9. For two analyses of the Grameen Bank, the best known of the micro-credit efforts, see M. A. Baqui Khalily, Mahmood Osman Imam, and Salahuddin Ahmed Khan, "Efficiency and Sustainability of Formal and Quasi-formal Microfinance Programmes—An Analysis of Grameen Bank and ASA," in *The Bangladesh Development Studies* 26, nos. 2 & 3, (June–Sept. 2000): 103–46, and Imran Matin, "Rapid Credit Deepening and a Few Concerns: A Study of a Branch of Grameen Bank," in *The Bangladesh Development Studies* 26, nos. 2 & 3 (June–Sept. 2000): 147–72.

10. Peter Berger and Thomas Luckmann, *The Social Construction of Reality: A Treatise in the Sociology of Knowledge* (Garden City, NY: Doubleday, 1966). If taken too far, Berger and Luckmann's basic insight could be employed to argue that there is *nothing* to life beyond humans' created meaning—rejecting God's action in the world. This, however, is not a necessary result of the insight.

11. Berger and Luckmann, *The Social Construction of Reality*, 58–60.

12. Several of the examples in this section are taken from Mary Murray Bosrock's series of books, *Put Your Best Foot Forward* (St. Paul, MN: International Educational Systems). See also Mary Murray Bosrock, *Asian Business: Customs & Manners* (New York: Meadowbrook, 2007).

13. Charles R. Taylor, Thomas A. Claus, and Susan L. Claus, *On-Premise Signs as Storefront Marketing Devices and Systems* (Washington, DC: U.S. Small Business Administration, 2005), 9.12–9.13.

2

How a Living Tradition Means

Americans generally need to be taught in school how to experience both poetry and the opera. In Milan, on the other hand, no one need go to school in order to learn how to experience an opera; the Milanese do not study opera, they inhale it. They would have to go to school to learn, for example, how to watch a baseball game in an experienceable way. Certainly no one in the Bronx need go to that school: in the Bronx it is baseball that is inhaled as a living thing, and opera and poetry that have to be learned.

–John Ciardi[1]

The late poet and literary scholar John Ciardi wrote a wonderful little book titled *How Does a Poem Mean?* Ciardi's title puts the reader on edge, since this is not the way we ordinarily talk about meaning. For those of us who have not grown up "inhaling" poetry, poems *have* meanings; there are meanings *written into* poems, and we can discuss *what* a poem means. Can we even understand his question, "How does a poem mean?" Ciardi's point, of course, is to cause exactly this sort of reaction in his readers. His title calls us to stop and think again about a set of relationships that we thought we had already understood. Instead of the expected, he proposes a way to think about how meaning emerges in poetry quite differently than we nonpoets typically assume. His unusual question opens up a possibility that wasn't there before.

The title for this chapter borrows from Ciardi's insight: How a Living Tradition Means. We really cannot say *what* the Christian tradition on economic life means for us today until we explore *how* this tradition means, how those meanings operate. And this task is far more difficult—though not impossible—for those Christians today who haven't grown up "inhaling" the Christian tradition. Learning from a living tradition involves exploring it from the inside, coming to understand what it calls us to today by understanding first what our spiritual ancestors in the tradition understood it to be calling them to in their day.

Thus there are three main questions we need to deal with in this chapter. The first concerns the nature of a tradition; the second, what a "living" tradition is; and the third, how it could be that a very old living religious tradition could have implications for how we think and act in daily economic life today.

What is a tradition?

There are many kinds of traditions: national, historical, philosophical, family, etc. In just about every case, they entail a lengthy history of people, ideas, and customs that predate the current generation, sometimes by a few decades, sometimes by many centuries. It might be your family's tradition to gather at your grandmother's house every Thanksgiving, a tradition strengthened by the fact that your grandmother used to do the same thing as a child at *her* grandmother's house.

But just doing the same thing over and over does not create a tradition. How you brush your teeth is a habit, not a tradition. Not only does a tradition require a kind of intergenerational continuity, but there has to be a significant story related to it as well. There is always a kind of respect that more recent entrants into this tradition have for the tradition itself and for earlier generations that have done this before. A college student living on campus might come to a greater awareness of this sort of respect for tradition if he proposes to visit a friend's home over the Thanksgiving holiday and then is surprised by his mother's insistence that he come home instead. "Thanksgiving is a time for family," he may be told. "It's a tradition."

We don't just "have" a tradition; we belong to that tradition. In a sense, the tradition has us.

The Christian tradition—or the Jewish and Christian tradition, to be more exact—begins with the Hebrew Bible and extends through more than 3000 years of human history. Those of us who are members of this tradition look back to the events that occurred and the texts that existed long before our birth as having a particular authority in our lives. We know of course that there are other religious traditions such as Buddhism and Islam and other intellectual traditions such as those arising out of Plato, Aristotle, or Karl Marx. There is much we can learn from other traditions, but somehow they do not have the same kind of authority over us that our own tradition does.

This is a bit like the difference between listening to our grandparents tell us stories about their childhood and listening to the stories of that nice elderly couple who live next door to our grandparents. It isn't that our grandparents are better at telling stories than their neighbors, as it's quite possible that the neighbors are great storytellers. The difference is that our grandparents' stories are in an important way *our* stories. Those events did not happen to us, of course, but they did happen to our family and thus are more engaging, more relevant, and more powerful in our lives today, especially if we're willing to take time to listen and reflect on them—and on what it means for us to be part of *our* family's traditions.

The same thing happens within the Christian tradition. When we read about the Israelites escaping slavery in Egypt under the leadership of Moses, we understand that these are our spiritual ancestors. When Paul and Peter struggled to discern what faith in Jesus would mean in the non-Jewish Roman world, we understand their efforts as our own. When we learn about Christians struggling to understand their own faith and live it out responsibly in the medieval period or during the Protestant Reformation or the French Revolution or in debates about slavery in 1850, we know that we are listening to the voices of our own spiritual ancestors struggling to discern what God was calling them to.

WHAT MAKES A LIVING TRADITION ALIVE?

This very sense that through our reading we can come to understand the intellectual and personal struggles of Christians in earlier generations is part of what keeps the Christian tradition alive. The difference between a living and a dead tradition is that the former continues to evolve over time while the latter is frozen in history. The historian Jaroslav Pelikan put this in a different way when he said that "tradition is the living faith of the dead; traditionalism is the dead faith of the living."[2] An interesting example of this difference was presented to my wife and me when we were deciding between two preschools for our son many years ago. One option was a "traditional" Montessori school, where the teachers strove to educate their students just as Maria Montessori had done in the early twentieth century in Italy, where she developed creative "child centered" methods of teaching. Our second option was the "American" Montessori school, which did most things the way Maria had, but where teachers felt free to add new developments. For example, there was much greater use of music than Maria herself had employed. Whereas the original Montessori approach aimed to maintain what Maria Montessori did as exactly as possible, the American Montessori decided to do things the way they figured Maria would be doing them now if she were still alive today. Both wanted to be faithful to her approach to educating children; they simply disagreed on what faithfulness means. Both aimed to "do what she did." One group understood this as doing the same things she did; the other stressed that she decided what to do based on her circumstances and so true faithfulness to her required them to take new circumstances into consideration in deciding how to teach.

This difference between two types of Montessori schools illustrates a larger pattern in traditions of all kinds. To take a secular political movement, consider Marxism. There have been many options in Marxist history, but most divide into two camps. The first are the "orthodox" Marxists, who aim to maintain the intellectual structure created by Karl Marx. The second are the "revisionist" Marxists, who do maintain most of that structure but alter parts of it. They assert that if Marx were alive today he would surely see things differently than he did originally, because his analysis was developed in dialogue with his historical context and that context has changed. Just about every tradition, whether or not it employs the words *orthodox* and *revisionist*, has this very same kind of debate. This is true whether the original expert was Abraham Lincoln, John Locke, the founding fathers of the United States, or the entrepreneur who founded a family business three generations ago.

Of course we see this in the Christian tradition as well. At one extreme is the strictly originalist perspective represented by a few small Pentecostal "apostolic" churches that recognize no doctrinal developments after the death of the twelve apostles. These reject, for example, even the Nicene Creed as an unwarranted novelty. They consider it unfaithful to biblical revelation, since it was composed at the Council of Nicea in 325. At the other extreme are the most liberal of Christians who feel free to reinterpret or even reject many beliefs (for example, the divinity of Christ) that Christians around the world proclaim each Sunday morning in the Nicene Creed.

The Christian tradition has indeed evolved over time, and we are aware that the very same Holy Spirit who inspired the Fathers of the early church to articulate the philosophical subtleties of the Nicene Creed remains active in the church today. One recent example relevant to economic life occurred when Pope John Paul II declared that the year 2000 would be a "Jubilee year." In this, he called upon an idea that existed three millennia before him in the Hebrew Scriptures. As we will see in more detail in the next chapter, the Jewish law directed that a Jubilee year was to be celebrated every forty-nine years. It required that any land that had been sold since the last Jubilee year should be returned to its original owner. However, the pope did not identify the return of land as a goal of Jubilee 2000, but instead quite explicitly identified debt relief for poor countries as its primary economic goal. Times have changed; farming and the ownership of land are not as central today as they were in ancient Israel, an agricultural society where not owning land meant you couldn't provide for yourself and your family. Pope John Paul's Jubilee proclamation amounted to doctrinal development of the idea of the Jubilee observance, a rough equivalent of such help in the twenty-first century: debt relief for poor nations to allow national governments to spend their scarce resources on education and healthcare rather than on interest payments for the national debt.

At a number of points in the history of Christianity, changing conditions in the world have brought about changes in moral teaching. In Chapter 11 we will examine changes in teaching on such issues as slavery and usury (the charging of interest when lending money). We will see that even where one answer was given for centuries and another answer was eventually provided by official church teaching, the essence of change in a living tradition is that change occurs in basic continuity with the past. Thus the traditional 3000-year-old teaching that slavery was morally acceptable in certain circumstances was eventually rejected when Christians institutionalized the understanding that all human beings are more fundamentally equal as children of one God than they are different, and that they all share the same God-given human dignity and all are redeemed in Christ. As we will see, most of the Christian churches came to this insight only after a number of other changes occurred in our understanding: that some races are not genetically inferior to others, that privilege, not biology, made some classes of people "superior" to others, and that the essence of democracy requires that every adult have the same rights before government. Once the situation changed, Christians recognized that slavery actually contradicted their most basic principles.

The point here is that in a living tradition, fundamental commitments and values remain respected as time goes on. However, changes in the world and in our understanding of our own inconsistencies periodically bring about changes—in our case, in Christian teaching on moral issues. Change occurs, but always in continuity with the tradition's most basic commitments. Most often, that change occurs because those most basic commitments *can't* be kept without the change.

How a living tradition has implications for us today

The most fundamental question of this book is: What does the Christian tradition mean for economic life today? Because we learn about this tradition through texts written over the centuries, it is helpful to start to answer this question by thinking more generally about our relationship to all kinds of older Christian texts, whether from the Bible or from Christian bishops and scholars in later centuries.

Here it will be helpful to employ a notion used by biblical scholars: the hermeneutic (or "interpretive") circle, which is a way of understanding how we should interpret these ancient texts—whether from the Bible, the early church, the Middle Ages, or even a decade ago. This helps us to both be faithful to the most fundamental commitments and values of our Christian tradition and at the same time be realistic about how those commitments and values should be worked out in a different context today.

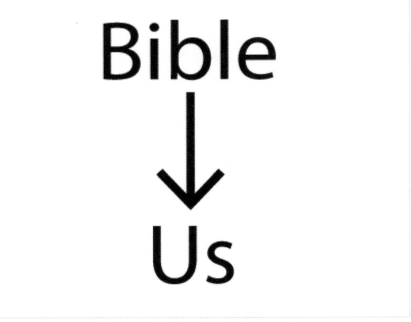

Figure 1. The Pre-Modern Presumption

In simplified terms, Figure 1 depicts the traditional, historical understanding of the relation between Christians and the biblical texts. The large arrow from the text toward us indicates the authority of the Bible under which all Christians stand. For centuries it was presumed that the Bible provided the truth not just about God and our faith but also about the physical universe: astronomy, physics, biology, etc.

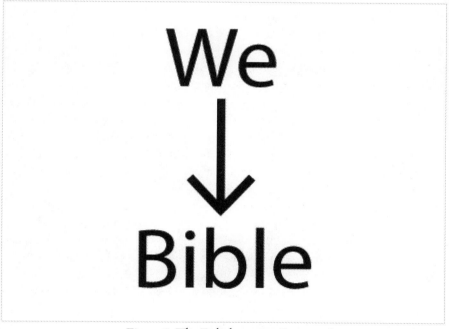

Figure 2. The Enlightenment Presumption

Figure 2 indicates roughly what happened for many who lost their faith with the arrival of the secular Enlightenment when, over several hundred years, the awareness grew that the Bible was wrong about many issues of astronomy, cosmology, biology, and geology—as modern science came to understand things more adequately. Many people took these failings as evidence that the Bible was untrustworthy and ought to be rejected. This led many intellectuals to a purely secular view of life and a rejection of religion as superstition: an outmoded, erroneous way of thinking. Thus the large arrow in Figure 2 indicates the authoritative judgment that intellectually responsible individuals were supposed to employ in critiquing the texts of the tradition so that, for example, they do not simplistically come to believe that the earth is at the center of the universe or that creation occurred 6000 years ago.

But we should not think of this drive toward science and toward a critique of the excesses of religion as simply arising outside of Christianity. The philosopher Charles Taylor argues persuasively that such impulses began *within* Christianity, for example with eleventh- and twelfth-century efforts to get the ordinary Christian to take faith more seriously and to purify the faith and reduce "magical" influences in Christian rituals. Thus the rise of science and even the Enlightenment's critique of religion can better be seen as arising out of the internal dynamics of Christian culture.[3]

The long slow move toward a rejection of religion on the part of many Western intellectuals took place over several centuries. The most extreme views in this direction occurred in the first half of the twentieth century, with the development of a philosophical system called logical positivism. Best represented by "the Vienna Circle," these philosophers and scientists declared that the goal of intellectual understanding of the world required the building up of all conviction starting with empirically certain facts. The hope was that all human knowledge could then be constructed based on such facts and thus there would be no need to rely on less trustworthy sources such as religion, tradition, or even scientific guesswork.

However, this extreme attempt at objectivity ultimately failed for two reasons. The first was that this philosophical movement came to an end when one of its members, Kurt Gödel, proved conclusively, by what came to be called Gödel's Theorem, that there could be no intellectual system that was based only on its own internal resources.[4] Every system of thought would require assumptions that could not be justified within the system itself. Thus nearly all philosophers today agree that logical positivism was a naïvely optimistic hope for a purely objective scientific view of the world.[5]

However, perhaps more important for the failure of this simplistic hope for objectivity through the natural sciences was a second development, in social science. The very same forces that generated a secular scientific Enlightenment deeply interested in objectivity also produced the disciplines of sociology and anthropology, scientific efforts that eventually demonstrated to us that even our "modern" understandings of how things work cannot be truly "objective." As we reviewed in the previous chapter, scientific insights, though valuable, always occur from one perspective and not from others. Every intellectual conviction, every insight, can only occur based upon a constellation of assumptions that we often call one's "perspective." And no attempt to eliminate our biases can ever eliminate the basic fact that every act of seeing is done from a particular perspective, bearing the biases and characteristics that this angle of vision entails.

As we saw in Chapter 1, many people learn this in their first experience overseas. We learn that some of the things we thought were just "how things are done" are instead really "how *we* do things." Thus we encounter personally the insights of the "social construction of reality" that we also saw in the previous chapter. The experience of another culture doesn't prove that our way of doing things is wrong, but it does raise for us the possibility that it might be. We can see that things can be done differently than they're done in our culture, and we are then able to ask a question that didn't—and perhaps couldn't—even occur to us before our travels: maybe there's a better way to do this. This phenomenon, of course, was the reason G. K. Chesterton observed that "the whole object of travel is not to set foot on foreign land; it is at last to set foot on one's own country as a foreign land."[6]

Insight into the sociology of knowledge—how knowledge is generated, organized, and passed on to others—has come to affect how scientists now understand science. Notions about the "facts" of science of a century ago have given way to the understanding that except for the most elementary of insights (for example, there are not four but three apples in the bowl on the kitchen counter), the facts science knows are always embedded in theories and do not possess the kind of abstract objectivity that some philosophers of science once thought possible. For example, what we know from radio telescopes about black holes in space and from electron microscopes about the shape of minute structures at the atomic level are not in any sense "simply the facts," but are facts embedded in a theoretical structure without which we could not make sense of or even know about black holes and atoms. And as we will see later in discussions of contemporary economic science, claims to objectivity or "value-free" economics are deeply flawed. Standard economics employs and promotes an inadequate view of the human person, and while it is very helpful for many purposes, it can also misdirect our attention and misguide public policy.

Returning to the hermeneutic circle, we now can understand that it is no longer adequate for intellectuals to think that they can simply sit in objective judgment over ancient texts like the Bible. Because our interpretation of the Bible is coming from a particular perspective, we now become aware that access to other perspectives is important in deciding whether our own is adequate. And just as a traveler can fly to another part of the world to see cultures different from one's own, so a reader today can "travel" to another time and read about how people back then understood the world and can use those views from an earlier era to challenge the reader's own cultural presumptions. This could happen when reading a wide variety of ancient wisdom, whether from Plato, the Hebrew Scriptures, or the Bhagavad Gita. But as we have just seen in the notion of belonging to a living tradition, for Christians, the Bible and the other texts in our tradition have an authority over us that neither Plato nor the Buddha possesses.

Thus the best way to understand our relationship with these ancient texts is through the hermeneutic circle in Figure 3. On the one hand, responsible for careful thinking about our lives, we must make judgments about these ancient texts in their own context. We can judge that the book of Genesis does not provide us with an adequate geology or biology, and we also conclude that the holding of slaves endorsed in the Bible is morally unacceptable today. On the other hand, we stand under the authority of this tradition and its texts and thus we have a responsibility to attend to the views articulated there that critique our own assumptions and relationships—so that those texts can shape our views about what we should be doing in economic life today. For example, what does it mean for us today that our God commanded the ancient Israelites to return all land to its original owners every forty-nine years? Does this imply that we have an obligation to the homeless today?

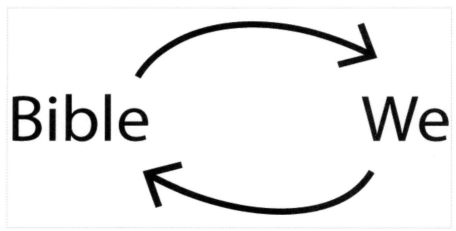

Figure 3. Today's Situation for Christians

This understanding of the hermeneutic circle does not give us easy answers, but it does provide us with a way forward. Unlike biblical fundamentalism, which claims that we should do exactly what was taught in the Bible, we understand that our task is more difficult. In fact, we understand that fundamentalism itself is not consistent, since there are many things that were taken for granted in the Bible that even most fundamentalists today would no longer endorse, such as the holding of slaves or the treatment of women and girls as the property of husbands and fathers. Thus our task is a difficult one, but it is the only responsible one left to us: to read carefully the views of our spiritual ancestors about economic life, to compare those views with the ones held in our culture today, and to discern carefully what those ancient texts mean for our life now.

In this process we have the advantage of commentaries written over many centuries that were themselves efforts to interpret earlier texts. Some of those authors lived in the early centuries of the church, others in the Middle Ages or during the Reformation. Still others lived in the twentieth century, much closer to our own day, and we can see them already struggling with many of the questions we wrestle with now.

The Catholic tradition has a special word for the *official* reflection on this tradition: the magisterium. This is the official teaching of the Roman Catholic Church on issues of all sorts. In this book we will be especially concerned with what the magisterium has taught about economic life. These official positions are commonly referred to as "Catholic social teaching." "Catholic social thought" contains this teaching but is larger, also including the work of scholars who were not popes or bishops. What we will come to see, of course, is that popes, bishops, and scholars in the church over the centuries have faced many of the same kinds of problems that we face today in trying to interpret what ancient texts mean for daily life.

CONCLUSION

In this chapter we have investigated the notion of a living tradition and how such a tradition can be helpful in thinking about economic issues today. As we have seen, this is essential to avoid both fundamentalism (so we shouldn't be trying to pass laws to return land to whoever owned it forty-nine years ago) and any arrogant dismissal of biblical wisdom (so it's important to understand God's purpose for the Jubilee year and to consider alternate ways to accomplish that aim in a modern market economy).

In the chapters that follow, we will review a wide variety of texts, and in the final chapters of the book will identify a number of conclusions for an ethical economic life today. This complexity can sometimes cause a reader to feel overwhelmed due to having to keep track of many independent but interrelated ideas and commitments. While this is one possible reaction, a better one is an appreciation of an attractive richness that simply cannot be embodied in one or two principles more important than the rest. The theologian Hans Urs von Balthasar has employed a felicitous phrase to name this: that Christian thought has "a symphonic nature." That is, the various elements of the traditions, though diverse, depend upon one another for their meaning, harmony, and effect.

This process of learning to hear and appreciate the symphony is not an easy one, particularly for those who did not grow up "inhaling" the music. But careful attention to the various elements within that tradition can do more than inform us of what the tradition has said explicitly about economic life in the past. If we learn to listen for *how* the tradition means, we will be able to make the careful judgments necessary to decide what this tradition should mean for economic life today.

Notes

1. John Ciardi, *How Does a Poem Mean?* (Boston: Riverside, 1959), 66.

2. Jaroslav Pelikan, *The Emergence of the Catholic Tradition 100–600*, vol. 1, *The Christian Tradition: A History of the Development of Doctrine* (Chicago: University of Chicago Press, 1973).

3. Charles Taylor, *A Secular Age* (Cambridge, MA: Harvard University Press, 2007), 154–58.

4. For an introduction to Gödel's Theorem, see Torkel Franzén, *Gödel's Theorem: An Incomplete Guide to Its Use and Abuse* (Wellesley, MA: A. K. Peters, 2005).

5. We must recall, however, that this philosophical insight isn't always recognized by natural scientists even today. Many sociobiologists, for example, are profoundly reductionistic, describing human intellectual and moral life as little more than the effects of "selfish" genes trying to perpetuate their lineage.

6. G. K. Chesterton, *Tremendous Trifles* (Salt Lake City: The Project Gutenberg Literary Archive Foundation, 2005, originally published 1909), www.gutenberg.org/files/8092/8092-h/8092-h.htm. Accessed January 29, 2012.

PART II

From the Bible to the Reformation

3

The Hebrew Scriptures

The history of Christian views of economic life began long before Christianity existed. Like the first Christians, we today are deeply indebted to the Jewish tradition out of which Christianity has flowed. Jesus himself continually employed the wisdom of his own Jewish tradition. Even modern popes have referred to Jews today as elder brothers in the faith.[1]

The Hebrew Scriptures (the Old Testament) are a collection of writings that include a wide variety of literary genres, from law to history to poetry and more. Though dating from centuries before the birth of Jesus, the Hebrew Scriptures in a real sense also belong to Christians and are critically important for the faith and life of Christians today. For our purposes, we will focus on a few of the major elements of this tradition, those that most directly address economic life.

THE CREATION STORY

The Bible begins with two versions of the story of God's creation of the world in the book of Genesis. Scripture scholars now understand that these stories were not from the earliest of Israelite history but came into being much later. Nonetheless, they convey fundamental insights for Jewish and Christian theology.

CREATION, NOT CREATIONISM

All Christians believe that God created the world. This is the doctrine of creation. Only fundamentalist Christians believe in "creationism," the belief that God created the world in seven twenty-four-hour days, about 6000 years ago. Fundamentalist Christians interpret the Bible literally and hold that the truth of the Bible requires that we believe that everything happened exactly as the biblical texts relate.

Catholics and mainline Protestants do not see the Bible as designed to provide a scientific description of events but as a religious statement, inspired by God to reveal religious truth to its readers. Modern science has learned that the rocks of the earth are billions of years old, that fish, cattle, and humans evolved over millions of years, and that the earth revolves around the sun and not the other way around.

Many atheists today argue that because the Bible is wrong scientifically, Christian faith is based on an illusion. Ironically, creationists share with these atheists a presumption about the bible and science—because these two sources provide different accounts of the earth and the cosmos, they cannot both be true. But fundamentalists argue that since the bible *must* be literally true, science must be in error.

It is far better to understand religion and science as two different ways of understanding the world—each with its own means for perceiving and articulating what is true.

THE WORLD IS GOOD.

The creation stories in Genesis leave us with two broad principles that are immediately relevant to economic life today. While neither can tell us exactly what to do in concrete situations, each contributes to a proper attitude and provides an important background conviction that should influence how we approach daily economic decisions.

The first principle is that the world is good. The first creation story tells us that at the end of each day of creation, God "saw that it was good" (Gen. 1:1-31). What does this mean for us today? Basically this goodness says that plants and animals, and even rocks and soil, are religiously significant, religiously important. Thus the life of the Israelite then and of the Christian today must take into consideration God's evaluation of the material world. This has important implications for our view of environmental problems today. But even broader than this is the conviction that religious faith is thoroughly tied to the material world. Most basically, we humans are not simply spirits but are body/spirits. That is, our physical body is just as much "who we are" as our spiritual side.

The most important aspect of the goodness of creation is articulated when the creation story says that humans have been created "in the image and likeness of God." Because of this unique characteristic of humanity, we have a fundamental dignity, not arising from what we do or from what others think of us but simply from what we are. But this dignity does not diminish the importance of the physical world—which is also religiously important. There are some world religions where the goal of religious faith is to somehow withdraw from "the world" into a spiritual place where the believer can more purely understand humanity's spiritual destiny. But this has not been a part of the authentic Christian tradition. Although our ultimate destiny is to be with God, Christianity remains respectful of and involved in worldly life. This is not an "otherworldly" religion.

Thus for example, the importance of the work we do, the respect we have for the material things we own, the care we take for the natural world, all these arise from this fundamental conviction that the material world is good.

In premodern times there clearly was no awareness of the great extent to which human life and technology today can threaten natural systems and the biosphere as a whole, but there was nonetheless an awareness of a connection between human evil and the natural world.

Human evil threatens nature.

Hear the word of the Lord, you Israelites, because the Lord has a charge to bring against you who live in the land:

"There is no faithfulness, there is only cursing, lying and murder, stealing and adultery; they break all bounds, and bloodshed follows bloodshed.

Because of this the land dries up, and all who live in it waste away; the beasts of the field, the birds of the sky, and the fish of the sea are swept away.

Hosea 4:1–3

The most basic statement of the relation between humans and the natural world was given in the first creation story when God tells the first humans to "be fruitful and increase in number; fill the earth and subdue it. Rule over the fish in the sea and the birds in the sky and every other living creature that moves on the ground" (Gen. 1:28).

The Hebrew word translated as "rule" has sometimes been translated as "have dominion." In either case, however, Scripture scholars remind us that in a world where humans were too insignificant to cause environmental damage, this sense of human superiority over the natural world was quite ordinary. Today, Christian theologians recognize the importance of not simply having dominion over the natural world but living in accord with the order there that God has established. Thus a greater sense of humility is required of people today in light of the capacity of our technology to impose immense risks and costs on our planetary biosphere. God's directive (in Gen. 2:15) to "tend the garden" requires a care for nature often absent in economic development today.

In their appreciation for the natural world, the ancient Israelites recognized that the creatures around them had an existence that had meaning for God, independent of the actions of humans. Recall what the psalmist says:

All creation praises God.

Let them praise the name of the LORD, for at his command they were created, and he established them for ever and he issued a decree that will never pass away. Praise the LORD from the earth, you great sea creatures and all ocean depths, lightning and hail, snow and clouds, stormy winds that do his bidding, you mountains and all hills, fruit trees and all cedars, wild animals and all cattle, small creatures and flying birds, kings of the earth and all nations, you princes and all rulers on earth, young men and women, old men and children. Let them praise the name of the LORD, for his name alone is exalted; his splendor is above the earth and the heavens. And he has raised up for his people a horn, the praise of all his faithful servants, of Israel, the people close to his heart.

Ps. 148:5-14

Later Christian theology understands the natural world sacramentally. Nature not only praises God, but is itself translucent to the divine light, showing God's splendor and power. This sacramentality of creation arises from the biblical account and has important implications for our view of environmental issues today. The natural world is not simply a mine from which we can take whatever we wish or a dump into which we can put any waste we may generate. A responsible environmental ethic—and an appropriate environmental policy—will require a careful interplay of scientific analysis and moral vision.

THE WORLD IS A GIFT.

The second theological principle arising out of the doctrine of creation is that the world is a gift. Christian theology understands all of creation—the physical world around us and even our own lives—as a gift created and given by God. We do not understand our presence in the world as simply the outcome of some sort of cosmic lottery. Although chance plays an important role in the evolution of the universe, our world, and our personal lives, Christians believe that the benevolent creative intention of God stands underneath all of this. Creation by

God signifies that there is a meaning to our being here, that our very existence is a gift.

Paul Camenisch has articulated an understanding of gift that is quite helpful here. Camenisch points out that gift giving is not simply a transfer of an object from one person to another, but is part of a deeper relationship. A thing becomes a gift because of the intention of the giver, and when the recipient accepts it, the intentions of the giver become part of the thing possessed. The gift is transferred for the benefit of the recipient and comes at some cost to the giver, but "to accept the gift is on some level to consent to that total complex reality and to consent to become part of it."[2]

Consider an example. We sometimes give a gift for a birthday or Christmas simply because we are expected to. However, this is a cheap version of gift. In its best sense, a gift is a transfer of something from one to another with a special meaning attached, a meaning that corresponds to the relationship that exists between the two people. We are most aware of that when we choose a gift for someone we love deeply. The ideal gift to give is not something that you care greatly about but the recipient doesn't like, nor is it simply something that the recipient cares much about but which you abhor. Rather, a gift is best when you value it as a representation of your willingness to give of yourself to the other and when it is also deeply valued by the one to whom you give it.

Have you ever received a gift—say, a small figurine from an aunt—that did not fit your expectations very well? Perhaps you didn't like it, but you felt an obligation to appreciate it, simply because you knew that your aunt was trying hard and intending the best in the gift. Perhaps you even now put that gift out on a table when your aunt is about to visit. Such times are awkward, but they remind us that the meaning of a gift is not simply the value of the thing given but rather the relationship expressed in the gift. And even when we receive a wonderful gift—where we greatly value the thing itself—the fact that it expresses a relationship makes it even more valuable.

Now we are able to consider what it means that the Israelites understood the world as a gift from God. They felt indebted to God, of course, for having been given this land when they had been slaves in Egypt, unable to escape the Pharaoh. But even more, because the Israelites recognized the presence of God in their lives, the gift of the land that they used each day in raising their crops and shepherding their flocks had a deeper meaning because it was being used in the presence of the giver. For this reason, the conditions that God had set for the use of such gifts had a much stronger resonance, the sort of "tremor and draw" we saw in the poem at the start of Chapter 1. Those conditions—moral expectations expressed in Israelite law and culture—arose from the gift-character of the world. Morality arose primarily from internal gratitude, not from a fear of punishment when violating laws imposed from the outside. "Morality is secondary to God's founding initiative, which we express theologically in terms of gift, . . . the consequence of the experience of God, more precisely the God-given experience of an entirely unmerited gift."[3]

The same is true for Christians today when we employ the material world to meet our needs and even to enjoy life to the full. At our best, we recognize that it is a gift from God who is present in our lives. If we remain appropriately attentive to our situation and appropriately grateful for what we receive each day, we will strive to live up to God's expectations for how we use his gifts to us.

In sum then, the fact that the world is good and that it is a gift to us from God imbues all of our economic activity with religious meaning. Our jobs, what we buy and enjoy, and any future economic security we might hope for—all can be seen as good and as gifts due to God's action in our lives. It is simultaneously a good thing that we enjoy the material world and that we understand that the gifted nature of that world requires us to respect its integrity and share its gifts with those who are unable to meet their own needs.

THE COVENANT

There is nothing more basic to understanding the character of Israelite religious faith than the relation between the Jewish people and their God, expressed in the Covenant. Passed on in oral tradition from generation to generation long before any of the events and stories were put in writing, the Covenant between God and his people fundamentally shaped the understanding of Israel as a whole and of each individual Israelite.

Biblical scholars tell us that many of the ideas of the Hebrew Scriptures can be found in other Near Eastern religions, where a covenant between human beings was widespread in the region, whether in simple agreements or more formal relationships such as contracts or treaties. In addition, the notion of a formal relationship with their gods was familiar in many nearby civilizations. At the same time the notion of a true Covenant—between divine and human *partners*—is unique to the Bible.[4]

The same can be said about the relation of biblical ideas to the wider religious myths prevalent in the Mesopotamian culture of the time. In other Near Eastern cultures, the primary role of human beings was to serve their gods by providing sacrifices. Thus the sacrifice of animals in Israelite culture was not unique. However, scholars point out that there are indeed two elements of the Hebraic notion that are unique in the region: God's care for humanity and humans' responsibility to continue God's creation.[5] Communal identity, formed through covenant as a member of the people of Israel, was more important than individual identity. This communal identity stands beneath the sense of obligation that Israelites had and supports an indictment of the sort of thoughtless individualism that even many Christians exhibit today.

One of the most important parts of the Covenant was expressed in law, the Torah, where Israel's faithful relationship with God is spelled out in detail. There were laws about worship, diet, and family relations, but we shall focus here on those related to economic life.

Protection for the poor

Do not mistreat or oppress a foreigner, for you were foreigners in Egypt.

Do not take advantage of the widow or the fatherless. If you do and they cry out to me, I will certainly hear their cry. My anger will be aroused, and I will kill you with the sword; your wives will become widows and your children fatherless.

If you lend money to one of my people among you who is needy, do not treat it like a business deal; charge no interest.

Exod. 22:21-25

For the LORD your God . . . defends the cause of the fatherless and the widow, and loves the foreigner residing among you, giving them food and clothing. And you are to love those who are foreigners, for you yourselves were foreigners in Egypt.

Deut. 10:17-19

Do not deprive the foreigner or the fatherless of justice, or take the cloak of the widow as a pledge. Remember that you were slaves in Egypt and the LORD your God redeemed you from there. That is why I command you to do this.

When you are harvesting in your field and you overlook a sheaf, do not go back to get it. Leave it for the foreigner, the fatherless and the widow, so that the LORD your God may bless you in all the work of your hands. When you beat the olives from your trees, do not go over the branches a second time. Leave what remains for the foreigner, the fatherless and the widow. Remember that you were slaves in Egypt. That is why I command you to do this.

Deut. 24:17-22

> When you reap the harvest of your land, do not reap to the very edges of your field or gather the gleanings of your harvest. Do not go over your vineyard a second time or pick up the grapes that have fallen. Leave them for the poor and the foreigner. I am the LORD your God.
>
> Lev. 19:9-10

The Deuteronomic code, a principal part of the law, specifies a number of concrete economic restrictions. When a farmer harvested his field of grain, he was required to leave the corners of the field unharvested for the poor of the day: the widow, the orphan, and the resident alien. He was similarly obligated to leave in the field any overlooked sheaves for those people who had no other source of support.

And it was not only the grain farmer who faced such requirements. When harvesting grapes from one's vineyard, the law required that the harvesters not return a second time to pick the grapes that had not yet been mature when the main harvest occurred. Here again, those grapes were to be left on the vine, available for picking by the widow, the orphan, and the resident alien.

Why these three groups? In every civilization, orphans live a difficult life without parents to look out for them. Widows too, particularly in a patriarchal society, will be in dire straits if they do not have children ready to care for them. And foreigners in most countries are treated as lesser persons, often exploited greatly. Thus this typical and often-repeated triad of persons—the widow, the orphan, and the resident alien—are the very concrete indicators in ancient Israel for those we today would call "the poor."

Many texts of the Torah express concern for the foreigner living in Israel. "Do not oppress a foreigner; you yourselves know how it feels to be foreigners, because you were foreigners in Egypt" (Exod. 23:9). The Lord often reminded the Israelites that his concern for the foreigner was mandatory for them as well. Why? The text provides as its rationale the fact that God had taken the Israelite nation out of subjection in Egypt and brought them into a land of their own.

However, the Scriptures also urge Israelites to go beyond simply treating an "outsider" with decency. They are to treat them as an "insider." "When a foreigner resides among you in your land, do not mistreat them. The foreigner residing among you must be treated as native-born. Love them as yourself, for you were foreigners in Egypt. I am the Lord your God" (Lev. 19:33-34). In this way, Israelites were challenged to understand the resident aliens among them not simply as deserving some attention in justice, but as one of their own. Today, many citizens of the U.S., Europe, and elsewhere often look with suspicion upon foreign residents who are undocumented workers in their midst. The Scriptures remind us that as spiritual descendants of the Israelites saved through the exodus, we too have special obligations to immigrants and even "illegal aliens" among us.

Another central feature of Israelite life was the notion of the Sabbath. Just as God had rested on the seventh day of creation in the Genesis story, the Israelite people were required to abstain from work every seventh day, on the Sabbath. This day of rest was not intended to criticize the hard work required to meet basic needs, but was to be a reminder that for all the striving God intends as part of the life of his people, those same people need to stop and consider the ultimate purpose of such effort.

In a similar way, the law required that the land itself have a sabbatical every seven years. On the seventh year, all fields were to be left untilled, with the poor being allowed to eat whatever crops might grow on them. All debts were to be forgiven, including the release of debt slaves, people in such dire straits that they sold themselves as servants to their fellow Israelites. Even more dramatic than the sabbatical year was the law's requirement of a "Jubilee" year, which was to occur every seventh sabbatical year. In the Jubilee year, all of the observances of the sabbatical were to occur and all land that had been transferred since the last Jubilee was to be returned to its original owner. There is no evidence in the Bible that the Jubilee year was ever enacted, but it represents a fundamental limitation on the meaning of economic ownership. In a culture based on subsistence agriculture, if a family was in such dire condition that they had no option but to sell their land, they would then never again be self-sufficient. This requirement in the law that land be returned to its original owners stands as a rejection of growing class differences and an affirmation that in God's plan, every family can take care of itself by its own productive work.[6]

A similar protection for the poor can be found in the prohibition against usury—the taking of interest on a loan of money. In an agricultural society, it was the destitute who had to resort to such loans, and Torah forbade the wealthy from taking advantage of the plight of their fellow Israelites. As we will see, this biblical teaching on usury would be maintained as a standard part of Christians' view of economic life for many centuries.

THE PROPHETS

In every human society in history, the highest moral advice for how a people should live has often been ignored, particularly by those who have the wealth and power to rise above their fellow citizens. At various points in the history of Israel, the Scriptures themselves identify this kind of problem. They recount the words of strong prophetic voices recruited by the Lord to publicly criticize the people of Israel, and in particular the wealthy, for placing their own comfort and social status above the requirements of the Covenant. Justice, then, is central to the concern of the prophets.

Woe to evildoers

Woe to those who make unjust laws, to those who issue oppressive decrees, to deprive the poor of their rights and withhold justice from the oppressed of my people, making widows their prey and robbing the fatherless. What will you do on the day of reckoning, when disaster comes from afar? To whom will you run for help? Where will you leave your riches? Nothing will remain but to cringe among the captives or fall among the slain.

Isa. 10:1-4

Woe to you who are complacent in Zion, and to you who feel secure on Mount Samaria, you notable men of the foremost nation, to whom the people of Israel come! You lie on beds adorned with ivory and lounge on your couches. You dine on choice lambs and fattened calves. You strum away on your harps like David and improvise on musical instruments. You drink wine by the bowlful and use the finest lotions, but you do not grieve over the ruin of Joseph. Therefore you will be among the first to go into exile; your feasting and lounging will end.

Amos 6:1, 4-7

Amos, Isaiah, and the other prophets called the well-to-do of their day to break out of their own comfort and to respond to the grieving of the poor. As a part of this indictment of the wealthy for having forgotten to care for the widow, the orphan, and the resident alien, the prophets Isaiah and Jeremiah spoke for God in their rejection of any attempts at sacrificial worship without an active concern for these poor in the land. Then as now, liturgical rites without justice are empty.

Justice, not sacrifice

Hear the word of the LORD, you rulers of Sodom; listen to the instruction of our God, you people of Gomorrah! "The multitude of your sacrifices—what are they to me?" says the LORD. "I have more than enough of burnt offerings, of rams and the fat of fattened animals; I have no pleasure in the blood of bulls and lambs and goats. When you come to appear before me, who has asked this of you, this trampling of my courts? Stop bringing meaningless offerings! Your incense is detestable to me. New Moons, Sabbaths and convocations—I cannot bear your worthless assemblies. Your New Moon feasts and your appointed festivals I hate with all my being. They have become a burden to me; I am weary of bearing them. When you spread out your hands in prayer, I hide my eyes from you; Even when you offer many prayers, I am not listening. Your hands are full of blood! Wash and make yourselves clean. Take your evil deeds out of my sight; stop doing wrong. Learn to do right; seek justice. Defend the oppressed. Take up the cause of the fatherless; plead the case of the widow. Come now, let us settle the matter," says the LORD. "Though your sins are like scarlet, they shall be as white as snow; though they are red as crimson, they shall be like wool. If you are willing and obedient, you will eat the good things of the land; but if you resist and rebel, you will be devoured by the sword." For the mouth of the Lord has spoken.

Isa. 1:10-20

"Is not this the kind of fasting I have chosen: To loose the chains of injustice and untie the cords of the yoke, to set the oppressed free and break every yoke. Is it not to share your food with the hungry and to provide the poor wanderer with shelter? When you see the naked, to clothe him, and not to turn away from your own flesh and blood?"

Isa. 58:6-7

A POSITIVE VIEW OF ECONOMIC LIFE

Given both the Torah's restrictions on the actions of the wealthy and the prophetic denunciation of their abuse of the poor, a careful reader might think that the Hebrew Scriptures have a largely negative view of economic life and prosperity. However, this would be completely false. In many ways the Bible is quite positive in its treatment of what we today would call business acumen and economic growth.

Economic historians have understood for centuries that one important prerequisite of prosperity in any nation is the presence of clear laws and a dependable monetary system. Systems of barter—trading one good for another—can occur without money, but this is awkward and often not very helpful, since what I may have to exchange with you may be something that you really don't want to receive in trade. With money, either of us can trade a good in return for money, and can then take the money elsewhere to purchase the things we actually want. Thus the monetization that occurred in Israel, as a part of the historical move to centralize worship in the nation, had the effect of improving the economic health of the nation.[7]

Similarly, the treatment of resident aliens and women in this period was an improvement over what occurred in many other Near Eastern societies and even earlier in Israel's own history. We look back today and find the holding of slaves and the treatment of women in Hebrew culture inconsistent with their stated values, an embarrassment, but it is important to recognize the ways in which Israel did improve cultural respect for these lower-status people.[8] This created a greater social and economic mobility than would have been possible without these changes. And, of course, the law established legal definitions for personal property claims, creating the predictability necessary for economic development.

It was even the case that there were fewer economic restrictions on the sale of houses inside a walled town than in rural areas where such a house would be tied to the land around it.[9] The importance of land for survival in an agricultural society led to the restrictions we have just seen entailed in the Jubilee year. However, the lesser restrictions within towns allowed for a greater flexibility in economic life and tell us that economic transactions there were a normal part of life.

An example of business acumen

"Let me go through all your flocks today and remove from them every speckled or spotted sheep, every dark-colored lamb and every spotted or speckled goat. They will be my wages. And my honesty will testify for me in the future, whenever you check on the wages you have paid me. Any goat in my possession that is not speckled or spotted, or any lamb that is not dark-colored, will be considered stolen."

"Agreed," said Laban. "Let it be as you have said." That same day he removed all the male goats that were streaked or spotted, and all the speckled or spotted female goats (all that had white on them) and all the dark-colored lambs, and he placed them in the care of his sons. Then he put a three-day journey between himself and Jacob, while Jacob continued to tend the rest of Laban's flocks.

Jacob, however, took fresh-cut branches from poplar, almond and plane trees and made white stripes on them by peeling the bark and exposing the white inner wood of the branches. Then he placed the peeled branches in all the watering troughs, so that they would be directly in front of the flocks when they came to drink. When the flocks were in heat and came to drink, they mated in front of the branches. And they bore young that were streaked or speckled or spotted. Jacob set apart the young of the flock by themselves, but made the rest face the streaked and dark-colored animals that belonged to Laban. Thus he made separate flocks for himself and did not put them with Laban's animals.

Whenever the stronger females were in heat, Jacob would place the branches in the troughs in front of the animals so they would mate near the branches, but if the animals were weak, he would not place them there. So the weak animals went to Laban and the strong ones to Jacob. In this way the man grew exceedingly prosperous and came to own large flocks, and maidservants and menservants, and camels and donkeys.

Gen. 30:32-43

Although fidelity to the Covenant was the primary concern of the Israelite nation, there is also a positive assessment of business acumen that an individual might demonstrate, an ability that often led to economic prosperity. The patriarch Jacob spent time in voluntary exile as a young man and, in spite of the inaccurate science in the quotation above, the Scriptures report that he became wealthy due to his skills as a breeder, herdsman, and shrewd businessman—even if somewhat deceitfully.

In a similar fashion, Joseph, after being sold into Egyptian slavery, came into political and economic power under the Pharaoh. There is no doubt that his ability to interpret the Pharaoh's dream and to make wise decisions was reliant on God's help, but the Scriptures nonetheless speak positively about Joseph's talent and savvy in becoming such an administrative success in planning for a famine.

An example of administrative ability

There was no food, however, in the whole region because the famine was severe; both Egypt and Canaan wasted away because of the famine. Joseph collected all the money that was to be found in Egypt and Canaan in payment for the grain they were buying, and he brought it to Pharaoh's palace. When the money of the people of Egypt and Canaan was gone, all Egypt came to Joseph and said, "Give us food. Why should we die before your eyes? Our money is used up." "Then bring your livestock," said Joseph. "I will sell you food in exchange for your livestock, since your money is gone." So they brought their livestock to Joseph, and he

> gave them food in exchange for their horses, their sheep and goats, their cattle and donkeys. And he brought them through that year with food in exchange for all their livestock. When that year was over, they came to him the following year and said, "We cannot hide from our lord the fact that since our money is gone and our livestock belongs to you, there is nothing left for our lord except our bodies and our land. Why should we perish before your eyes—we and our land as well? Buy us and our land in exchange for food, and we with our land will be in bondage to Pharaoh. Give us seed so that we may live and not die, and that the land may not become desolate." So Joseph bought all the land in Egypt for Pharaoh. The Egyptians, one and all, sold their fields, because the famine was too severe for them. The land became Pharaoh's, and Joseph reduced the people to servitude, from one end of Egypt to the other. Joseph said to the people, "Now that I have bought you and your land today for Pharaoh, here is seed for you so you can plant the ground. But when the crop comes in, give a fifth of it to Pharaoh. The other four-fifths you may keep as seed for the fields and as food for yourselves and your households and your children." "You have saved our lives," they said. "May we find favor in the eyes of our lord; we will be in bondage to Pharaoh."
>
> Gen. 47:13-25

We see in the Hebrew Scriptures the conviction that the upright person must live in accord with the Covenant, assisting those unable to care for themselves. But at the same time the tradition praises the business and administrative acumen of those who are both faithful and economically successful.

THE PROBLEM OF FAITH AND PROSPERITY

Building from the respect for economic success that we have just seen, the Hebrew Scriptures at times go further and articulate the view that anyone who is faithful to the Covenant will find economic prosperity. However, as attractive as such a view is for those who enjoy such prosperity, the Scriptures do not present this view so simply. The Book of Job presents the ultimate challenge to the naïve view, preserved even today in some Christian fundamentalist circles, that if you are faithful you will be prosperous.[10]

Job is a successful man in just about every way conceivable. He has lands and livestock, children and grandchildren, and the respect of all around him. Job is thoroughly faithful, but in the face of great suffering and deprivation is tempted to curse his God. He can answer the questions of his doubting friends by pointing to his virtuous record, but he cannot make sense of the calamities that have befallen him. The dramatic power of the story arises from the extent of the general presumption throughout Israelite history, and indeed throughout the Near East in that period, that virtue and economic success will go hand in hand. It is Job's unbending fidelity to God in the face of the greatest of sufferings that speaks the strongest message of the story. No human success—economic, familial, social, or otherwise—is to stand in the way of the fundamental fidelity of every Israelite to the Lord, whose ways are mysterious. Thus while the relation of economic prosperity and religious faith may be more complex than that anticipated by the dominant biblical view of the world, the primacy of faithfulness to the Covenant remains the basic message.[11]

SLAVERY

Slavery was accepted as a common practice in ancient Israel, as it was to one degree or other in just about every culture in the premodern period. According to the Hebrew Scriptures, there were several reasons why another person might be held as a slave. It was possible to hold other Israelites as slaves either as a judicial penalty (Exod. 22:2) or due to a voluntary sale in poverty (Lev. 25:39; Exod. 21:2-4; Amos 2:6; 8:6). Foreigners could be held as slaves for life (Lev. 25:46), as well as any children born to parents in slavery (Exod. 23:12; Lev. 22:11). In addition, foreign slaves could be acquired by purchase or by right of conquest as prisoners of war (Lev. 25:44-46; Num. 31:26; Deut. 20:11).[12]

Although Israel approved slavery, a practice that we find morally unacceptable today, there was in the Bible a clear sense of making the life of the slave less harsh and less demeaning than was true in many Near Eastern cultures at the time.[13] Some scholars argue that the Bible represents the first appeal in world literature "to treat slaves as human beings for their own sake and not just in the interests of their masters."[14] Nonetheless, the very approval of an extensive system of slavery in ancient Israel stands as a reminder that we should not naïvely hope to transport special moral teachings from biblical times to our own. A careful discernment is required.

CONCLUSION

The Hebrew Scriptures cover a wide variety of concerns and speak in a number of different literary voices. However, most basic is the relationship of the Hebrew people with the Lord in the Covenant, generating both daily meaning for individual persons and a set of communal expectations and laws embodying what God requires of them.

Many people in the twentieth-first century, including many Christians, have identified themselves as individuals first and only secondarily as members of a community. Even then, many see their membership in a community as simply a voluntary decision they have made to accomplish their own goals by cooperating with others. The Hebraic and Christian view of human life begins in a very different place. Israelites most fundamentally understood themselves as members of a family and a community in relationship with God. The moral requirements they faced, whether in culture or law, were not seen as impositions by some foreign power or distant deity but rather they were understood as expectations rising quite naturally out of a relationship with a God whose most fundamental characteristic was his care for Israel itself. Thus the norms of the society were seen not as logical consequences of philosophical reflection but instead as a kind of precious inheritance that each generation receives from its ancestors, dating back to God's ancient relationship with the Israelite people.

The understanding of the material world as good and as a gift to be cherished arises from, and only makes sense within, this fundamental relationship with God. Even more importantly, the commitment to the widow, the orphan, and the resident alien—the poor in the ancient world—is also rooted in this covenantal relationship. The God of Israelites and Christians is a God who sides with the oppressed, the ignored, and the outcast. Concern for these marginalized people is not simply an ethical principle; it is a religious principle, rooted in the nature of the God we worship. For this reason, the treatment of the poor becomes the central test—the gold standard—for how well a society conducts its economic life. For this reason, the prophets of the Hebrew Scriptures—and prophets up to our own day—have challenged the prosperous to transform "business as usual" in favor of those harmed or simply left behind by the economic activities of the privileged.

Christians today have much to learn from the view of economic life presented in the Hebrew Scriptures. We ought not naïvely attempt to apply today all the particular practices of our Israelite ancestors, but the fundamental orientations articulated in the Hebrew Scriptures stand as a challenge to easy consciences today.

Notes

1. John Paul II, "Address to the Jewish Community," at the Great Synagogue in Rome, April 13, 1986, in *Spiritual Pilgrimage: Texts on Jews and Judaism, 1979–1995*, ed. Eugene Fisher and Leon Klenicki (New York: Crossroad, 1995), 60–66.

2. Paul Camenisch, "Gift and Gratitude in Ethics," *Journal of Religious Ethics* 9 (1981): 1–34.

3. Pontifical Biblical Commission, *The Bible and Morality: Biblical Roots of Christian Conduct* (Libreria Editrice Vaticana, 2008), para. 4.

4. Ibid., para. 17.

5. Ibid., para. 106.

6. See, for example, Leslie J. Hoppe, "The Torah Responds to the Poor," *Bible Today* 32 (Sept. 1994): 277–82.

7. Barry Gordon, *The Economic Problem in Biblical and Patristic Thought* (Leiden: E. J. Brill, 1989), 18.

8. John Maxwell, *Slavery and the Catholic Church* (Chichester and London: Barry Rose, 1975), 22–23.

9. Gordon, *The Economic Problem*, 18ff.

10. The story of Job is a poem, set between two prose texts—the prologue and epilogue—that describe Job's travail as a test of faithfulness to God. The story itself, however, can stand on its own *theologically* without the "happy ending" provided by the epilogue.

11. Daniel K. Finn, "Economic Order," in *The New Dictionary of Catholic Social Thought*, ed. Judith A. Dwyer (Collegeville, MN: Liturgical, 1994), 311–12.

12. Maxwell, *Slavery*, 22–24.

13. Ibid., 22–23.

14. Muhammad A. Dandamayev, "Old Testament Slavery," in *The Anchor Bible Dictionary* 6, ed. David Noel Freedman et al. (New York: Doubleday, 1992), 65.

4

The New Testament

The Old Testament, what is today called the Hebrew Scriptures, is part of the body of Christian texts. Still, the New Testament—today typically called the Christian Scriptures—constitutes the most fundamental set of documents for Christians today. It includes a wide range of literary genres, from the oldest stories about Jesus to the sophisticated theological analyses of the Pauline epistles and the Gospel of John, to the apocalyptic view of the end of the world in the Book of Revelation. Not all of these texts address economic life, but many do. Here, we will attend to just three of those sources, the Gospels, the Acts of the Apostles, and the Pauline epistles.

THE MISSION OF JESUS

The Gospel of Luke tells us that at the very beginning of Jesus' ministry, immediately after his baptism by John in the Jordan and his temptation by the devil in the desert, Jesus' first act was to travel in Galilee, where he had grown up as a child. He went to his hometown of Nazareth and entered the synagogue on the Sabbath. Luke recounts that he did this in other towns as well, but there can be little doubt that the stakes were highest in his own village, where everyone knew him as "the carpenter's son."

The mission of Jesus

He went to Nazareth, where he had been brought up, and on the Sabbath day he went into the synagogue, as was his custom. And he stood up to read. The scroll of the prophet Isaiah was handed to him. Unrolling it, he found the place where it is written:

The Spirit of the Lord is on me, because he has anointed me
to preach good news to the poor. He has sent me to proclaim

---

freedom for the prisoners and recovery of sight for the blind, to release the oppressed, to proclaim the year of the Lord's favor.

Then he rolled up the scroll, gave it back to the attendant and sat down. The eyes of everyone in the synagogue were fastened on him, and he began by saying to them, "Today this scripture is fulfilled in your hearing."

All spoke well of him and were amazed at the gracious words that came from his lips. "Isn't this Joseph's son?" they asked.

Jesus said to them, "Surely you will quote this proverb to me: Physician, heal yourself! Do here in your hometown what we have heard that you did in Capernaum."

"I tell you the truth," he continued, "no prophet is accepted in his hometown. I assure you that there were many widows in Israel in Elijah's time, when the sky was shut for three and a half years and there was a severe famine throughout the land. Yet Elijah was not sent to any of them, but to a widow in Zarephath in the region of Sidon. And there were many in Israel with leprosy in the time of Elisha the prophet, yet not one of them was cleansed—only Naaman the Syrian."

All the people in the synagogue were furious when they heard this. They got up, drove him out of the town, and took him to the brow of the hill on which the town was built, in order to throw him down the cliff. But he walked right through the crowd and went on his way.

Luke 4:16-30

Scripture scholars agree that Luke's intention in putting this story at the start of Jesus' ministry was to identify what Jesus himself saw as his mission in the world. And of course we can see two separate parts of that quotation from the prophet Isaiah which Jesus chose to read aloud. The first identifies the special relationship that Jesus has with God as the bearer of the Spirit of the Lord, something that Luke already identified in the baptism by John in the Jordan.

The second portion of the quotation, however, might be a bit surprising, since it specifies what Jesus says he has been sent to do. Christians who tend to interpret faith as entailing only a deeply personal relationship with God might be surprised that Jesus does not say that his mission is to bring people closer to God or to get them to be more careful in their prayers or to persuade them to attend to their liturgical responsibilities more faithfully. No, instead he says that his mission is to relieve the suffering and oppression of those most ignored, rejected, or persecuted. He says that these actions proclaim the year of the Lord's favor—that is, they proclaim the "good news," the gospel, of the Lord.

It is tragic that Jesus' listeners in Nazareth were unable to imagine that this local boy could now be speaking to them in God's name. They drove him out of town. Their focus, of course, was on his claim to have this special relationship with God. Interestingly, those Christians who overemphasize the importance of their personal relationship with Jesus Christ as their savior and who downplay his mission to the poor and oppressed make the same error as the people of Nazareth did. They focus so much on Jesus' special relationship with God that they too fail to hear all that Jesus said he was about.

Thus we have at the very beginning of Jesus' public ministry a proclamation that what matters to him is his relationship to the Father and the release of captives, the recovery of sight of the blind, and the end of oppression.

This fundamental setting of priorities for all his followers by Jesus himself is vividly important as we ask what Christian faith means for economic life. Like Jesus, we must keep prayer and our relation with God as the foundation for who we are and all we do, but Jesus himself held up the treatment of the least among us as similarly primary to his mission. Those who intend to follow him, then, would seem to be required to approach economic life—and all of life—keeping vividly in mind Jesus' own priorities.

THREE BASIC THEMES

There has been a lively debate among biblical scholars for decades about what parts of the Gospels represent the most authentic parts of Jesus' own message and which parts may have been embellished, quite properly, by subsequent theological reflection in the Christian community before the biblical texts were written down. Biblical scholar John R. Donahue, S.J., summarizes scholarly consensus when he identifies three separate themes generally understood to be among the most basic and authentic materials from the oldest stories about Jesus that we have: the proclamation of the Kingdom, the call to fellowship with tax collectors, and a call to discipleship.[1]

THE KINGDOM OF GOD

The Kingdom

"The time has come," he said. "The kingdom of God is near. Repent and believe the good news!"

Mark 1:15

> From that time on Jesus began to preach, "Repent, for the kingdom of heaven is at hand."
>
> Matt. 4:17
>
> This, then, is how you should pray: Our Father in heaven, hallowed be your name, your kingdom come, your will be done on earth as it is in heaven. Give us today our daily bread. Forgive us our debts, as we also have forgiven our debtors. And lead us not into temptation, but deliver us from the evil one. For if you forgive others when they sin against you, your heavenly Father will also forgive you.
>
> Matt. 6:9-14

The notion of the "kingdom of God" has roots in the Hebrew Scriptures, since it is often said there that God is the sovereign Lord of all the earth. Although a minor theme in the Hebrew Scriptures, the kingdom of God is a central metaphor of Jesus' ministry. In the New Testament it is understood as "the equivalent of the presence of God himself who comes to conquer evil and transform the world."[2]

Jesus taught that "the kingdom of God is at hand." The phrase "is at hand" reminds us that there is a double sense of presence of the reign of God in our lives. First, it is currently active; it invades and shapes the present situation, and thus calls for a response on the part of Jesus' disciples, both in his day and ours. Second, it is not yet a reality; Christians have long understood that the kingdom of God will never exist in its fullness on this earth. This "already, but not yet" characteristic of the reign of God in Jesus' preaching stands as a challenge to how disciples live their lives in the present and as an eschatological promise that God will ultimately bring about the Kingdom. As the Pontifical Biblical Commission puts it,

> The real and definitive destiny of humankind, when evil will have been vanquished, justice reinstated, and humanity's craving for life and peace fully satisfied, remains a future experience, but the contours of this future—a future that reveals God's entire purpose for humanity—contribute to defining what human life should be already in the present.[3]

Christians living in modern democracies today, with no experience of an all-powerful monarchy, can only stretch their imaginations to understand this use of the word *kingdom* as a symbol. But as Donahue explains, the use of this symbol in a world where kings and emperors are well known clearly brings to mind a sense of "the active exercise of God's sovereignty."[4] Today, of course, in recognition that God is neither male nor female, the phrase "kingdom of God" is often translated as "the reign of God."

When Jesus responds to the request that he teach his disciples how to pray, he gives them the Lord's Prayer, the most fundamental of Christian prayers. In it, Jesus tells his disciples to pray "Thy Kingdom come," meaning that they express their sincere intention that the reign of God become present in their lives and in this world. And as if to anticipate the tendency of some of his followers to think that the Kingdom would be only something that happens in the afterlife, he tells his disciples to pray for God's will—God's sovereignty—to come "on Earth as it is in heaven." These are extremely powerful words that we often fail to notice simply because we say them so often and so routinely.

Do not be anxious.

Someone in the crowd said to him, "Teacher, tell my brother to divide the inheritance with me."

Jesus replied, "Man, who appointed me a judge or an arbiter between you?" Then he said to them, "Watch out! Be on your guard against all kinds of greed; a man's life does not consist in the abundance of his possessions."

And he told them this parable:

"The ground of a certain rich man produced a good crop. He thought to himself, 'What shall I do? I have no place to store my crops.'

"Then he said, 'This is what I'll do. I will tear down my barns and build bigger ones, and there I will store all my grain and my goods. And I'll say to myself, "You have plenty of good things laid up for many years. Take life easy; eat, drink and be merry."'

"But God said to him, 'You fool! This very night your life will be demanded from you. Then who will get what you have prepared for yourself?'

"This is how it will be with anyone who stores up things for himself but is not rich toward God."

Then Jesus said to his disciples: "Therefore I tell you, do not worry about your life, what you will eat; or about your body, what you will wear. Life is more than food, and the body more than clothes. Consider the ravens: They do not sow or reap, they have no storeroom or barn; yet God feeds them. And how much more valuable you are than birds! Who of you by worrying can add a single hour to his life? Since you cannot do this very little thing, why do you worry about the rest?

"Consider how the lilies grow. They do not labor or spin. Yet I tell you, not even Solomon in all his splendor was dressed like one of these. If that is how God clothes the grass of the field, which is here today, and tomorrow is thrown into the fire, how much more will he clothe you, O you of little faith! And do not set your heart on what you will eat or drink; do not worry about it. For the pagan world runs after all such things, and your Father knows that you need them. But seek his kingdom, and these things will be given to you as well."

Luke 12:13-31

The reign of God entails not only living our lives in accord with God's will in the sense of ceasing to mistreat others and reaching out in generosity, but also includes a much more serene view of daily life. God cares for the lilies in the field, so surely God looks out for us. That is, Jesus tells us to worry less about what the future may bring for us. He says this not to prevent us from prudent savings for the future in a commercial culture, but rather to say that whatever we do, we should do it without the anxiety that blocks the way of faith. The problem, of course, as theologian Reinhold Niebuhr put it, is that human freedom and intelligence—our capacity for transcendence—allows us to anticipate the future and thereby leads us to become anxious about things over which we lack control.[5] Jesus wants his followers to be prudent but to do so without a self-destructive and sinful craving for a temporal security that is illusory. Buying more and more things cannot make us truly secure. Only God can provide that. Our ultimate security will come only in life with God after our earthly existence ends, but the challenge of the Kingdom is "to adopt a way of life that reflects now the future reality of the Kingdom."[6]

Committed believers must be realistic enough to recognize that the Kingdom will not fully arrive prior to the Lord's second coming, but they must also be committed enough to prepare for God's reign which is already breaking into our earthly reality. This entails "the obligation to create an order increasingly similar to that for which the Savior died, and for which he goes on working day by day until its complete manifestation."[7] Material goods are not evil—recall that Jesus provided extra wine at the wedding feast at Cana. But followers of Jesus must keep them properly ordered—to our true and final end in God. Later in history—as we will see in the next chapter—when Christians have responsibility for political power, the meaning of this "order" we are called to create moves beyond the Christian community itself and out into the realm of economic and political life more broadly.

FELLOWSHIP WITH TAX COLLECTORS

> ### Jesus and the tax collectors
>
> As Jesus went on from there, he saw a man named Matthew sitting at the tax collector's booth. "Follow me," he told him, and Matthew got up and followed him.
>
> While Jesus was having dinner at Matthew's house, many tax collectors and sinners came and ate with him and his disciples. When the Pharisees saw this, they asked his disciples, "Why does your teacher eat with tax collectors and sinners?"
>
> On hearing this, Jesus said, "It is not the healthy who need a doctor, but the sick."
>
> Matt. 9:9–12
>
> "To what can I compare this generation? They are like children sitting in the marketplaces and calling out to others: 'We played the flute for you, and you did not dance; we sang a dirge and you did not mourn.' For John came neither eating nor drinking, and they say, 'He has a demon.' The Son of Man came eating and drinking, and they say, 'Here is a glutton and a drunkard, a friend of tax collectors and sinners.' But wisdom is proved right by her deeds."
>
> Matt. 11:16–19

The second basic theme of the Gospels is fellowship with tax collectors. It is important to recall that tax collection in the Roman Empire in New Testament times did not occur through an Internal Revenue Service the way it does in the U.S. today. The Roman system was harsh and shrewdly effective. Once they conquered a local tribe or nation, the Romans did not directly deal with all the members of that society but instead deputized elites from that society to do their business for them. Thus for example, we know that although Pontius Pilate was the Roman administrator of Palestine at the time of Jesus' ministry, the Romans left the local political structure, King Herod and the religious authorities, in place and used them to rule the people of Israel.

Tax collection was handled similarly. Local individuals were empowered to collect the taxes owed to the Empire, but they were allowed to increase their own income by increasing the tax rate that they imposed on their fellow countrymen. And they did. Thus there was great personal animosity against these tax collectors—far beyond the irritation of a taxpayer today who learns that the I.R.S. is about to audit his tax return. The tax collector of Jesus' day was considered a lowlife who imposed the unfair Roman tax burden on his countrymen and became wealthy by increasing the tax rate even further. Tax collectors were despised as traitors.

Zacchaeus the tax collector

Jesus entered Jericho and was passing through. A man was there by the name of Zacchaeus; he was a chief tax collector and was wealthy. He wanted to see who Jesus was, but being a short man he could not, because of the crowd. So he ran ahead and climbed a sycamore-fig tree to see him, since Jesus was coming that way.

Jesus reached the spot, he looked up and said to him, "Zacchaeus, come down immediately. I must stay at your house today." So he came down at once and welcomed him gladly.

All the people saw this and began to mutter, "He has gone to be the guest of a sinner."

But Zacchaeus stood up and said to the Lord, "Look, Lord! Here and now I give half of my possessions to the poor, and if I have cheated anybody out of anything, I will pay back four times the amount."

Jesus said to him, "Today salvation has come to this house, because this man, too, is a son of Abraham. For the Son of Man came to seek and to save what was lost."

Luke 19:1-10

When encountering the chief tax collector Zacchaeus, Jesus does not ignore or condemn him for his exploitation of the Jewish community and his service to the Roman oppressor. Rather, Jesus joins Zacchaeus back at his home and invites him to greater responsibility. Zacchaeus explains that he will give half of his goods to the poor and will correct any fraud by repaying the debt fourfold. Jesus does not speak directly about Zacchaeus's economic plans, but he clearly approves of Zacchaeus's conversion, and in the process we find that Zacchaeus becomes a faithful "steward" of his goods. He does not offer, nor does Jesus ask him, to give up everything he owns, but he does convert to living a life of righteousness.

The message that Jesus gave to his disciples then—and gives to us now—is that no one should be treated as a legal or cultural outcast and that everyone who is willing to live virtuously qualifies for Jesus' approval. We see a similar insistence on inclusion in Jesus' treatment of many others who were looked down upon in Israelite society, including prostitutes, lepers, the physically handicapped, and resented outsiders, such as the Samaritan woman. Jesus' mission certainly challenges us today—both us as individuals and our economic system—when we demean or ignore individuals around us, whether that is the homeless man loitering on a downtown street, the undocumented immigrant woman who speaks no English, or the custodian who cleans the toilets in the building where we work.

THE CALL TO DISCIPLESHIP

Discipleship

Jesus went through all the towns and villages, teaching in their synagogues, preaching the good news of the kingdom and healing every disease and sickness. When he saw the crowds, he had compassion on them, because they were harassed and helpless, like sheep without a shepherd. Then he said to his disciples, "The harvest is plentiful but the workers are few. Ask the Lord of the harvest, therefore, to send out workers into his harvest field."

Matt. 9:35-38

"If you obey my commands, you will remain in my love, just as I have obeyed my Father's commands and remain in his love. I have told you this so that my joy may be in you and that your joy may be complete. My command is this: Love each other as I have loved you. Greater love has no one than this, that he lay down his life for his friends. You are my friends if you do what I command. I no longer call you servants, because a servant does not know his master's business. Instead, I have called you friends, for everything that I learned from my Father I have made known to you. You did not choose me, but I chose you and appointed you to go and bear fruit—fruit that will last. Then the Father will give you whatever you ask in my name. This is my command: Love each other."

John 15:10-17

The third basic theme in the oldest accounts of the life of Jesus is the call to discipleship. Time and again through the Gospels, we hear Jesus calling those around him to be his disciples, that is, to be learners in the disciplines of life that Jesus teaches. At bottom this includes a willingness to give up the convictions and advantages that the fortunate carry with them whenever they stand in the way of a deeper commitment to Jesus and his mission.

Jesus called everyone to discipleship, to a life oriented by love of God and neighbor. In response, some gave up all their material belongings, leaving behind family and friends; yet others do not. All disciples are expected to contribute heartily from what they have in order to assist others in need. This understanding of discipleship from an economic point of view is critically important if we are to understand the later developments in Christianity with regard to wealth and economic life more generally.

IMPLICATIONS

A critically important insight into the implications of these three themes—the kingdom of God, fellowship with tax collectors, and the call to discipleship—is given by the parable of the last judgment, the only time Jesus ever identified how individuals will be judged by God at the end of their lives. Students today often ask their teachers, "What will be on the test?" Here Jesus goes so far as to tell us explicitly the questions that will be on life's final exam.

The last judgment

When the Son of Man comes in his glory, and all the angels with him, he will sit on his throne in heavenly glory. All the nations will be gathered before him, and he will separate the people one from another as a shepherd separates the sheep from the goats. He will put the sheep on his right and the goats on his left.

Then the King will say to those on his right, "Come, you who are blessed by my Father; take your inheritance, the kingdom prepared for you since the creation of the world. For I was hungry and you gave me something to eat, I was thirsty and you gave me something to drink, I was a stranger and you invited me in, I needed clothes and you clothed me, I was sick and you looked after me, I was in prison and you came to visit me."

Then the righteous will answer him, "Lord, when did we see you hungry and feed you, or thirsty and give you something to drink? When did we see you a stranger and invite you in, or needing clothes and clothe you? When did we see you sick or in prison and go to visit you?"

The King will reply, "I tell you the truth, whatever you did for one of the least of these brothers of mine, you did for me."

Then he will say to those on his left, "Depart from me, you who are cursed, into the eternal fire prepared for the devil and his angels. For I was

---

> hungry and you gave me nothing to eat, I was thirsty and you gave me nothing to drink, I was a stranger and you did not invite me in, I needed clothes and you did not clothe me, I was sick and in prison and you did not look after me."
>
> They also will answer, "Lord, when did we see you hungry or thirsty or a stranger or needing clothes or sick or in prison, and did not help you?"
>
> He will reply, "I tell you the truth, whatever you did not do for one of the least of these, you did not do for me."
>
> Then they will go away to eternal punishment, but the righteous to eternal life.
>
> Matt. 25:31-46

Implicit in this story are the three fundamental themes we have just reviewed. The kingdom of God is at hand; all disciples should be living up to the standards of the Kingdom here on earth in anticipation of its coming. Because we are called to fellowship with those who are outcast and looked down upon, Jesus reminds us that how we treat those "least" in our society will determine how we are judged in the end. And, of course, the call to discipleship is exactly what is being examined in this judgment, since disciples are those who lead their lives the way Jesus wants them to, in accord with his own mission. These teachings comport well with those Jesus gave in the Sermon on the Mount, when in the Beatitudes (Matt. 5:3-12; Luke 6:20-22) he recommends that his disciples be joyous in leading a virtuous life, poor in spirit, meek, merciful, peaceful, and willing to undergo persecution for the sake of righteousness.

The Gospels do not address concretely many of the economic issues we face today, such as how to deal with environmental degradation, what intellectual property rights should entail, or how to structure the provision of necessities for those who cannot provide for themselves in the twenty-first century. However, a basic outline is provided in the Gospels and it is then up to disciples today to answer the question about how to implement the commitments to which Jesus calls us. This book is an attempt to address that question.

Does God love the poor more than the rich?

Both the Hebrew and Christian Scriptures often attest to God's particular concern for the poor and outcast. Jesus' own words make clear their special place in his mission. As we will see later, both liberation theologians and popes today speak of God's "preferential option for the poor." Thus a question often arises about whether this means God actually loves poor people more than wealthy ones.

We know from both Scripture and tradition that God does not have favorites and loves every person with an infinite love. But how can God then have a particular concern for some of his children?

In his workshops on parish social ministry, the educator Jack Jezreel includes a wonderful interpretation of this apparent contradiction. He asks us to consider a father with three young daughters, all of whom he loves greatly—and equally. If while the three are playing outdoors, one of them falls, hits her head on the sidewalk, and lies there unconscious, it will be no surprise to witness the father rushing to her side, focusing almost exclusively on her because her needs at this point are so much greater than her sisters'. This, Jezreel says, is what God does in particular concern for the poor and outcast. God loves us all equally, and that is why we recognize a divine "preferential option" for the least among us.

THE ACTS OF THE APOSTLES AND EPISTLES

The descriptions of the earliest Christian communities in the Acts of the Apostles and in the Pauline epistles show Christians of intense faith who are struggling to work out the meaning of Jesus' mission for their own lives after he was gone. Scripture scholars tell us that many people's behavior was influenced by the widespread belief among early Christians that Jesus' second coming would happen before long, almost surely within their own lifetimes. It is impossible to sort out today either the strength of this belief in a quick second coming of the Lord or the influence of that belief on daily life, but scholars tell us that it had significant impact.

One central theme made clear in the teachings of Paul is that we have been redeemed in Christ and this makes all the difference for our lives. This redemption is a free gift offered by God in Christ and there is nothing we can do to earn or deserve it. Nonetheless, in redemption in Christ, God accepts our daily moral conduct not as causing redemption but as a witness to the salvation already operative within us. Thus living out our faith in ordinary economic life is always understood as a loving response to a generous God.

SHARING GOODS IN THE JERUSALEM COMMUNITY

One of the most important stories in the Acts of the Apostles related to economic life is a description of the holding of goods in common within the community of Christians in Jerusalem.

Pooling resources

All the believers were together and had everything in common. Selling their possessions and goods, they gave to anyone as he had need. Every day they continued to meet together in the temple courts. They broke bread in their homes and ate together with glad and sincere hearts, praising God and enjoying the favor of all the people. And the Lord added to their number daily those who were being saved.

Acts 2:44–47

There were no needy persons among them. For from time to time those who owned lands or houses sold them, brought the money from the sales and put it at the apostles' feet, and it was distributed to anyone as he had need.

Joseph, a Levite from Cyprus, whom the apostles called Barnabas (which means Son of Encouragement), sold a field he owned and brought the money and put it at the apostles' feet.

Acts 4:34–37

The fact that the members of the Jerusalem community met every day in the temple may indicate that they had given up their ordinary daily work and focused almost completely on living in accord with Jesus' call. Later in the Christian tradition there are two fundamental interpretations of this intense sharing of their resources to meet the needs of everyone. On the one side are those who argue that because Christians in Jerusalem seemed to be consuming the capital stock of the community in an unsustainable way, they must have assumed that the second coming of Christ would occur soon and, using today's terminology, there would be little reason to save for retirement. From this perspective, later Christians should not follow their example. The second interpretation is that their behavior is the recommended way for all Christians to live in all eras: with simple needs and the guarantee that all persons' needs would be met through the pooling of everyone's resources into a common fund.

Whatever the proper interpretation of this "primitive communism" within the early Jerusalem community, it is clear that the great apostle Paul did not recommend this ethic for economic life when he established new Christian communities around the Mediterranean.[8] There are no reports in the New Testament of any other communities pooling their resources so dramatically, though there is a consistent appeal for the well-to-do to share their goods with the poor. In each community, Paul took up a collection to support the "saints in Jerusalem" (e.g., Rom. 15:23-27), in accord with an earlier agreement he made when Peter and the other leaders in Jerusalem affirmed their support for Paul's mission to the Gentile world (Gal. 2:10). Thus it was no surprise that Paul chastised the Christians in Corinth (1 Cor. 11:17-34) for severing the relationship between compassion toward the needy and celebrating the Eucharist in memory of Christ's death. As was true for the prophets of the Hebrew Scriptures, liturgy must be tied to justice. Paul consistently taught that Christians ought to live a transformed life, be obedient to God, and generously give of themselves to their brothers and sisters.

THE IMPORTANCE OF WORK

Work

In the name of the Lord Jesus Christ, we command you, brothers, to keep away from every brother who is idle and does not live according to the teaching you received from us. For you yourselves know how you ought to follow our example. We were not idle when we were with you, nor did we eat anyone's food without paying for it. On the contrary, we worked night and day, laboring and toiling so that we would not be a burden to any of you. We did this, not because we do not have the right to such help, but in order to make ourselves a model for you to follow. For even when we were with you, we gave you this rule: "If a man will not work, he shall not eat."

We hear that some among you are idle. They are not busy; they are busybodies. Such people we command and urge in the Lord Jesus Christ to settle down and earn the bread they eat. And as for you, brothers, never tire of doing what is right.

If anyone does not obey our instruction in this letter, take special note of him. Do not associate with him, in order that he may feel ashamed. Yet do not regard him as an enemy, but warn him as a brother.

2 Thess. 3:6–15

Many scholars tell us that Paul himself was a tent maker and continued to work in this occupation so that he would not be an economic burden on the communities he visited. The context of Paul's words indicates that he was trying to offset the view that, since the second coming would soon occur, believers could give up their daily work and focus only on their heavenly destiny. Paul makes clear an insight that even today stands behind the right to food, clothing, and shelter: that ordinarily all should provide these for themselves and their families, but if they are unable, the community is obliged to provide for them.

KOINONIA AND DIAKONIA

Two of the most important themes in the Pauline epistles are *koinonia* and *diakonia*. Together, these two articulate both the internal dynamics of the Christian community and its orientation to those outside.

Koinonia is a rich Greek word that is variously translated in English as community, communion fellowship, sharing, or joint participation. The most basic form of communion of the faithful is that which occurs at the Eucharist.

Koinonia

Is not the cup of thanksgiving for which we give thanks a participation in the blood of Christ? And is not the bread which we break a participation in the body of Christ? Because there is one loaf, we, who are many, are one body, for we all partake of the one loaf.

1 Cor. 10:16–17

Thus the notion of *koinonia* includes both liturgical relationships and fellowship within the church at all times, emphasizing that the relationship among Christians themselves is intimately tied to their common relationship with Jesus Christ.

Diakonia is the Greek word for service. The very same bonds of community that tie us so intimately in faith with the Lord also call Christians to service to one another and to all who have unmet needs. The collection that Paul took up in his various communities to support the church in Jerusalem was a fundamental form of *diakonia*. This was, however, simply a part of a broader demand of Christian life that each should live in service to others, both in their own local community and beyond. Paul's own mission to the Gentiles arose out of his understanding that the gospel of Jesus extends beyond the Jewish community to all in the world. Thus Christians today maintain the same view that this life of faith should never be centered on the community of Christians themselves, important as that is. It always entails an outward directedness, a form of service, to all they come in contact with.

These two fundamental notions of *koinonia* and *diakonia* together identify both the internal vitality and external orientation of the Christian church. Without the communion in the life of Christ, the Christian church would be empty. Without the mission of service to all, not simply within the community but outside as well, the mission of Christ to the world would be forgotten.

SLAVERY

Unlike the more humane requirements for the keeping of slaves in the Hebrew Scriptures, the Roman civil law that predominated in the Mediterranean area during New Testament times allowed for a far harsher version of human slavery. The slave had no rights and was simply a piece of property owned by the master. In this situation, the New Testament teaching on slavery takes on an important nuance.

Scripture scholars sometimes distinguish two different levels within the Pauline tradition on slavery.[9] The first would be a more fundamental theological view of slavery and the other what we might call a more "pastoral" view of the moral requirements that masters and slaves should face. As Paul describes the fundamental theological reality, he reminds his readers that within Christian life there is no distinction between Jew and Greek, male and female, slave and free. Rather all are equal in the eyes of God.

Sons of God

You are all sons of God through faith in Christ Jesus, for all of you who were baptized into Christ have clothed yourselves with Christ. There is neither Jew nor Greek, slave nor free, male nor female, for you are all one in Christ Jesus. If you belong to Christ, then you are Abraham's seed, and heirs according to the promise.

Gal. 3:26–29

For we were all baptized by one Spirit into one body—whether Jews or Greeks, slave or free—and we were all given the one Spirit to drink.

1 Cor. 12:13

Thus from this most fundamental point of view it would seem that Christians should not hold slaves and therefore should free any they have at the time of their conversion to the Christian faith. However, this was not the general teaching of the early church, and the recognition of this accommodation to the dominant culture appears in the later Pauline epistles, which scholars tell us may not have been written by Paul himself but by his disciples.

Slaves and masters

Slaves, obey your earthly masters in everything; and do it, not only when their eye is on you and to win their favor, but with sincerity of heart and reverence for the Lord. Whatever you do, work at it with all your heart, as working for the Lord, not for men, since you know that you will receive an inheritance from the Lord as a reward. It is the Lord Christ you are serving. Anyone who does wrong will be repaid for his wrong, and there is no favoritism.

Col. 3:22-4:1

Slaves, obey your earthly masters with respect and fear, and with sincerity of heart, just as you would obey Christ. Obey them not only to win their favor when their eye is on you, but like slaves of Christ, doing the will of God from your heart. Serve wholeheartedly, as if you were serving the Lord, not men, because you know that the Lord will reward everyone for whatever good he does, whether he is slave or free.

And masters, treat your slaves in the same way. Do not threaten them, since you know that he who is both their Master and yours is in heaven, and there is no favoritism with him.

Eph. 6:5-9

All who are under the yoke of slavery should consider their masters worthy of full respect, so that God's name and our teaching may not be slandered. Those who have believing masters are not to show less respect for them because they are brothers. Instead, they are to serve them even better, because those who benefit from their service are believers, and dear to them. These are the things you are to teach and urge on them.

1 Tim.6:1-2

Teach slaves to be subject to their masters in everything, to try to please them, not to talk back to them, and not to steal from them, but to show that they can be fully trusted, so that in every way they will make the teaching about God our Savior attractive.

Titus 2:9-10

This advice is in many ways similar to the advice given to slaves and slaveholders in the Hebrew Scriptures. It calls for a respectful relationship without urging either the slaveholder to free the slave or the slave to resist the master's control. In this, contemporary Christian Scripture scholars recognize the "household codes" of the early Roman Empire, which in this case controlled the relationship of slavery but also imposed upon women the patriarchal culture of the Roman era even though in Christian principle, men and women were of equal dignity before God.[10]

It is in the end impossible to know precisely the mind of Paul or the other early church leaders on the issue of slavery. On the one hand, their insight into the fundamental equality of all would seem to imply that Christians should not tolerate anything like slavery. Yet their advice to slaves and slaveholders about how to treat the other does not usually reflect any ultimate sense that slavery itself is an evil institution. Perhaps the best that can be said is that the cultural conditioning to which all human knowledge and language are subject can be so powerful that it is quite difficult for us to understand our own cultural biases. As we will see later in the book, the ongoing development of world history often provides a vision of the possibility for a different set of cultural standards. This happened in the history of Christian teaching of slavery, something we will return to in Chapter 11.

THE DEVELOPMENT OF DOCTRINE

One of the important themes in a responsible economic ethic today is the development of Christian teaching over time as circumstances change. In later chapters we will look at changes concerning economic issues such as slavery, usury (the charging of interest when lending money), and the very idea of human rights. Here, however, it will be helpful to note briefly some examples of the development of doctrine within the Christian Scriptures.

One such example arose when Paul challenged the requirement that Gentile males should be circumcised when they become Christians. The apostles in Jerusalem were inclined to insist that all Christians follow Jewish law, while Paul, the apostle to the Gentiles, argued that the life and teaching of Jesus instead called not for a commitment to Jewish law but to living a faithful life as a disciple of Jesus himself. This dispute was important enough for the early Christians that it takes up nearly the entire fifteenth chapter of the Acts of the Apostles. Paul won this argument. The apostles and elders in Jerusalem eventually allowed Gentile Christians to remain uncircumcised as long as they followed the Mosaic law in abstaining from "food sacrificed to idols, from blood, from the meat of strangled animals, and from sexual immorality" (Acts 15:29).

Another example is recounted in Paul's letter to the Galatians where he describes how he confronted Peter, the leader of the Christian church. Paul reports that "when Peter came to Antioch, I opposed him to his face, because he was clearly in the wrong" (Gal. 2:11). The issue was whether Christians should be allowed to eat with Gentiles. Paul was arguing they should, whereas Peter had lapsed into the practice of avoiding such meals in order to respect the traditions of those Jewish Christians who continued to keep the kosher laws of the Jewish tradition. Although Peter was in charge, Paul showed him no deference on this issue since he was convinced that the gospel of Jesus transcends these traditional dietary restrictions and should not be a barrier for Gentile Christians. Peter and the whole church eventually agreed, and we observe in this incident not only an important development in Christian doctrine but an important lesson for church authority to humbly rethink its positions when confronted with an inconsistency between its teaching and the fundamental message of the gospel.

A third example of the development of Christian teaching occurs in Paul's frequent use of secular Greek philosophy in his teaching to Christians in Greek cities around the Mediterranean. In this, Paul found particularly useful the teaching of the Stoic philosophers, one of the most pervasive points of view about the moral life in the Greek world of his day. For example, in describing how Christians need not be subject to the complete Mosaic law, he argued that the requirements of God's law are "written on the hearts" of all persons, whether Jew or Gentile (Rom. 2:14-15). Similarly, Scripture scholars note that in his frequent listing of moral virtues, and in the importance of freedom from passions as fundamental to the moral life, Paul borrowed liberally from Stoic ideas in articulating the fundamental moral teaching of Jesus (e.g., Gal. 6:1-10; 1 Cor. 5:1). Paul is not here adding to Christian teaching anything that would contradict what Jesus taught his disciples, but he has begun a tradition, which we will see in more detail in the next chapter, of articulating a fundamental message employing the dominant language and modes of thought of the Greek listeners to whom he is preaching.

Thus both in loosening the requirements of the Mosaic law for Christians and in incorporating local language and modes of thought in Christian preaching, the Christian community was on its way to becoming a world church.

CONCLUSION

This chapter has provided a brief summary of some of the themes in the Christian Scriptures relevant to the fundamental question of this book: the implications of Christian faith for economic life in the twenty-first century. While there is in the New Testament no explicit description of economic globalization, CEO pay, or global warming, there is a wealth of material relevant to our understanding of these and other issues we confront today.

Most basic, as we have seen, is Jesus' mission in the world, which he explicitly described for his disciples. He is here to bring people to the Father and to release captives, give sight to the blind, and free the oppressed. He teaches that God's judgment of each of us on the last day will ask not how much we prayed but whether we responded to the needs of the poor, despised, and marginalized. The themes of the Kingdom, fellowship with tax collectors, and the call to discipleship each deepen the believer's understanding and commitment to this vision.

And as we have seen in the early Christian communities through the Acts of the Apostles and the letters of Paul, a fundamental part of Christian discipleship has always been concern for others, most especially those who are unable to provide for their own basic needs. Christians in every age are called to "put on the mind of Christ," challenging us to live our lives self-consciously centered on the example and teaching of Jesus. Any Christian view of a proper economic life today will have to sustain these basic New Testament commitments.

Notes

1. John R. Donahue, S.J., "Biblical Perspectives on Justice," in *The Faith That Does Justice: Examining the Christian Sources for Social Change*, ed. John C. Haughey (New York: Paulist, 1977), 68–112.

2. Pontifical Biblical Commission, *Bible and Morality: Biblical Roots of Christian Conduct* (Libreria Editrice Vaticana, 2008), para. 42.

3. Ibid.

4. Donahue, "Biblical Perspectives," 86.

5. Reinhold Niebuhr, *Moral Man and Immoral Society: A Study in Ethics and Politics (1932)* (New York: Charles Scribner's Sons, 1995).

6. Pontifical Biblical Commission, *Bible and Morality*, para. 102.

7. Ibid., para. 148

8. Barry Gordon employs this evidence to dismiss the argument that Christians should emulate the sharing of the early Christian community in Jerusalem. See Gordon, *The Economic Problem in Biblical and Patristic Thought* (Leiden: E. J. Brill, 1989), 78.

9. For a discussion of the complexity of Paul's stance on slavery in the midst of the Roman system of slavery, see "The Letter to Philemon in the Context of Slavery in Early Christianity," in D. Francois Tolmie, ed., *Philemon in Perspective: Interpreting a Pauline Letter* (New York: De Gruyter, 2010), 142–68; and J. Albert Harrill, "Paul and Slavery," in J. Paul Sampley, *Paul in the Greco-Roman World: A Handbook* (Harrisburg, PA: Trinity Press International, 2003), 575–607.

10. See, for example, Elisabeth Schüssler Fiorenza, *In Memory of Her: A Feminist Theological Reconstruction of Christian Origins* (New York: Crossroad, 1983).

5

The Early Church

Christian Faith and Concern for the Poor

The New Testament recounts the spread of Christianity out of Israel and around the north side of the Mediterranean Sea, through what is now Lebanon, Syria, Turkey, Greece, and Italy. This process owed much to the energies of the apostle Paul. However, the next few centuries saw developments that even Paul himself would not have dreamed of.

THE DEVELOPMENT OF CHRISTIAN DOCTRINE

In broad strokes, Christianity adopted Greek modes of thought and expression—it became "Hellenized"[1]—when it expanded from Jerusalem westward. The Hebraic faith of Jesus and the twelve, articulated in parables and wisdom sayings, came to be expressed in an ordered rationality, cultivated in ancient Greece and its intellectual successor, Rome. That is, the Greek way of thinking was employed to articulate Christian theology and the self-understanding of people of faith. This was not a sellout of Christian faith but rather the expression of the wisdom and insight contained in a biblical faith within the more rational and intellectually sophisticated language of Greek, and within the philosophical and rhetorical traditions of ancient Greece. All of the seven great ecumenical councils of the early church—from the First Council of Nicea in 325, through councils at Constantinople, Ephesus, and Chalcedon, to the Second Council of Nicea in 787—were held in what is today Greece and Turkey. Greek was the language employed in both oral debates at the councils and in their written decrees and creeds.[2]

The spread of Christianity around the Mediterranean world took place, of course, through the local conversion of individuals to the Christian faith. Christianity began as a religion of poor people, but as more and more Roman citizens became Christians, both poor and wealthy joined this new faith community. And the wealthy, who have always educated their children well, ended up combining within themselves the fundamental faith convictions of Christian life and the intellectual point of view that they inherited from the school system in the Roman world. Understanding this interaction between Christian faith and the structures of Greek and Roman thought—and how Christian theology changed in this context—is critical to an adequate grasp of how Christian faith today should relate to secular intellectual analysis in the twenty-first century. Such an understanding is essential for answering the basic question of the book: What does the history of Christian teaching on economic life mean for economic life in the twenty-first century?

Scholars today who downplay or even deny the development of Christian doctrine over the centuries often describe the movement of the early church from Hebraic wisdom teaching to sophisticated Greek philosophical doctrines as a process in which early Christian leaders chose carefully among the resources of the Greek and Roman intellectual traditions. According to this account, the secular world didn't influence or alter Christian thought. Instead, the bishops of the early church shrewdly used appropriate parts of secular thought to express the insights already contained within Christian teaching.

There is a great deal of truth in this account. However, it is inadequate without a complementary second account, recognizing that a reciprocal influence did occur: with Greek and Roman modes of thought shaping how Christians came to understand their faith.

This second account is rooted in the sociology of knowledge, which, as we saw in Chapter 1, is part of the sociological understanding of the "social construction of reality." Our words do not simply name our experience and the world around us. The words and modes of thought available to us determine not just how we describe things; they also shape how we experience the world and our lives, including our faith. Thus the influence of Greek and Roman thought left us with a theology, liturgy, and church quite different from what it would have been if, say, China or India had controlled the Mediterranean world of Jesus' day and Paul had traveled east instead of west in spreading the gospel.

This second account is hard to accept for some "conservative" Christians who fear it would undermine the certainty and security they identify with church teaching that has always simply articulated the truth handed on by Jesus Christ to his disciples. The Christian rule of faith and the truth of revelation have indeed been handed on, under the influence of the Holy Spirit. But to understand how the cultural context is a part of this process, it is helpful to consider the most influential persons in this handing on of the tradition—the bishops of the early church, who generally were highly educated men from wealthy families.

Some early bishops, like Gregory of Nazianzus, grew up as Christians, in addition to being educated in the best schools of the Greek and Roman world. Although the reciprocal influence of faith and culture surely occurred in the lives of these bishops, it is possible for a scholar today to hold out hope that these bishops incorporated into their worldviews only those elements of Greek and Roman intellectual life that their early schooling in Christian faith would authorize. But many other bishops had been non–Christian adults before they converted to Christianity, after having their intellectual frame of mind thoroughly formed by a secular education prior to any influence by Christianity. Perhaps the best single example here is Ambrose of Milan, but also included are Cyprian of Carthage, John Chrysostom, Justin Martyr, and Tertullian. Those who knew them generally recognized a basic continuity in these persons before and after their encounters with Christianity. There can be little doubt that many of the habits of mind held before their conversions remained with them afterwards.

Ambrose of Milan

Ambrose of Milan was born in the year 340. His father was Prefect of Gallia, a territory including land in France, Spain, Britain, and Africa. Educated in Rome, Ambrose was made governor in northern Italy when he was thirty-two years old.

A man of great wisdom and administrative ability, he was asked to mediate a dispute over who should be the next Bishop of Milan. Contrary to his own plans at age thirty-four, the people and clergy of Milan chose him. He was baptized, ordained as a priest, and then consecrated as bishop within a week. He gave his worldly possessions to the poor and his land to the church.

Ambrose was influential; for example, he threatened to excommunicate Emperor Theodosius over the deaths of 7000 people and the killing of a Roman governor. After the Emperor did penance for several months, Ambrose allowed Theodosius to return to the Eucharist. Ambrose's teaching and example brought Augustine to the Christian faith. Ambrose died in 397 at age fifty-seven.

It was under the leadership of bishops that the new church was forced to think through its convictions and had to distinguish between correct and incorrect belief (defining orthodoxy and heresy). In thinking through controverted issues, there was not simply Hebrew wisdom at work but also the deeply philosophical frame of mind that these Christian leaders absorbed from the culture they grew up in. For example, quite important in the lives of many of the early church Fathers was the influence of Stoic philosophy, a branch within the Greek and Roman philosophical traditions that stressed the importance of living simply in order to keep one's intentions clearly focused on the most important elements of life. The Fathers, of course, had a higher notion of those most important elements, namely one's relationship with God, in a way the Stoic philosophers themselves did not.

The articulation of Christian belief within Greek and Roman modes of thought is what generated the highly sophisticated intellectual clarifications of Christian doctrine that we find in the great early councils such as Nicea and Chalcedon. It was the bishops who developed these precise doctrinal phrasings about the three persons in one God and the two natures of Christ and a number of other subtle philosophical distinctions that the original apostles, uneducated fishermen as they were, would never have thought of.

Just as important for the purposes of this book is the development of a remarkable cultural synthesis in the joining of the Hebraic mindset with the Greek and Roman views of the world. Historians of culture have often pointed back to this creative synthesis as the most fundamental reason that the Western world has had a different economic and technological trajectory than have other cultures around the globe, even though many of those other cultures were scientifically advanced in many ways.

As Mircea Eliade has argued, most ancient cultures had a cyclical view of time, focusing on the repetition that goes on year after year, based on the patterns of sun and moon, and on planting and harvest cycles.[3] The Israelites' view of time, however, added something different, because God had broken into their lives and had made a difference in their history and insisted that their future be different from their past. This Hebrew attitude about time as moving forward to something different from the past had a very powerful influence when combined with the rational philosophical analysis that so typified the Greek and Roman approach to intellectual life. Thus some scholars have argued that the rise of science and technology in the West—from Roger Bacon in the thirteenth century to the Industrial Revolution five hundred years later—was made possible by this remarkable combination of an analytical rationality with a religious view of the unfolding of history.

For the purposes of this chapter, our focus will be on the relation of faith and economic life in the early church. Traditionally, this era in the church is called "the patristic period," based on the Latin word "pater," father. Most of the leaders of the early Christian community—and all of the bishops—were men, following the patriarchal cultural forms of the secular world at the time. There were women leaders in the church too—including the "desert mothers" who led early religious communities of women—but not many of their writings have been preserved.[4] The writings we do have come largely from sermons by various bishops of the early church. Most of the quotations in this chapter and the next come from Peter Phan's very helpful book, *Social Thought*.[5]

To understand the view of economic life in the early church, it is essential to start with God, the focus of any life of faith.

THE CENTRALITY OF GOD

The essence of Christian faith has always been tied to our dependence on God and God's gracious concern for us, both in this life and eternally. Thus it is important to recognize that, in understanding the actions of day-to-day life, the church Fathers were always insistent that Christians keep a proper perspective, knowing that their ultimate hope and destiny is with God and not with this earth.

One of the most vivid ways of speaking about this perspective in economic life came from Augustine of Hippo, who distinguished between two ways of relating to the goods humans have available to them. Augustine employed the Latin word *uti* to identify the "use" of a good for some higher purpose and used the word *frui* to identify the enjoyment of something for its own sake, with no higher purpose behind it. For Augustine, only God is to be "enjoyed"; our ultimate fulfillment, or happiness, can only occur in relation with God. Too many people, he argued, misunderstood this: "They want to be happy, even while living a life that will not make them so."[6] Thus Augustine understood sin as "disordered love," our misguided grasping for fleeting pleasures that cannot satisfy the human heart, something only God can do.

Using and enjoying

There are, then, some things which are to be enjoyed, others which are to be used. . . . Those which are to be enjoyed make us happy. Those which are to be used help us as we strive for happiness and, in a certain sense, sustain us, so that we are able to arrive at and cling to those things which make us happy.

To enjoy anything means to cling to it with affection for its own sake. To use a thing is to employ what we have received for our use to obtain what we want, provided that it is right for us to want it. A bad use ought rather to be termed an abuse.

But, if we who enjoy and use things, living as we do in the midst of both classes of things, strive to enjoy the things which we are supposed to use, we find our progress impeded and even now and then turned aside. As a result, fettered by affection for lesser goods, we are either delayed in gaining those things which we are to enjoy or we are even drawn away entirely from them.

Augustine of Hippo, *Christian Instruction*[7]

Augustine here presses in a religious context a distinction between more and less important goals in life that dates back to Aristotle's *Nichomachean Ethics* and Xenophon's *Education of Cyrus*.[8] He instructs his listeners that we should enjoy only God; in fact, it is our destiny to be with God and enjoy God forever. All other goods are to be used—in order to reach our highest goal, union with God. Thus all earthly pleasures—whether from friendship, alcohol, or good literature—should be "used," employed in the proper place and time. Here he does not mean what we today sometimes mean by "using people"—a manipulation of them with no concern for their own good. Rather he challenges us to understand that all things around us should be subordinate to the importance of God. If our relationships to people around us do not lead us closer to God, then we have misused those people. Our language today says that, at our best, we "encounter God in others," but Augustine's intention here is similar, even though expressed in the language of a different era.

Augustine of Hippo

Augustine was born in 354 in North Africa (in what is today Algeria). He studied law in the secular center of Carthage, where he led a profligate life, including much sexual promiscuity (as he explains in his autobiography, *The Confessions*). Although a successful young professor of rhetoric in Carthage, he decided to move to Italy in 383 for the simple reason that he was fed up with the unruliness of the students.

In Italy he was quickly named professor of rhetoric at the Imperial school in Milan, where he met Ambrose. He was eventually baptized and returned to North Africa as a dedicated Christian, distributing his goods to the poor. Within three years he was ordained a priest, and five years later a bishop. His insight and erudition made him one of the most influential theologians in the history of Christianity. Augustine also established a religious community of men, and thus was simultaneously a bishop in the public sphere and the equivalent of an abbot of a local community.

Augustine lived through tumultuous times. While he was Bishop in Hippo, the Visigoths invaded and sacked the city of Rome, the first time a foreign power had controlled that city in eight hundred years. He died at age seventy-six as the "barbarian" forces were overtaking most of Northern Africa.

Another theme stressed in the early church is that of the self-sufficiency of the Christian. Here, the teaching of Clement of Alexandria is a helpful illustration of this theme and of the influence of Stoic philosophy on Christian faith.

Autarkia: self-sufficiency

Those concerned for their salvation should take this as their first principle, that, although the whole creation is ours to use, it is made for the sake of self-sufficiency, which anyone can obtain with a few things. Those who take delight in what they have hoarded up in their storehouses are foolish in their greed.

Clement of Alexandria, *The Tutor*[9]

It is quite remarkable that Clement would claim that if you're worried about your eternal salvation the first thing you should be thinking about is self-sufficiency (*autarkia* in Greek). He does not speak here of going to church or saying your prayers. What he has in mind, of course, is the great advantage of living simply, because a simple life requires less energy and time to gather the few material things we really need, and leaves more time and energy for God in our lives. Here we see the influence of Stoic philosophy, which had a similar principle for living simply, without anxiety. Although Jesus hadn't talked about "self-sufficiency," his parable of the lilies of the field, which we saw in the previous chapter, taught simplicity and a reduction of anxiety that a simpler life effects.

Clement of Alexandria

Clement of Alexandria was born to a non-Christian family around the year 150. His later conversion to Christian faith was a turning point in his life, as he had been restless and moved often in search of knowledge and instruction from different teachers. He did not find the peace he was looking for until he met Pantaenus, in Alexandria, a cultural hub and trading port. Pantaenus had founded the important school of Alexandria, Egypt, and Clement took over for Pantaenus as the director of this school when he was forty years old. Well educated and familiar with Greek thinking, Clement employed many dimensions of Greek philosophy in his writings. He died in his sixties, around the year 215.

Time and again the Fathers urge detachment from possessions and a conversion of heart that allows the Christian to live in the world and use the things of the world, while keeping both mind and heart on that which is most important, God. This need for detachment, along with God's concern for the poor, creates an obligation for the wealthy. According to the early second-century document, *The Shepherd of Hermas*, "It is for this purpose that the Master has made you wealthy, to perform this ministry for him."[10] Although this perspective left the social relations of wealthy and poor intact, the Fathers understood that God works in the world through his people, and in this case, through their use of wealth, which is to be distributed to assist those whose needs are unmet.[11]

The importance of God in the life of a Christian should not be underestimated, but we must keep in mind that the Fathers did not preach a religion that calls for individuals to escape from the world.

The proper treatment of earthly goods

Thus some men make evil use of these things, and others make good use. And the man who makes evil use clings to them with love and is entangled by them (that is, he becomes subject to those things which ought to be subject to him, and creates for himself goods whose right and proper use require that he himself be good); but the man who uses these rightly proves that they are indeed goods, though not for him (for they do not make him good or better, but become better because of him).

Therefore he is not attached to them by love, lest he make them limbs, as it were, of his spirit (which happens if he loves them), and lest they weaken him with pain and wasting when they begin to be cut off from him.

Instead, let him be above temporal things completely. He must be ready to possess and control them, and even more ready to lose and not to possess them. Since this is so, you do not think, do you, that silver or gold should be blamed because of greedy men, or food and wine because of gluttons and drunkards, or womanly beauty because of adulterers and fornicators?

Augustine of Hippo, *On Free Choice of the Will*[12]

The goods of the earth are not to be looked down upon but appreciated for their goodness. One of the classic patristic sayings was that "goods are called goods because they do good."[13] Although being with God is the ultimate aim of all humanity, there is no rejection of the material world. In fact, the proper use of goods becomes one of the primary standards for understanding whether one has lived a life that accords with God's intentions. Augustine himself points to the standard that Jesus first taught in the parable of the last judgment, which we saw in the previous chapter.

The standard of judgment

There are others who have not won the crown of martyrdom, who have not taken to heart the high and noble counsel of perfection by selling their goods, yet they are free of deeds deserving damnation; they have fed Christ hungry, given drink to Him thirsty, clothed Him naked, received Him a wanderer, and, although they will not sit with Christ on a throne when He comes to judge, they will stand at His right to receive the judgment of mercy: "Blessed are the merciful for they shall obtain mercy" (Mt 5:7), and "Judgment without mercy to him that has not done mercy, but mercy exalts itself above judgment" (James 2:13).

Augustine of Hippo, *Letters*[14]

The Fathers closely related faith in God with treatment of the poor. This link has its roots, as do most of their moral teachings, in both the gospel message of Jesus and the understanding of the world drawn from Greek thought. Thus with Paul, the Fathers understood that in Christ there is neither Jew nor Greek, slave nor free, male nor female. But at the same time it built upon well-established Greek ideas, originating in Plato and Aristotle, that "something divine is present in man" regardless of the person's immediate situation.[15]

Every person possesses dignity.

I have no contempt for anyone, for every person is worthy of our attention as a creation of God, even the lowest among the slaves. I am not concerned with the social position of a person but with a person's virtue. I do not look at a master or a slave but a human person. It is for the human being that the heaven opened, the sun shines, the moon rises, the air fills everything, the springs well-up water, the sea stretches out immeasurably. It was for the human person that the only begotten son of God became human. My Lord shed his blood for the human being. Who am I to have contempt for any human being? How should I expect to be forgiven if I would do so?

John Chrysostom, *In Lazarum*[16]

CONCERN FOR THE POOR

Poverty and homelessness are serious problems today, and some people talk as if they are simply creations of a modern economic system. But the Fathers of the church knew well from pastoral experience the suffering that attends the lives of the poor. Consider the words of Gregory of Nyssa.

The poor

These days have brought us naked and homeless men in plenty; a host of captives is at everyone's door; strangers and fugitives are not lacking, and on every side their begging and stretched-out hands are there to see.

Their house is the open air; their lodgings are the arcades, the streets, the deserted corners of the markets; they lurk in holes like owls and birds of the night. Their clothing is tattered rags; their means of subsistence, the sympathy of the compassionate. Their food is anything thrown by the passers-by; their drink, the springs they share with the beasts. . . .

They live a wild and vagabond life, not by habit but because need and misfortune have brought them to it.

Gregory of Nyssa, *Love of the Poor*[17]

In a similar manner, John Chrysostom describes the plight of those who have no home to go to.

The contrast of wealth and poverty

Why do you choose to be rich through covetousness? To hoard up gold and silver for others and innumerable curses and accusations for yourself? The poor man whom you have defrauded is suffering anguish because of the lack of the necessities of life, and is lamenting, and drawing down upon you the curses of thousands.

He may go about the market place at fall of evening and not knowing where he is going to spend the night. How can the unhappy fellow sleep, with pangs in the belly, tortured by hunger, while it is freezing and the rain is coming down on him?

And while you are coming home from the bath, clean and dandy, dressed in soft clothes, full of contentment and happiness, and hastening to sit down to splendidly prepared dinners, he is driven everywhere about the market place by cold and hunger, with his head hung low and his hands outstretched. The poor man does not even have the courage to ask for the necessary food from one so well fed and so well rested, and often has to withdraw, covered with insults.

When, therefore, you have returned home, when you lie down on your couch, when the lights around your house shine bright, when your table is well prepared and plentiful, at that time remember that poor miserable man wandering about like dogs in the alleys, in darkness and in mire, and from these alleys he goes back, not to his house, his wife, or his bed, but to a pile of straw, like those dogs which we hear baying all through the night.

And you, if you see but a drop of water falling from the ceiling, you would throw the whole house in confusion, calling for the slaves and disturbing everything, while he, laid in rags, and straw, and dirt, has to bear the bitter cold.

John Chrysostom, *Homilies on the First Letter to the Corinthians*[18]

Here we understand the care with which the early church Fathers understood the plight of the poor and the scandal it causes when Christians do not come to their aid.

Today we periodically read in news stories from very poor nations around the world where the father of a family has sold a child into slavery or, what often amounts to the same thing, into prostitution. We are appalled that a parent could ever do this and many have decried this as a terrible problem of the modern age, which it certainly is. But we find that the same was true in the days of the early church, as was made clear in the writings of Basil the Great, who presents us with heart-rending description of the problem that sounds like it could have been written today.

The plight of a poor man considering the sale of a child

The bright gleam of gold delights you; you are heedless of all the lamentation of the needy that rises loud in your wake. How can I bring home to you what the poor man's sufferings are?

He casts his eyes round the house, sees that he has no gold and never will have; his clothes and furniture are what the poor's always are—worth a few pennies altogether. What then? What is left? He looks at his sons, and thinks he may stave off death by selling them in the market-place.

Watch the battle between starvation and fatherhood. The one threatens him with the most pitiful of deaths, the other holds him back and bids him die with his children; again and again he starts forward, again and again he checks himself; but the stress of pitiless want is on him, and he succumbs at last.

And what are his thoughts! "Which shall I sell first? Which will please the corn merchant best? Shall I take the eldest? He has rights I dare not violate. The youngest then? I pity his youth, still innocent of misery. This one is his parents' living image; this other is ripe for schooling. What hopelessness! What am I to do? Can I turn against any of them? Can I become a brute beast? Can I forget nature? If I cling to them all, I shall see them all wasting away with hunger. If I sacrifice one, with what face can I look at the others? They will suspect me of treachery at once. How can I stay in a house which I myself have orphaned? How can I sit down to my table when there are the means of filling it?"

The poor man goes off in tears to sell his darling son; but you—you are cold to his misery, you feel no touch of nature. He, poor wretch, is starving; and you keep him in suspense; you beat about the bush, drawing out his agony. To keep alive, he offers his own flesh and blood; and you, whose very hand should be palsied at receiving the price of such wretchedness, you haggle about the bargain, you try to give less than you get, and in every way you can make the poor creature's burden worse. Tears do not move you, groans do not soften your heart, you are unrelenting and pitiless.

Basil the Great, Homily, "I Will Pull Down My Barns"[19]

The Fathers clearly show a compassion for the suffering of the poor, and they are equally aware that the suffering can prevent a person from focusing on the higher things of life. As Clement of Alexandria put it, "when someone lacks the necessities of life he cannot but be broken in spirit; he will have no time for better things since he will make every effort to procure what he needs however and whenever he can."[20]

The Fathers continually reminded their listeners of God's concern for the poor, using many of the sources that we ourselves reviewed in the last two chapters on the Scriptures. Although the early church did not use the phrase "human dignity" to discuss the value of the poor person who is to be assisted, the underlying idea was not foreign. As Augustine said, "there is no one in the human race to whom love is not due, either as a return of mutual affection or in virtue of his share of our common nature."[21]

Basil the Great

Basil the Great was born to a wealthy family in Caesarea (in modern-day Turkey) about the year 329. He attended Greek schools there with his younger brother, Gregory of Nyssa, where he met Gregory (eventually to be known as Gregory of Nazianzus), who was to become a lifelong friend. Basil and Gregory soon moved to Constantinople and later to Athens in pursuit of higher education. Afterwards, Basil returned to Caesarea to practice law and teach rhetoric.

In his mid-twenties he had a religious conversion ("I awoke as out of a deep sleep") and was baptized. He then visited monasteries in Egypt, Palestine, Syria, and Mesopotamia. Upon his return he opened his own monastery in Pontus, thus becoming known as the father of Eastern monasticism. At age forty-one, he was chosen as Bishop of Caesarea. Basil expended great energy in service to the poor of the region. His time as bishop was short; he died less than nine years later.

As a part of their concern for the poor, the Fathers insisted that all should work and not remain idle. Just as today, the goal is for each family to support itself. Many of the poor are too old, too young, or too infirm to do this, but others who need assistance are to be helped toward self-sufficiency, a teaching affirmed in the *Didache*, the oldest surviving catechism in Christianity.

Against idleness

Let everyone who comes in the name of the Lord be received; after that, when you have tested him, you will know what he is like.

If the one who comes is a traveler, help him as much as you can, but he shall not stay with you more than two or three days if this is necessary. But if he wants to settle with you, and he is a craftsman, let him work and so eat. If he has no craft, see to it in your own understanding that no one lives among you in idleness because he is a Christian. If he is unwilling to do this, he is trading on Christ. Be on your guard against such people.

Didache 12.1–12.5

One final way in which the church Fathers were concerned about the poor is in their prohibition of usury: the charging of interest when lending money. In this, the Fathers followed the teaching of both the Hebrew Scriptures and the classical Greek argument against usury. Like the Israelites, the Fathers understood that in a traditional economic system, those who most frequently turned to borrowing were the poor who were forced to do so out of misfortune or abuse. The prosperous were encouraged to make a loan to a poor person in distress but were not to add an additional charge. Like the Greeks, they held that it was simply wrong to make money for these reasons, the taking of interest on a loan of money was strictly forbidden.

CONCLUSION

During the second through the fifth centuries, Christianity moved from being a small "third world" religion centered in Jerusalem to being the received religion of both wealthy and poor throughout the Roman Empire. The Fathers of the church, bishops educated in the best Greek and Roman schools, came to articulate the fundamentals of the faith received from Jesus in the language of Greek philosophy, developing the doctrines and creeds still at the center of Christian faith today.

This chapter has made clear that for the Fathers of the early church, faith in God is the bedrock of the Christian life—trusting in a God who created the world and who plans an eternal destiny for his people. That ultimate goal acts as a rule or standard against which the daily lives of believers are measured, calling each of us to dedicate ourselves to treasures that will not rust, instead of to the baubles and ballyhoo that so often distract us with their lure. Service to the poor, then, is not understood as a burden reducing the economic well-being of the prosperous but as a call from God that leads to a more secure happiness for those willing to take it on. An important part of this patristic analysis is the character of ownership and wealth, which the next chapter will address.

Notes

1. *Hellas* is the Greek word for Greece.

2. For a popular description of the rise of Greek and then Latin in early church life, see Thomas G. Casey, "Ave Atque Vale," *America* 200, no. 18 (June 8, 2009): 16–18.

3. Mircea Eliade, *The Myth of the Eternal Return, or Cosmos and History*, trans. Willard R. Trask (Princeton: Princeton University Press, 1974). We should note that there is considerable support for Eliade's view of a cyclical time, for example, Gideon Goosen, *Spacetime and Theology in Dialogue* (Milwaukee: Marquette University Press, 2008). At the same time, some scholars doubt so vivid a portrayal of cyclical time. See, for example, Sasha Stern, *Time and Process in Ancient Judaism* (Oxford: The Littman Library of Jewish Civilization, 2003).

4. See, for example, Mary Forman, O.S.B., *Praying with the Desert Mothers* (Collegeville, MN: Liturgical, 2005) and Laura Swan, *The Forgotten Desert Mothers* (New York/Mahwah, NJ: Paulist, 2001).

5. Peter Phan, *Social Thought*, vol. 20, *Message of the Fathers of the Church* (Wilmington, DE: Glazier, 1984). Most of the Patristic texts in chapters 5 and 6 are from this very helpful volume. This and all excerpts from Phan's *Social Thought* are being used with permission from copyright by the Order of Saint Benedict. Published by Liturgical Press.

6. Augustine of Hippo, *The City of God*, XIV, 4 (New York: Modern Library, 1950).

7. Augustine of Hippo, *Christian Instruction* 1, 3, 3 in Phan, *Social Thought*, 216–17.

8. I am indebted to Brian Matz for this insight.

9. Clement of Alexandria, *The Tutor*, Section 2, 3:38 in Phan, *Social Thought*, 66.

10. The Shepherd of Hermas, in Phan, *Social Thought*, 53.

11. For a review of the various explanations for the existence of poverty in the biblical world, ranging from a more radical criticism in the Book of Revelation to the milder acceptance of social conditions in the Shepherd of Hermas, see Steven J. Friesen, "Injustice or God's Will? Early Christian Explanations of Poverty," in *Wealth and Poverty in the Early Church and Society*, ed. Susan R. Holman (Grand Rapids, MI: Baker Academic, 2008), 17–36.

12. Augustine of Hippo, *On Free Choice of the Will*, I, VI, 15 in Phan, *Social Thought*, 202–3.

13. Clement of Alexandria, *Quis Dives Salvetur?*, 14, in Charles Avila, *Ownership: Early Christian Teaching* (Maryknoll, NY: Orbis, 1983), 43.

14. Augustine of Hippo, *Letters*, in Phan, *Social Thought*, 214–15.

15. For a fuller investigation of the Hellenic background to these Patristic ideas, see Demetrios J. Constantelos, chapter 13, "The Hellenic Background and Nature of Patristic Philanthropy in the Early Byzantine Era," in *Wealth*, ed. Susan Holman, 187–208.

16. *In Lazarum*, PG 48:1029. Cited in Demetrios J. Constantelos, "Hellenic Background," 204.

17. Gregory of Nyssa, *Love of the Poor*, in Phan, *Social Thought*, 131.

18. John Chrysostom, Homilies on the First Letter to the Corinthians, in Phan, *Social Thought*, 152–53.

19. Basil the Great, Homily, "I Will Pull Down My Barns," in Phan, *Social Thought*, 116–17.

20. Clement of Alexandria, *Who Is the Rich Man That Is to Be Saved?*, in Phan, *Social Thought*, 73.

21. Augustine of Hippo, *Letters*, in Phan, *Social Thought*, 207.

6

The Early Church

Patristic Teaching on Ownership and Wealth

Readers today are sometimes shocked to discover how harshly the early church Fathers spoke about those wealthy Christians who did not share their wealth with the needy. From the beginning, the Christian community understood assistance for the poor as among the most fundamental of obligations.

OBLIGATIONS OF THE WEALTHY

The Fathers quite frequently argued that it was in the eternal self-interest of the rich to share with the poor, and that, in addition, a life of financial moderation was essential for proper moral development, reflecting insights from both the gospels and the Stoic tradition.[1]

Sharing of riches is the duty of justice.

Now I say that every man should be relieved in his difficulties. For a person who is in need and suffers inconveniences in his daily life is in torment and anguish. Whoever delivers a needy man from his necessities draws great joy for himself. For the man who is harassed by this kind of misfortune suffers the same torture and affliction as the man in prison. Indeed, many who are incapable of enduring these calamities take their own lives.

Therefore, whoever knows of the misfortune of such a person and does not release him, commits a serious sin and is guilty of that man's blood.

The Shepherd of Hermas[2]

What you rich give to the needy brings profit to yourself; for your own possessions are increased when they are diminished. You yourself are fed by

---

the bread you give to the poor, because whoever has mercy on the poor is himself sustained by the fruits of his compassion.

Mercy is sown on earth and sprouts in heaven; what is planted in the poor produces in front of God. "Do not say, I will give tomorrow," says the Lord (Prov 3, 28). If God does not allow you to say: "I will give tomorrow," how can he bear you to answer: "I will not give"?

When giving to the poor man you are not giving him what is yours; rather you are paying back to him what is his.

Indeed what is common to all, and has been given to all to make use of, you have usurped for yourself alone. The earth belongs to all, and not only to the rich; yet those who do enjoy it are far fewer than those who do not. You are paying back, therefore, your debt; you are not giving gratuitously what you do not owe.

Ambrose of Milan, *On Naboth*[3]

But we possess many superfluous things, unless we keep only what is necessary. For if we seek useless things, nothing suffices . . . the superfluous things of the wealthy are the necessities of the poor. When superfluous things are possessed, others' property is possessed.

Augustine of Hippo, *Reflections on Psalm 147*[4]

And since we are human beings, we must pay our debt of goodness to our fellow human beings, whatever the cause of their plight: orphanhood, exile, cruelty of the master, rashness of those who govern, inhumanity of tax-collectors, brutality of blood-thirsty bandits, greediness of thieves, confiscation, or shipwreck. All are equally miserable and look up to our hands in the same way as we look up to those of God whenever we stand in need of something.

Gregory of Nazianzus, *On the Love for the Poor*[5]

THE PATRISTIC VIEW OF OWNERSHIP

The ownership of things in the early church was controlled by Roman law, which articulated strong claims for owners, without emphasis on social obligations to the poor. The Fathers taught that the Roman view of ownership was a faulty one, because it violated what God himself intended in the creation of the world.

Central here is the fundamental conviction, inherited from biblical faith, that God has given the earth to humanity in order that everyone's needs be met. Property ownership is understood as a helpful invention of humans, but it should not violate God's fundamental intention for the earth, and thus any property ownership system would have to be subject to a judgment about whether it helps or hinders the meeting of human needs of all.

As we shall see, some of the statements of the Fathers in condemning those wealthy Christians who did not share their surplus with the poor might be interpreted by readers today as a simple condemnation of private property ownership. Indeed, there were more radical and in some cases heretical groups that held the wealthy responsible for the existence of the poor, and called for a renunciation of all wealth.[6] However, if we consider all the writings of each of the Fathers, it is clear that they did not condemn personal ownership itself but rather its abuse in hoarding. In general, the view of property ownership in the early church can be summarized by the following rule of thumb: "If I have more than I need and you have less than you need, I am obliged to share my surplus with you, because God has given the earth to humanity, and my wealth to me, to meet the needs of all."

The selfish rich man

"I am wronging no one," you say; "I hold fast to my own, that is all." Your own! You gave it to yourself to bring into life with you? You are like a man who takes a seat in a theatre and then keeps out newcomers, claiming as his own what is there for the use of everyone. Such are the rich; they seize what belongs to all and claim the right of possession to monopolise it; if everyone took for himself enough to meet his own wants and gave up the rest to those who needed it, there would be no rich and no poor.

Did you not come naked out of the womb, and will you not go back naked to earth again? Whence came the riches you have now? If you say from nowhere, you deny God, you ignore the Creator, you are ungrateful to the Giver. But if you acknowledge they came from God, tell us the reason for your receiving them. Is God unjust when he distributes the necessaries of life unequally?

Why are you rich and another poor? Surely it is that you may win the reward of charitableness and faithful stewardship, and the noble prizes of patience? And yet you store up everything in the pockets of insatiable covetousness and think you wrong no one when you are defrauding so many.

Who is the covetous man? One for whom plenty is not enough! Who is the defrauder? One who takes away what belongs to everyone. And are not you covetous, are not you a defrauder, when you keep for private use what you were given for distribution? When someone strips a man of his clothes we call him a thief. And one who might clothe the naked and does not—should not he be given the same name?

The bread in your cupboard belongs to the hungry, the cloak in your wardrobe belongs to the naked, the shoes you let rot belong to the barefoot, the money in your vaults belongs to the destitute. Everyone you might help and do not—to all these you are doing wrong.

Basil the Great, Homily, "I Will Pull Down My Barns"[7]

Here we see Basil taking an approach employed by church Fathers throughout both East and West. The rich did not come into life bringing their wealth with them but found it here, largely wealth inherited within the family. The Fathers did not condemn such inherited wealth as long as the heir employed it for the good of both his family and others. Irenaeus even compared the offering of inherited wealth to God to the Israelites' use of the goods taken from the Egyptians in order to build the Temple in Jerusalem.[8] Thus there is a very strong obligation to share one's wealth, if there are others who have unmet needs.

Ambrose of Milan has similarly strong language when he speaks about the obligation to help the poor.

The rich man's concerns

You give coverings to walls and bring men to nakedness. The naked cries out before your house unheeded; your fellow-man is there, naked and crying, while you are perplexed by the choice of marble to clothe your floor. A poor man begs for money in vain. Your fellow-man is there, begging bread, and your horse champs gold between its teeth. Other men have no corn; your fancy is held by precious ornaments.

What a judgment you draw upon yourself! The people are starving, and you shut your barns; the people are groaning, and you toy with the jewel upon your finger. Unhappy man, with the power but not the will to rescue so many souls from death, when the price of a jeweled ring might save the lives of a whole populace.

Ambrose of Milan, *On Naboth*[9]

The obligations of prosperity are strong and created by God—to be acted upon by those who have a surplus in the presence of needy people. It was rare for the Fathers to articulate just how much the wealthy ought to give away, but Clement of Alexandria specifically identified jewelry, makeup, and silver dishware as items no one needs to own.[10] Gregory of Nyssa proposed an even broader standard.

Beastly selfishness

But if one man should seek to be an absolute possessor of all, refusing even a third or a fifth to his brothers, then he is a cruel tyrant, a savage with whom there can be no dealing, an insatiate beast gloatingly shutting its jaws over the meal it will not share. Or rather he is more ruthless than any beast. Wolf does not drive wolf from the prey, and a pack of dogs will tear the same carcass; this man in his limitless greed will not admit one fellow-creature to a share in his riches.

Gregory of Nyssa, *Love of the Poor*[11]

John Chrysostom suggested that even if the wealthy were to keep their capital, they should at least be willing to give away much of the annual income generated by it.

Giving from annual income

I am not constraining you to lessen your capital, not because I do not wish it, but because I see you are very recalcitrant. I am not then saying this. No. But give away the revenues; keep nothing of these. It is enough for you to have the money of your income pouring in on you as from a fountain; make the poor sharers with you, and become a good steward of the things God has given you.

John Chrysostom, *Homilies on the Gospel of Matthew*[12]

COMMON OWNERSHIP

The Fathers knew the Scriptures well and understood that the Acts of the Apostles reported that the Jerusalem community pooled resources to meet everyone's needs. Even though this was an exception and not the norm for the Christian world, a number of Fathers refer to this possibility.

Cyprian of Carthage pointed to the early Jerusalem community, which, he said, "flourished with greater virtues when the faith of believers was warm with a fervor of a faith still new."[13] All the Fathers recognized the temptation to covetousness on the part of the rich.

John Chrysostom

John Chrysostom was born about the year 347 in Antioch (in modern-day Turkey). His father was a high-ranking military officer. He received a classical Greek education and was deeply shaped by Greek philosophy. His life changed at age twenty when he met a bishop, Meletius. He was baptized about age twenty-three and eventually went to live as simply as one could, in a cave outside of Antioch. He lived there for two years but eventually returned to Antioch to recover his health, which had been damaged by fasting and exposure. John then stayed in Antioch where he served as a deacon and priest for several years and at age fifty was ordained Archbishop of Constantinople, a position he at first refused to accept. His preaching was so eloquent and persuasive that he become known as "Chrysostom," meaning "golden-mouth." Committed to Jesus' teaching about service to the poor, he ended the tradition of lavish dinners hosted by the bishop for the wealthy and he instituted a series of reforms. As archbishop he was fearless in accosting the rich—some would say tactless—and many wealthy resented him deeply, particularly members of the imperial family, whom he frequently criticized. He was twice driven out of Constantinople by the imperial court (on charges of heresy) but was reinstated from exile because of citizens' outrage at the injustice. He died at age sixty during his journey to a third exile. Three decades later his body was moved back to Constantinople and laid to rest in honor in the Church of the Apostles.

John Chrysostom, the most radical of the Fathers regarding the dangers of personal ownership, was convinced that "concerning things that are common, there is no contention, but everything is peaceful. But as soon as someone attempts to possess himself of anything to make his own, then contention is introduced as if nature itself protests against the fact."[14]

At one point, Chrysostom proposed to his listeners a thought experiment about common ownership, suggested by the early Jerusalem community.

The dispersion of property is the cause.

And if you please, let us now for a while depict it in words, and derive at least this pleasure from it, since you have no mind for it in your actions. For at any rate this is evident, even from the facts which took place then, that by selling their possessions they did not come to be in need.

Let us imagine things as happening in this way: All give all that they have into a common fund. No one would have to concern himself about it, neither the rich nor the poor. How much money do you think would be collected? I infer—for it cannot be said with certainty—that if every individual contributed all his money, his lands, his estates, his houses (I will not speak of slaves, for the first Christians had none, probably giving them their freedom), then a million pounds of gold would be obtained, and most likely two or three times that amount. Then tell me how many people our city [Constantinople] contains and how many Christians? Will it not come to a hundred thousand? And how many pagans and Jews! How many thousands of pounds of gold would be gathered in! And how many of the poor do we have? I doubt that there are more than fifty thousand. How much would be required to feed them daily? If they all ate at a common table, the cost could not be very great. What could we not undertake with our huge treasure? Do you believe it could ever be exhausted?

And will not the blessing of God pour down on us a thousand-fold richer? Will we not make a heaven on earth? Would not the grace of God be indeed richly poured out?

If this turned out so brilliantly for three or five thousand (the first Christians) and none of them was in want, how much more would this be so with such a great quantity? Will not each newcomer add something more?

John Chrysostom, *The Dispersion of Property*[15]

Although the Fathers were highly critical of the prevailing individualistic view of private property ownership, they did not call for abolishing it in favor of a system of common ownership of goods. Some even appealed to the Greek and Roman traditions, where there was a great suspicion about the holding of goods in common. As Lactantius put it, "private property contains the matter of both vices and virtues but communal property sharing holds nothing but license for vices."[16]

Thus the possibility of common ownership is periodically mentioned in the early church but it is not endorsed as something Christian discipleship requires.

OTHER ARGUMENTS FOR HELPING THE POOR

> *Rich and poor the same*
>
> First of all, take ornaments away from a woman, and servants from a master, and you will discover that the master is no different from the slaves he has bought neither in bearing, nor in look, nor in voice. In fact, he is very similar to his slaves in all these things. He differs from his slaves in one respect only, namely, he is weaker, and, because of his upbringing, more susceptible to sickness.
>
> Clement of Alexandria, *Homilies on Second Corinthians*[17]

The Fathers rarely wrote formal analyses or treatises. What most have left behind is their sermons. Thus we can understand that they employed a wide variety of approaches in trying to persuade the wealthy to assist the poor, some of which are best understood when we envision them making these arguments as part of a Sunday morning sermon, with some less-than-generous wealthy Christians occupying the places of honor in church.

Thus one frequently recurring argument, illustrated in many of the quotes above, is that it is in the interest of the wealthy themselves to be generous with their goods. As we have seen, this is often phrased as a wise concern about one's eternal salvation, but the Fathers at times go into greater detail about the ways in which the poor can serve the rich in return. It was a consistent theme throughout patristic literature that on the day of judgment the poor can speak to God, the judge of all, about the virtues of those wealthy individuals who assisted them during their lives on earth.

> *How the poor help the rich*
>
> The poor are the treasurers of the good things that we look for, the keepers of the gates of the kingdom, opening them to the merciful and shutting them on the harsh and uncharitable. They are the strongest of accusers, the best of defenders—not that they accuse or defend in words, but that the Lord beholds what is done towards them, and every deed cries louder than a herald to him who searches all hearts.
>
> Gregory of Nyssa, *Love the Poor*[18]
>
> The rich man has great wealth, but, so far as the Lord is concerned, he is poor, because, distracted as he is by his wealth, he can offer only a very limited praise and prayer to God; and when he does, his praise and prayer is

brief and weak and has no power to come before God. So when a rich man goes to a poor man and gives him what he needs, he can be confident that what he does for the poor man can obtain a reward from God (for the poor man is rich in his prayer and in his praise, and his prayer has great power with God). With this faith, then, the rich man does not hesitate to supply the poor man with everything.

On the other hand, the poor man who has been assisted by the rich intercedes for him and gives thanks to God for his benefactor. And the latter is more committed to help the poor man, so as not to let him want for anything during his life, because he knows that the poor man's prayer is acceptable and rich in God's eyes.

Both fulfill their duties in this way: the poor man offers his prayers—these are his riches—and gives back to the Lord the gift of prayers that he has received. In the same way the rich man unhesitatingly gives to the poor the riches he has received from the Lord. This is a great and acceptable deed in the sight of God because the rich man knows how to administer his riches correctly and distributes to the poor God's gifts and rightly accomplishes the Lord's ministry.

The Shepherd of Hermas[19]

In addition, the Fathers sometimes appealed to the sense of mastery that the wealthy are often quite proud of. The way to prove one is in charge of one's wealth—and not its servant—is to give it away.

Possessed by one's possessions

A possession ought to belong to the possessor, not the possessor to the possession. Whosoever, therefore, does not use his inheritance as a possession, who does not know how to give and distribute it to the poor, he is the servant of his wealth, not its master.

Ambrose of Milan, *The Earth Belongs to All* [20]

One fascinating part of the concern of the early Fathers for the poor is the founding of charitable institutions, a tradition that has been carried on throughout Christian history, even to this day. Peter Phan describes how Basil the Great set up institutions for the organized administration of charity.[21] All bishops appointed deacons to provide services to the poor, but Basil also constructed buildings on the edge of the city to receive travelers, including lepers, and gathered the resources necessary to provide staff to take care of them.

THE NATURAL WORLD

In the twenty-first century, we face a number of very serious environmental problems that never entered the consciousness of the Fathers of the early church. As a result, when we look for assistance on ecological problems today among the writings of the Fathers, we must examine the presuppositions that the early church held about the natural world, even though they had no worries at the time about the capacity of humanity to destroy it.

The goodness of creation

The earth is good by the height of its mountains, the moderate elevation of its hills, and the evenness of its fields; and good is the farm that is pleasant and fertile; and good is the house that is arranged throughout in symmetrical proportions and is spacious and bright; and good are the animals, animate bodies; and good is the mild and salubrious air; and good is the food that is pleasant and conducive to health; . . . and good is the heaven with its own sun, moon and stars.

Augustine of Hippo, *De Trinitate*[22]

After the creation of everything on the sixth day, "God saw everything he had made, and behold, it was very good."

What could match this for reliable comment, when the Creator of all gives the verdict in person and says that everything created is good, and even very good? So, whenever you see someone moved by his own reasoning and intent on contradicting Sacred Scripture, shun him like a lunatic.

John Chrysostom, *Homilies on Genesis*[23]

Jame Schaefer has argued that, although the Fathers were not facing the environmental problems we face today, there are consistent themes in their work that indicate several ecologically important assumptions made in the early church. The first of these is the goodness of creation.

Arising as it does out of the Hebrew Scriptures, the Christian understanding of creation based in the creation story in Genesis is that God "saw that it was good." This insight lies behind the sacramental view of the world that characterizes Catholic theology: that even the material world reveals God's gracious gift of self. As Paul Tillich once put it, the material world is "translucent to the divine."[24] This notion that the material world is good is critically important in any Christian understanding of an economic ethic today. Christianity does not withdraw from the material world as somehow evil or even neutral. It understands the human person as both spiritual and material and thus appreciates the engagement in the physical world even while acknowledging that our ultimate destiny will transcend the bounds of the physical Earth.

Even mute creatures praise their Creator.

Let your mind roam through the whole creation; everywhere the created world will cry out to you: "God made me." Whatever pleases you in a work of art brings to your mind the artist who wrought it; much more, when you survey the universe, does the consideration of it evoke praise for its Maker. You look on the heavens; they are God's great work. You behold the earth; God made its number of seeds, its varieties of plants, its multitude of animals. Go around the heavens again and back to the earth, leave out nothing; on all sides everything cries out to you of its author; nay the very forms of created things are as it were the voices with which they praise their Creator.

Augustine of Hippo, *On the Psalms*[25]

Thus the central patristic gift to theological reflection on the environment today is the awareness that we live in a world created by God that has a dignity independent of our own. This means that we ought to appreciate the beauty and goodness of creation and ought to use it with gratitude, respect, and restraint.

FREEDOM AND SLAVERY

We have seen that one of the arguments to persuade the wealthy to share their goods with the poor was that the wealthy ought not to be possessed by their possessions.

Freedom and slavery

If anyone considers dispassionately and serenely all the words of Job, he will see the worth of those things over which men wish to gain power, and to which they are so attached by cupidity that they become slaves to mortal

> things even as they imprudently seek to master them. . . . For to possess
> such things without clinging to them is much more praiseworthy than not
> to possess at all.
>
> Augustine of Hippo, *The Way of Life of the Catholic Church*[26]

In this caution about "slavery" to material goods there is an understanding
of freedom for the Christian that conflicts with the dominant secular view
in Augustine's day. Freedom should be understood as the free choice to live
morally, in a way that will make us truly happy, and not simply the free
choice to enjoy whatever we might like. The Fathers advocate possessing things
without clinging to them because clinging to them leads the owner to be less
free.

Today we witness a similar discrepancy between the dominant secular
view of freedom and the understanding of freedom in the Christian tradition.
In our time, freedom tends to be understood as what we might call "self-
initiation." That is, most people today think you are free as long as whatever
you do is what you yourself have chosen to do. However, the Christian view
of freedom has always been better understood as "self-perfection." Servais
Pinckaers has called this notion "freedom for excellence," and describes the
musician's freedom to play whatever she wishes on the piano.[27] The untrained
face no physical restrictions and can hit any piano keys they wish, but this
absence of physical restriction is a pale version of the freedom that comes with
effort expended in seeking excellence. We are free when we choose that which
fulfills us, that which leads us to live as God has intended, that which brings us
true happiness.

A quick illustration of the difference between these two approaches to
freedom can be seen in the realm of addiction. Ask yourself whether you
could freely choose to become addicted to drugs (whether "hard" drugs or
alcohol). On the one hand, you would have done it yourself and thus in
the contemporary view of freedom you acted "freely." However, in a more
adequate view of freedom, we must ask whether becoming a slave to drugs
can possibly be understood as a free act. Those in the world most enamored
of the view of freedom as self-initiation—often called libertarians in the United
States—sometimes go so far as to defend voluntary slavery. That is, I might offer
to pay you $3 million a year for the next five years, if you agree, beginning
in year six, to be my slave for the rest of your life. The libertarian philosopher
Robert Nozick, for example, defends this as a perfectly moral offer and believes
that governments should leave me free to offer it and you to accept.[28] However,

the Christian view of freedom would say this should be prohibited by law since such choices are not free, and are almost always made out of desperation. Allowing even nondesperate voluntary slavery is based in a distorted view of what it means to be human.

The condemnation of slavery as a violation of human freedom did not appear in the early church or for that matter in nearly all religious and secular premodern conversations. The Fathers of the church, like their secular Roman counterparts, accepted the institution of slavery as perfectly moral in limited circumstances, generally due to the outcome of war and the consequence of sin. Several of the Fathers instructed slaves to obey their masters "for the glory of God."[29] This is yet another example of the influence of the social construction of reality on religious thinking. In the premodern era it was beyond the imagination of most Christians, including bishops and popes, that slavery should be abolished completely.

Thus the Christian view of freedom insists that individuals make their own decision but recognizes that not every decision being made is a free one. We are free when we actively choose to do what fulfills ourselves, in accord with God's plan.

Is there hope for the rich?

The Fathers of the church are so strong in their condemnations of those wealthy who do not share from their surplus that one might be tempted to think that they see no hope for the rich. Indeed those who do not open their purse to help the poor are destined for a life apart from God, because as Clement of Alexandria put it, such a man "carries in his heart not the Spirit of God but the spirit of gold or land."[30]

However, the Fathers condemned neither the wealthy nor commerce. Time and again the Fathers acknowledge that although there is a great danger in the creation of a private property system, it need not be spiritually fatal, since as Clement said, "from this unrighteousness it is possible to perform a deed that is righteous."[31] Clement says elsewhere, "The Lord, therefore, does not forbid us to be rich but to be rich unjustly and insatiably."[32] Throughout, there is a clear conviction that wealth can be used well as an instrument.

The meaning of the story of the rich young man in Matt. 19:16-22

What was it that turned him [the rich young man] to flight and made him abandon his teacher, and reject his entreaty, his hope, his life, and his past achievement?—"Sell your possessions." But what does this mean? It is not, as some hastily interpret it, a command that he should throw away what he possesses and renounce his wealth.

What he is told to banish from his soul are his notions about wealth, his attachment to it, his excessive desire for it, his morbid excitement over it, and his anxieties—those thorns of existence which choke the seed of true life.

There is nothing great or enviable about having no money, unless it is for the purpose of gaining true life. Otherwise it must be said that people with nothing at all, the destitute who beg for daily bread in abject poverty by the roadside, even though they are ignorant of God and of God's righteousness, would be the most blessed of men, the dearest to God, the sole possessors of eternal life, merely in virtue of their complete lack of any ways or means of livelihood and of their want of the smallest necessities.

Clement of Alexandria, *Who Is the Rich Man That Is Saved?*[33]

Augustine says that we can learn a similar lesson from the Scriptures. Many of the leading figures of the Old Testament—such as Abraham, Isaac, and Jacob—were wealthy individuals, but they lived properly, and this is the key. He says, therefore, that it is not necessary for the rich young man to sell all of his goods, but what is necessary is that he be willing to share from his surplus with those who have unmet needs.[34]

A NOTE ON ECONOMIC INEQUALITY

Discussions today about poverty often include discussions of economic inequality. The difference, of course, is that poverty refers to the condition of persons whose basic needs are not met, and this may occur regardless of whether their incomes are very much different from the wealthiest people in their society. Economic inequality refers to the difference between the incomes of the poorest and the wealthiest of people and thus one could imagine a society in which no one has unmet needs but where there were indeed differences in income between the richer and the less prosperous.

It is important to keep these two ideas separate as we consider the discussion of poverty in the early church. In fact, in all the premodern authors we will see, there is no discussion of economic inequality. That is, the key issue is always whether people's needs are met, not whether some are less wealthy than others.

The difference in focusing on one or the other is that if we were to consider all economic inequality as a bad thing, this would imply that the only good situation is when everyone has an equal income. The Christian tradition has never endorsed this idea. Rather, the goal has always been that everyone's needs should be met, with the presumption that if everyone's needs were in fact met, there would be much less problem, if any, with the fact that some people had more money than others. We will return to this topic in the last chapters of the book.

NATURAL FACTS AND THE MORAL LIFE

Nature's moral clues

Clothing and gold and silver, food and drink and covering—we are born without them all; naked nature receives her children into the tomb, and no one can enclose his acres there.

Nature, impartial at our coming, is impartial at our going; she bears us all equal, and entombs us equal in her bosom. Who can tell class from class among the dead? Open the earth again and find your rich man if you may; excavate a tomb a short while after, and if you know the man that you see, prove by token that he was poor. The sole difference is that the rich has more to waste away with him.

Ambrose of Milan, *On Naboth*[35]

Just as the foot is the measure of the sandal, so the physical needs of each are the measure of what one should possess. Whatever is excessive . . . is a burden for the body.

Clement of Alexandria, *The Tutor*[36]

Ambrose, Clement of Alexandria, and others of the Fathers often argued that starting with the fact that everyone is born naked, we can conclude the wealthy are not a better kind of people than the poor. The Fathers use this Stoic notion of a "natural fact" about our birth (that everyone is born naked) as a kind of clue, left in nature by God, about the moral life we should live. The rich should not think of themselves as so different from the poor.

In a similar moral argument, Clement of Alexandria argued that sandals have something to teach us. Consider yourself going into a shoe store to buy a new pair of athletic shoes. Once you pick out the shoe you like best, you discover that for the same price you can buy a much larger shoe than the one that best fits your foot. Since you would be "getting more for your money," why wouldn't you choose the biggest size you could get for the price? The answer, of course, is that it would be foolish to have a shoe you would be slopping around in as you walked. Buying "more shoe" than you need would be a big mistake; no doubt you would stumble and be badly served by your new shoes. Clement's point is that just as you would not choose a sandal that is too large for your foot, so you should not seek material goods that exceed your needs. His view is that you would simply be "slopping around" in too many things in your life and you may stumble on the path to your ultimate goal. Having too many things gets in the way of what is really important in life.

This use of natural facts is an ethical method that the Christian church adopted from the Stoic tradition of Greek philosophy. For Christians, of course, it is God who put these moral clues into nature and, if we are sensitive and look for them carefully, we can find indications in nature for how we ought to live our lives. We will see in Chapter 8 how Thomas Aquinas, several centuries later, expands on this idea of moral clues in nature and develops an ethical analysis based on the natural law.

CONCLUSION

Who is a Christian?

Let no one, therefore, deceive or lead another person astray, for, unless a man has been just, he does not have life in him; unless he has observed the commandments of Christ in every respect, he cannot have part with Him; unless he has despised earthly possessions, he will not gain heavenly ones; unless he has scorned human considerations, he will not have divine blessings.

Let no one declare himself to be a Christian unless he both follows the teaching of Christ and imitates His example.

Do you think that man is a Christian who nourishes no needy person with his bread, who refreshes no thirsty person with his wine, whose table no one shares, under whose roof no stranger or wayfarer abides, whose garments clothe no naked person, whose helping hand assists no pauper, whose blessings no one experiences, whose mercy no one feels, who imitates the good in no way but rather laughs and mocks and persistently harasses the poor? Far be such an attitude from the minds of all Christians, far be it that such a one should be called the child of God.

He is a Christian who follows the way of Christ, who imitates Christ in all things, as is written: "He who says that he abides in Christ ought himself to walk just as he walked" (1 Jn 2:6).

He is a Christian who shows mercy to all, who is not disturbed by any injury, who does not permit the poor to be oppressed in his presence, who assists the wretched and succors the needy, who sympathizes with the sorrowful and feels the grief of another as his own, who is reduced to tears by the weeping of another, whose house is common property for all, whose door is never closed to anyone, whose table is shared by every poor person, whose food is offered to all, whose goods all share and no one feels slighted, who serves God day and night, who meditates upon and considers His precepts ceaselessly, who makes himself poor in this world so that he may become rich in the eyes of God, who suffers himself to be considered of no account among men so that he may be acceptable before God and the angels, who seems to hold nothing concealed in his heart, whose soul is simple and spotless, whose conscience is faithful and pure, whose whole thought is directed to God and whose whole hope is in Christ, who desires heavenly rather than earthly possessions, who despises earthly goods so that he may acquire divine.

Augustine of Hippo, *A Christian Life*[37]

In conclusion, we have heard the Fathers of the church calling their listeners, the early Christians, to be people of faith, deeply prayerful and dedicated to the way of true life shown to them by God in Jesus Christ. That way entails an attentive care to the needs of the poor, which the Fathers endorse not only through their preaching of the gospel but also in their intellectual analysis of the character of property ownership. Because God has given the world to all so everyone's needs would be met, those who own more property than they need—whether landed estates, grain stored in barns, or lavish household goods—actually have a debt to those whose needs are unmet. In the early church, as in the Hebrew Scriptures, care for the needs of the poor might be described as the gold standard for assessing economic life. The Fathers remind us, of course, that this obligation should be taken up gladly by the believer in an effort to imitate Christ.

We saw how John Chrysostom appealed to the holding of wealth in common in the first Jerusalem community, but neither he nor the other Fathers in the end rejected personal ownership as the normal way to organize economic life. Instead they taught that those individual owners share their surplus with the needy—even describing this sharing as the test determining whether the owner is master of his wealth or its servant.

We who have our needs met face the same temptations as the prosperous in the early church. Thus the teaching of the Fathers stands as a challenge for us Christians today, as we put to ourselves the same question that they asked: What are the implications of Christian faith for economic life today?

Notes

1. Brian Matz, "Alleviating Economic Injustice in Gregory of Nyssa's *Contra Usurarios*," *Studia Patristica* 45 (2010): 549–53.

2. The Shepherd of Hermas, 114, 4, 2, in Phan, *Social Thought*, 55.

3. Ambrose of Milan, *On Naboth*, in Phan, *Social Thought*, 173–74.

4. Augustine of Hippo, *Reflections on Psalm* 147, in Avila, *Ownership*, 113.

5. Gregory of Nazianzus, *On the Love for the Poor*, XIV, 6, in Phan, *Social Thought*, 123.

6. See, for example, the anonymous Pelagian treatise, "On Riches," which holds this view of the relation of the wealthy and poor. In addition, Epiphanius of Salamis's *Panarion* refers to some fringe Christian groups who continue the practice of renunciation of all wealth, which the author judged as a faulty literal reading of the story of Jesus and the rich young man in Mark 10. Private correspondence with Brian Matz, July 7, 2010.

7. Basil the Great, Homily, "I Will Pull Down My Barns," in Phan, *Social Thought*, 117.

8. Irenaeus, *A.H.* IV.30.3. Frank Williams, "The Panarion of Epiphanius of Salamis, Books II and II," *Nag Hammadi and Manichaean Studies* 36 (Leiden: E. J. Brill, 1994), 116. I am indebted to Brian Matz for these references.

9. Ambrose of Milan, *On Naboth*, in Phan, *Social Thought*, 175.

10. Clement of Alexandria, *Quis Dives Salvetur* 13, *Paidagogos* 2.3, 2.12, and 3.7, and *Stromata* 6.12, in Phan, *Social Thought*, 63–75.

11. Gregory of Nyssa, *Love of the Poor*, in Phan, *Social Thought*, 133.

12. John Chrysostom, *Homilies on the Gospel of Matthew*, Homily LXVI, 3, in Phan, *Social Thought*, 145.

13. Cyprian of Carthage, *On Works and Almsgiving*, in Phan, *Social Thought*, 90.

14. John Chrysostom, *The Meaning of Private Property*, in Phan, *Social Thought*, 160.

15. John Chrysostom, *The Dispersion of Property*, in Avila, *Ownership*, 100–101.

16. Lactantius, *Div. Inst.*, 3, 33, in Phan, *Social Thought*, 36–37.

17. Clement of Alexandria, "Homilies on the Second Letter to the Corinthians," in Phan, *Social Thought*, 67–68.

18. Gregory of Nyssa, "Love the Poor," in Phan, *Social Thought*, 132. See also Susan Holman, *The Hungry Are Dying: Beggars and Bishops in Roman Cappadocia* (Oxford: Oxford University Press, 2011).

19. *The Shepherd of Hermas*, in Phan, *Social Thought*, 53.

20. Ambrose of Milan, *The Earth Belongs to All*, in Avila, *Ownership*, 67.

21. Phan, *Social Thought*, 27.

22. Augustine of Hippo, *De Trinitate*, 17–18, in *The Trinity*, trans. Stephen McKenna, CSSR, (Washington, DC: Catholic University of America Press, 1963), 10.12, 135–37, cited in Jame Schaefer, *Theological Foundations for Environmental Ethics: Reconstructing Patristic and Medieval Concepts* (Washington, DC: Georgetown University Press, 2009), 105.

23. John Chrysostom, *Homilies on Genesis*, 1–17, Homily 10:12–13, translated by Robert C. Hill (Washington. DC: Catholic University of America Press, 1986), 137.

24. Paul Tillich, "Rejoinder," *Journal of Religion* 46, no. 1 (January 1966).

25. Augustine, *On the Psalms*, Ancient Christian Writers 29 (New York: Newman, 1960), 272, cited in Schaefer, *Theological Foundations*, 105.

26. Augustine of Hippo, "The Way of Life of the Catholic Church," in Phan, *Social Thought*, 203–4.

27. Servais Pinckaers, O.P., *The Sources of Christian Ethics* (Washington, DC: Catholic University of America Press, 1995), 354–78.

28. Robert Nozick, *Anarchy, State, and Utopia* (Oxford: Blackwell, 1974), 331.

29. Basil the Great, *De Spiritu Sancto*, 20; *Moralia*, 75, 1, in Phan, *Social Thought*, 34.

30. Clement of Alexandria, *The Stromata*, in Phan, *Social Thought*, 76.

31. Clement of Alexandria, *Quis Dives Salvetur*, in Avila, *Ownership*, 44.

32. Clement of Alexandria, *The Stromata*, in Phan, *Social Thought*, 70.

33. Clement of Alexandria, "Who Is the Rich Man That Is Saved?" in Phan, *Social Thought*, 72.

34. Augustine of Hippo, *Letters*, in Phan, *Social Thought*, 209.

35. Ambrose of Milan, *On Naboth*, in Phan, *Social Thought*, 168.

36. Clement of Alexandria, *The Tutor*, 3, 7, in Avila, *Ownership*, 42.

37. Augustine of Hippo, *A Christian Life*, in Phan, *Social Thought*, 231–32.

7

The Beginnings of Monastic Life

Every organization has some members who are more dedicated to its purpose than others. In the first three centuries of Christianity, the Christian community often found itself persecuted by the Roman authorities. With their lives in danger, there weren't many halfhearted Christians. Even when persecutions weren't raging, Christians were clearly a small group identified by a religion that arose out of one of the backwaters of the Roman Empire; it got little respect in the broader culture. No one became a Christian to improve their social status.

All this changed when the Emperor Constantine declared himself a Christian in the year 313. Prior to Constantine, there was often a very high price to be paid for being a Christian. After his conversion, just the opposite occurred: it was not only socially acceptable but socially obligatory to become a Christian for anyone who wanted to maintain status within the imperial system. This influx of so many new members had both good and bad effects upon Christianity. The good effect, of course, was that there were many more people following "the way" Jesus taught, and Christian values had a greater prospect of transforming the lives of more people. The downside, however, was that there were lots of people going to church who really didn't take it very seriously. Thus those Christians who were most convinced about taking their religion seriously had to either put up with Christian communities that were quite diverse in their degree of dedication or had to establish new ones.

There are examples of Christian ascetics and monastics prior to Constantine, but since monastic life arises out of this desire to dedicate oneself more and more thoroughly to a life of faith, changes in the fourth and fifth centuries increased the number of monastic communities. There was great diversity in early monasticism both in men's monasteries and women's. Because of limitations of space in this volume, we will restrict our treatment of early monasticism to two of the most famous rules of conduct for monastic life: those of Benedict of Nursia and Augustine of Hippo. Benedict's rule eventually became immensely influential and was adopted by literally thousands of communities of men and women around the world. Augustine's rule has been less influential, partly because of the hybrid life that Augustine himself led, being both an active bishop engaged in all the affairs of the church in the world and the head of a community of men. Both bear important insights into economic life that are relevant far beyond the cloister walls.

THE PURPOSE OF MONASTIC LIFE

Monastic motivation

The chief motivation for your sharing life together is to live harmoniously in the house and to have one heart and one soul seeking God.

Live then, all of you, in harmony and concord; honor God mutually in each other; you have become His temples.

The Rule of St. Augustine, Chapter 1

Listen carefully, my son, to the master's instructions, and attend to them with the ear of your heart. This is advice from a father who loves you; welcome it, and faithfully put it into practice. The labor of obedience will bring you back to him from whom you had drifted through the sloth of disobedience. This message of mine is for you, then, if you are ready to give up your own will, once and for all, and armed with the strong and noble weapons of obedience to do battle for the true King, Christ the Lord.

Therefore we intend to establish a school for the Lord's service. In drawing up its regulations, we hope to set down nothing harsh, nothing burdensome. The good of all concerned, however, may prompt us to a little strictness in order to amend faults and to safeguard love. Do not be daunted immediately by fear and run away from the road that leads to salvation. It is bound to be narrow at the outset. But as we progress in this way of life and in faith, we shall run on the path of God's commandments, our hearts over-flowing with the inexpressible delight of love. Never swerving from his instructions, then, but faithfully observing his teaching in the monastery until death, we shall through patience share in the sufferings of Christ that we may deserve also to share in his kingdom.

The Rule of St. Benedict, Prologue[1]

The fundamental purpose of monastic life is for each monk to seek God in community with others. There is always a kind of humility about the possibility for knowing God in the monastic tradition, always a sense that it is a lifelong effort and not something that one accomplishes at some point in one's life and then simply lives with from then on. There is no confident talk about having found God. The faithful monk seeks God.

WORK AND PRAYER

A balance of prayer and work

First of all, every time you begin a good work, you must pray to him most earnestly to bring it to perfection. In his goodness, he has already counted us as his sons, and therefore we should never grieve him by our evil actions. With his good gifts which are in us, we must obey him at all times that he may never become the angry father who disinherits his sons, nor the dread lord, enraged by our sins, who punishes us forever as worthless servants for refusing to follow him to glory.

The Rule of St. Benedict, Prologue

The Prophet says: Seven times a day have I praised you. We will fulfill this sacred number of seven if we satisfy our obligations of service at Lauds, Prime, Terce, Sext, None, Vespers and Compline, for it was of these hours during the day that he said: "Seven times a day have I praised you." Concerning Vigils, the same Prophet says: "At midnight I arose to glorify you." Therefore, we should praise our Creator for his just judgments at these times: Lauds, Prime, Terce, Sext, None, Vespers and Compline; and let us arise at night to give him praise (Ps 118:61).

The Rule of St. Benedict, Chapter 16

Be assiduous in prayer at the scheduled hours and times. . . .

When you pray to God in psalms and hymns, the words you sing should be alive in your hearts. . . . Keep to the prescribed text when you sing; avoid texts which are not suited for singing.

The Rule of St. Augustine, Chapter 2

It is the abbot's care to announce, day and night, the hour for the Work of God. He may do so personally or delegate the responsibility to a conscientious brother, so that everything may be done at the proper time.

The Rule of St. Benedict, Chapter 47

The monk's life was to be characterized by both work and prayer. This is a surprise to some people today because of a stereotype that monks simply sit around (or kneel!) and pray all day. However, this insistence on labor and prayer brings a balance to the daily life of the monastery and is rooted in the fundamental religious conviction that worship and work are not by any means in conflict. They are two ways of giving praise to God. This is important to understand because while some people interpret the whole monastic experience as a rejection of "the world," and a withdrawal into some sort of spiritual place, this was not at all the self-understanding of the monks involved. Rather, Christian faith was to be based in an integrated life, one that involves both body and spirit, both work and prayer, throughout each day.[2]

And pray they did. Benedict insisted that the community gather seven times each day to pray. The first prayer service of the day, "Lauds," occurred during the middle of the night as a reminder that even in our sleep we are in a relationship with God and thus it is appropriate to praise him for his goodness in our lives at all hours of the day and night. The monks then went back to bed and gathered again at dawn and several times during the day for the other prayer times, ending with Compline before retiring for the night.

The central portion of these daily prayers was and remains today the recitation of the Psalms, with the monks praying all 150 Psalms in the course of each week. The Psalms were chosen by Benedict because of their ability to address the diversity of themes in the Christian life. As the great monastic scholar of the fifth century, John Cassian put it, the songs are best for the prayer of the monk:

> Penetrating into all the sentiments of the Psalms, he will begin to sing them in such a way that he pours them forth with the deepest compunction of heart, not his words composed by the psalmist, but as if he had written them himself as his own prayer.[3]

ASCETICISM AND PERSONAL VIRTUE

Counsel for daily life

Renounce yourself in order to follow Christ (Matt 16:24; Luke 9:23); discipline your body (1 Cor 9:27); do not pamper yourself, but love fasting. You must relieve the lot of the poor, clothe the naked, visit the sick (Matt 25:36), and bury the dead. Go to help the troubled and console the sorrowing.

The Rule of St. Benedict, Prologue

To the extent that your health allows, subdue your flesh by fasting and abstinence from food and drink. If anyone is unable to fast, let him at least take no food between meals, unless he is sick.

The Rule of St. Augustine, Chapter 3

Your way of acting should be different from the world's way; the love of Christ must come before all else. You are not to act in anger or nurse a grudge. Rid your heart of all deceit. Never give a hollow greeting of peace or turn away when someone needs your love. Bind yourself to no oath lest it prove false, but speak the truth with heart and tongue.

You must not be proud, nor be given to wine (Titus 1:7; 1 Tim 3:3). Refrain from too much eating or sleeping, and from laziness (Rom 12:11). Do not grumble or speak ill of others. . . .

Place your hope in God alone. If you notice something good in yourself, give credit to God, not to yourself, but be certain that the evil you commit is always your own and yours to acknowledge.

The Rule of St. Benedict, Prologue

Either have no quarrels or put an end to them as quickly as possible, lest anger grow into hatred, making timber of a splinter, and turning the soul into the soul of a murderer. Thus you read: "Anyone who hates his brother is a murderer."

Whoever has offended another with insults or harmful words, or even a serious accusation, must remember to right the wrong he has done at the earliest opportunity. The injured must remember to forgive without further bickering. If they have offended each other, they shall mutually forgive their offences.

An individual who is prone to anger, yet hastens to beg forgiveness from someone he has consciously harmed, is better than another who is less inclined to anger and less likely to ask pardon. An individual who absolutely refuses to ask pardon, or does so without meaning it, is entirely out of place in the monastery.

The Rule of St. Augustine, Chapter 6

As a matter of fact, every other vice produces evil deeds with a view to doing evil, but pride sets a trap for good deeds as well, with a view to destroying them. What benefit is there in giving generously to the poor and becoming poor oneself, if the pitiful soul is more inclined to pride by rejecting riches than by possessing them?

The Rule of St. Augustine, Chapter 1

These precepts should be read to you once a week, so that you will see yourselves in this little book as in a mirror and not neglect anything through forgetfulness.

The Rule of St. Augustine, Chapter 8

Central to the life of a monk is a disciplining of one's own thoughts and desires in order to be less distracted by felt needs and more focused on the call of Christ to seek God and love one's neighbor. Physical asceticism is one of the stereotypes of monastic life, sometimes depicted in the extreme as a fundamental hatred of the body and the physical life. However, in the monastic tradition, disciplining the body—fasting, sleeping on a thin mattress or a board, going without an extra cloak on a cold day—does not reject the human body. It recognizes that our bodily desires can easily preoccupy us and lead us to focus on our own needs rather than the needs of others and our journey toward God. Thus it is quite significant that Benedict's prologue combines the need to discipline one's body with the commitment to relieve the poor and sick. This renunciation is, then, rooted in its ability to help each monk more fully live out the gospel call. Even those of us who are not monastics can see in monastic life a helpful understanding of the relation between a simpler life and service of others.

Both Benedict and Augustine attempt to address all the ordinary problems that persons have with each other. In any group, there are always quarrels and misunderstanding and so both of these rules provide guidelines for how best to deal with such recurrent problems of human life. Each monk is called to a responsible interaction with his brothers and in the end to deference to the abbot when individual monks are unable to resolve the problem themselves.

It is possible, of course, that a monk could live up to the rule, but might do so with pride, in which case he violates the spirit of the rule even while fulfilling it. Thus both Benedict and Augustine are careful to warn their monks against thinking too well of themselves, always calling them to humility and service to others. And because this series of disciplines and attitudes requires a lifelong dedication, not something one accomplishes in a week or a year, both Augustine and Benedict instruct their members to listen to the reading of the rule frequently so that they can internalize it, not as simply a list of things that must be done but as a spirit for engaging life each day. This kind of advice, of course, is good for any of us, whether inside a monastery or not.

The cellarer and material goods

As cellarer of the monastery, there should be chosen from the community someone who is wise, mature in conduct, temperate, not an excessive eater, not proud, excitable, offensive, dilatory, or wasteful, but God-fearing, and like a father to the whole community. He will take care of everything, but will do nothing without an order from the abbot. Let him keep to his orders.

He should not annoy the brothers. If any brother happens to make an unreasonable demand of him, he should not reject him with disdain and cause him distress, but reasonably and humbly deny the improper request. Let him keep watch over his own soul, ever mindful of that saying of the Apostle: He who serves well secures a good standing for himself (1 Tim 3:13). He must show every care and concern for the sick, children, guests and the poor, knowing for certain that he will be held accountable for all of them on the Day of Judgment.

He will regard all utensils and goods of the monastery as sacred vessels of the altar, aware that nothing is to be neglected. He should not be prone to greed, nor be wasteful and extravagant with the goods of the monastery, but should do everything with moderation and according to the abbot's orders.

The Rule of St. Benedict, Chapter 31

The "cellarer" had responsibility for everything kept in the cellar, where the monastery would store most of the tools, implements, and other things the monastery owned. The abbot delegated to the cellarer, a person who today is usually called the "prior," the responsibility for much of the daily oversight of the monastery related to various kinds of work monks do and the tools and other things they need in doing so.

Note one critically important phrase in Benedict's description of how the cellarer is to treat the utensils and tools and other things that the monastery employs in its daily life. He says that the cellarer should "regard all utensils and goods of the monastery as sacred vessels of the altar." Implicit in this reference to the chalice (the cup that holds the consecrated wine) and ciborium (which holds the consecrated bread) used at Mass is an important insight into the monastic understanding of economic life.

This reference to sacred vessels of the altar was immediately understandable by all Catholics up until the second half of the twentieth century. Prior to the Second Vatican Council, only the priest was authorized to handle these vessels, and those assistants, "altar boys," who moved the chalice from one place to another as needed, were always instructed to employ a small white cloth between the hand and the chalice so that the importance and dignity of the chalice would not be lost. Thus when Benedict says that even the tools of the monastery are to be treated as sacred vessels of the altar, he is telling the cellarer and all the monks about the religious importance of even the most menial tools used in daily farm work. Once again, we see here not an escapist rejection of the material world but rather an acknowledgment that the material world, even in the form of the most humble shovel or hoe, is to be treated with great respect. Part of this might be attributable to a shrewd interest in taking good care of the tools and utensils of the monastery, but at the same time it is a spiritual affirmation of the material world as sacramental, pointing to a divine reality beyond (or beneath) themselves. If members of an ancient monastic community could see the religious significance of their daily work and tools, surely those of us who live "in the world" should do the same.

Monastic hospitality

All guests who present themselves are to be welcomed as Christ, for he himself will say: I was a stranger and you welcomed me (Matt 25:35). Proper honor must be shown to all, especially to those who share our faith (Gal 6:10) and to pilgrims.

Once a guest has been announced, the superior and the brothers are to meet him with all the courtesy of love. First of all, they are to pray together and thus be united in peace, but prayer must always precede the kiss of peace because of the delusions of the devil.

All humility should be shown in addressing a guest on arrival or departure. By a bow of the head or by a complete prostration of the body, Christ is to be adored because he is indeed welcomed in them. After the guests have been received, they should be invited to pray; then the superior or an appointed brother will sit with them. The divine law is read to the guest for his instruction, and after that every kindness is shown to him. The superior may break his fast for the sake of a guest, unless it is a day of special fast which cannot be broken. The brothers, however, observe the usual fast. The abbot shall pour water on the hands of the guests, and the abbot with the entire community shall wash their feet. After the washing they will recite this verse: God, we have received your mercy in the midst of your temple (Ps 47:10).

The Rule of St. Benedict, Chapter 53

Hospitality is one of the most important themes in Benedictine monasticism. Here too, the stereotype of monks trying to escape the world gets proven wrong. As Kathleen Norris has pointed out, cult groups—such as the California cult called "Heaven's Gate" that committed mass suicide in 1992—often aim to escape the world. Thus they don't welcome guests from that world into their midst.[4] Benedict teaches that the treatment of guests is at the center of what it means to live a faithful monastic life. Thus this fundamental outward orientation again presents a lesson to the rest of the Christian church. If monks, even in the midst of their setting up separate communities off the beaten path, emphasize the importance of welcoming strangers from the outside, surely those of us who live "in the world" should do at least as much. As we will see in Chapter 18, this ancient insight into the centrality of hospitality in monastic life has much to teach us about the moral standards for healthy organizational life in the twenty-first century. It is a needed antidote to much of the harshness and demonization of opponents that characterizes so much of contemporary discussion of public policy, even within Christian circles.

PRIVATE PROPERTY

Against personal property

Above all, this evil practice must be uprooted and removed from the monastery. We mean that without an order from the abbot, no one may presume to give, receive, or retain anything as his own, nothing at all—books, writing tablets, or stylus—in short, not a single item, especially since monks may not have the free disposal even of their own bodies and wills. For their needs, they are to look to the father of the monastery, and are not allowed anything which the abbot has not given or permitted. All things should be the common possession of all, as it is written, so that no one presumes to call anything his own (Acts 4:32).

But if anyone is caught indulging in this most evil practice, he should be warned a first and a second time. If he does not amend, let him be subjected to punishment.

The Rule of St. Benedict, Chapter 33

Do not call anything your own; possess everything in common. Your superior ought to provide each of you with food and clothing, not on an equal basis to all, because all do not enjoy the same health, but to each one in proportion to his need. For you read in the Acts of the Apostles: "They possessed everything in common," and "distribution was made to each in proportion to each one's need."

Those who owned anything in the world should freely consent to possess everything in common in the monastery.

The Rule of St. Augustine, Chapter 1

Although the respect for the material objects in the monastery was great, Benedict and Augustine were convinced that personal ownership of goods by individual monks would be destructive of the community. Their thinking here is that if I own this thing and you don't, this thing easily becomes an object of contention between you and me. If such a dispute is resolved as it usually is "out in the world," based on the interests of the person who owns it, not only will ownership become too important, but personal interest will become the rule by which the use of things get decided. Both Benedict and Augustine are completely clear that there ought to be no private property in the monastery. Each monk should ask to use whatever he needs. Things should be used based on who needs to use them and not on any other basis.

ATTITUDES TOWARD SERVICE

Kitchen service

The brothers should serve one another. Consequently, no one will be excused from kitchen service unless he is sick or engaged in some important business of the monastery, for kitchen service increases reward and fosters love. Let those who are not strong have help so that they may serve without distress, and let everyone receive help as the size of the community or local conditions warrant. If the community is rather large, the cellarer should be excused from kitchen service, and, as we have said, those should also be excused who are engaged in important business. Let all the rest serve one another in love.

The utensils required for the kitchen service are to be washed and returned intact to the cellarer, who in turn issues them to the one beginning his week.

On Sunday immediately after Lauds, those beginning as well as those completing their week of service should make a profound bow in the oratory before all and ask for their prayers. Let the server completing his week recite this verse: "Blessed are you, Lord God, who have helped me and comforted me" (Dan 3:52; Ps 85:17). After this verse has been said three times, he receives a blessing. Then the one beginning his service follows and says: "God, come to my assistance; Lord, make haste to help me" (Ps 69:2). And all repeat this verse three times. When he has received a blessing, he begins his service.

The Rule of St. Benedict, Chapter 32

In a community where there were only men, the traditional services of meal preparation and cleanup afterwards could not be assigned to women, even though that was the cultural norm of the day. If this work were to be done, men would need to do it. The monastic rules insisted that this sort of work should be shared by everyone, regardless of status. But a further insight is offered to us here when we consider the peculiar practice of praying for and with those serving in the kitchen.

Lauds was the first prayer of the day and Sunday the first day of the week. Thus we have to ask ourselves what it means that Benedict would have the kitchen servers from the previous and the coming week stand before the community during the first prayer service on Sunday, the day of the Lord's resurrection. The custom sends a powerful message even to those of us who are not monastics.

Kitchen work, especially the washing of dirty pots and pans, has never had a high status. Helpful in understanding this is the experience in the typical Israeli kibbutz, a collective village founded to create community, beginning with the presumption that all necessary jobs should be equally respected and valued. Most of the jobs of a kibbutz have been able to be allocated to persons without implying that one has greater status than another.[5] Thus the farm worker has no less stature in the community than the physician. But it has been nearly impossible for these communities to think of the menial kitchen labor of cleaning up after meals as having the same status as other jobs in the community. Thus even when intense efforts are made by religious communities, there seems to be something about kitchen labor that resists transformation of respect. We might imagine, even further, that in a monastic community of men in the early church, this tendency to look down upon menial parts of kitchen labor would be quite strong.

Thus it is noteworthy that Benedict does not treat kitchen labor as unfortunately distasteful work which we simply have to divide up because it has to get done. Rather he provides public recognition of this kind of work. Once again, Benedict thwarts our stereotypes if we think that the point of monastic life was to escape from the realities of life "in the world." Instead, Benedict celebrates work, even menial work, as religiously important, as something that is raised to the highest awareness the first time the community gathers on the first day of each week. What would our lives be like if we began thinking the same about all the forms of monotonous or menial work we do week after week?

THE STANDARD OF NEED

Needs, not wants

It is written: Distribution was made to each one as he had need (Acts 4:35). By this we do not imply that there should be favoritism—God forbid—but rather consideration for weaknesses. Whoever needs less should thank God and not be distressed, but whoever needs more should feel humble because of his weakness, not self-important because of the kindness shown him. In this way all the members will be at peace. First and foremost, there must be no word or sign of the evil of grumbling, no manifestation of it for any reason at all. If, however, anyone is caught grumbling, let him undergo more severe discipline.

The Rule of St. Benedict, Chapter 3

If food, clothes, a mattress, or blankets are given to those who come to the monastery from a more comfortable manner of life, the more robust individuals, to whom such things are not given and who are on this account more fortunate, ought to recall how much affluent people have altered their lifestyle in order to embrace the present one, even though the frugality practiced by the stronger brothers continues to elude them. No one should desire the extras given to a few, since this is done more out of tolerance than out of deference. Deplorable disorder would occur if the monastery provided a setting . . . where the wealthy become workers, while the poor become pampered.

No one is to be annoyed, nor should it seem to be unjust when a special diet is provided for brothers whose health has been adversely affected by their former status in life. A different background endows some people with greater physical strength. These should not consider others fortunate because they see concessions granted to their brothers and not to themselves. Let them be thankful rather that they have the strength to endure what others cannot.

The Rule of St. Augustine, Chapter 3

Sick people necessarily take less food so as not to aggravate their condition. During convalescence they are to receive such care as will quickly restore their health, even if they come from the lowest level of poverty in the world. Recent illness has afflicted them with the same frailty which the wealthy possess from their previous manner of life. When sick people have fully recovered, they should return to their happier ways, which are all the more fitting for God's servants to the extent that they have fewer needs. Food formerly necessary to remedy their illness should not become a pleasure which enslaves them. They should consider themselves richer, since they are now more robust in putting up with privations. For it is better to need less than to have more.

The Rule of St. Augustine, Chapter 3

The monastic tradition is, of course, deeply embedded in the Scriptures. The monks pray all of the psalms each week and regularly hear readings from other parts of the Bible. Thus it is no surprise that Benedict and Augustine taught that need must be the standard for what persons should receive, just as the Scriptures had stressed. They are careful to argue that those who do not need as much—whether because of their good health or their robust character—should not resent the fact that others—whether because of their ill health or their weak constitution from their prior life in a wealthy family—are given extra to meet their needs.

The abbot tells those who receive less not simply that they shouldn't grumble but also that they ought to be glad they are better off than those who need more, since the discipline of the body aims to remove such needs from one's concern so that the monk can more wholeheartedly seek God in his daily life. Those who need more, for whatever reason, are at a disadvantage in their journey toward God; those who need less should be grateful.

Those of us who do not live in monasteries do not have an abbot to decide what our needs are. These are choices we make for ourselves. However, the insight of the monastic orders into need presents a lesson even for us. That is, "it is better to need less than to have more." The more things we own, the more our cares and concerns are centered around maintaining those things and obtaining even more. And in an era when we overuse environmental resources and give up a perfectly useful cellphone for the latest model, needing less is an important part of our way forward. If needs can be kept simple, our life journey can be simpler and more responsible.

INCENTIVES

The motivation for effort

In this way, let no one work for himself alone but all your work shall be for the common purpose, done with greater zeal and more concentrated effort than if each one worked for private purpose. The Scriptures tell us:

"Love is not self-seeking." We understand this to mean: the common good takes precedence over the individual good, and the individual good yields to the common good. Here again, you will know the extent of your progress as you enlarge your concern for the common interest instead of your own private interest; enduring love will govern all matters pertaining to the fleeting necessities of life.

The Rule of St. Augustine, Chapter 5

Just as there is a wicked zeal of bitterness which separates from God and leads to hell, so there is a good zeal which separates from evil and leads to God and everlasting life. This, then, is the good zeal which monks must foster with fervent love: They should each try to be the first to show respect to the other (Rom 12:10), supporting with the greatest patience one another's weaknesses of body or behavior, and earnestly competing in obedience to one another.

The Rule of St. Benedict, Chapter 72

Many people today have come to understand human incentives quite differently than did the ancient world. Today, we have some insights that were not widely grasped in the premodern world. One of those is that people can act in their own self-interest in the market and, when the market and its context are properly structured, can do so without harming others, and in fact can help create prosperity for others. But one of the costs of this focus on self-interest as a motivating factor is that it tends to blind us to the many places in life where self-interest is not and should not be the most powerful of motivations. Augustine and Benedict were vividly aware that a concern for the common purpose—"the common good"—can bring greater zeal and effort than simply working for private purpose.

This tends to be a counterintuitive insight for many people today, partly because we have become so accustomed to the presumption that people will work harder for themselves than they will for others. But we might think of the players on a college sports team, and ask what that football or soccer player is thinking during those long practices in preparation for the big game. Surely there are many times when personal physical fatigue is great and where, if the athletes decided based only on their own self-interest, any one of them might choose to leave practice early that day and take a rest. Instead, they decide to carry on for the good of the team. This certainly happens during the big game, where players push on with a kind of energy that often surprises even themselves, but the fact that it happens so regularly in practice is an important insight. It is simply not true that in all cases working for oneself generates more energy than working for others. This is an insight from the ancient world of Christian life that modern Christians need to take seriously. This is not to say that the modern understanding of self-interest is empty, but rather that a balance is needed. It would be a big mistake for Christians today to adopt unselfconsciously a simplistic view of human life that says effort for self will always exceed effort for common purpose.

Conclusion

We see through the monastic rules of Benedict and Augustine how communities of men and women were set up in the early centuries of the church in order to live the Christian life more fully. Stress was put on disciplining one's body to prevent bodily cares and desires from overtaking what is more important in life, the search for God. Monks were known for both prayer and work, praying several times a day in common and working to support the monastery. The community was dedicated not just to its internal life but also to hospitality and service to the poor in the area.

The rules of Benedict and Augustine contradict the prevailing stereotype today that monasteries embody a rejection of the world, and in particular a rejection of the material world. On the contrary, the material goods of the monastery and the work of the monks are understood as spiritually significant. This is not a view of religion that aimed to escape the material cares of the world or even to simply put up with them as unfortunately necessary for a spiritual life. Instead, from a monastic viewpoint, work and the material things needed for daily life are an essential part of one's faith life and there is no bright line dividing the material from the spiritual. As Jon Gunnemann has put it, "the created world is material all the way up and spiritual all the way down."[6] Daily life involves a continual moving back and forth between work and prayer, between economically productive labor and praise of the Lord, integrating the two in a single daily rhythm, so that prayer is part of daily work and work itself is a prayer in the Lord.

Thus those of us who do not live in a monastery have something very important to learn about our own economic life today. If these men and women living in separate monastic communities, often far from the nearest city, understood this religious importance of work and the material world, surely we who are engaged more directly in the world ought to live out a similar integrity of our daily lives, recognizing how our daily employment can be a vibrant part of a life of faith.

Notes

1. *The Rule of St. Benedict*, trans. Timothy Fry, O.S.B. (Collegeville, MN: Liturgical, 1982). Reprinted with permission.

2. For a helpful history of one Benedictine abbey and its embodiment of this integration, see Colman James Barry, *Worship and Work: Saint John's Abbey and University, 1856–1956* (Collegeville, MN: Saint John's Abbey, 1956).

3. John Cassian, *Conf.*, 10, 11, cited in Claude J. Peifer, O.S.B., *Monastic Spirituality* (New York: Sheed & Ward, 1966), 423.

4. Kathleen Norris, *Amazing Grace* (New York: Riverhead, 1998), 262–67.

5. Michael Walzer, *Spheres of Justice* (New York: Basic, 1983), 172–73.

6. Jon Gunnemann, "Capital, Spirit, and Common Wealth," in *The True Wealth of Nations: Catholic Social Thought and Economic Life*, ed. Daniel K. Finn (New York: Oxford University Press, 2010), 290.

8

The Medieval Period

Thomas Aquinas and Natural Law Ethics

INTRODUCTION

The medieval period in Christian history includes many thinkers and a number of different perspectives. The limitation of space here requires us to focus our treatment on only one of the most important of these figures, Thomas Aquinas. One indication of the importance of this man is that when scholars today refer to "Thomas," it's clear that they don't mean Thomas Hobbes, Paine, Jefferson, or Pynchon. They mean Thomas Aquinas.

This chapter will present an overview of Aquinas's ethical theory, based on the natural law. The next chapter will examine four economic problems he addresses with this approach: property ownership, the just price, slavery, and usury. All have important implications for economic life in the twenty-first century.

Thomas Aquinas

Thomas was born to a noble family in Aquino, in southern Italy, about the year 1225. From early childhood, his parents educated him at the Benedictine abbey of Monte Cassino and wanted him to become a Benedictine monk. However, he eventually prevailed in his own desire to become a member of the Order of Preachers, a Dominican priest. He was educated at the University of Paris and taught in Rome and Paris for many years.

Thomas was an enthusiastic student of the Greek philosopher Aristotle, combining that secular perspective with the Christian view of God as Creator and ruler of the universe. Although Thomas was critical of those who adopted too much of the pagan philosopher's worldview, his own

---

work was condemned by the Archbishop of Paris, Étienne Tempier, for holding "heretical" pagan ideas. History vindicated Aquinas, as his theology became broadly influential and he was declared a saint within a half century of his death and within two centuries a doctor of the church, a status on a par with Ambrose and Augustine. Although he died before he reached the age of fifty, Thomas's many writing have set the course of much of Roman Catholic theology over the seven centuries since he died.

Natural law ethics

Thomas Aquinas developed a method for thinking through moral issues that has remained central to Roman Catholic moral theology for seven hundred years: the ethics of the natural law. As we saw in Chapter 6, several of the church Fathers drew heavily on the Stoic tradition of natural law—and the treatment of "natural facts"—in their teaching and preaching about how Christians ought to live their lives. Aquinas takes a large step forward in developing these notions by combining the philosophical framework of Aristotle with the Christian conviction that God is Creator of all that exists. (In fact, Thomas's debt to Aristotle is so great that he simply refers to him as "the Philosopher.") In doing so, Thomas proposes an ethic of virtue—arguing that only virtuous behavior is ultimately fulfilling for humans, precisely because it corresponds to human nature, as God intended it in creation.

In arguing that human reason unaided by biblical revelation can understand the natural law, Thomas does not reject that revelation. He insists that God's grace daily acts to "perfect" nature and that the Christian must always stand in faith in daily life. Nonetheless, because this volume focuses on economic life and because Thomas treats economic issues such as property, the just price, and usury without explicit recourse to these theological resources, we will focus here on his natural law ethics.

To understand this perspective, we will look in turn at Thomas's view of eternal law, natural law, and human law and then we'll also review his treatment of "the divine law," that is, God's law as revealed in the Scriptures. As we shall see, Thomas has a thoroughly theistic view of existence and yet develops a powerful method for addressing moral problems that is based in human reason, a method available even to those who do not have divine revelation.

THE ETERNAL LAW

Whether the eternal law is a sovereign plan existing in God?

Just as in every artisan there pre-exists a plan of the things that are made by his art, so too in every governor there must pre-exist the plan of the order of those things that are to be done by those who are subject to his government. And just as the plan of the things yet to be made by an art is called "the art" or exemplar of the products of that art, so too the plan in him who governs the acts of his subjects bears the character of a law.

Now God, by His wisdom, is the Creator of all things in relation to which He stands as the artisan to the products of his art. Moreover He governs all the acts and movements that are to be found in each single creature. Therefore as the plan of the Divine Wisdom, inasmuch as by it all things are created, has the character of art, exemplar, or idea; so the plan of Divine Wisdom, as moving all things to their proper end, bears the character of law.

Accordingly the eternal law is nothing else than the plan of Divine Wisdom, as directing all actions and movements.

Thomas Aquinas, ST (*Summa Theologica*), I-II, q. 93, a. 1.

As Thomas explains, the most fundamental kind of law is eternal law. Just as the members of the city council have in mind a plan for automobile traffic that is embodied in the laws creating one-way and two-way streets, so God's plan for the universe—how everything from gravity to photosynthesis to human freedom will work—has the character of a law. And since God is all-powerful, his plan for how things are to unfold is a law embodied in "the nature" of each creature. Whether rocks or trees, water or people, stars or mountains, every created thing in the universe is understood by Thomas as fulfilling a part of God's plan. In summary, eternal law is the plan for the universe in the mind of God.

THE NATURAL LAW

Whether there is in us a natural law?

Since all things subject to Divine providence are ruled and measured by the eternal law, as was stated above, it is evident that all things partake somewhat of the eternal law, namely, from its being imprinted on them: they derive their respective inclinations to their proper acts and ends. Now among all others, the rational creature is subject to Divine providence in the most excellent way, in so far as it partakes of a share of providence, by being provident both for itself and for others. Thus, it has a share of the Eternal Reason, whereby it has a natural inclination to its proper act and end: and this participation of the eternal law in the rational creature is called the natural law.

Hence the Psalmist after saying (Ps. 4:6): "Offer up the sacrifice of justice," as though someone asked what the works of justice are, adds: "Many say, Who showeth us good things?" in answer to which question he says: "The light of Thy countenance, O Lord, is signed upon us": thus implying that the light of natural reason, whereby we discern what is good and what is evil, which is the function of the natural law, is nothing else than an imprint on us of the Divine light.

It is therefore evident that the natural law is nothing else than the rational creature's participation in the eternal law.

Even irrational animals partake in their own way of the Eternal Reason, just as the rational creature does. But because the rational creature partakes thereof in an intellectual and rational manner, therefore the participation of the eternal law in the rational creature is properly called a law, since a law is something pertaining to reason. Irrational creatures, however, do not partake thereof in a rational manner, so there is no participation of the eternal law in them, except by way of similitude.

Thomas Aquinas, ST, I-II, q. 91, a. 2.

Each creature is structured as God intends. For example, oaks and elms and other deciduous trees in the Northern Hemisphere regularly put out green leaves in the spring that turn brown in the fall, before the trees stand dormant in winter. Trees also are phototropic; they grow toward the sun, not along the ground. This is part of the nature of the tree, as Thomas explains it, and we can learn about that nature—how trees are supposed to be—by observing both healthy and unhealthy trees. If a particular oak tree puts out leaves in the spring but we find them turning brown three weeks later, we understand that something has gone wrong. We might not know whether it is a disease or an insect or human damage behind this problem, but we know that this oak tree is not healthy; it is not flourishing. Experts who study trees can discover what helps or hinders an oak tree to thrive. In Thomas's words, they come to understand the nature of trees. This articulates in philosophical language the divine rootedness of physical creation that in systematic theology is sometimes called the sacramental character of reality: that God's gracious gift of self is intimately tied to the gift of the physical world. As Michael and Kenneth Himes have put it, "Sacraments are not intrusions into the secular world; they are points at which the depth of the secular is uncovered and revealed as grounded in grace."[1]

Thomas argues that the same is true for humans. Certain ways of life are natural for us, i.e., are a part of human nature. For example, we are social animals in that we naturally congregate with others. We live in families, with parents taking care of their young children. We are destined, he says, to want to know about the world around us, including about our Creator. And just as with the oak tree, we can learn about healthy human beings by studying both healthy and sick ones. Physicians, of course, do this all the time. They understand physical health and disease by understanding carefully those who are well and those who are ill. But Thomas argues that the same is true in a moral sense.

Consider the person you may know who, whenever he gets into a jam, will make up "a little white lie" to explain the situation, in hopes of avoiding responsibility for something he's done wrong. Although this might work once or twice with each person he meets, soon nearly everyone knows he lies to cover up his mistakes. At that point it no longer works—and even worse, he is known as an untrustworthy person in everyone's eyes. We all understand that this is a kind of moral sickness and it undermines both the person and the human community, which depends so much on people being able to trust what others say. Just as the natural law for trees is to put out green leaves in the spring, so Thomas argues that the natural law for humans is to tell the truth—which implies a prohibition against lying—because lying undercuts human flourishing. Thus honesty is a virtue because it conduces to human fulfillment. Virtuous behavior is not a burdensome requirement but the path to true happiness.

As Thomas notes in the last part of the quotation above, because "law" technically relates to rational decisions, it is not literally true to say that the tree "follows" a law, since trees can't make decisions. However, Thomas applies the notion of law as an analogy to "irrational" creatures such as trees or rocks or water. And thus we can say that the oak tree fulfills its nature, that it follows the natural law, when it does things trees ordinarily do. In the centuries since Thomas's day, this stretching of the language has become so commonplace that today we have no problems saying that rivers flow downhill because water follows the law of gravity.

In a virtuous life, we keep the many good things of daily existence—persons, things, experiences—in a proper order, with lesser goods subordinated to greater goods, and to our ultimate good in God. Thus this ethic of virtue is teleological, from the Greek *telos*, meaning goal or end. The right thing to do is to respect the hierarchy of goods, for this will make us truly happy.

Whether the natural law contains several precepts, or only one?

Good is the first thing that falls under the apprehension of the practical reason, which is directed to action: since every agent acts for an end under the aspect of good. Consequently the first principle of practical reason is one founded on the notion of good, namely that "good is that which all things seek after."

Hence this is the first precept of law that "good is to be done and pursued, and evil is to be avoided." All other precepts of the natural law are based upon this: so that whatever the practical reason naturally apprehends as man's good (or evil) belongs to the precepts of the natural law as something to be done (or avoided).

Since, however, good has the nature of an end, and evil the nature of a contrary, all those things to which man has a natural inclination are naturally apprehended by reason as being good (and consequently as objects of pursuit), and their contraries as evil (as objects of avoidance). Thus the order of natural inclinations is the order of the precepts of the natural law.

There is in man first of all an inclination to good in accordance with the nature which he has in common with all substances: inasmuch as every substance seeks the preservation of its own being, according to its nature: and because of this inclination, whatever is a means of preserving human life, and of warding off its obstacles, belongs to the natural law.

Secondly, there is in man an inclination to things that pertain to him more specially, according to that nature which he has in common with other animals: and in virtue of this inclination, those things are said to belong to the natural law, "which nature has taught to all animals," such as sexual intercourse, education of offspring, and so forth.

Thirdly, there is in man an inclination to good, according to the nature of his reason, which nature is proper to him: thus man has a natural inclination to know the truth about God, and to live in society: and in this respect, whatever pertains to this inclination belongs to the natural law; for instance, to shun ignorance, to avoid offending those among whom one has to live, and other such things regarding the above inclination.

Thomas Aquinas, ST, I-II, q. 94, a. 2

The most striking feature of Aquinas's natural law ethics is that the cues about how to live our lives morally are already built into us as natural inclinations, in accordance with our God-given nature. Thomas argues that, like all creatures, we have the inclination to preserve our being (even rocks "try" to stay in one piece). And like the larger animals, we are naturally inclined toward sexual intercourse in the creation of offspring, toward care for the young, etc. And he argues that as the only rational creatures on earth, humans have inclinations not shared by other earthly beings. These are the inclinations to want to know about God, to live in society—and out of this, the inclination to shun ignorance and to avoid offending others. That is, humans have a natural inclination to virtue.

Critical here is Thomas's presumption that "the good is that which all things seek." This might at first seem simply untrue, since we know that at times we ourselves do not do what is good but do what is evil. Thomas, of course, knew the reality of sin, so what does he mean when he says that everyone pursues the good? To ask this question most dramatically, we might think of the most evil persons we have ever met—or read about in history. Consider, for example, Adolf Hitler, at whose command millions perished. Thomas's concept of pursuing the good can be applied to Hitler, in that Hitler saw the attractiveness of the goals he was pursuing. Hitler believed that a pure Aryan race was highly desirable, a great good for humanity. So in this sense, Hitler too sought the good. But would this mean Hitler was right? Did he seek the good rightly? The answer, of course, is "No."

For Thomas, our natural inclination toward the good does not guarantee that our intellect will properly perceive what is truly good and, even if we do perceive it, the inclination doesn't guarantee that our will is strong enough to act properly in seeking the good. These are things that our intellect and will must work hard at. But the basic point here is that built into us are natural inclinations toward what is good for us.

What sort of moral principles might be derived from this way of thinking about the moral life? Let's return to the example of lying. Thomas might ask us to consider the fact that we as humans are social animals and that we live in groups. For a community to thrive, people must trust one another and thus as we just saw, lying is something that is morally objectionable because it breaks down the trust that people have in one another. We know upon reflection that each of us is better off if we do not lie about our misdeeds but instead admit them and commit ourselves to avoiding them in the future. Covering up our mistakes is not only dishonest, breaking down trust, but also creates in us a self-image that is illusory and leaves us insecure about our own identity. Morally healthy people—virtuous people—make mistakes but admit them and are worthy of our trust. This is how and why lying is understood to be immoral within natural law reasoning—and why honesty is a virtue to be embodied in daily life.

Whether the natural law is the same in all men?

The practical reason is busied with contingent matters, about which human actions are concerned: and consequently, although there is necessity in the general principles, the more we descend to matters of detail, the more frequently we encounter defects. Accordingly then in speculative matters truth is the same in all men, both as to principles and as to conclusions: although the truth is not known to all as regards the conclusions, but only as regards the principles which are called common notions. But in matters of action, truth or practical rectitude is not the same for all, as to matters of detail, but only as to the general principles: and where there is the same rectitude in matters of detail, it is not equally known to all.

Thus it is right and true for all to act according to reason: and from this principle it follows as a proper conclusion, that goods entrusted to another should be restored to their owner. Now this is true for the majority of cases: but it may happen in a particular case that it would be injurious, and therefore unreasonable, to restore goods held in trust; for instance, if they are claimed for the purpose of fighting against one's country. And this principle will be found to fail the more, according as we descend further into detail, e.g. if one were to say that goods held in trust should be restored with such and such a guarantee, or in such and such a way; because the greater the number of conditions added, the greater the number of ways in which the principle may fail, so that it be not right to restore or not to restore.

Consequently we must say that the natural law, as to general principles, is the same for all, both as to rectitude and as to knowledge. But as to certain matters of detail, which are conclusions, as it were, of those general principles, it is the same for all in the majority of cases, both as to rectitude and as to knowledge; and yet in some few cases it may fail, both as to rectitude, by reason of certain obstacles (just as natures subject to generation and corruption fail in some few cases on account of some obstacle), and as to knowledge, since in some the reason is perverted by passion, or evil habit, or an evil disposition of nature; thus formerly, theft, although it is expressly contrary to the natural law, was not considered wrong among the Germans, as Julius Caesar relates (*De Bello Gall.* vi).

Thomas Aquinas, ST, I-II, q. 94, a. 4

Although Thomas is convinced that we can learn much about the character of morality through the natural law analysis, he cautions us that only the most general principles are absolutely certain and that as we get into more concrete situations, we will have to employ prudent judgment in making decisions about what is right and wrong. This is not to say that we are left with moral relativism, the mistaken notion that people get to decide as they wish what is right and wrong. Rather, because general principles are applied in concrete situations, we must be careful not to fall into the trap of legalism, the mistake of applying general principles without exceptions and without attention to the immediate circumstance.

Whether the natural law can be changed?

A change in the natural law may be understood in two ways.

First, by way of addition. In this sense nothing hinders the natural law from being changed: since many things for the benefit of human life have been added over and above the natural law, both by the Divine law and by human laws.

Secondly, a change in the natural law may be understood by way of subtraction, so that what previously was according to the natural law, ceases to be so. In this sense, the natural law is altogether unchangeable in its first principles: but in its secondary principles, which, as we have said (A. 4), are certain detailed proximate conclusions drawn from the first principles, the natural law is not changed so that what it prescribes be not right in most cases. But it may be changed in some particular cases of rare occurrence, through some special causes hindering the observance of such precepts, as stated above (A. 4).

A thing is said to belong to the natural law in two ways. First, because nature inclines thereto: e.g. that one should not do harm to another. Secondly, because nature did not bring in the contrary: thus we might say that for man to be naked is of the natural law, because nature did not give him clothes, but art invented them. In this sense, the possession of all things in common and universal freedom are said to be of the natural law, because the distinction of possessions and slavery were not brought in by nature, but devised by human reason for the benefit of human life. Accordingly the law of nature was not changed in this respect, except by addition.

Thomas Aquinas, ST, I-II, q. 94, a. 5

Thomas explains that although the most basic principles of natural law do not change, there may be additions to the natural law, in the sense of human inventions that do not contradict the natural law. Everyone is born naked—and thus clothing is not natural in this sense—yet clothing is a wise addition to the natural law, especially appropriate in colder climates.

We should note that Thomas's other examples of "useful additions to the natural law" are both telling: private property and slavery. He notes in passing that "universal freedom" (where no one is a slave) is natural, and that human institutions have created slavery. In Thomas's day, it was generally presumed by both Christians and others that slavery was a natural and moral part of life, in certain circumstances. The second example of an addition to natural law is personal property ownership. As Thomas indicates, "the possession of all things in common" (no one owns any particular part of the natural world) is presumed to be the natural state. That is, systems of property ownership don't occur in nature but are established in human law and practice. From Thomas's point of view this is quite appropriate, and we will examine his treatment of property in the next chapter. His point here is that while property ownership is not a part of the natural law as God created it, it is something that is rightfully added "over and above" by humans for the benefit of humanity.

HUMAN LAW

Whether every human law is derived from the natural law?
Every human law has just so much of the nature of law as it is derived from the law of nature. But if in any point it deflects from the law of nature, it is no longer a law but a perversion of law.

Thomas Aquinas, ST, I-II, q. 95, a. 2

Whether it belongs to the human law to repress all vices?

> Human law is framed for a number of human beings, the majority of whom are not perfect in virtue. As a result, human laws do not forbid all vices, from which the virtuous abstain, but only the more grievous vices, from which it is possible for the majority to abstain; and chiefly those that concern harm to others, without the prohibition of which human society could not be maintained: thus human law prohibits murder, theft and the like.
>
> Thomas Aquinas, ST, I-II, q. 96, a. 2

Human laws are laws created by those persons who have responsibility for a local or national community. In Thomas's day, these were kings and princes, whereas in our day, they are city councils and local, state, and national legislatures. Human laws are designed to make the requirements of the natural law more concrete and to decide a huge number of particular issues, each of which could be resolved in more than one way. The natural law reveals murder as immoral, and the human law specifies this by distinguishing between first-, second-, and third-degree murder. To take a less critical example, human law decides whether we are to drive on the right- or the left-hand side of the road. As natural as it seems to people in North America to drive on the right side of the road, we know that people in England drive on the left. Such decisions are clearly arbitrary and, while critically important for the harmony and well-being of the community, they could have been decided the other way around.

It is essential that human law flow from the natural law. If it should violate the natural law, it is not authentically a law at all but is, as Thomas puts it, "a perversion of law." This is the foundation for the Christian notion of civil disobedience. Whether in opposition to an unjust war or some other destructively immoral policy of a government, civil disobedience, whereby citizens break a law to formally protest that law's injustice, has a long and respectable history. The tradition has always expected those who engage in civil disobedience to pay the price for breaking the law, rather than simply breaking it and running away. In our language today, we speak of such a law as being immoral, unjust, or illegitimate, whereas in Thomas's language, it is not a law at all. Perhaps the two greatest examples of civil disobedience of the past century have been movements led by Mahatma Gandhi in India and Martin Luther King Jr. in the United States. Both protested—and eventually changed—unjust laws that oppressed large numbers of citizens.

DIVINE LAW

Whether there was any need for a divine law?

Besides the natural and the human law, it was necessary for the directing of human conduct to have a divine law. And this for four reasons.

First, because it is by law that man is directed how to perform his proper acts in view of his ultimate goal. And indeed if man were ordained to no other end than that which is proportionate to his natural faculty, there would be no need for man to have any further direction of the part of his reason, besides the natural law and human law which is derived from it. But since man is ordained to an end of eternal happiness which is beyond the understanding of man's natural faculty, as stated above, it was necessary that, besides the natural and the human law, man should be directed to his end by a law given by God.

Secondly, because, on account of the uncertainty of human judgment, especially on contingent and particular matters, different people form different judgments on human acts; thus different and contrary laws result. In order, therefore, that man may know without any doubt what he ought to do and what he ought to avoid, it was necessary for man to be directed in his proper acts by a law given by God, for it is certain that such a law cannot err.

Thirdly, because man can make laws in those matters of which he is competent to judge. Man is not competent to judge interior movements that are hidden, but only exterior acts which are visible: and yet for the perfection of virtue it is necessary for man to conduct himself aright in both kinds of acts. Consequently human law could not sufficiently curb and direct interior acts; and it was necessary for this purpose that a divine law should supervene.

Fourthly, because, as Augustine says, human law cannot punish or forbid all evil deeds: since while aiming at doing away with all evils, it would do away with many good things, and would hinder the advance of the common good, which is necessary for human intercourse. In order, therefore, that no evil might remain unforbidden and unpunished, it was necessary for the divine law to supervene, whereby all sins are forbidden.

Thomas Aquinas, ST, I-II, q. 91, a. 4

The last kind of law Thomas treats is "divine law," by which he means the law of God as revealed in the Bible. Divine law is like the natural law, in that both flow from the eternal law—and both help us understand God's plan. But while the natural law can be understood by any human person exercising reason, divine law can be known only by those with access to biblical revelation.

Thomas gives four reasons why divine law is necessary for humans. The first is that without revelation, relying only on our natural capacities, we humans would never imagine our ultimate goal, unity with God for all eternity. Second, there is always a degree of uncertainty with human reasoning, whereas revelation, such as the Ten Commandments, can give us confidence in its content. Third, moral restrictions apply not only to outward actions, but to interior motivations, thoughts, and decisions as well. But since humans cannot judge the mental states of other humans, there is no way for the community to enforce any human prohibition against evil thinking. Thus it is appropriate that God should more directly prohibit and punish such "internal" actions as immoral.

Fourth, although human law always aims to cause the effects that the lawgiver intends, it also often has other effects. Because the unintended consequences of human laws are important, Thomas says that human law could not attempt to punish all evil actions without significant damage to the common good. A good example here is the teaching on lying that we just reviewed. Only a few forms of lying have been made illegal: for example, lying under oath and in contracts. If all acts of lying were made illegal, the courts would be bogged down with a myriad of lawsuits initiated by one person against another. In addition, those of us who wish never to lie would have to be as careful in our daily speech as we now must be under oath. There would be no room for jokes, exaggerations, or even inexact speech if every word from our mouth had to be the literal truth. Thus there is great wisdom in Thomas's understanding that human law should not try to prohibit all evil. Human law can set minimum conditions for the moral life but should never be expected to define all of morality. The rest is left to personal moral commitment.

Thomas's observation that the law should not and must not try to prohibit all evil things means that those who want to be moral can never be satisfied with simply "following the law." As we will see later in this book, this is particularly needed in twenty-first-century public life—both political and economic. All too many business and political leaders who have acted immorally think it is a sufficient defense to say that they haven't broken any laws. This represents a fundamental misunderstanding of both morality and law. Law is essential for a moral society, but the law provides only a moral floor below which society will not allow human conduct to fall. However, the requirement of the law falls far short of what a moral life demands.

PRUDENCE

One final element is needed in this summary of Thomas's approach to the moral life. Once we are clear about the moral values we hold, we need a way to decide what to do about them. For example, in deciding whether any one particular value should be embodied in law (say, the prohibition against murder) or not (for example, the prohibition against lying to a friend). The key virtue (or "habit" of judgment) is prudence.

In defining prudence, Thomas quotes the seventh-century bishop, Isidore: "A prudent man is one who sees as it were from afar, for his sight is keen, and he foresees the event of uncertainties."[2] Prudence is the virtue that enables us to apply general principles in resolving particular practical issues. Prudence doesn't decide on those principles but, as Thomas puts it, prudence decides "in what manner and by what means" those principles will be implemented in concrete situations.

The uncertainties that complicate the application of principles arise from two sources, because life is complex both morally and empirically. On the one hand, there are often several important goods at stake in any concrete situation, and accomplishing one of those values to a greater extent often means accomplishing others less well. For example, we could save lives from traffic accidents by reducing the speed limit on freeways to forty miles an hour, but this will impose the very real cost of increased time required in getting people and goods from one place to another.

On the other hand, even if we know how to resolve the problem of the interrelation of goods, things are further complicated by the uncertainty of the empirical situation. The result of taking this or that proposed action is itself usually unclear and often in dispute. For example, differences in competing moral evaluations about international trade today typically involve differences about what trade accomplishes; some say it harms ordinary workers around the world, while others say it helps them.

Thus two people who hold the same moral principles could disagree on how to resolve the conflicts that occur among basic values and/or the conflicts entailed in trying to estimate what will be the outcome of any particular effort to implement those values. Prudence is the virtue that assists us to make those judgments.[3]

Prudence requires wisdom and careful discernment. It is not easy to teach. But at our best, we become like the man Isidore holds up as an example for us: one who sees as it were from afar, for his sight is keen, and he foresees the event of uncertainties.

CONCLUSION

We have seen a brief overview of the virtue-based natural law system of ethics proposed by Thomas Aquinas—founded on the understanding of eternal, natural, and human law. By means of this approach to morality, Thomas says that we can use human reason to understand certain moral requirements for human life that are, in a sense, built into our nature as humans. That is, what we "ought to do" is to act virtuously, which is what will fulfill us as human persons. Vice isn't wrong because God just declared some actions to be sins. Vice is wrong because it ultimately makes us unhappy—it subverts true human flourishing. Thomas applies this system of ethical analysis to four concrete economic issues, topics we will examine in the next chapter.

Notes

1. Michael J. Himes and Kenneth R. Himes, *Fullness of Faith: The Public Significance of Theology* (New York, Paulist, 1993), 82–83.

2. Thomas Aquinas, *The Political Ideas of Thomas Aquinas* (New York: Hafner, 1974), II-II, q. 47, a. 1.

3. William C. Mattison defines prudence as that virtue which "disposes us to see rightly (accurately) the way things are in the world around us, and to employ that truthful vision to act rightly." *Introducing Moral Theology: True Happiness and the Virtues* (Grand Rapids, MI: Brazos, 2008), 98.

9

The Medieval Period

Thomas Aquinas on Four Economic Issues

Thomas Aquinas applies the natural law analysis to four major economic issues: personal ownership of property, the just price to charge for anything bought or sold, slavery, and the charging of interest when lending money (usury). We will examine these issues in this chapter and then in the next will investigate how Christian teaching about two of these (slavery and usury) changed in later centuries. These provide a model for the development of moral doctrine that will be helpful in considering, at the end of this volume, whether and how any other economic teachings should change in the twenty-first century.

PROPERTY OWNERSHIP

Whether it is lawful for a man to possess a thing as his own?

Two things are competent to man in respect of exterior things.

One is the power to procure and dispense them, and in this regard it is lawful for man to possess property. Moreover this is necessary to human life for three reasons. First because every man is more careful to procure what is for himself alone than that which is common to many or to all: since each one would shirk the labor and leave to another that which concerns the community, as happens where there is a great number of servants. Secondly, because human affairs are conducted in more orderly fashion if each man is charged with taking care of some particular thing himself, whereas there would be confusion if everyone had to look after any one thing indeterminately. Thirdly, because a more peaceful state is ensured to man if each one is contented with his own. Hence it is to be observed

> that quarrels arise more frequently where there is no division of the things
> possessed.
>
> Thomas Aquinas, ST, II-II, q. 66, a. 2

Thomas approaches the question of the ownership of property (i.e., "external" things, like tools, clothing, animals, houses, or land) in a very practical manner. He endorses the notion that individuals can and should own property, though we should recall that in Thomas's day those "individuals" were almost always males, who owned all the property of their family, a much more hierarchical and much less widely distributed kind of property than we take for granted today. Nonetheless, the reasons Thomas gives for why personal ownership is moral are what we today might call "economic efficiency" reasons. He says, first, that people are more likely to put in the effort to create or purchase things ("procuring" them) if they are themselves going to own them than if ownership were going to be in common among all. Second, owners are far more likely to take care of their own property than are people who use common property. Third, there is a great advantage to knowing who will decide on the use of each thing ("dispensing" it), and with personal property ownership, it is the owner who makes that decision. This avoids any disputes about who should decide on who gets to use what.

To take a contemporary example, we might ask what life would be like if all the students in a college residence hall who own a car transferred ownership to the group of all students who live there, a kind of common ownership, so no one had more claim on any one car than anyone else. In Thomas's account, far fewer students would be inclined to buy a car. Second, when it was time for the oil to be changed in that blue Toyota, no one may step forward to see that it is done. And third, on Saturday evening, when many students might want to use one of the cars to go to a movie, without individual ownership there could be both confusion and even quarrels about who gets to use the final car left in the parking lot when two or three different groups arrive at the same time to use it.

Thus Thomas endorses the ownership of property by individuals, and he sounds, at least in the paragraph just quoted, as if he supports the individualistic view of personal ownership that typifies our culture today, the sort that says "it's mine and I can do whatever I want with it." However, this is not the full story, as he continues:

The second thing that is competent to man with regard to external things is their use. In this respect man ought to possess external things, not as his own, but as common, so that he is ready to communicate them to others in their need. Hence the Apostle says (1 Timothy 6:17-18): "Charge the rich of this world . . . to give easily, to communicate to others," etc.

Thomas Aquinas, ST, II-II, q. 66, a. 2

After endorsing the personal ownership of property for obtaining things and deciding who is to use them (for "procuring and dispensing" them), Thomas then says that when we consider the *use* of that property, the owner ought to employ it "as common" and "not as his own." This is surely cold water in the face of the individualist view of property ownership predominant today. But in making this argument, Thomas remains consistent with the earlier traditions we have seen from the Hebrew and Christian Scriptures and the early church. As we might expect, Thomas's reasons for holding this to be true are rooted in the natural law.

We saw the early church's rule of thumb for property owners: God has given the earth to humanity—and my wealth to me—to meet the needs of all, and for that reason if I have more than I need, I have an obligation to share with you if you have less than you need. Thomas has taken this fundamental argument to an even deeper level. God's intention that the things of the earth should meet everyone's needs is not simply an idea of God's that individuals ought to take into consideration when they decide how to live their lives. Thomas's understanding of natural law says that God's ideas about material things are actually built into the nature of those things themselves: it is the nature of material goods that they should meet the needs of all. His argument in favor of a system of personal ownership of property, outlined above, refers to an important human law, a prudent one for the administration of property. However, as we have seen, no human law should ever violate the natural law and thus it is presumed that any system of private property should ensure that the nature of the material goods involved be respected. That is to say, a system of private property can only be justified if it leads to meeting the needs of all.

Whether theft is always a sin?

If anyone considers what is meant by theft, he will find that it is sinful on two counts. First, because of its opposition to justice, which gives to each one what is his, so that for this reason theft is contrary to justice, through being a taking of what belongs to another. Secondly, because of the guile or fraud committed by the thief, by laying hands on another's property secretly and cunningly. Thus it is evident that every theft is a sin.

Thomas Aquinas, ST, II–II, q. 66, a. 5

Because Thomas intends a property system that would unfold justly, he endorses the rights of property owners and considers theft a sin. It is morally wrong to steal what belongs to others.

But since the natural law assigns to individual property owners the obligation to share their surplus with those who have unmet needs, it might happen, due to sin, that those who have a surplus refuse to share it with those in need, and thus Thomas describes a surprising possibility.

Whether it is lawful to steal through stress of need?

Things which are of human right cannot derogate from natural right or Divine right. Now according to the natural order established by Divine Providence, inferior things are ordained for the purpose of meeting man's needs by their means. Therefore the division and appropriation of things which are based on human law do not preclude the fact that man's needs have to be remedied by means of these very things. Hence whatever certain people have in superabundance is due, by natural law, to the purpose of helping the poor. For this reason Ambrose says, "It is the hungry man's bread that you withhold, the naked man's cloak that you store away; the money that you bury in the earth is the price of the poor man's ransom and freedom."

Since, however, there are many who are in need, while it is impossible for all to be aided by means of the same thing, each one is entrusted with the stewardship of his own things, so that out of them he may come to the aid of those who are in need.

Nevertheless, if the need be so manifest and urgent, that it is evident that the present need must be remedied by whatever means be at hand (for instance when a person is in some imminent danger, and there is no other possible remedy), then it is lawful for a man to meet his own need by means of another's property, by taking it either openly or secretly: nor is this properly speaking theft or robbery.

Thomas Aquinas, ST, II–II, q. 66, a. 7

Thomas asks whether someone in extreme and urgent need might ever morally take property belonging to someone else without permission. In developing his answer, he first summarizes the understanding of property that we have already seen.

God created the natural order, giving material things ("inferior" things) a nature designed to meet the needs of all humans. Human law has wisely created a system of personal ownership. But human law must never contradict natural law. Thus any human system for private property, as wise as it may be, must be set up so as to respect the nature of the material world as the source of the things everyone needs. This "system" includes not simply the laws but also what we today might call personal morality of the "culture." That is, a moral property system requires not only good laws, but good people who are willing to live up to their personal obligations—such as sharing one's surplus with others whose needs are unmet. Thus Thomas says that if someone is in extreme and urgent need, that person can morally take what is needed. This very possibility is perhaps most famously raised by Jean Valjean's theft of a loaf of bread to feed his starving family in Victor Hugo's novel, *Les Misérables*. Note that Thomas is not saying we can simply take what we want—and not even saying we can take whatever we need. But if the danger is grave and imminent—i.e., a life-threatening situation—such taking can be moral.

Although this teaching of Thomas is somewhat surprising to many of our contemporaries, it was not simply an invention of his. The basic argument that approves of the taking of others' goods in a life-threatening situation was quite common among experts in law in the century before Thomas himself lived and worked. Scholars such as Huguccio, Ricardus Anglicus, Alanus, and Laurentus all took a similar point of view.[1] Whereas among the church Fathers, for example, the description of this phenomenon was that the rich man was stealing from the poor if he did not share his surplus, some scholars in this later era began to speak about the action of the poor man and quite understandably argue that "the poor man did not steal because what he took was really his own *iure naturali*"—which could mean either "by natural right" or by "natural law."[2] This may at first seem very wrong, as we in the West are taught to respect private property, and we live in a culture that tends to think of the control by owners over their property as nearly absolute. But consider an example.

You are riding in a friend's car in a very rural area. Your friend swerves off the road to avoid a deer, hitting a tree, wrecking the car, and very seriously injuring himself. You, fortunately, have escaped injury and are now convinced that you must get your friend to the hospital as soon as possible or he will likely die. By chance, there is another car just across this rural road, and as you investigate, you discover the driver is nowhere around but the keys are in the ignition. The question here is this: Would you help your friend into the passenger seat of the other car and then take the car to drive to the hospital?

It is not your car and thus you would be stealing it. The owner of the car might later take you to court for theft. If you believe owners should have complete control over their property, you would be wrong to take that car and you must instead find another solution, for example hoping that another car will come along this desolate stretch. But let's also assume you do in fact wait for fifteen or thirty minutes for another car to come by and there is no traffic whatsoever. You become more worried that your friend is dying and thus more inclined to steal the other car.

An absolutist view of private property would say that the control of property owners over their property is so important that you should sit there with your friend dying and wait for a driver to come by. Thomas's view of property, however, says that this makes no sense—if we understand that physical things are intended to meet human needs, and in this case there is an urgent human need that this physical thing, the car, can help meet. So you may find yourself taking the car, agreeing with Thomas that private property rights are limited and the rationale for this limitation is the ultimate subordination of material things to meeting human needs. And this, Thomas says, is not theft.

We can even make our example more difficult. Some people might be willing to take the car only on the grounds that the owner of the car, were he present, would either drive you and your friend to a hospital or allow you to borrow the car to do so. That is, you might be willing to take the car solely on the grounds that you assume the owner *would* give you permission if he were present. So let us now change our example and say that the owner of that car is in fact nearby, perhaps collecting plant specimens for his biological laboratory. Let us presume too that you explain the situation and he refuses to allow you to use the car and refuses to interrupt his own scientific work to take your friend to the hospital. The question here is: Would you take the car anyway? To make things simple, let's presume that you are large of stature and the owner of the car is small and thus you have no worry that he might attack you if you begin to take the car. So the question is: Would you be willing to take the car to save your friend's life even if the owner refused to give you permission to do so? Here too, Thomas says you could morally take the car in this situation because the owner of the car is violating the nature of the thing he owns when he refuses to allow it to meet this urgent need. This, Thomas says, is not robbery but rather a moral use of property on your part. Thomas does not say what a civil magistrate would decide if the owner sues you in court for theft—and of course you might be found guilty, even if you did the morally right thing. But the issue here is the morality of taking the car, not the legality of doing so.

The Thomistic teaching on property, still endorsed by the Catholic Church today, is a significant challenge to the nearly absolute view of ownership so popular today.

We should note one element that does *not* appear in Thomas's argument about taking someone else's property in dire and urgent need. Thomas makes no mention of rights—either of the rights of the owner or the rights of someone in dire need. We will investigate this issue in Chapter 11, so here we need only notice that rights language—particularly the language of human rights or civil rights—was only beginning to be used in the medieval period. Ideas about such rights grew historically out of this earlier natural law analysis and should still today be seen in that context if rights talk is to be properly understood within the Christian tradition.

The just price

Whether it is lawful to sell a thing for more than its worth?

It is altogether sinful to have recourse to deceit in order to sell a thing for more than its just price, because this is to deceive one's neighbor so as to injure him. Hence Cicero says: "Contracts should be entirely free from double-dealing: the seller must not impose upon the bidder, nor the buyer upon one that bids against him."

But, apart from fraud, we may speak of buying and selling in two ways. First, as considered in themselves, and from this point of view, buying and selling seem to be established for the common advantage of both parties, one of whom requires that which belongs to the other, and vice versa, as the Philosopher states. Now whatever is established for the common advantage should not be more of a burden to one party than to another, and consequently all contracts between them should observe equality of thing and thing. Again, the quality of a thing that comes into human use is measured by the price given for it, for which purpose money was invented. Therefore if either the price exceed the quantity of the thing's worth, or, conversely, the worth exceed the price, there is no longer the equality of justice: and consequently, to sell a thing for more than it is worth, or to buy it for less than it is worth, is in itself unjust and unlawful.

Secondly we may speak of buying and selling considered as accidentally tending to the advantage of one party and to the disadvantage of the other: for instance, when a man has great need of a certain thing, while another man will suffer if he be without it. In such a case the just price will depend not only on the thing sold, but on the loss which the sale brings on the seller. And thus it will be lawful to sell a thing for more than it is worth in itself, though the price paid be not more than it is worth to the owner. Yet if the one man derive a great advantage by becoming possessed of the other man's property, and the seller be not at a loss through being without that thing, the seller ought not to raise the price, because the advantage accruing to the buyer is not due to the seller, but to a circumstance affecting the buyer. Now no man should sell what is not his, though he may charge for the loss he suffers.

Thomas Aquinas, ST, II-II, q. 77, a. 1,

Property ownership is not the only challenge that Thomas Aquinas presents to economic life today. Thomas's teaching on the just price objects to an overconfident view of markets that would claim that justice can be served regardless of the price at which something sells in the market as long as both parties agree to that price. Here Thomas's argument is once again rooted in Aristotle's: the fundamental point of economic exchange is to assist both parties. This is an older version of the modern economic notion that each party to a voluntary exchange will be better off afterwards than before, or else they would not have entered into the exchange. For Thomas, voluntary agreement isn't sufficient to guarantee justice.

To understand the difference that Thomas's perspective makes, it will be helpful to review one aspect of the modern view of the determination of prices within economic science. We take it for granted today that prices are set by the interaction of supply and demand. According to standard economic analysis, those who produce products (suppliers) will not produce them unless they can at least cover their costs and make an average profit (to make it worth their while to invest their money and time to make these products rather than others). Thus for producers of, say, wooden chairs, the higher the price they can sell chairs for, the more chairs they want to produce. The lower the sale price of chairs, the fewer they want to produce. For those who want to buy a product (demanders), the lower the price at which they can buy chairs, the more attractive is the purchase. The higher the price, the fewer will be demanded. Thus in an overall market, there is an impersonal process that occurs whereby the price is set depending on both the number and willingness of consumers to pay for such chairs at each possible price, and the number and willingness of those who make wooden chairs to produce chairs at each possible price.[3] The development of this economic insight took many decades, such that even brilliant economists like Adam Smith in the eighteenth century and David Ricardo in the nineteenth century were not themselves able to work this out fully. It was only in the late nineteenth century with advances by John Stuart Mill and the later introduction of "marginal utility theory" and "marginal productivity theory" that economists came to have a good explanation for how this price determination process links the desires of consumers with the desires of producers.

Thus it is no surprise that Thomas Aquinas, six hundred years earlier, did not understand how price determination in a market worked. In Thomas's day the weight of tradition was far heavier. Most people had the same jobs as their parents and grandparents, and prices didn't fluctuate much.

As the quotation above indicates, Thomas follows Aristotle in teaching that the price of something being sold should be a fair one, equal to its value. In a world where prices didn't fluctuate much, most people felt they understood by experience what the value of this or that thing should be. It seems clear that Thomas has in mind here what modern economists would call the long-run cost of production. That is, a good should sell for a price that will cover all of the expenses of producing it, including a moderate profit for the one who made and sold it. Unfortunately, a number of historians of economic thought have argued that the just price doctrine simply endorses the prevailing market price. As Stephen Worland put it, "The scholastic just price is, for all intents and purposes, substantially identical with the concept of 'normal price,' or 'long-run price,' analysis which has been ever since the days of Adam Smith one of the central concerns of economic science."[4]

However, this is an overstatement, since Thomas treats fluctuations in price differently, with the question being whether the seller can justly raise the price when conditions are different from normal. Thomas's view is that if the seller has a loss greater than usual when he sells it, then he may charge extra. But if he has no greater-than-usual loss, he should not charge extra, even if the buyer is willing to pay more than usual because the buyer has a greater-than-usual gain from buying the item. To see this, consider an example.

Let's say that a large storm passes through your neighborhood and, as a result, tree branches and rubbish are strewn all over your property, blocking your driveway and making life difficult. By chance, you bought a shovel last week that you now use to clean up. As you begin working, your neighbor, who has suffered a similar mess around his home, comes over to make you an offer.

He asks you whether you'd be willing to sell him your shovel because he needs one to clean up his own property. You explain that you just bought the shovel last week and are now happy you did because you need it to clean up around the yard. He asks you how much you paid, and you respond, "Thirty dollars, at Mr. Hanson's hardware store." So your neighbor offers you thirty dollars to purchase the shovel from you. Thomas's question is whether you might justly charge more than thirty dollars at this point, and his answer is "yes." Today you have an unusual need for the shovel, unlike the ordinary day, and if you were to give up the shovel now your loss would be greater than usual; so the shovel is worth more than usual. Thus you would be allowed to charge more if you decided to sell it.

However, to consider the second aspect, let's say your neighbor instead drives down to Mr. Hanson's store to buy a shovel for himself this morning after the storm. He finds that the price for all these shovels is now forty dollars, because Mr. Hanson raised the price after the storm hit. Here, Thomas argues that Mr. Hanson is acting immorally. The hardware store owner has no greater loss today than last week when he gives up a shovel, so he should keep the price at $30. He bought them all at the wholesaler's a month ago for $22, and knew that he would make a reasonable profit on the shovel at thirty dollars. For him today to raise the price to $40 would be taking advantage of the plight of people in his area without himself having any greater loss at doing so. In Thomas's words, he may not charge for a loss he does not incur. This argument of Thomas's is largely ignored by those commentators who simplistically assert only that the just price is generally equivalent to the market price.[5] Perhaps the best evidence against this error is provided by Albino Barrera when he asks, "What function is served by the just price doctrine if it simply calls on people to pay the price that the market sets?"[6]

As with private property, Thomas's teaching on the just price conflicts with many modern views, particularly those of mainstream economics today. We learn in an introductory college economics course that it is the interaction of supply and demand that results in a market price. If, as in our example, the demand for shovels rises after a storm, the price will quite naturally tend to rise. Contemporary economics, aiming to be a value-neutral science, wants to avoid any talk of what is fair or just, and instead simply aims to describe what occurs. As economists put it, they leave talk of what's right and wrong to philosophers and theologians. And yet built in to this analysis is almost always the presumption that there can be no "just price" other than the market price, because the very notion of a just price implies a static view of demand and supply conditions. Even if prices were quite stable in Aquinas's day, economists say, they certainly are not today, so how could anyone define a just price?

However, from a moral point of view, modern society maintains a sense that markets alone can generate unjust prices. Even today we have examples of widespread public resistance to thinking that the market price, whatever it is, is always just if the buyer voluntarily agrees to pay it. Thomas clearly thought some prices charged by some sellers were unjust for taking advantage of needy buyers and this remains true today, even if it is impossible to draw a precise line between justice and injustice here.

For example, the state of Florida has a law under which "price gouging" carries a penalty of $1000, and instances of deceptive business practices a penalty of $10,000. Thus after just about every hurricane, one can find news stories recounting complaints about the price of small household generators jumping from $250 to $2000. Similarly, as motel owners inland know that people who live along the coast will often have to leave their homes during a hurricane and find lodging elsewhere, there are regularly lawsuits about price gouging by motels. In one typical case that went to court, the motel charged $109 for rooms even though the sign outside still said "All Rooms: $39.99."[7] Thus although economic science does not address the potential injustice of prices, and although we all get used to paying high prices in places where there is no competition (for example, think of the price of a hot dog at the baseball park), our culture has not lost the sense that some prices are indeed unjust and that in some cases those who charge them should be punished.

The teaching about just price (including the idea of a just wage, since the wage is the price of labor) is the single most difficult issue in applying Christian social thought to the market economy today. We will return to this issue in later chapters of this volume.

SLAVERY

A thing is said to belong to the natural law in two ways. First, because nature inclines thereto: e.g. that one should not do harm to another. Secondly, because nature did not bring in the contrary: thus we might say that for man to be naked is of the natural law, because nature did not give him clothes, but art invented them. In this sense, the possession of all things in common and universal freedom are said to be of the natural law, because the distinction of possessions and slavery were not brought in by nature, but devised by human reason for the benefit of human life.

Thomas Aquinas, ST, I-II, q. 94, a. 5

Considered absolutely, the fact that this particular man should be a slave rather than another man, is based, not on natural reason, but on some resultant utility, in that it is useful to this man to be ruled by a wiser man, and to the latter to be helped by the former, as the Philosopher states.

Thomas Aquinas, ST, II-II, q. 57, a. 3

Nothing prevents a thing being against nature as to the first intention of nature, and yet not against nature as to its second intention. Thus, all corruption, defect, and old age are contrary to nature, because nature intends being and perfection, and yet they are not contrary to the second intention of nature, because nature, through being unable to preserve being in one thing, preserves it in another which is engendered of the other's corruption. . . . I say then in like manner that slavery is contrary to the first intention of nature. Yet it is not contrary to the second, because natural reason has this inclination, and nature has this desire—that everyone should be good; but from the fact that a person sins, nature has an inclination that he should be punished for his sin, and thus slavery was brought in as a punishment of sin.

Thomas Aquinas, ST, Supp. III, q. 53, a. 1

Thomas Aquinas explains his views on slavery by once again appealing to the natural law. As we saw earlier in this chapter, he reminds his reader that there is a distinction between what arises in nature and what can be added over and above the natural law through human wisdom. Thus he says that neither clothing nor private property nor slavery is part of the natural law, in the sense that without human intervention those things don't arise. However, they are additions to natural law, which he says are helpful for humanity. Here Thomas follows the predominant view of both the ancient Greeks and the earlier Christian tradition that slavery in certain circumstances is morally appropriate. The most broadly accepted circumstance was when enemy combatants were captured in a war, but slavery was frequently accepted as the fate of those who aided enemy combatants or who were children of slaves.

Another way that Thomas gets to the same distinction is in his description of the first and second "intention" of nature. Here the same sort of defense of slavery is maintained. According to God's original plan there would be no slaves, but in the presence of the sin that characterizes the human condition, it is appropriate and even for the benefit of some to become slaves and be taken care of by others.

In summary, Thomas adds little new to the traditional Christian view of slavery. It is a relationship between master and slave that should be characterized by the appropriate care on the part of the master and respectful obedience on the part of the slave, and in this sense a form of slavery less harsh than in some other parts of the world, but slavery nonetheless.

Usury

Unlike the use of the word today, in the premodern world *usury* was defined as charging an extra amount (typically called "interest") when one lends money. Today, of course, usury means charging an unfair or exorbitant rate of interest, and "usury laws" today typically impose a cap on how high a rate of interest anyone can charge. Thus the reader must shift gears here and enter into the mindset of the medieval world where charging any amount of interest when lending money was considered deeply immoral.

We saw in Chapter 3 that in the Hebrew Scriptures the people of Israel were prohibited from charging interest when they lent to one of their fellow Israelites. The reason was that in a fundamentally agrarian economy, the most frequent reasons that someone would need to borrow were poverty and economic hardship, as may happen after a crop failure for a farm family of modest means. The only way to make it through the winter until next year's harvest may be to borrow from a well-to-do family in the community. Thus the primary reason for the prohibition against usury in ancient Israel was that it represented an abuse of the poor, and a shirking of the obligation of every Israelite to assist those in need.

The Fathers of the early church taught that usury was immoral for largely the same reasons. Their presumption was that anyone who had the resources to lend to someone in serious need should lend without interest or, better yet, should give what is needed, in accord with the general principle that if I have more than I need and you have less than you need, I should share with you from my surplus. The Fathers considered usury so destructive that Ambrose of Milan actually made an exception for lending to the enemy, because "interest is a sort of war, where one strikes one's enemy without using the sword."[8]

However, the treatment of usury in Thomas Aquinas departs from that of his predecessors in the Christian tradition largely because he distinguishes the moral issues related to property ownership from those related to usury and thus presumes that the property ownership responsibilities will take care of the needs of the poor and that the issue of usury can be analyzed on other grounds altogether.

UNDERSTANDING WHAT IT MEANS TO BORROW IN GENERAL

Before addressing the question of the moral manner in which one might lend or borrow money, Thomas asks his readers to ignore money completely and instead begin with a more general question of what is involved in borrowing or lending anything whatever. In this, he once again follows Aristotle's lead.

There are certain things the use of which consists in their consumption: thus we consume wine when we use it for drink and we consume wheat when we use it for food. Thus in such things, the use of the thing must not be reckoned apart from the thing itself, and whoever is granted the use of the thing, is granted the thing itself and for this reason, to lend things of this kind is to transfer the ownership. Accordingly if a man wanted to sell wine separately from the use of the wine, he would be selling the same thing twice, or he would be selling what does not exist, wherefore he would evidently commit a sin of injustice. . . .

On the other hand, there are things the use of which does not consist in their consumption: thus to use a house is to dwell in it, not to destroy it. Therefore in such things both may be granted: for instance, one man may hand over to another the ownership of his house while reserving to himself the use of it for a time, or vice versa, he may grant the use of the house, while retaining the ownership. For this reason a man may lawfully make a charge for the use of his house, and, besides this, reclaim the house from the person to whom he has granted its use, as happens in renting a house.

Thomas Aquinas, ST, II-II, q. 78, a. 1

There are certain things whose use is their consumption, and which do not admit of usufruct, according to law. Thus, if such things be extorted by means of usury, for instance money, wheat, wine and so forth, the lender is not bound to restore more than he received (since what is acquired by such things is the fruit not of the thing but of human industry), unless indeed the other party by losing some of his own goods be injured through the lender retaining them: for then he is bound to make good the loss.

On the other hand, there are certain things whose use is not their consumption: such things admit of usufruct, for instance house or land property and so forth. Thus, if a man has extorted from another his house or land, he is bound to restore not only the house or land but also the fruits accruing to him therefrom, since they are the fruits of things owned by another man and consequently are due to him.

Thomas Aquinas, ST, II-II, q. 78, a. 3

Thomas argues that when it comes to borrowing and lending, all goods can be divided into two groups: those that are used up when they are used and those that are not. Thomas distinguishes these because, he says, borrowing and lending goods like wine (which is used up once drunk and nothing is left afterwards) is quite different from borrowing and lending something like a house, which is not used up when being used. Thus it will help us to understand Thomas's argument if we think through the situation of borrowing and lending of wine and houses in Thomas's day.

Consider the loan of a bottle of wine. Let's say that you are a householder in thirteenth-century Paris (where Thomas taught) and a neighbor knocks on your door one afternoon. He reports that he will have friends coming over for dinner and just now realizes that he has red wine but no white. He thinks that one of his guests will prefer white wine and thus asks if he can borrow a bottle of white wine from you. You agree and invite him to accompany you down to your wine cellar. There you find a number of bottles of wine, both red and white, and you choose a bottle of white from the wine rack and hand it to him. He leaves and goes home with the wine.

After some time, whether tomorrow morning or a few days later, your neighbor returns, knocking on the door to pay back his loan. From Thomas's point of view, it would not matter much whether it was the very same bottle that he borrowed (if his guest in fact did not want white wine and he never opened the bottle) or whether it is an identical bottle that he purchased in town after he used up the bottle he borrowed from you. In either case, you take the bottle down to your wine cellar and put it back on the rack with the others.

The key question Thomas asks is whether you could rightfully insist on an extra charge when your neighbor returns the bottle of wine. Thomas employs here implicitly the same logic that we saw in the last chapter concerning the just price. Because you have had no loss, it would be immoral for you to charge something extra when your neighbor returns the bottle of wine. The same analysis would apply to any other goods that are used up when used, such as a sack of flour or a gallon of gasoline. Today we would call these "consumption goods."

We should note that the same logic of just price would indicate that if you had a need for that bottle of white wine the same day that your neighbor wanted to borrow it—perhaps you yourself were planning a dinner party and you had only enough white wine to serve your own guests—then you would indeed have had a loss from not having it available. In this situation, Thomas would certainly have allowed you to charge extra if you and the neighbor agreed to the lending of a bottle of white wine that day. However, Thomas's analysis here covers the more general case where such unusual (or as he says, "contingent") circumstances do not obtain.

The second type of good that Thomas considers regarding borrowing and lending is any good that is not used up when used. Here, he points to the lending of a house. Thomas is no doubt aware that houses eventually get worn out and used up, but that occurs over decades or even centuries. Thus he ignores issues of material depreciation in considering the typical, temporary loan of a house. Similarly if the borrower of the house damages it during use, the owner can rightfully charge extra to fix it, but this is not essential to the lending/borrowing process, and so Thomas ignores it as well.

When we lend a house to another person, we allow them to live in it for a time with full rights to its use but without transferring any ownership to them. In Thomas's language, the house generates "usufruct" (it is "fruitful"), in the sense that it produces a service to the residents of the house. Thomas reports that in this case it is quite moral to charge something extra in addition to simply receiving the house back when the borrower is finished with it. This something extra we ordinarily call "rent," and even though we don't usually think of the rental of a house as an act of "borrowing," that is certainly what renting is: borrowing something where we pay for the privilege of the loan.

Thomas sees the house (and everything in this second category of goods) as producing what in modern economic terms we would call a "stream of services." This makes the second group "capital goods," in economic parlance, as they are not directly used up in consumption but instead produce services that are valuable to us. The same analysis would apply to other goods not used up when used, such as a table, an automobile, or a refrigerator.[9]

Thus in sum, Thomas says that if we look at borrowing in general, there are two kinds of goods: consumption goods and capital goods. When we lend a consumption good, something used up when it is used, we should ask for nothing extra when it is returned. However, when we lend capital goods, we are allowed to charge extra because during that time of the loan we are giving up the stream of services that the good generates.

BORROWING AND LENDING MONEY

Now money, according to the Philosopher, was invented chiefly for the purpose of exchange: and consequently the proper and principal use of money is its consumption or alienation as it is sunk in exchange. Hence it is by its very nature unlawful to take payment for the use of money lent,

> which payment is known as usury: and just as a man is bound to restore other ill-gotten goods, so is he bound to restore the money which he has taken in usury.
>
> Thomas Aquinas, ST, II-II, q. 78, a. 1

Once Thomas has developed his basic analysis of borrowing based on two types of goods, the only question left in addressing usury is: "Which kind of good is money?" Thomas's answer is: "the first kind." To think this through, it is helpful to consider what would have happened in Thomas's day when someone asked to borrow money.

Just as before, let us say your neighbor knocks on your door and asks if he may borrow three gold coins, which he will need first thing in the morning. If you agree to the loan, you will do something quite similar to what you did when he asked to borrow that bottle of wine. You will go down to your cellar where you keep your gold coins. You pull three gold coins out of your strongbox and give them to your neighbor, who leaves with the money you have lent him. Sometime later, whether the next day or a month or year later, he appears at your door and hands you three gold coins in repayment. These may be the same three coins (if it turned out he didn't need to use them) or, more likely, three equivalent coins. In either case, you take the coins downstairs, just as you did the wine, and put them back in the strongbox. Thus Thomas argues that in lending the wine and the gold coins, you have had no loss. You were temporarily without them but without any loss to you.

Once again, Thomas would certainly say that if you yourself needed those gold coins for some purpose at the time when your neighbor wanted to borrow them, you would be right in asking for some extra payment to compensate for your loss. However, in the general case, you have gold coins in your strongbox and you simply return the ones he borrowed to that place when he is finished with them. Because you have no loss, you should not charge anything extra. In Thomas's words, money is "sterile," in that it does not produce "usufruct." Thus it is immoral to charge extra when one lends money to another; usury is immoral.

CONCLUSION

Thomas concludes that the personal ownership of property is a good thing and that property does not have to be owned in common to be moral. In this, of course, he rejects the view of that tiny minority in Christian history that considers the holding of goods in common as exemplified in the Jerusalem community to be the norm for responsible Christian life. He cites three efficiency reasons why this is the case and thus supports one of the most fundamental institutions of market economies: private property. However, Thomas adds that all material goods have a purpose as part of God's creative intention for them: a destiny to meet human needs. As we will see later, Pope John Paul II quite characteristically referred to this as "the universal destination of goods." That is, as a property owner, I am obliged to use the goods I own in a way that respects God's intention for all the goods on the earth: material goods are to be used to meet the needs of all. Thus if others have unmet needs and I have extra, I have an obligation in justice to share my surplus with them.

Concerning the just price, Thomas taught that a price is allowed to be higher than normal if that higher price compensates the seller for some unusual loss. However, it would be wrong to charge more simply because a buyer has an unusual need and thus is willing to pay more than the usual price—because the seller would be charging for a loss he does not incur.

If we ask about the implications of these teachings for economic life today, we can see two important effects. Concerning private property, the Thomistic view of property ownership by individuals would oppose many restrictions on private property—for example, that an individual cannot start a business—that might be proposed by, say, communist governments. However, property ownership also entails a strong moral obligation—to share a surplus. This in turn is a fundamental part of the justification of government taxation of the prosperous to support programs that pay for services that poor families need, whether education, healthcare, or others. There is no willingness here to create a dependent class of persons who don't have to work for themselves, but the insight that we owe something to those who are unable to meet their own needs carries over vividly into the modern world.

The second implication concerns the notion of the just price. This remains a difficult problem because, unlike the understanding of the obligations of property, the obligations of the just price do not fit well at all within a market society. Today, producers of goods and services compete in a worldwide market and often find that the products they need as inputs for their own production fluctuate in price, requiring producers to make adjustments. The market for selling their goods is also global, and thus producers often find themselves unable to sell their product without reducing the price. The notion that there simply is a just price for every product and service is one that does not match well with a market economy. This does not mean that there is no solution here, but we will need to wait until later in the book to understand the kind of solution that might work: relying on the market to set prices but understanding that the fundamental obligation behind a just price must still be respected in a market system, requiring community involvement, whether through government or voluntary organizations.

Concerning slavery, Thomas agreed with the common teaching on the topic that Christians and others had long held: that under certain conditions—particularly following a war—it was perfectly moral for one person to own another. It took nearly six hundred years after Thomas's day for the world to reject slavery in every situation, an important change in doctrine that we will discuss in more detail in Chapter 11.

Concerning usury, Thomas followed the lead of Aristotle in his opposition to the taking of interest on a loan of money. Unlike the biblical and patristic opposition to usury because of its abuse of the poor, Thomas depended on the doctrine of property ownership to engender support for those with unmet needs. His analysis of usury centered on the character of money. And it is the later historical change in the character of money that eventually led to a change in church teaching on usury, also in Chapter 11.

As one of the most influential voices in the history of Christian social thought, Thomas Aquinas provides methods for thinking about economic life still today. We will return to contemporary reliance on Aquinas in later chapters.

Notes

1. See Chapter 2, "Origins of Natural Rights Language," in Brian Tierney's *The Idea of Natural Rights* (Atlanta: Scholars, 1997), especially 72–73.

2. Tierney, *Natural Rights*, 73.

3. See chapters on supply and demand analysis in any introductory textbook, for example Robert H. Frank, Ben S. Bernanke, and Louis D. Johnston, *Principles of Economics: Brief Edition* (New York: McGraw-Hill Irwin, 2009), chapter 3.

4. Stephen Theodore Worland, *Scholasticism and Welfare Economics* (Notre Dame: University of Notre Dame Press, 1967), 231.

5. Ibid.

6. Albino Barrera, *Economic Compulsion and Christian Ethics* (New York: Cambridge University Press, 2005), 102.

7. *New York Times*, August 18, 2004.

8. Ambrose of Milan, *De Tobia*, 14, 51, in Phan, *Social Thought*, p. 41.

9. Today, items like refrigerators are called "consumer durables" to distinguish them from simple consumption goods. Refrigerators and washing machines are typically purchased by consumers; they are a form of capital.

10

The Protestant Reformation

One of the most important events in the history of Christianity was the Protestant Reformation, literally a protest by Christians in the sixteenth century against the rites, customs, and prevailing theology of the Roman Catholic Church. Historians have typically dated the start of the Reformation from the posting of ninety-five theses on the door of the castle church in Wittenberg, Germany, by a young Augustinian monk named Martin Luther on October 31, 1517.

As dramatic as the events of the sixteenth century were, they were not the first efforts at reform within the Christian church in the West. Historians recount a long series of efforts to reform Christian faith and practice over several hundred years prior to Luther's birth, beginning perhaps with the decision of the Lateran Council of 1215 to make auricular confession universal, encouraging all Christians to confess their sins personally in an effort to move toward more responsible Christian daily life. The call of Francis of Assisi to his followers to choose lives of simplicity and poverty was another part of this process. Charles Taylor sees this "individuating" of Christianity as a critical step, on the one hand, in reform movements—of which the Reformation is the most dramatic—and, on the other, in the later rise of secularism and atheism as cultural rivals to Christian faith.[1]

Still, many of the popes and leading bishops of the church in the fifteenth and sixteenth centuries looked and acted more like the princes of Europe than servants of God's people. Thus it is understandable that at some point the accumulation of protests would result in more fundamental changes in European church and society. There are many important figures in the Protestant Reformation, but the constraints of space require us in this chapter to focus on only two, Martin Luther and John Calvin. In these two great reformers we can see the mainstream Protestant view of economic life.

MARTIN LUTHER

Christians today sometimes picture Luther striding boldly to the front door of a cathedral with hammer and nail in hand, defiantly posting his theses for the world to see. In fact, things were not so dramatic, since he actually posted them on a side door and they were almost certainly just one of many things posted there. This door acted as a bulletin board for all sorts of announcements about discussions and debates in academic life that were happening in Wittenberg at the time.[2] Although the posting of the theses was much less dramatic than it may sound to us today, the impact of Luther's life was immense. The success of the Lutheran Reformation stands out as far more dramatic than any that had come before, dividing Europe into Catholic and Protestant, and eventually—contrary to Luther's intention—dividing the Protestant world into a number of different denominational visions of what Christian faith ought to mean.

Martin Luther

Martin Luther was born in 1483 in Eisleben, Germany, then part of the Holy Roman Empire. His father wanted him to have a career in the law, and Martin took a standard course of study at the University of Erfurt, followed by entrance into the school of law there. However, he quickly decided that the law was not for him and pressed toward philosophy and theology, joining an Augustinian monastery at age twenty-two. He was ordained a priest and then studied and taught theology at the University of Wittenberg.

Although he fasted and prayed as required by the Rule of St. Augustine, seen in Chapter 7, Luther found no consolation but largely religious despair in monastic life. When a Dominican priest, Johann Tetzel, was sent to Germany to raise money to rebuild St. Peter's Basilica in Rome, offering indulgences in return, Luther began an escalating series of complaints to church authorities about the evils of selling indulgences, since the practice contradicted basic Christian belief that salvation was a gift of God. At age thirty-three, he posted his famous theses, leading eventually to his excommunication by the pope and his being outlawed by the Emperor.

Receiving considerable support from many in Germany, Luther gave structure to a renewed Christianity where faith in God was central, and the Bible—translated into German by Luther himself to make it directly accessible to the faithful—was the living word of God. He died at age sixty-two.

A GENERAL OVERVIEW OF THE PROTEST

Two of the most important of Luther's objections in the ninety-five theses concerned the status of the laity. First, he argued that it was a serious mistake to think of the Christian population as divided into two great orders, one a holier and more religiously important group of bishops, priests, brothers, and nuns, and the other, the less important laity. The second was that Roman authorities reserved the interpretation of the Bible to church experts and did not encourage the average Christian to engage the text directly.

Underlying both of these objections was the more fundamental argument Luther made that the salvation which comes to us in Jesus Christ is a free gift from God, not something that humans themselves can bring about. Here he was objecting strenuously to the sale of indulgences in the medieval church.

Scholars point out that in the late medieval period, popular piety developed a fascination with the question of what occurs after one's own death, out of which arose an intense concern about purgatory, a sort of in-between existence after one dies but before one enters heaven, during which one pays a price for the sins of one's life. It is in this spiritual context that the notion of an indulgence arose, as Christians could reduce their "time" in purgatory by saying particular prayers or making particular pilgrimages.

The greatest abuse arose when popes and bishops offered indulgences simply for the contribution of money to help erect cathedrals and other church buildings. It was this which most angered Luther, as it implied that the wealthy would have an easier time getting into heaven than the poor, something that Jesus himself had said would simply be the other way around. (Recall his teaching that it is easier for a camel to pass through the eye of a needle than for a rich man to enter heaven.)

For Luther, "God justifies by imputing righteousness from outside us. Justification by faith is a relation, not a substantial amalgamation."[3] That is, Luther objected to the prevailing vision of an economy of salvation where contemporary church practice implied that one could be more or less saved, more or less ready to be with God in heaven, depending on what one did or the prayers one said. Luther rejected the notion that one might accumulate some sort of credits in the eyes of God and instead argued for the more fundamental understanding that justification is a relationship between God and the human person, dependent only on God's gracious love and not on some quantifiable balance sheet of assets and debits.

Salvation, faith, and works

From this absolute God everyone should flee who does not want to perish, because human nature and the absolute God—for the sake of teaching we use this familiar term—are the bitterest of enemies. Human weakness cannot help being crushed by such majesty, as Scripture reminds us over and over.

Martin Luther, *Commentary on Psalm 51*[4]

For the righteousness of God is not acquired by means of acts frequently repeated, as Aristotle taught, but it is imparted by faith, for "He who through faith is righteous shall live" (Rom. 1:17). . . . Therefore I wish to have the words "without work" understood in the following manner. Not that the righteous person does nothing, but that his works do not make him righteous, rather that his righteousness creates works. For grace and faith are infused without our works. After they have been imparted the works follow.

Martin Luther, *Heidelberg Disputation*[5]

For Luther, the most fundamental mistake of the Roman church was to forget that salvation comes from a gratuitous act of God. No work that we do could possibly bring about salvation, since we are insignificant and thoroughly unneeded from God's point of view. At the same time, however, Luther argued strenuously against those who would claim that all one needs is faith and not acts of service to others. As he explains, action cannot bring about salvation, but anyone with faith and a grace infused by God will certainly be engaged in good works, following the example of Jesus.

Thus the implication of Christian faith for economic life remains important for Luther, because a person living in faith in Jesus Christ will be energized by the promise inherent in the "good news" of God's future for all of creation.[6]

THE COMMITMENT TO ACTION IN THE WORLD

The shift in the understanding of justification—as brought about through grace alone and not works—relieved the faithful of the anxiety that their ultimate salvation depended upon the actions that they took in their daily lives. However, following Christ still left the Christian intimately aware of human inadequacy. In addition, this shift of attention away from spiritual works aimed at salvation opened up greater awareness of the importance of one's daily work and even entailed a broadening of the meaning of the request for "our daily bread" in the Lord's prayer.

Our daily bread

When you pray for "daily bread," you pray for everything that is necessary in order to have and enjoy daily bread and, on the contrary, against everything that interferes with enjoying it. You must therefore enlarge and extend your thoughts to include not only the oven or the flour bin, but also the broad fields and the whole land which produce and provide for us our daily bread and all kinds of sustenance. For if God did not cause grain to grow and did not bless and preserve it in the field, we could never take a loaf of bread from the oven to set on the table.

To put it briefly, this petition includes everything that belongs to our entire life in this world; only for its sake do we need daily bread. Now, our life requires not only food and clothing and other necessities for our body, but also peace and concord in our daily business and in associations of every description with the people among whom we live and move—in short, everything that pertains to the regulation of our domestic and our civil or political affairs. For where these two relations are interfered with and prevented from functioning properly, there the necessities of life are also interfered with, and life itself cannot be maintained for any length of time.

Martin Luther, *Large Catechism*[7]

A cobbler, a smith, a peasant—each has the work and office of his trade, and yet they are all alike consecrated priests and bishops. Further, everyone must benefit and serve every other by means of his own work or office so that in this way many kinds of work may be done for the bodily and spiritual welfare of the community, just as all the members of the body serve one another (1 Cor. 12:14-26).

Martin Luther, *To the Christian Nobility*[8]

For Luther, every individual has a "vocation." Coming from the Latin word *vocare*—to call—a vocation is God's calling to each Christian to a particular set of activities in life and to living out those roles as well as possible. And because the acts of prayer, penance, and pilgrimage cannot bring about one's salvation, there is no reason to distinguish the spiritual roles of priests and nuns from those of the "ordinary" roles of cobbler, farmer, and homemaker. No one Christian is superior to any other based on occupation, and thus Luther brought about the closure of monasteries and the great simplification of the system of clergy.

Later scholars have noted that this new emphasis on the spiritual meaning of one's everyday work had an important impact on the economy as a whole.

Whereas in the pre-Reformation church the ordinary jobs could be looked down upon as inferior to those of priests and bishops, they were now highly respectable jobs and the ones that God wants us to live out. Thus the economic system came to bear a spiritual dignity that was not nearly so clear in the earlier system. There was still a long way to go before Christians would articulate more carefully the spiritual significance of markets themselves, but this shift on the part of Lutheran spirituality was a critically important first step.

CONCERN FOR THE POOR

In spite of the changes that the Lutheran Reformation brought about for the ordinary understanding of salvation and economic life, and in spite of Luther's rejection of scholastic philosophy, the fundamental obligation of the well-to-do toward the poor remained critical to Lutheran teaching. Luther drew this from "the pure study of the Bible and the Fathers of the church."[9]

The dangers of wealth

It is exceedingly difficult for a rich person to be righteous and godly, because idolatry and contempt for one's brother are associated with wealth. . . . The common danger for rich people is the sin of omission, where they do not come to the aid of the poor and needy, even though God has sternly commanded it.

Martin Luther, *Lectures on Genesis*[10]

The rich man who "feasted sumptuously every day" was not condemned for his riches but because he sinned by omission: he did not feed the hungry man sitting at his gate. He was not damned because he robbed or did evil with respect to these goods. . . . He was damned rather because he did not do good to his neighbor, namely, Lazarus. This parable adequately teaches us that it is not sufficient merely not to do evil and not to do harm, but rather that one must be helpful and do good.

Martin Luther, *Sermon on the Rich Man in Luke 16*[11]

Beware! God will not ask you at your death and at the Last Day how much you have left in your will, whether you have given so and so much to churches . . . he will say to you, "I was hungry, and you gave me no food; I was naked, and you did not clothe me" (Matt 25:42-43). Take these words to heart!

Martin Luther, *Trade and Usury*[12]

Luther, of course, turns to the gospel for guidance, here examining the story of Lazarus (the poor man sitting outside the door of the rich man who ignored him) and the parable of the Last Judgment in Matthew 25. Every good Christian should feel an obligation to help the poor meet their needs. Luther quotes Ambrose of Milan in saying, "Feed the hungry: if you do not feed him then as far are you concerned, you have killed him."[13] These, of course, are harsh words and not typical of everything that Luther said about the poor, but clearly a part of his fundamental message.

Luther's condemnation of usury on the basis of the biblical precedent follows closely Christian tradition to this point: that usury was an exploitation of the poor and thus a destructive economic practice. At the same time, Luther's traditionalism left him unable to support the rebellion of peasants against their civic overlords out of a concern for stability and a skepticism of "the people" that is quite reminiscent of similar arguments made by Thomas Aquinas centuries earlier.[14] Thus although Luther is deeply committed to service to the poor as a part of any responsible active life of faith, this concern does not yet extend to any transformation of political or economic structures, a change in Christianity that later leaders would have to propose.

John Calvin

The second great figure of the Protestant Reformation was John Calvin. Like Luther who came before him, Calvin shared the critique of the Roman church and the great abuse of indulgences that put true Christian faith to shame. However, Calvin was an attorney: a man of the law and a far more practical intellect than the theologian Luther. Thus we find in Calvin a far more developed understanding of the ethical implications of the reformed faith. For example, Calvin and Christians in his community strove to transform the city of Geneva, Switzerland, into an example of what the Christian church as a social organization could be at its best. As we will see, Calvin brings about some important shifts in Christian history, including a reevaluation of the teaching on usury. And because of this sort of development of the tradition, Calvin stands as a more significant person in the history of Christian views of economic life than Luther, whom the great scholar Ernst Troeltsch described as fundamentally traditional.[15]

John Calvin

   Born Jean Cauvin in 1509, the reformer we know as John Calvin was a French lawyer who broke with the Roman Catholic Church at age twenty-one and became a Protestant theologian and pastor. Like Luther, he stressed the sovereignty of God and the free gift of salvation, and unlike Luther, the doctrine of predestination. Calvin's faith stressed the insignificance of humans in the face of an all-powerful God.

Calvin was the central religious figure in the transformation of the city of Geneva, Switzerland, into a deeply religious community, though he himself did not have a formal civil role in city governance. His very practical background as an attorney led him to develop a sophisticated social ethic—integrating proper civic governance into a broader vision of Christian faith. He eventually split with Luther over the meaning of the Eucharist and became internationally known as an independent Protestant leader, due to whom several of today's Protestant denominations call themselves Calvinist. He died at age fifty-four.

GENERAL OVERVIEW

Sin and salvation

We must, therefore, acquiesce in the judgment of God, which pronounces man to be so enslaved by sin that he can bring forth nothing sound and sincere. Yet, at the same time, we must remember, that no blame for that is to be cast upon God. . . . And further it must be noted, that men are not exempted from guilt and condemnation, by the pretext of this bondage: because, although all rush to evil, yet they are not impelled by an extrinsic force, but by the direct inclination of their own hearts; in short, they sin . . . voluntarily.

John Calvin, *Commentary on Genesis*[16]

All those who think they can merit something before God and make him their debtor are condemned of depraved pride. . . .

God receives nothing extra from us but only gathers the legitimate fruits of his lordship. Therefore we must grasp these two things: that God owes us nothing naturally nor is any service that we pay him worth a hair.

John Calvin, *Commentary on Luke*[17]

Calvin was convinced of three principles often forgotten by the Roman church: that humans are insignificant in the sight of God, that salvation comes as a free gift of God, and that nothing we do can make God love us more—or less—than he already does. At the same time, however, Jesus Christ established a church on earth and within the church there is the possibility of living out a responsible life in accord with God's will. As André Biéler has argued, "[T]his partial restoration here on earth of the primitive natural social order prefigures its complete restoration with the final arrival of the Kingdom of God."[18] This is by no means easy, but the problem, as Calvin saw it, was that the leaders of the church in Rome were far more interested in their own wealth and ease than in the responsible life of the church as a whole.

Christians in civil government

And you, Christian kings, princes and lords, ordained by God to punish the wicked and uphold the good in peace, in accordance with the Word of God, are responsible for having that so useful and essential sacred doctrine published, taught and understood throughout all your lands, regions and domains. . . .You must realize that there is no better or firmer foundation than to have him as Head and Master, and to govern your peoples under his hand, in order to keep your domains truly prosperous.

John Calvin, *Preface to the New Testament*[19]

Calvin's view of Christian life recognizes that there would be a government outside of the church and that one could expect more from government than Luther thought possible, but clearly not as much as is possible within the church itself. Thus although Calvin was the dominant figure in Geneva for most of his life, he never held political office. At the same time, he did appear before the Council of Government and argued persuasively for this or that change in public policy, often bringing about the change, given his influence in the city. Calvin saw not only the leaders of the city of Geneva, but kings and princes everywhere, as ordained by God, and he challenged Christians in government to live up to the commandments of God.

For all the change that Calvin brought about and the much more active way in which Calvinist Christianity had implications for government, we must not make the mistake of thinking of Calvin as an advocate of democracy. He aimed to reform government and was no "flatterer of princes," but at the same time he understood those in civil authority, whether elected by the people or hereditary monarchs, to be in their place because of the rule of the Lord. Thus we find Calvin's attitude toward tyranny is quite close to that of Thomas Aquinas, three hundred years earlier. Few leaders—religious or secular—in the premodern era trusted "the people" to take the law into their own hands and to overthrow even an unjust tyrant.

Civil government

The function of civil government . . . is not merely to see to it that people eat, drink, and be sustained in their life, even though it embraces all these activities when it provides for their living together. It does not, I repeat, look to this only, but . . . prevents the public peace from being disturbed; it provides that each may keep his property safe and sound; that people may carry on intercourse among themselves without fraud or harm; that honesty and modesty may be preserved among them.

John Calvin, *The Institutes*[20]

Whenever it is a matter of good and upright government, God points to strangers and orphans and widows; for through them the character of the public government can easily be seen. For when others obtain their right, it is no matter of wonder, since they have advocates to defend their cause, and also their friends are assembled. . . . But when strangers and orphans and widows are not unjustly dealt with, it is an evidence of real integrity. . . .

But today we see the poor so given over to fraud and mischievousness—it is awful; they are small-time thieves and crooks. If a person has fields and vineyards by the villages, he will be constantly cheated out of some of his property, just as if he was in the land of the enemy. Why? Because the poor allow themselves such freedom and think they can take advantage of the rich to plunder and steal everything they can.

John Calvin, *Sermons on Deuteronomy*[21]

Calvin understands the function of government as providing the structure necessary for ongoing daily life. Included here is the attention of government to the treatment of the poor and outcast, with Calvin referring to the biblical trio of the poor: orphans, widows, and resident aliens. Their treatment, he says, is the test for the integrity of civil government.

However, in a move that departs from the view of Aquinas on theft, Calvin allows no room for the poor person in dire need to legitimately steal from others. Here he expects the discipline of the church to be sufficient to provide for the needs of all, and as a former attorney, he does not want to risk the flouting of human law that such doctrines might encourage.

THE WEALTHY, THE POOR, AND CALVIN'S VIEW OF PROPERTY OWNERSHIP

The rich

Accordingly, [the prophet Isaiah] describes the feelings of those who never have enough, and whom no wealth can satisfy. So great is the keenness of the covetous that they desire to have everything, just for themselves, and reckon everything which others have to be something they are missing. Hence the perspicacious observation of Chrysostom, that "the covetous would willingly take the sun from the poor if they could," for they envy others even what is common to all, and would gladly steal it from them to enjoy it all by themselves.

John Calvin, *Commentary on Isaiah*[22]

God could very well give each person plenty so that no one would need help from anyone else, but he wants to test the love and fraternity we have together when we thus communicate with each other as he commands us to do. . . . For otherwise they are like murderers if they see their neighbors wasting away and yet do not open their hands to help them. In this, I tell you, they are certainly like murderers.

John Calvin, *Commentary on Matthew*[23]

We know well enough that it is a common vice which prevails upon the rich to spend too sumptuously and excessively on banquets and well-garnished tables. Though the Lord permits them to live abundantly and generously at his supply, yet one must ever beware of being lavish, and keep respect for plain living. Not for nothing does the Lord by his prophets throw sharp words at those who sleep on ivory couches, who pour on precious unguents, who entrance their palates with sweetness to the notes of the zither, to all intents like fat cattle in rich pastures (Amos 6:4).

John Calvin, *Commentary on James*[24]

Like the biblical and patristic witnesses long before him, Calvin is vividly clear on the dangers of wealth and the tendency of the wealthy to try to justify their exploitation of the poor. He will have nothing of it.

Assistance to the poor

God makes provision for everyone without distinction from what the earth produces.

John Calvin, *Commentary on Exodus*[25]

> We must consider that what each person possesses has not come to him by mere chance but by the distribution of the supreme master and Lord of all.
>
> John Calvin, *The Institutes*[26]
>
> Let everyone regard himself as the steward of God in all things which he possesses.
>
> John Calvin, *Commentary on Genesis*[27]

Calvin thus provides two critical reasons why the rich should support the poor who are unable to take care of their own needs. First, God has provided the earth to meet the needs of all his children and thus everyone—in particular each Christian—has a duty to see to it that God's will in this regard is carried out. Second, all that anyone owns is given by God. Humans are thus stewards of the things they own, not absolute owners.

Even though Calvin was convinced that the prosperous Christian must freely share with those unable to meet their own needs, he was quite explicit in rejecting the call of those reformers who argued that the example of the Jerusalem community as reported in the Acts of the Apostles required the common ownership of goods. Calvin's response is included in his analysis of the teaching of St. Paul, who had referred back to God's provision of manna in the desert when the Israelites were escaping slavery in Egypt.

Property ownership

When they had all worked together to gather the manna, the whole amount was found sufficient to fill an omer for every individual. For they did not each of them collect a private store; but, when all had applied themselves to collecting the manna at length, they took their prescribed portion from the common heap. . . .

Only let us remember that this is done figuratively. . . . The manna was a food differing from what we commonly use, and was given daily into their hands without tillage or labor. . . .

The logic of ordinary production is different; for it is necessary if people's needs are to be supplied in friendship and peace that each should possess what is his own, that there should be buying and selling, that heirs should inherit that to which they are entitled, that there be gifts, that each should be able to increase his resources in proportion to his diligence, strength, dexterity or other means. In short, policy requires that each should enjoy what belongs to him; and hence it would be absurd to prescribe, as to our ordinary needs, the law which is here laid down as to the manna.

And St. Paul, also, wisely makes the distinction, in enjoining that there should be an equality, not arising from a promiscuous and confused use of property, but by the rich spontaneously and happily relieving the wants of their brethren, and not grudgingly and with regret or under constraint. In this way he reminds us that whatever goods we possess flow from the bounty of God, like the manna; but, since each now possesses privately and separately whatever is theirs, there is not today the same requirements to put all goods in common, which God laid upon his ancient people.

John Calvin, *Commentary on Exodus*[28]

Luke does not mean that the faithful sold all that they possessed, but only so far as need required. It is most likely that there were many who made no inroads upon their possessions.

John Calvin, *Commentary on Acts*[29]

Practical man that he was, Calvin distinguished between God's free gift of manna in the desert and the "logic of ordinary production" that God expects us to employ in providing for human needs today. Here, Calvin is aware of the difference in incentives necessary for a system of economic production, largely agricultural in his day, as opposed to the simple redistribution of freely given manna from God.

Similarly, Calvin interprets the actions of the Jerusalem community, described in the Acts of Apostles, not as the common pooling of all resources but rather as a response to the needs of others. Calvin would say that the wealthy must be willing to give up even the land they own if the needs around them require it. Here, we find him laying the groundwork for an economy based on personal ownership and individual initiative, all the while tied to a strong commitment to sharing one's goods with those whose needs are unmet.

WORKS AND WAGES

God's role in human work

No one excels even in the most despised and humble craft, except in so far as God's Spirit works in him. For, although there are diversities of gifts, still it is the same Spirit from whom they all flow (1 Corinthians 12:4).

John Calvin, *Commentary on Exodus*[30]

> Since however God ordained that man should be exercised in cultivating the ground, he condemned in his person all indolence and idleness. Wherefore, nothing is more contrary to the order of nature, than to consume life in eating, drinking, and sleeping, while in the meantime we propose nothing to ourselves to do.
>
> John Calvin, *Commentary on Genesis*[31]

Arising out of Calvin's understanding of God, creation, the fall, and redemption is a view of work and productivity that leaves the Christian called to work diligently. Here Calvin endorses Luther's notion that each Christian has a vocation from God and that how one conducts oneself in daily economic life is religiously important. And since we are called in this way, it is important that people work energetically, without too much enjoyment (or even too much sleep), which can interfere with our commitment to live out a responsible life in our vocation.

Calvin's view of economic life also had important implications for the kind of wage that employers would pay their workers.

> *Wages*
>
> Moses admonishes us that this tyranny on the part of the rich shall be punished if they do not supply their workers with the means of subsistence, even if they are not called to account before earthly justice. Hence we infer that this law is not political, but altogether spiritual, and binding on our consciences before the judgment seat of God.
>
> John Calvin, *Commentary on Deuteronomy*[32]
>
> For that is how the rich so often behave . . . A rich man will note this: "That fellow lacks everything: I shall have him for a bite of bread, for he must offer himself to me even if it means gritting his teeth—I will give him half a wage and even so he will have to count himself satisfied." . . .
>
> If there is a poor man earning his living as a laborer day by day, who hasn't a penny to his name, he will be forced to sell [himself] at a low price. Purchasing in these circumstances, knowing his need very well, is clearly oppression, and we shall be able to say, as the proverb puts it, this virtually is to throttle him—it is a kind of robbery. That, I say, is what one would say when someone buys the labor of those in want who are so constrained that they can do nothing else, and have no other resource than to do what they do not want to do.

John Calvin, *Sermon on Deuteronomy*[33]

In addressing wages so explicitly, Calvin makes an important step forward in the history of the Christian view of economic life. Traditionally, most people were farmers, subsisting on their own land or, if tenant farmers, living on a share of what they produce on someone else's. Understanding that individuals in cities are dependent on earning money and not growing food, Calvin addresses the issue of wages explicitly. The same issue can, of course, occur with agricultural workers in rural areas, but in that situation the traditions of recompense tended to be more stable. The arrangements for wages in nonfarm work were more temporary and less predictable. A wage laborer uses the wage to purchase the necessities of life, and since God intended that all humans have their needs met, the payment of a sufficient wage is essential to a well-functioning economic system. For this reason, Calvin also proposed initiatives in Geneva for the creation of jobs for those who didn't have them.[34]

Practically minded as he was, Calvin was intimately aware of how the employer could take advantage of workers when there were more people looking for work than there were jobs. He is always clear that Christians should choose to remunerate their workers properly out of a loving decision in accord with the free invitation of Christ. Thus he resists setting up a series of religious laws that people have to follow, but instead holds out a standard for responsible Christian conduct that all persons are called to live up to freely. At the same time, however, they *are* expected to live up to them and there is strong disapproval of those who don't.

USURY

Usury and economic context

Those who do not take this view will reply that we simply have to go along with the judgment of God, generally forbidding all forms of usury to his people. My answer is that only the poor are referred to, and therefore if we have dealings with wealthy people, we may lend to them at interest; for in condemning a vice, the lawmaker clearly appears not to be condemning things about which he says nothing.

John Calvin, *Commentary on Psalm 15*[35]

One place where scholars universally agree that John Calvin brought something novel to the Christian economic ethic is in his treatment of usury, the charging of something extra when one lends money.

The Scriptures are fundamentally important for Calvin, as they were for Luther, and thus his interpretation of the scriptural prohibition of usury is central. Calvin interprets God's Old Testament prohibition of charging interest on loans between Jews as part of the civil arrangements of the biblical period, not essential to biblical theology. That is, he points to the contextual character of this prohibition and we can understand that argument easily. Old Testament society was poor and thoroughly agricultural, and those who looked for loans did it out of economic desperation in order to make it through to the next harvest. In that earlier era, Calvin argued, God saw it appropriate to simply prohibit usury. However, in a different situation—such as in the urban economy of sixteenth-century Geneva—that may not be needed.

The function of a loan to a prosperous man

I get an income from renting out a house. Is this to make money grow? Does money not bear more fruit in goods than any possessions one might mention? Is it to be permissible to rent a piece of ground and unlawful to take some profit from money? What!? If one buys a field, will the money not produce more money? How do merchants add to their possessions?

Nobody borrows from us in order to sit on the idle money without making a gain from it. Hence what is produced is no longer money but income.

John Calvin, *Letter to Claude de Sachin*[36]

If a wealthy man in easy circumstances, and wanting to buy a good farm, borrows part of the amount from his neighbor, why can the lender not gain some profit from the income till he has received his own money? Every day many instances like this occur, in which as regards fairness, interest is not worse than making a purchase.

John Calvin, *Commentary on Leviticus and Deuteronomy*[37]

Calvin bases his approval of taking interest on an important shift in the economic system. His practical experience in economic life told him that there are many occasions when a well-to-do person borrows money from another well-to-do person in order to make an investment. Here there is little worry about the exploitation of the borrower by the lender. And since the purpose for such a loan would be to make some sort of profitable investment by the borrower, it makes little sense, Calvin argues, that the borrower could use the loan to make a profit but the lender was forbidden to share in that profit because he decided to lend money rather than make an investment directly himself.

This analysis was new in the Christian tradition and it was the one that eventually won out, largely because Calvin understood sooner than other Christian leaders that the function of money was changing. While loans to the poor were still to occur without charging interest, Calvin saw a good reason to allow for the lending of money in a way that rightfully pays interest to the lender.

Yet in spite of his approval of usury for commercial loans, Calvin did not approve of professional bankers, only of loans between individuals. He has not yet carried his argument to its logical conclusion: that, if done responsibly, the occupation of the banker can be morally respectable. Here, Calvin retains the traditional Christian suspicion of commerce and greed. As we shall see, it is not until the twentieth century that Christians make a sustained and explicit argument in favor of commerce and profit-making.

CONCLUSION

The reformers Martin Luther and John Calvin had severe criticisms of the Roman Catholic Church—and received severe criticisms in return—particularly over the nature of Christian faith and the role of the church. However, when it came to what that faith should mean for economic life, there was far more agreement than conflict.

Luther's approach to economic issues was largely indistinguishable from official Roman teaching—on property ownership, fair business practices, usury, etc. Calvin was more attuned to the institutional needs of the growing commercial sector, and while supporting most traditional positions, he did approve of charging interest on loans between business people, anticipating changes in the Lutheran and Catholic positions on usury that would not occur until much later in history. Both Luther and Calvin maintained the foundation of the Christian view of economic life: love of neighbor. As James M. Childs puts it, "If the engines of economic life are not driven by some sense of communal caring or responsibility for one another, then greed, individual and systemic, proceeds unabated and disparities are increased."[38]

This chapter has focused on two giants of the Protestant Reformation, ignoring other important reformers and later leaders of Protestant denominations due to the constraints of space. Yet nearly all would agree with the basic outlines of Christian responsibility in economic life sketched above. A commitment to the poor was universal, derived directly from Jesus' own life and teaching. Economic life was not looked down upon, but economic success bore the same dangers that the church Fathers had chronicled many centuries earlier. As the founder of Methodism, John Wesley, put it, sharing with the poor is essential for a faithful Christian.

> Do you gain all you can, and save all you can? Then you must, in the nature of things, grow rich. Then if you have any desire to escape the damnation of hell, give all you can; otherwise I can have no more hope of your salvation than for that of Judas Iscariot.[39]

The history of Christian views of economic life bears a remarkable consistency on the basic issues: the character of property ownership and the obligation of the well-to-do to assist those unable to provide for their own needs. Over the centuries, development in some of the teaching has occurred, with Calvin leading the way on usury and with changes on slavery and human rights to come later. Before turning to review Christian texts from the modern period, it will be helpful to examine in the next chapter the character and causes of those developments.

Notes

1. Charles Taylor, *A Secular Age* (Cambridge, MA: Harvard University Press, 2007), 68–75.

2. Samuel Torvend, *Luther and the Hungry Poor* (Minneapolis: Fortress Press, 2008), 13. I am indebted to Torvend for much of the analysis and many of the concrete references to the works of Martin Luther that appear in this chapter. Quotations used with permission.

3. Jared Wicks, *Luther and His Spiritual Legacy*, Theology and Life Series 7 (Wilmington, DE: Glazier, 1983), 139, cited in Torvend, 33.

4. Martin Luther, "Commentary on Psalm 51," in *Luther's Works*, ed. J. Pelikan (Philadelphia: Muhlenberg, 1962), hereafter cited as "LW," cited in Torvend, 51.

5. "Heidelberg Disputation," in *Martin Luther's Basic Theological Writings*, ed. Timothy F. Lull (Minneapolis: Fortress Press, 1989), 46–47.

6. See James Childs, "Ethics and the Promise of God: Moral Authority and the Church's Witness," in *The Promise of Lutheran Ethics*, ed. Karen L. Bloomquist and John R. Stumme (Minneapolis: Fortress Press, 1998), 97–114.

7. Martin Luther, *Large Catechism*, 449–50, cited in Torvend, 82.

8. Martin Luther, "To the Christian Nobility," LW, 44:130, cited in Torvend, 50.

9. Martin Luther, *Luther Werke, Kritische Gesamtausgabe, Briefwechsel* (Weimar: Hermann Böhlaus Nachfolger, 1930), l.74, 33, cited in Torvend, 61.

10. Martin Luther, *Lectures on Genesis*, LW, 4:38l, cited in Torvend, 81

11. Martin Luther, "Sermon on the Rich Man in Luke 16," LW, 51:8.

12. Martin Luther, *Trade and Usury*, LW, 45:286.

13. Martin Luther, LW, 44:109, cited in Torvend, 77.

14. One of the reasons Thomas gave in disapproving of tyrannicide was that allowing for such actions would lead the worst elements of society to irresponsibly take such matters into their

own hands. St. Thomas Aquinas, "On Kingship," Book 1, Chapter 6, in *The Political Ideas of St. Thomas Aquinas*, ed. Dino Bigongiari (New York: Hafner, 1974), 188–92.

15. See Ernst Troeltsch, *The Social Teaching of the Christian Churches* (Chicago: University of Chicago Press, 1976), 575–76.

16. John Calvin, "Commentary on Genesis," in André Biéler, *Calvin's Economic and Social Thought* (1961), ed. Edward Dommen, trans. James Greig (Geneva: World Alliance of Reformed Churches, World Council of Churches, 2005), 386. Quotations used with permission.

17. John Calvin, "Commentary on Luke," N.T. Commentaries, *Harmony of the Gospels*, Luke 17:7, in Biéler, *Calvin's Economic Thought*, 366–67.

18. Biéler, *Calvin's Economic Thought*, 304.

19. John Calvin, Preface to the New Testament, *Op. Calv.*, IX, 818f., in Biéler, *Calvin's Economic Thought*, 248.

20. John Calvin, *Institutes* (1560), IV, xx, 3 and 9, in Biéler, *Calvin's Economic Thought*, 333.

21. John Calvin, "Sermon on Deuteronomy 24:19-22," *Op. Calv.*, XXVIII, 199, in Biéler, *Calvin's Economic Thought*, 336 and "Sermon CXXXVI on Deuteronomy 23:24f. and 24:1-4," *Op. Calv.*, XXVIII, 138, in Biéler, *Calvin's Economic Thought*, 294.

22. John Calvin, "Commentary on Isaiah," in Biéler, *Calvin's Economic Thought*, 298.

23. John Calvin, "Commentary on Matthew," Sermon XLIV on the Harmony of the Gospels, Matthew 3:9f., *Op. Calv.*, XLVI, 552, in Biéler, *Calvin's Economic Thought*, 299.

24. John Calvin, "Commentary on James," N.T. Commentaries, James 5:5, in Biéler, *Calvin's Economic Thought*, 281.

25. John Calvin, "Commentary on Exodus 23:10f.," in Biéler, *Calvin's Economic Thought*, 206–7.

26. John Calvin, *Institutes* (1560), II, viii, 45, in Biéler, *Calvin's Economic Thought*, 309.

27. John Calvin, "Commentary on Genesis 2:15," in Biéler, *Calvin's Economic Thought*, 309.

28. John Calvin, "Commentary on Exodus 16:13-18," in Biéler, *Calvin's Economic Thought*, 295–96.

29. John Calvin, "Commentary on Acts," N.T. Commentaries, Acts 4:32 and 34, in Biéler, *Calvin's Economic Thought*, 312.

30. John Calvin, "Commentary on Exodus," O.T. Commentaries (*Harmony of the Law*), Exodus 31:2, in Biéler, *Calvin's Economic Thought*, 353.

31. John Calvin, "Commentary on Genesis," O.T. Commentaries, Genesis 2:15, in Biéler, *Calvin's Economic Thought*, 359.

32. John Calvin, "Commentary on Deuteronomy 24:14," in Biéler, *Calvin's Economic Thought*, 370.

33. John Calvin, "Sermon CXL on Deuteronomy 24:14-18," *Op. Calv.*, XXVIII, 188, in Biéler, *Calvin's Economic Thought*, 371.

34. Ernest Troeltsch, *The Social Teaching of the Christian Churches*, vol. 2 (London: Westminster John Knox, 1992), 642.

35. John Calvin, "Commentary on Psalm 15:5," in Biéler, *Calvin's Economic Thought*, 412.

36. John Calvin, "Letter to Claude de Sachin," in Biéler, *Calvin's Economic Thought*, 405.

37. John Calvin, "Commentary on Leviticus 25 and Deuteronomy 23," in Biéler, *Calvin's Economic Thought*, 411.

38. James M. Childs Jr., *Greed: Economics and Ethics in Conflict* (Minneapolis: Fortress Press, 2000), 64.

39. "Causes of the Inefficacy of Christianity," *The Works of John Wesley*, vol. 4, ed. Albert C. Outler et al. (Nashville: Abingdon, 1984), 95–96.

PART III

Resources for Interpretation

11

The Development of Moral Teaching

The basic aim of this book is to ask what Christian faith means for economic life today. To answer this question, it is essential to apply some of the most fundamental and ancient principles in the Christian tradition to our economic setting today, much different from the cultural and institutional circumstances where these principles were first articulated. To decide how they should apply today we need to understand past examples of "doctrinal development"—how basic teaching can change in some less important ways to better implement the teaching of more fundamental insights in a new era. We saw in earlier chapters two important examples of the development of doctrine in the early church. The first, described in Chapter 4, was the decision not to require Gentile Christians to be circumcised. Acts 15 describes how the apostles and elders eventually agreed with Paul's proposal to exempt Gentiles from many of the requirements of the Mosaic Law, but they were to avoid eating meat that had been sacrificed to Roman idols (though this prohibition also disappeared, after the apostolic era).[1] The second, noted in Chapter 5, occurred when the men chosen to be bishops in the early church were already well educated in the best Greek and Roman schools. Some, like Ambrose and John Chrysostom, were well-formed adults living successful secular lives in the Roman world before their conversion to Christianity. When they became bishops, they did not give up their modes and structures of thought, but began to articulate Christian belief in a more precise language and philosophical system that Peter, James, and John would have found inscrutable. The results were the doctrinal formulations of the great Councils of Nicea, Chalcedon, and others.

There are other, less dramatic examples of the development of doctrine scattered throughout Christian history. One such example would be the difference in the church's attitude toward civil government during the first three centuries of Christian life and the time afterward. At the beginning, of course, Christians were a tiny minority, periodically persecuted by the Roman Empire. In this era, the church generally took a stance of noninterference between church and state because of the hostility. However, with the adoption of Christianity by the Emperor Constantine in 315, church leaders began developing a political theory about the need for collaboration and the distinction of powers between church and state. Gustavo Gutiérrez has pointed out that, as a part of this process, the very understanding of freedom in the early church developed over time. During the times of persecution, the notion of freedom was closely tied with the right of every citizen to his own religion, and the Roman state was kept at arm's length with the argument that its competence did not include religious matters. However, once the Empire became officially Christian, the distance between church and state was reduced and the emperors came to regulate the freedom to practice one's religion rather than allow it in an untrammeled way, since the Empire now served some of the interests of the church and vice versa.[2] This and other examples where a change in the church's own situation brought about a change in teaching are well known.[3]

This chapter will examine three examples of the development of moral teaching beginning with the work of Thomas Aquinas: the teaching on usury, slavery, and human rights. In each case, although Thomas's positions might appear to the casual observer as standing in contradiction to the later developments in Catholic teaching, a more careful look will demonstrate the continuity that always endures in the development of doctrine within a living tradition.

Usury

Today there are very few Christians who think that the taking of interest when making a loan of money is immoral. The moral judgment today is that a reasonable rate of interest is quite legitimate, although it would be immoral to charge "exorbitant" rates of interest, which is the meaning of "usury" today. Limits on these rates are prudent since some are tempted to exploit the poor, who often have little choice but to borrow in the midst of hardship. However, the shift from a general condemnation of taking interest to a general approbation of it took many centuries and much debate.

The biggest single change in this process was the shift from a largely traditional and agrarian economy to the more urban, industrial, and finance-oriented economy of the modern world. Even in the era of Thomas Aquinas, the cities were growing, and in the centuries following, the growth of cities and the expansion of commerce were powerful forces in the development of European history. The key issue concerning usury is that money has changed in character from Thomas's day to our own. The most important evidence for this is that we no longer keep our money in a strong box in the cellar, or as was said earlier in industrial history, we don't keep it "under the mattress."

The difference, of course, is that over several hundred years money was transformed so that it was not simply a piece of precious metal that people valued, but it came to be understood as a claim on resources that could be put to work even for short periods of time. Today we know that we can invest our money in a mutual fund that in turn invests that money halfway across the world, and then we can move that investment tomorrow if we wish. Put in the vocabulary of Aquinas, today money is more like the house than the wine. It produces a stream of services, usufruct.

With highly flexible financial markets, business people who need to borrow money, say, to build a new factory, now can look to "the market" to borrow the money they need, intending to pay it back when the investment pays off. Thus millions of individuals, each willing to lend a small amount, can be "brought together by the market" to form a large loan of money, even if those individuals are intending to lend their money for different lengths of time. Money invested overnight or over a year provides a stream of services, and the value of these services rises and falls with the likely prospect of business success. Those who lend money now undergo a loss of those services—they could otherwise invest the money themselves. This is a significant change since the days when people would simply store their gold coins in a strongbox in the cellar.

explanation of the market. [margin note]

As we saw in the previous chapter, the first Christians to understand this sort of positive role for lending and taking of interest were the followers of that great figure of the Protestant Reformation, John Calvin, in Geneva. But eventually the other Christian churches followed Calvin's lead in understanding that the taking of interest on a loan can be a morally healthy part of a business enterprise and even part of responsible consumer spending, as long as the interest rates are not too high and those who are in financial distress are not abused in the process.

Usury is a helpful example of how moral doctrine can change over time: a change that occurs in continuity with the past. Here we can see that the world changed—money changed in character—and so the condemnation of usury needed to end, based on the Thomistic analysis that in an earlier era had led to that condemnation.

SLAVERY

One of the best-known examples of a change in moral teaching within the Christian tradition is the evaluation of slavery. We have moved from a situation where it was considered fully moral in some circumstances for one person to own another, to our situation today where slavery is universally condemned as immoral. We do not have space here to recount the long history of the change in teaching on this matter. However, we can review some part of that history, focusing particularly on the Roman Catholic Church.[4]

As we saw earlier, slavery was accepted as common practice in both the Hebrew Scriptures and the New Testament. Among the Israelites, there were several reasons why another person might be held as a slave.[5] It was possible even to hold other Israelites as slaves either as a judicial penalty or due to a voluntary sale in poverty for a fixed number of years. Foreigners and any children born of parents in slavery could be held as slaves for life. In addition, foreign slaves could be acquired by purchase or by right of conquest as prisoners of war.

In the New Testament, we saw the treatment of slaves largely in the letters of Paul, where some scholars today distinguish two levels of teaching, sometimes referred to as "the dogmatic theology of slavery," and "a pastoral theology of slavery."[6] These two are distinguished in that most fundamentally (the dogmatic view) Paul understood that all who are baptized as Christians are equal in the sight of God, whether slave or free, male or female, Jew or Greek (Galatians 3:26–28; Colossians 3:11; 1 Corinthians 12–13). But the second, more pastoral approach included moral directives for how slaves and masters should treat each other. This approach recognized the power of prevailing Roman law allowing slavery, and took for granted that the small band of Christians was not likely to bring about a change in the empire. As we saw in Chapter 4, Paul encouraged Philemon to treat his slave Onesimus kindly and advised Onesimus to respect the authority of his master. It is a matter of some debate today to what extent Paul was himself aware of this distinction and understood his "pastoral" advice as simply a concession to an evil institution (and whether it was Paul or his disciples who gave the pastoral advice). Some would claim that Paul, like others in the early church, endorsed slavery as a normal part of our sinful human condition.

Similarly, we saw that the early church Fathers accepted slavery in much the same way, as a common practice within the empire but one that would require Christian slaves and Christian masters to treat each other with respect. This was a teaching both of individual Fathers as well as church councils. Thus for example, in 340 ce, the Council of Gangra declared that "if anyone, on the pretext of religion, teaches another man's slave to despise his master, and to withdraw from his service, and not to serve his master with good will and all respect, let him be anathema."[7] The Fathers were convinced that masters and slaves share the same status in God's eyes, even though they taught slaves that they should be respectfully subject to their masters. The historical record indicates that many of the popes owned slaves, including Pope Gregory the Great in the sixth century.[8]

Among the explanations given by the Fathers is that slavery as an institution is a consequence of Original Sin. That is, God's intention for humanity, as expressed in life in the Garden of Eden before Adam's sin, was that all humans should live in harmony as equals. However, the Fathers taught that with the arrival of Original Sin, there was a distortion of the fundamental harmony of nature. A part of that distortion was the creation of the institution of slavery as a morally appropriate part of human life, justly imposed on serious sinners, such as those who wage unjust war. It was also taught that slavery could be an appropriate status not only for the vicious, but also for stupid persons who will do better under the strict control of a wiser person than they would on their own.

However, in spite of the general endorsement of the possibility of a just slavery, there were a number of counter-elements in the patristic period that stand out as early indications of an eventual shift in a teaching. Not only were both Christian slaves and masters equally children of God, but masters who freed their slaves were often praised for their generosity. One of the strongest statements against slavery in the early church came from Gregory of Nyssa:

> You condemn a person to slavery whose nature is free and independent, and you make laws opposed to God and contrary to his natural law. For you have subjected one who was made precisely to be lord of the earth, and whom the Creator intended to be a ruler, to the yoke of slavery, in resistance to and rejection of this divine precept. . . . For the only proper slaves of mankind are the animals devoid of intelligence.
>
> Gregory of Nyssa, *Homily on Ecclesiastes*[9]

Among the most radical teachings against slavery in the first millennium of Christianity was one provided by Benedictine Abbot Smaragdus of Saint-Mihiel, who in a book he wrote about the year 830, advised the Emperor that "every man should let his slaves go free, in consideration of the fact that it was not nature but sin which subjected such slaves to him, for we are all created of equal status but sin has subjected some people to others; and also in consideration of the fact that if one forgives, one will be forgiven."[10] Abbot Smaragdus was not, however, articulating official church teaching on slavery.

Medieval Christianity largely repeated the attitudes about slavery inherited from the early church. With the revival of interest in Roman civil law in the eleventh through fourteenth centuries and the simultaneous reappropriation of the work of Aristotle, nearly all the classic arguments for and against slavery were once again articulated by theologians and canonists. John Maxwell summarizes the conditions under which slavery was generally accepted as moral within the medieval church. These could include captivity in war, a penalty for severe crimes, a judgment against a debtor unable to pay his debts, the voluntary sale of children by destitute parents, the voluntary sale of oneself by a destitute pauper, and anyone born to a mother who was herself a slave.[11]

As we saw in the previous chapter, Thomas Aquinas himself maintained the rough distinction created in the Pauline tradition by distinguishing a "first intention" of nature in which all are equal in the state of original innocence in the garden, and the "second intention" of nature, which occurred after original sin where slavery and other institutions such as private property were created to deal with the sinful character of human life.

One of the major driving factors in the analysis of slavery in the medieval church was a series of wars between Christian and Islamic nations, the most important of which were the Crusades. It was common practice on both sides that a victory was followed by the enslavement of many of the enemy, both combatants and often noncombatants, including women and children. Time and again, popes and church councils affirmed the morality of taking slaves in war.

In general, Christians were not included in this teaching, and a winning Christian army was not to enslave any Christian populations. But in 1179, the third Council of the Lateran specified enslavement as a penalty for any Christians who, during a war, had been providing Muslims with materials and services for repairing their ships or who had been piloting those ships for financial gain.[12] Thus the general teaching was that for a serious enough violation of morality, slavery is a just penalty for anyone.

The rule of much of the Western Hemisphere by the Catholic nations of Spain and Portugal raised for the Roman Catholic Church many issues regarding treatment of the indigenous peoples. One important context for the slavery issue there was the preexisting slave trade out of West Africa that occurred as early as the fifteenth century, where one African tribe would raid another, capture slaves, and sell them to oceangoing Europeans, who then would resell them elsewhere in the world. The popes at times issued approval of this process, though often due to a misrepresentation made by the slave traders themselves. The Portuguese traders, for example, informed the Vatican that these slaves were Muslim and thus their capture and sale was part of the broader Mediterranean struggle between Christianity and Islam. Under these conditions, the popes granted to the kings of Portugal an authority to enslave Muslims and other non-Christians in West Africa. For example, in 1452 Pope Nicholas V wrote to the King of Portugal saying "we grant you by these present documents, with our Apostolic Authority, full and free permission to invade, search out, capture and subjugate the Saracens and pagans and any other unbelievers and enemies of Christ wherever they may be, as well as their kingdoms, duchies, countries, principalities, and other property . . . and to reduce their persons into perpetual slavery."[13]

Many historians now conclude that had the pope been more accurately informed that the Africans involved had nothing to do with Islam, such broad endorsements of slavery would not have occurred. And there is ample record of the many attempts by popes during the sixteenth through eighteenth centuries to reduce the weight of oppression of Spanish and Portuguese conquerors on the indigenous peoples of the Western Hemisphere, at times explicitly prohibiting enslavement of them.

Thus the general stance of the Catholic Church was that there were indeed conditions under which slavery could justly occur and the great debate was over whether new situations fell under those conditions or were different enough that slavery should be forbidden.

The eventual change in humanity's attitude toward slavery arose most vigorously not from the Roman Catholic Church or mainline Protestant churches but from two other sources: the Quakers (the Religious Society of Friends) and from secular society with the philosophical leadership of Montesquieu, Rousseau, and others during the eighteenth and nineteenth centuries. Quakers argued that our equality under God was so important that it would be a violation of the gospel and God's intention for humanity to hold slaves. Thus the Quakers became the first significant group of the "abolitionists."[14] The secular or "humanist" antislavery movement made much the same argument without reference to God. That is, the essence of human identity is rooted in the freedom of each individual. Slavery is such a violation of freedom that, as Rousseau argued, it is "incompatible with human nature."[15]

The development of antislavery opinion within the Catholic Church clearly had roots that go all the way back to the Bible. However, in the modern period, the general prohibition of slavery was slow in coming. Those Catholic moral theologians who first favored a condemnation of slavery often also recognized that this stance was unacceptable within the church. Thus such important moral theologians as Alphonsus Liguori (1696–1787) simply avoided the topic of slavery in their books as a way of not endorsing the common teaching of the church as it had existed for hundreds of years.

Further complicating the development of teaching on slavery was the fact that the Roman Catholic Church largely sided with the monarchies of Europe against the various pro-democracy (and antislavery) movements that occurred on the continent in the eighteenth and nineteenth centuries. Most secular critics of slavery were strongly antireligious, and the Catholic Church sided with the nondemocratic forces in the period. Before the theological arguments were sorted out in the Catholic world, nations around the globe began making slavery illegal. The United States did this at the end of the Civil War, in 1865, but other nations such as Venezuela, Argentina, Ecuador, the Dominican Republic, Spain, and Chile did so in the early 1800s.

The first formal, official condemnation of slavery in all its forms and in all situations within the Catholic Church did not occur until 1965, when the Second Vatican Council declared that "whatever violates the integrity of the human person . . . whatever insults human dignity, such as subhuman living conditions, arbitrary imprisonment, deportation, slavery, prostitution, the selling of women and children . . . all these things and others like them are infamous."[16] Here, for the first time in official Catholic teaching, is an exceptionless condemnation of slavery, without any pointing to the unfortunate existence of human institutions that we must live with and try to make more humane.

There is still something of a dispute about this history of the slow development of an antislavery doctrine within Catholic theology and Canon law. As early as the eighteenth century, a number of historians produced very selective histories in which the antislavery statements of popes and councils were emphasized, while statements to the contrary were simply ignored. This general view, and the widespread conviction that the church does not change its teachings over time, led Pope Leo XIII to make the unwarranted statement that "from the beginning, almost nothing was more venerated in the Catholic Church, which embraces all men with motherly love, than the fact that she looked to see slavery eased and abolished which was oppressing so many people . . . she undertook the neglected cause of the slaves and stood forth as a strenuous defender of liberty . . . she made every effort to ensure that the institution of slavery should be abolished where it existed and that its roles should not revive where it had been destroyed."[17] This inaccuracy by Leo XIII is repeated in a number of efforts to retell the history of the Catholic teaching on slavery.[18]

Both the change in the political situation (where slavery was legal in fewer and fewer nations of the world as time passed) and in popular opinion (where ordinary people came more and more to see slavery as a violation of the freedom and dignity of persons) form the backdrop to eventual changes in formal church teaching. However, a second important factor—delaying change for a time—was what John Maxwell describes as "the overriding influence of the principle of continuity of doctrine." What Maxwell means by this, and by its influence in slowing the change of the teaching on slavery, is that "popes, bishops, canonists and moralists in the eighteenth and nineteenth century could not easily accept that a moral doctrine which had been commonly taught for over 1400 years could possibly be mistaken."[19] The process of change was a slow one, but in the end, change occurred.

HUMAN RIGHTS

In our culture, the notion of universal human rights is so thoroughly taken for granted that it is hard for us to imagine a world where such talk did not occur, where the average person didn't think of all humans having certain basic rights. But that was exactly the situation in both church and society prior to the modern age.

A right is a claim which a person has that other persons have a moral obligation to respect. In the premodern world there were certainly rights, but these were claims held by particular persons because of particular situations and not claims that everyone could make simply because they were human. The owner of an estate or the Archbishop of Paris or the king himself had various rights. Thus in accord with local and national property laws, the owner of a parcel of land had the right to exclude others from building on the land that the owner possessed. However, the notion of "human rights" is far broader, in that *every* human is presumed to have such rights simply because they are *human* persons, and it is this broader notion of rights that we do not find in Aquinas or in most other scholars, religious or secular, in the premodern world.

Today, both secular philosophy and Christian theology endorse rights and the presumption that all humans have certain rights. For Christians, such rights have their origin in God. For many secular theorists, rights seem to have no origin, no explanation other than the claim that people simply *have* rights.[20]

To understand this shift to universal rights, consider Thomas's explanation (which we saw in Chapter 9) for why someone in dire and urgent need might morally take the property of others who have refused to share it voluntarily.

Whether it is lawful to steal through stress of need?

Things which are of human right cannot derogate from natural right or Divine right. Now according to the natural order established by Divine Providence, inferior things are ordained for the purpose of meeting man's needs by their means. Therefore the division and appropriation of things which are based on human law do not preclude the fact that man's needs have to be remedied by means of these very things. Hence whatever certain people have in superabundance is due, by natural law, to the purpose of helping the poor.

Since, however, there are many who are in need, while it is impossible for all to be aided by means of the same thing, each one is entrusted with the stewardship of his own things, so that out of them he may come to the aid of those who are in need. Nevertheless, if the need be so manifest and urgent, that it is evident that the present need must be remedied by whatever means be at hand (for instance when a person is in some imminent danger, and there is no other possible remedy), then it is lawful for a man to meet his own need by means of another's property, by taking it either openly or secretly: nor is this properly speaking theft or robbery.

Thomas Aquinas, ST, II–II, q. 66, a. 7

Here we see Thomas's general summary of his view of property ownership. God has created the material world to ensure that all humans have their needs met and this capacity to meet needs is built into the nature of those goods that sustain human life. If you can't find employment and are hungry, and I have a surplus of bread in my pantry, I am under a moral obligation to share that bread with you. No human system of property ownership ought to violate the natural law, founded on God's intention for the world, and thus no property ownership system should define ownership in so absolute a way that the well-to-do have no obligation to assist those who through no fault of their own are unable to meet their needs.

For Thomas, the key issue here is that if I do not share the extra bread in my pantry with a starving child, I am violating the nature of the bread, since material things are ordained for the purpose of meeting needs. However, he does not say that the child has "a right to food," even though this is common parlance in Christian conversation today. So how do we explain this shift in moral argumentation in Christian history, such that something premodern people would hardly even think of saying has become a standard part of contemporary Christian teaching?

One of the best ways to think about this is to realize that in Thomas's analysis the focus of the moral spotlight was on the nature of the bread (and the consequent obligations of the owner of the bread), while in the modern world our focus has turned more toward the person in need. Thomas, of course, was a theologian, not a lawyer. But experts in canon law were even in Thomas's day discussing these same issues and in their legal discourse there was indeed attention to the perspective of the poor person whose needs Thomas so clearly discussed. According to intellectual historian Brian Tierney, these discussions among canonists in the twelfth and thirteenth century represented the medieval beginnings of the later seventeenth-century endorsement of universal natural rights.[21] There was no clear endorsement of these rights in the earlier period, but canonists were clearly aware of the conflict between the moral judgment that the poor man in dire and urgent need could justly take from the rich man and the fact that the civil magistrates would probably jail the man who committed such a theft if he were ever caught. The canonists did not have a good solution for this problem (they sometimes argued that the poor man could appeal to his bishop, who might then with church authority command the intransigent wealthy man to help the poor), but their work began an effort to see the issue from the point of view of the person in need, eventually opening the door to the more explicit understanding of natural rights that developed in the modern period.[22]

There was a slow transition through the use of the language of natural rights, with the Latin word "ius" often being used ambiguously as referring to either the natural "law" or a natural "right." Brian Tierney cites Hostiensis (a thirteenth-century scholar and canonist who worked in England, France, and Italy, eventually becoming an archbishop) as among the very first to use the unambiguous language of natural rights when he described the action of the poor man who steals in desperate need: "One who suffers the need of hunger seems to use his right rather than to plan a theft."[23] As Godfrey of Fontaines put it,

> On account of this, that each one is bound by the law of nature to sustain his life, which cannot be done without exterior goods, therefore also by the law of nature each has dominion and a certain right in the common exterior goods of this world, which right also cannot be renounced.[24]

This perspective was a minority point of view for a long time. As Jean Porter has summarized the situation, "Although the scholastic concept of natural law does not necessarily imply a doctrine of subjective natural rights, there are some generally recognized natural law claims which do function much like subjective rights." Speaking of universal subjective rights was not widely accepted until the seventeenth century, but the roots are clearly there in medieval thought.

Historians of culture have long debated how and why the modern focus on the individual person arose, but there are a number of elements of that transition that are clear enough. This shift toward the perspective of the individual poor person in discussions of property was part of a broader set of changes that scholars identify as taking place in the twelfth and thirteenth centuries, changes that took greater note of the thoughts and feelings of individual persons—what is often referred to as the rise of Christian humanism. The twelfth century saw the rapid development of a literature about courtly love that explored both the pains and joys of human relationships. Religious piety came to emphasize more a personal, and even emotional, relationship between the individual believer and Jesus himself. The Lateran Council of the early thirteenth century made personal private confession a common practice in Europe.[25] Thus we should understand that these changes, which hundreds of years later eventuated in the individualism of the modern world, arose out of developments within the medieval Christian tradition.

Another way to understand this transition is by considering the rise of democracy. Throughout most of human history in most of the world, there was very little interest in or respect for democracy, understood as the political control of a nation by all the people who live there. Far more frequent and far more frequently justified was the presence of kings, princes, emperors, or simply the nobility, who held political authority. At the dawn of the modern world there arose a concern for the average person in a way that was not there before. (Even in the democracy of ancient Athens, it was not all persons who had democratic rights but only an elite group of males who owned property.)

The British political philosopher Thomas Hobbes was among the most influential to make arguments that stressed consideration of the rights of individual citizens to control their own lives; indeed, he defined freedom as simply the absence of law.[26] In *Leviathan*, published in 1651, Hobbes proposed that his readers should begin thinking about political authority by imagining a time before there were any governments whatsoever (investigating here a question that many scholars had earlier posed).[27] In this "state of nature," Hobbes argued, each individual would have a natural right to defend himself. Yet in the absence of any government to enforce law, those who were strongest and meanest would become the thugs who control the lives of others. Thus he hypothesized that people's existence in the state of nature would be "solitary, poor, nasty, brutish, and short." Unless you were among the thugs yourself, your life would be pretty miserable.

In response, Hobbes argued, individuals would be quite willing to hand over to a king (the "leviathan" of the book's title) their right to defend themselves and thereby promise to follow the king's rules in return for the imposition of law and order. Hobbes didn't call for the overthrow of the king and the establishment of democracy, but his ideas were radical in that they based the legitimacy of monarchy not in God or in tradition but in the (hypothetical) decision of individual citizens.

Much more could be said about his argument, but the point here is that beginning in the late medieval period political philosophers and other intellectuals began thinking about the rights and roles of individual citizens in national political life. Hobbes was simply the most famous of a number of intellectuals since the early fourteenth century who argued that the right to rule needed to be confirmed by the consent of the governed.[28] Slowly through this long process, these thinkers turned the spotlight of attention away from a focus on an objective moral order and included the capacity of individual persons to freely choose to live a moral life. Eventually the spotlight shifts from the king to the ordinary person. Grotius moved the notion of "the right" from Thomas's sole focus on the objective "what is just" to a broader sense of "a moral quality of a person, enabling him to have or do something justly."[29] Of course, this resulted in political democracy at first including only the males of the landed gentry, but eventually men of all stations of life and, after that, women and minority groups in the nation.

This shift to greater respect and attention to individual persons brought about the use of the language of rights within the Christian tradition to articulate ideas that in the premodern world had been spoken of without reference to individual rights. Thus going back to Thomas's argument focusing on the nature of the bread in the pantry, modern Roman Catholic discourse talks not only about how the material world should meet human needs ("the universal destination of goods," as we will see in Chapter 17) but also about the claims (rights) of individuals to have their needs met. Persons have a corresponding duty to meet their needs by their own productive work—either producing what they need or earning money sufficient to buy it. But those who are unable to provide for themselves have a claim on what they need, corresponding to the obligation to share on the part of those who have a surplus. Thus Catholic social thought in the twenty-first century combines both elements in an integrated view of how human rights arise. One example of this is the right to food. No able-bodied person who refuses to work can rely on handouts, but those unable to support themselves—whether unable to work or unable to find jobs—deserve support from those who are prosperous.

It is interesting to note that the history of human rights runs counter to one widely accepted interpretation of rights today: that certain political rights of "noninterference" (such as freedom of speech, freedom of assembly, freedom of the press, etc.) are somehow more fundamental than "economic rights" (such as the right to food and clothing and shelter). Some political philosophers today assert that the former are more basic because they do not require anyone else to do anything except to not interfere. Some go so far as to reject economic rights altogether. However, as Brian Tierney argues persuasively, the first claim recognized as a broad human right of all human persons was the right to the food and other necessities required for human survival.[30]

The principal problem with the language of rights today is that many people have lost the notion of obligations that should accompany rights. The idea of rights has been abused by people who assume they have rights as humans but no or few obligations in addition. More accurately, the history of the Catholic view of rights within the natural law tradition says that every right is rooted in God's creative intention for the world, just as are the duties that God intends. Thus from an adequate perspective, rights and duties must be articulated together. As we will see later, Pope John Paul II reminded us of this in his articulation of the right to food, clothing, and shelter as rooted in "the universal destination of goods," harking back to Thomas's focus of the needs-meeting character of material goods, and the obligations of whoever owns them.

In sum, the Catholic view of human rights, civil rights, and economic rights has always been integrated into a more basic understanding of God's creative work.[31]

What would Thomas think?

Having seen these developments in the history of usury, slavery, and human rights, it is useful to ask what Thomas Aquinas might say about all this if he were alive today. In fact, the evidence is that he would approve.

Concerning the issue of slavery, Thomas made clear that the approval of slavery was not part of God's intention for humanity embodied in the natural law but was an addition to the natural law created by humans in the face of a sinful world. Like the long tradition before him, Thomas presumed that slavery was a given part of human culture, since it had been for millennia. It is not clear whether Thomas would have been an early abolitionist had he lived in the nineteenth century. Yet, it is likely that once human societies demonstrated that they could easily survive without slavery and once the premodern prejudices about the inferiority of other races were exposed for the ethnocentric bias they were, Thomas could easily argue that the sinful state of humankind does not require the existence of slavery. A slow improvement in the morality of our public institutions over time could accompany a rejection of slavery in a world already transformed in this regard. Thus if Thomas were alive and shared knowledge now widely taken for granted that was not available in his era, there is little doubt that his moral analysis would today condemn slavery as well. The change in the teaching on slavery can best be understood as a rejection of a less important earlier insight, that flawed institutions are necessary in a sinful world, in favor of a more fundamental insight, that all humans are equal in the sight of God and bear equal dignity as children of God.

Thomas's argument about usury focused on the character of the thing being borrowed. Money, he understood, was like the wine, in that money was sterile in Thomas's day. Today, however, given the immense transformation of the economy, money is not sterile. The best evidence of this is that no one keeps their money in the cellar or under the mattress any longer (except in times of terrible economic crisis) but instead invests most of it in the marketplace. Money today is like a house, providing a stream of services, because money itself is a claim on resources and that claim is valuable to have, even for a short while. Lenders of money incur a loss and can justly insist on compensation.

Thus if Thomas were alive today he could keep intact his analysis of borrowing and lending and simply conclude that in today's world, money is more like the house than the wine and thus the charging of interest would not be immoral.

Concerning the issue of human rights, it is clear that Thomas would be worried, as are our religious leaders today, about the use of rights language if there is no recognition of corresponding duties. A very important example here is the view of property ownership. Many people today have a very strong or even absolute understanding of the rights of a property owner. However, Thomas and contemporary Catholic social thought would argue that property ownership entails a fundamental obligation to share, whether directly with the poor or through communal taxation. Thus talk of the rights of property owners without talk of the duties of property owners is a moral mistake.

Nonetheless, Thomas would likely agree with contemporary teaching of the Catholic Church that one could indeed speak of the rights of needy persons, as this is simply a change in focus, not substance. Thomas focused on the nature of the goods, and the focus on the claim of the needy person fits well with the notion that God intended this person to have needs met, even though Thomas himself—like most in the premodern world—did not speak in those terms.

CONCLUSION

In this chapter, we have reviewed three significant shifts in the moral analysis of economic life that have occurred since the time of Thomas Aquinas, regarding usury, slavery, and human rights. There are two important lessons to be learned here.

The first is that every living tradition finds that its moral teachings will change over time as the context for human life changes. Usury gives a brilliantly clear example due to the change in the character of money over the seven centuries since Thomas addressed the issue. Because the world changed, the teaching changed—in order to remain faithful to the more important underlying commitments of the tradition.

The change in the teaching on slavery has been less dramatic, since the Christian tradition has historically criticized the more inhumane forms of slavery, from the Hebrew Scriptures onward. Nonetheless, the common teaching of the Catholic Church for nearly two millennia was that slavery was morally defensible in certain circumstances—and that is no longer the case. In the end, admittedly after prodding from sources outside the church, the most fundamental insight of human dignity and equality won out.

The example of human rights illustrates that large shifts in the cultural consciousness of a civilization may bring about changes in how religious leaders think and speak about fundamental moral realities. Because the Western world came to focus more on the role and dignity of the human person, Christian moral discourse found it helpful to take up the language of rights—and human dignity—in describing the moral life of individual persons.

It is immensely important to note that in all three cases there has occurred a development of moral doctrine in fundamental continuity with earlier doctrinal commitments. Thus for example, while it may seem to some people that the churches have simply rejected their earlier condemnation of usury, such a construal of what happened is simply wrong. The outcome may look contradictory, because now Christians are allowed to take interest when for so many centuries it was condemned. However, the fundamental argument within the Jewish and Christian traditions—that the wealthy have an obligation to care for the poor—can be fulfilled through the property ownership requirements and can thus allow for the charge of interest on a loan of money because of the new character of money in a commercial society.

The second general lesson to understand from this chapter relates back to our discussion of "how a living tradition means." That is, we face a number of questions about how to interpret today the fundamental moral commitments of our spiritual ancestors earlier in Christian history. One of the most important of these is the traditional doctrine of the just price. As early as the late fifteenth century, scholars in Spain—such as Luis Molina, S.J.—began to recognize a greater dynamism in economic life and no longer talked as Aquinas had about the economic value of a thing "in itself." Long before the nineteenth-century development of utility theory in British economics, Molina taught that the usefulness of an object (what economists today call its "utility") played an important part in its value. Molina himself did not question the traditional doctrine of just price,[32] but his insight into usefulness began a process of understanding prices as dependent on subjective factors, leading later economists to believe that there can be no objective "just" price anymore.

Today in a market economy, particularly in a global market economy where there is no overarching government able to set standards for the treatment of workers and the environment, manufacturers are under immense pressure to cut costs in order to compete with manufacturers on the other side of the planet who may not share their concern for workers and environment. Thus in the setting of prices, including wages for workers, the market system has no easy way of embodying the process of the just price, a topic we will take up again in the concluding chapters of this book.

If we are still to accomplish the most fundamental goals implicit in the just price doctrine, we will need to school ourselves in the examples from the past where development of moral doctrine has occurred in order to accomplish something similar today. This is no easy task, but at least in this chapter we have seen three examples of this kind of development of moral teaching and we are better prepared to face the questions of the development of moral doctrine in our own day.

Notes

1. Pontifical Biblical Commission, *Bible and Morality*, para. 214–15.

2. Gustavo Gutiérrez and Richard Shaull, *Freedom and Salvation: A Political Problem* (Atlanta: Knox, 1977), 6–15.

3. For further description, see Phan, *Social Thought*, 43. See also John Thomas Noonan, *A Church That Can and Cannot Change: The Development of Catholic Moral Teaching* (Notre Dame: University of Notre Dame Press, 2005).

4. The following history of the teaching on slavery owes much to the work of John Francis Maxwell, *Slavery and the Catholic Church: The History of Catholic Teaching Concerning the Moral Legitimacy of the Institution of Slavery* (Chichester and London: Barry Rose, 1975).

5. Maxwell, *Slavery*, 22–30.

6. Ibid.

7. Canon 3. *C.J.C. Decreti Gratiani*, II, C.XVII, Q.IV, c.37, cited in Maxwell, *Slavery*, 30.

8. Noonan, *A Church That Can and Cannot Change*, 36–40.

9. Gregory of Nyssa, Homily on Ecclesiastes, PG (Migne Patrologia Greca), 44, 665–67, cited in Maxwell, *Slavery*, 32.

10. Smaragdus of Saint-Mihiel, *Via Regia*, c.XXX. PL (Migne Patrologia Latina), 102, 967–98, cited in Maxwell, *Slavery*, 42.

11. Maxwell, *Slavery*, 45–46.

12. Third Lateran Council, Canon 24. *C.J.C. Decret. Greg.* IX, L.V, t.VI, c.6, Maxwell, *Slavery*, 48.

13. Nicholas V, *Dum Diversas*, June 16, 1452, Raynaldus (1747 edition) IX. Year 1452, 600, n. 11, Maxwell, *Slavery*, 53.

14. Maxwell, *Slavery*, 98.

15. Jean-Jacques Rousseau, *The Social Contract*, trans. Charles Frankel (New York: Hafner, 1947).

16. *Gaudium et spes*, para. 27, 29, Maxwell, *Slavery*, 12.

17. Pope Leo XIII, *Catholicae Ecclesiae*, November 20, 1890. *Leonis Papae Allocutiones*, 1898, IV, 112, Maxwell, *Slavery*, 117.

18. For a recent example of a selective history of Catholic teaching on slavery, see Joel S. Panzer, *The Popes and Slavery* (New York: Alba House, 1996).

19. Maxwell, *Slavery*, 13.

20. See, for example, Robert Nozick, *Anarchy, State and Utopia*, Introduction.

21. Brian Tierney, *The Idea of Natural Rights*, 74.

22. Tierney is persuaded that this rise of "juristic, distinctively non-Aristotelian theories of natural rights had grown up before Aquinas," but that Aquinas did not choose to include them in his Aristotelian synthesis. The later impact was clear, however, as this approach to speaking of natural rights did become part of the mainstream of Western political thought. Tierney, *Natural Rights*, 45.

23. Ibid., 73.

24. Ibid., 38.

25. Ibid., 55.

26. Thomas Hobbes, *Leviathan; or, The Matter, Forme and Power of A Common Wealth Ecclesiasticall and Civil* (1651), ed. Michael Joseph Oakeshott (Oxford: Blackwell, 1960). For Tierney's comments, see Tierney, *Natural Rights*, 51.

27. Tierney, *Natural Rights*, 131–35.

28. Tierney, *Natural Rights*, 182.

29. Tierney, *Natural Rights*, 325.

30. Tierney, *Natural Rights*, chapter 2.

31. For a contemporary Catholic view on the character and extent of human rights, see David Hollenbach, *Justice, Peace, and Human Rights: American Catholic Social Ethics in a Pluralistic World* (New York: Crossroad, 1988).

32. Molina explained that "an advantage or benefit accruing to the buyer does not justify a sale at a higher price." Luis de Molina, S.J., *La teoría del justo precio* (1593–1609) (Madrid: Editorial Nacional, 1981), *Disputa* CCCXLVIII, 6, "Que el precio común de los bienes no aumenta por el hecho de que le sean necesarios al vendedor, ni porque se le vendan a quien espera obtener de ellos un gran beneficio."

12

Engaging Controversies Today

The final chapters of this book will focus on the implications for economic life today that flow from the history we have reviewed in previous chapters. There is considerable diversity in how Christians today understand what that history should mean for the twenty-first century. Within the Catholic tradition, for example, neoconservatives claim that capitalism is the only truly Christian economic system while many liberation theologians argue that capitalism is immoral. Thus we must not only know the history but we also need a way to sort through the often-conflicting interpretations of that history.

This chapter will examine four separate conceptual frameworks or clusters of issues that help in that sorting process. The first will be the problems that every economy must solve. The second will be the issues that divide the various positions on what economic life should be like. The third is what sociologists have learned about the effects of social structures in the lives of individual persons. The fourth is the character of coercive power, an essential part of nearly every organization.

Every framework of ideas that we might employ to interpret what's going on around us will include certain presuppositions. It is impossible to have a perspective on the world that does not come from a particular angle and does not thereby partake of both the advantages and the limitations that this angle of vision entails. The key, however, is that the framework be carefully chosen with an aim to clarify the issues at hand. Thus one of the criteria employed in proposing the four frameworks of this chapter is that each helps to clarify the concerns of widely diverse intellectual positions on economic life today in ways that each position would recognize as an accurate summary of its views. This chapter aims to incorporate the primary empirical and moral concerns of these various perspectives and to make them comparable with each other, even though many partisans involved in these debates believe that their own views have little or nothing in common with those of their intellectual opponents.

This false assumption has led to a scandalous lack of real debate between left and right in Christian economic ethics.

A second criterion important for the choice of such frameworks is whether the framework will help the reader subsequently make moral decisions about economic life. Whether the issue is how to lead one's life as an individual in a job or what sorts of national economic policies ought to be supported, it is a primary interest of this volume that the reader come to be better able to make those decisions. Later chapters will propose answers to many of the questions raised in this chapter, but because the aim of this chapter is to explore four frameworks helpful in providing those answers, a more neutral explanation of issues will be provided here. That is, there will be no attempts in this chapter to identify what the Christian tradition would have to say about these issues.

THE FOUR PROBLEMS OF ECONOMIC LIFE

Economists have long begun their thinking about economic life by asking, "What are the problems that every economy needs to solve?" One typical list of such problems includes: What is to be produced? How much of it? By whom? And who gets to own the wealth generated? Other economists have had a slightly different list of questions. But one of the failings of nearly all such lists is that they tend to be limited to the concerns that mainstream economics is comfortable with. A better approach is to start with all the relevant problems, whether or not any one academic discipline can address them all. Thus we shall review here the four problems of economic life.

ALLOCATION

The first problem every economy must solve is allocation. This encompasses most of the questions that economists have addressed within economic science. Every economy needs to decide in some way what will be produced and how, and what resources will be used—human labor, soil, minerals, water, agricultural products, machines, etc.

Markets are remarkably good at solving problems of allocation. No one needs to tell the steel factory what inputs to use in making steel, nor does anyone need to tell the farmer how much wheat to grow. In a market, these decisions are made by those who run the factories and farms and they make their decisions based upon the prices they face. These will be prices for inputs to their production process (coal and iron ore for the steel factory; seed, fertilizer, and tractors for the farmer). But just as important is the price of the products they sell, for when the price of steel or wheat rises, these producers are immediately encouraged to produce more if they can.

The same is true for those who sell inputs that these producers employ. Workers are often willing to work more hours when wages are higher and may actually be willing to move to a different city for a better job. The companies that produce tractors notice when farmers have higher incomes (and will therefore be more likely to buy tractors) and will produce more tractors in anticipation. And consumers act in a similar way. When the price of green beans or pork or Pepsi in the grocery store rises, consumers will be tempted to switch to corn, chicken, and Coke—or to other products that are rough substitutes for the now higher-priced items.

All these decisions are made simultaneously by participants all over the globe. A change in price in one part of the world is quickly relayed to other regions and has immediate effects. Billions of adjustments occur in the behavior of producers and consumers each day within a network of intricate interactions that no central government planning agency could possibly come close to replicating. It is indeed the clumsiness of central planning that played so large a part in the demise of the Soviet Union.

At the same time, however, we must be aware that without important legal restrictions markets would carry out this allocation process in ways that violate the moral convictions of many people. We tend not to notice this because we often have already incorporated into law many restrictions that prevent such violations.

One general category of such restrictions are the things that society has decided ought not be bought and sold in the marketplace. Although there are debates about some of these restrictions, there is a wide-ranging consensus that many things ought not be bought or sold: children, votes, civic duties to serve (whether on a jury or in the military during a draft), hand grenades, ground-to-air missiles, sex, and the list goes on.

Although the market would on its own produce many things that people in their moral convictions decide ought not be bought and sold, it is also true that markets will not produce many things that most people in their moral convictions decide ought to exist. Thus markets do not generate sufficient numbers of homeless shelters or medical clinics for the poor, or drugs useful in combating diseases—like malaria—that plague mostly people too poor to buy them. If society decides that such things should be produced, it must find ways other than markets to do so—typically through a combination of private charity and government action.

And there are also goods that exist but cannot be easily traded in the marketplace. We all value clean air, rivers, lakes, and oceans, but these are not things that are for sale. Here too markets do not provide a good solution, since market decisions are made by participants to an exchange, and there are strong economic incentives for them not to notice any problems their exchange may cause third parties. The classic case here, of course, is air pollution arising from a factory smokestack. Economists sometimes note that, if the air and water were privately owned, markets would resolve the problem. But such observations are irrelevant and misleading in a world where citizens will never allow individuals to own the Mississippi River or the air over Pennsylvania. Some sort of nonmarket solution, typically government regulation of one kind or another, will be necessary (though the government may employ market-based methods—such as a carbon tax—to accomplish this goal).

Thus the current situation in most Western nations is that due to many prudent rules that structure markets, there are good reasons to trust markets to solve the problem of allocation in the vast majority of cases. However, we must simultaneously rely on both government and civil society organizations to solve those parts of the problem of allocation that markets cannot.

DISTRIBUTION

The problem of distribution addresses another central question about the things that are produced in the economy: Who gets what? Markets do indeed generate a distribution of income each year, and although in most cases citizens may find this morally appropriate, there are many situations where such a market-only distribution is judged morally inadequate by most people.

Thus it seems fair to most citizens that those who spend long years in medical school should generally earn higher incomes than those who have only a high school or college degree. Physicians typically have higher-than-average incomes. Those who work longer hours earn more than their co-workers who work fewer. Those who take greater economic risks, for example in starting a new business, can at times make above-average profits—which, because of the risk of failure, are morally justifiable in most cases.

At the same time, as we saw in earlier chapters, Christians have been deeply concerned about people who cannot care for their own economic needs and are ignored by the market because they have no marketable skills. Classic here are orphans who are totally dependent upon the assistance of others, and the elderly who are beyond the working age. Similarly, the unemployed who are actively seeking work but unable to find it are widely seen as appropriate recipients of help from the community, as are a number of other categories of people about whom there are more active moral debates.

The point of this chapter is not to resolve the question as to who should get what, but simply to point out that the question of distribution is one that every economy must and does answer. While the market handles many parts of the distribution problem well, other parts require action from citizens and their government.

SCALE

In the premodern world, humanity's efforts to produce goods and services to meet human needs occurred on a much smaller scale than today. There were examples in the premodern world of environmental problems, some quite dramatic, as that which about the year 1200 seems to have led to the departure of the Anasazi people who lived in cliff-side dwellings in the southwestern part of the United States.[1] But these problems were local, not global. It was only quite recently in world history that humans gained the capacity to damage the natural environment on a planetary scale.

When humans learned to generate power from fossil fuels—coal and oil predominantly—factories became much larger and the growing prosperity of so many generated severe threats to the Earth's biosphere. Problems include the depletion of the earth's water, soil, and ozone; the various dimensions of global climate change; and the wastes generated by prevailing modes of production and consumption, which are causing an unsustainable overload of the planet's capacity to absorb them.

We are unable to go into the details of the problem here, but as we just saw in the discussion of allocation, the problem of scale is one that markets do not handle well at all. Market transactions typically ignore any effects that occur in the lives of others not directly involved in the transaction. Thus we all drive our cars without much concern that the gases escaping from the tailpipe have significant negative effects on others and the environment.

Economists' theories are attuned to questions of scale within a business firm, modeling the decision of the heads of the organization to expand production up to the point where the cost of the extra resources invested will equal the value of the extra income generated by the expenditure. However, the only way for society at large to make a similar judgment about global pollution or climate change is for our government to make that assessment and set up rules that will limit or appropriately regulate market activity. Markets cannot and will not decide on the optimal size of the economy—our ecological "footprint"—in the biosphere.

There are great debates going on about the most appropriate policies for limiting the scale of the economy's impact within the biosphere—for example, employing "cap and trade" systems or a carbon tax or an outright prohibition of certain activities—but those details need not concern us in this chapter. The point is that finding the proper scale of the economy in the biosphere is one of the four problems that every economy must solve, and one that markets cannot solve on their own.

QUALITY OF RELATIONS

In every economy there is an interaction of persons who produce goods and services each day. Economics as a discipline has spent very little time considering the quality of those relations, but anyone who runs a firm knows that the efficiency of the business is deeply dependent upon the quality of relations among employees.

Thus although many economists would avoid this question of how humans relate to each other because it entails a number of moral issues, it is nonetheless immensely important for economic life because it plays such a large role in efficiency and in resolving the problems of allocation and distribution discussed above.

We can learn much from the efforts of large corporations that expend considerable resources to develop a good "corporate culture" to encourage individuality, creativity, cooperation, and participation of all employees in the overall mission of the firm. These characteristics are similarly valued within the moral perspective of Christianity and many secular value systems.

One way that economics has begun to move in this direction is in its discussion of trust and "social capital." Central to the notion of social capital is a lively sense of trust between individuals. In fact, we might think of social capital as a kind of "stock" of assets that an organization or society has, with trust as the "flow" that contributes to enlarging that stock of capital. Organizations and societies with greater social capital conduct daily life with efficiency and simplicity for many reasons. There is less need for surveillance and enforcement of rules, and individuals are more willing to work toward common goals.

Thus every economy faces this fourth problem of how best to structure and improve the quality of relationships. Different perspectives on the political spectrum provide different answers, and Christianity has from the earliest of times had much to say about the best way for those relationships to occur.

In summary, this framework of the four problems that every economy must solve does not by itself give us answers as to how to solve them. The point, however, is to be aware that all four problems need to be addressed, and we should not be so preoccupied with one that we lose sight of the others. Keeping these four problems in mind will assist in evaluating competing accounts of what the history of Christian teaching means for economic life today, since some of those accounts are provided by people who consistently ignore one or another of these fundamental problems.

THE MORAL ECOLOGY OF MARKETS

In attempting to provide solutions to the four problems of economic life just examined, individuals and groups have had strong disagreements as to what would be the best way to structure economy and society. We have answers that range from Marxist communism on the left to libertarian individualism on the right, with many alternative perspectives in between. One of the most difficult parts of entering into such disputes is the fact that many people involved in them are so overly confident in the truth of their own position. They not only fail to see any truth in the positions of others, but they are unable to see that they could even have a reasonable dialogue with their opponents because they begin from a radically different starting point.

The framework of a moral ecology of markets helps to overcome this apparent inability of intellectual opponents to talk to each other. It outlines four fundamental issues on which each perspective takes a position, even though at times only implicitly.[2]

One important feature to keep in mind is that not all markets are the same. How markets are defined and how they interact with other parts of human life can vary greatly. For example, economists Luigino Bruni and Stefano Zamagni have made a historical study of the rise of markets in Italy in the thirteenth through fifteenth centuries.[3] They argue that we today could learn much from those "civil markets" in how they integrated productive efficiency with moral values and the common good. Their claim that capitalist markets today are but one form of markets is the sort of insight that the framework of the moral ecology of markets can help make clear. Differences in the character of markets can be traced to differences in the four elements in the moral ecology of markets.

THE LEGAL DEFINITION OF THE MARKET

A market is a place where people can interact with each other, making economic offers to others and either accepting or declining offers they receive. There are, of course, many different kinds of markets, including markets for final goods and services, for labor, for natural resources, and for financial instruments. Each has unique elements, but here it is helpful to note a fundamental similarity in all of them and to talk of "the market." Whether it involves employers interacting with employees, producers with their suppliers, or consumers with the stores from which they buy products, the market is characterized by a great deal of freedom.

However, human history has demonstrated that if there are no restrictions on what market participants can legally do, some would resort to abuses: practices that are morally offensive. As a result, every nation has a list of activities that are forbidden because they are overly abusive. To take the most basic, no one would approve of a market where there was a legal acceptance of the assassination of one's economic competitors. Similarly, using physical force to press an employee or supplier or employer to act in a particular way is forbidden by law.

If we look at this question politically, it turns out that those on the far right have a very short list of activities that are so abusive they must be forbidden (murder, thuggery, fraud); other groups farther to the left have successively longer lists. In the United States, Republicans want to forbid insider trading and practicing medicine without a license, while Democrats would add restrictions to provide greater protection for the environment or to forbid the hiring of permanent replacement workers during a strike. Much farther to the left on the political spectrum, Marxists have a still longer list, with the former Soviet Union forbidding the private ownership of firms. But there was still a market in the U.S.S.R. Once those restrictions on the market were in place, individual citizens were free to take their rubles to the marketplace to buy from what was available according to their own choices.

Thus the first question in the moral ecology of markets concerns the rules that define markets.

However, just as the biologist knows, we cannot really understand any particular biological organism separate from its context, its ecology, so it is impossible to evaluate markets morally apart from their context, their moral ecology. The reason is that just about everyone's attitude about markets—and whether they think the markets they participate in are just—depends not simply on the definition of markets provided by the prohibitions enforced by law. Involved—at least implicitly—are three other concerns in every market's moral ecology.

THE PROVISION OF ESSENTIAL GOODS AND SERVICES

Everyone from left to right on the political spectrum recognizes that the market logic of exchange is not appropriate for all human interactions. In particular, there are certain goods and/or services that are considered so essential that everyone should have access to them, even people who are too poor to pay anything for them. Libertarians on the far right often claim that there are no "economic rights," no goods or services that government should provide. From their point of view, collecting taxes to pay for those goods or services would be a violation of the property rights of taxpayers. However, even libertarians consider the services of police and the courts so fundamental to justice that a good libertarian society would provide these services even to those who are too poor to pay any taxes. And, of course, that means even libertarians agree that collecting taxes from some citizens to provide services to other citizens is just.

Once again as we move farther left on the political spectrum, there are longer lists of goods or services that are considered essential. For example, Republicans in the U.S. consider education up to grade twelve so essential that it should be provided without charge, even to those who are too poor to pay taxes. Democrats have a longer list of such goods and services (e.g., medical care for all) and Marxist governments on the far left provide even more (e.g., apartments). Whether any person considers markets to be just will depend heavily on whether their economy and society—either through government or private organizations—provide "essential goods and services" in accord with that person's view of what is essential.

THE MORALITY OF INDIVIDUALS AND ORGANIZATIONS

Everyone involved in the discussion about the justice of markets takes a position on the morality of individuals and organizations. What that morality should be varies significantly, but everyone from libertarians to communists holds that individual virtue is essential for making any economic system work. For example, trustworthiness is morally essential for markets to operate. Even beyond the legal requirements of fairness, most people find that a good work situation requires that co-workers will not only not steal from them, but will cooperate and even lend a helping hand when appropriate.

Organizations understand the importance of the morality of their members. As we have seen, corporations often spend large amounts of money to develop an appropriate corporate culture. The key here is that whether the goal is purely economic efficiency or includes broader concerns about the morality appropriate for fully human life, everyone who participates in the discussion about the justice of markets includes certain presumptions about what should be the morality of individuals and groups.

THE CHARACTER OF CIVIL SOCIETY

Civil society is that network of organizations larger than the family but smaller than the national government that helps organize daily life. Whether these are the Chamber of Commerce and labor unions in the work world, or parent-teacher organizations at school, or churches, museums, and various service organizations, the quality of personal life and one's assessment of the moral quality of economic life are heavily dependent upon the richness of organizational life. Whether for hobbies or social mission or employment, a vibrant society has a wide variety of voluntary organizations that engage and help individuals in a number of ways.

Participants to the debate over markets on the far right tend to understand such civil society organizations as purely voluntary and intended only to help their members; individuals are understood to join such organizations simply to accomplish their goals. Persons politically farther to the left typically add to this functional approach a greater appreciation of the relationships that exist in civil society organizations. They appreciate this relatedness of persons to one another as itself part of human fulfillment. In addition, they frequently expect these organizations to serve the common good.

Summarizing, this framework of the moral ecology of markets is helpful in sorting through debates about the morality of the economy today. Every person has a view of how each of these four parts of life should best be structured, and if they were indeed structured that way, that person would judge markets to be just. As we shall see in later chapters, how to define markets, what goods and services should be communally provided, what ought to be the morality of individuals and their organizations, and what is the character of civil society will all play a role in answering the ultimate question of this book: What does the history of Christian views of economic life mean for the economic life of Christians today?

SOCIAL STRUCTURES AND PERSONAL AGENCY

A central issue in debates about the morality of economic life is the relation of persons as individual decision makers ("agents") to the social structures within which they live and work. The market is one such social structure, as are the institutions of government, business, civil society, and the family that help us solve other important problems of economic life.

There is a significant debate about this interaction of agency and structure, and it is helpful to turn to sociology for a view of causality in this interaction. And there is a range of positions within sociology on the issue. Some on the far left seem to treat individual persons as if they are merely pawns pushed around by social forces, while others on the far right would claim that social structures have no causal impact other than through the personal decisions of individuals, usually those who hold positions of authority within those structures.

A more moderate position, one presented by the British sociologist Margaret Archer, understands individual persons as the only true agents (i.e., actors, decision makers) in this process but recognizes that social structures have causal effects in the lives of persons.[4]

A central idea here is that certain characteristics of society "emerge" out of the interactions of individuals. Emergence is a process that characterizes both the natural and social worlds. In emergence, two or more "lower level" entities combine to create a "higher level" entity that has characteristic qualities that are different from and cannot be reduced to the qualities of the lower-level entities that interacted to create it.[5] Thus for example, water is an emergent from hydrogen and oxygen. It is truly different from those two elements. Hydrogen and oxygen are gases at room temperature, while water is a liquid. Both gases feed fires, while water puts fires out. Similarly, as Christian Smith argues, atoms are emergent from protons, neutrons, and electrons; hurricanes emerge from air and water, and lawn mowers are emergent from the various parts they're made of. Each example of emergence produces something quite real that has characteristics that cannot be simply explained as the characteristics of the parts that generate it. Thus we can also understand that social structures and their particular properties emerge from the interactions of persons.

The "emergent properties" of a social system are often completely unintended. Consider the sociologist's view of "enablements" and "restrictions."[6] Enablements are advantages that are conferred upon some individuals. Thus for example, because English has become the most universal language in the world, a tourist from the United States, Canada, or other English-speaking nations can travel to many other nations of the world that do not have English as their native language and yet can still find persons who speak English, making such travel much easier. This is an enablement that allows English speakers an ease of access to the world that others do not have.

If we consider a citizen of Italy or Brazil or Sri Lanka, we find that they face a corresponding "restriction" in travel. They are certainly free to go to other nations, but in most nations they are unlikely to find people who can speak their language. Thus to travel as easily as the English speaker can, these tourists have to pay a higher price: they will need to learn the local language or, more likely, learn English so they can speak with people in many countries around the world.

Much more could be said about this analysis within sociology, but the point here is to see its implications for economic life. The market is one of the most pervasive and influential social structures in human life today, and it is critical to understand that the market generates both enablements and restrictions in the sociological sense.

Markets, of course, operate within an existing culture and thus the pattern of enablements and restrictions of that culture will typically characterize the market as well. Thus the well-to-do tend to face far more enablements than the poor (consider the culture of achievement in strong suburban school districts or the reputational advantages of elite colleges) and typically far fewer restrictions (such as cultural suspicion directed at minority groups or dangerous neighborhoods that often plague the poor).

Supporters of markets prefer to depend on the individual decisions of market participants in order to respect the autonomy of all who participate. However, once we realize that existing social relationships are laced with restrictions and enablements that fall on different groups in different ways, we can understand that allowing everyone the freedom to make a market choice does not mean that everyone is being treated equally in markets.

Consider two eight-year-old girls who have the same IQ and the same enthusiasm, perseverance, and willingness to work in school, but one lives in a wealthy suburb and the other in a dangerous part of a low-income area of the city. We know that the child in the inner city will face far more restrictions and fewer enablements in her academic and personal development than will her counterpart in the suburbs. To fast-forward to age twenty-two, we can ask whether a simple openness to receive job applications from both young women can be considered evidence of the justice of a market when so many other parts of life, including the economic system, have treated these two so differently in the past. For example, Friedrich Hayek defends a libertarian perspective in arguing that only individuals and not social structures are causes, and only they can treat a person unjustly, whether at age eight or twenty-two.[7] John Rawls, on the other hand, argues that fair equality of opportunity requires that society address the imbalance between the two girls—for example, by providing better schools to inner-city children than to suburban—before justice can characterize an economic system where employers simply hire the best-qualified applicant.[8] Thus the insight into the importance of social structures in the economic success or failure of individual citizens raises the question of whether we have a common responsibility to shape those social structures in a way that generates more just opportunities for everyone.

THE IMPORTANCE OF COERCIVE POWER

Among the great debates today about how economic life should be structured is the role of government in structuring markets. Everyone agrees that government must play some role, but how large or active a role is widely debated, as we have seen in the prior discussion of the moral ecology of markets.

One of the fundamental differences between these positions concerns the very nature of government, and central to that issue is an understanding of the character of power that government wields. Some claim that the coercive power of government almost always restricts the freedom and rights of citizens, while others understand governmental power, properly employed, as actually serving the freedom of its citizens by imposing widely agreed-upon restrictions against the abuse of freedom.

We saw in Chapter 6 how an adequate Christian notion of freedom understands freedom as the choice for self-perfection or excellence. The presence of a moral standard existing outside of ourselves—and even of rules enforced by others—does not necessarily violate one's freedom. Those many today who think freedom is self-initiation—that anything one chooses to do is "freely" chosen simply because the individual is making the choice without interference—misunderstand the role of external standards in the moral life. The latter group more frequently misunderstands the nature of coercion, but even many in the former group do as well.

The dictionary defines a threat as the insistence that another person must do something, accompanied by the declaration that noncompliance will be accompanied by some harm. Coercion is a successful threat. It has two phases. First, person A tells person B to do X or else Y will happen. Second, person B then decides to do X rather than suffer Y. A classic example is the hoodlums who successfully extort weekly payments from shopkeepers, who decide to "pay up" in order to prevent threatened physical violence.

As philosopher Thomas Wartenberg points out, some people think coercion refers only to immoral threats, but this is to confuse the notion of a successful threat with the notion of right and wrong.[9] It is better to understand coercion as a descriptive notion—a successful threat—and then to follow up with a moral decision as to whether any particular act of coercion is moral or immoral.

The reason for this descriptive approach is that the moral use of coercion occurs in our lives all the time. Parents regularly coerce their toddlers and tell them that certain forbidden behaviors will be followed by other "logical consequences," penalties that the child will not like. The same occurs, though at a more sophisticated level, when parents attempt to discipline their teenagers.

Similarly, university professors employ coercion when they make the threat implicit in every syllabus that if the student does not fulfill the requirements of the course, he or she will receive an "F" for a final grade. Governments, too, use coercion, as when the threat of being stopped for speeding leads me to drive no more than five miles an hour over the speed limit, even when I'm late for a meeting and in a great hurry. In this case, I am coerced by state law for the common good. As Servais Pinckaers argues, when discipline, law, and rules are employed wisely, they foster freedom; they develop the "ability to perform actions of real excellence by removing dangerous excesses . . . which achieves harmony between freedom and law."[10]

Coercion can occur even in situations the individual voluntarily enters. Thus a student voluntarily matriculates at a college and then is subject to the coercive power of the grade. An employee voluntarily accepts a job but then lives under a number of threats from his or her employer. The presence of coercion, however, usually does not dominate our experience of human life, whether as students or employees or drivers on the highway. Human life is complex, and coercion is usually only present in the background. Thus parents love their children, and professors respect the autonomy of their students. Employers know that the workplace will be more productive if there is a good relationship between managers and workers. And police officers frequently work hard to be a nonthreatening presence when there is no criminal activity going on.

Although governments are different from other institutions in the seriousness of the penalties they can impose (e.g., incarceration), it is a mistake to *define* the relationship between governments and people in terms of the most severe forms of coercive power that governments have over citizens. In the vast majority of cases, those powers do not come into play. Thinking of government simply as the source of coercive power would be like thinking of the relationship of professor and student as essentially one of giving a passing grade or an "F." Or it would be similar to thinking of parents' relationship to their children as defined by the coercive power parents can exercise.

It is important to notice that in most organizations, coercive power is exercised through rules that bear specified penalties if broken—whether that is a club rule requiring members to pay dues or a highway speed limit or procedures at work. The organization typically identifies particular individuals—the club secretary, the highway patrol officer, the Human Resource manager—to enforce the rules. But the people taking on that role generally see themselves as having little choice in the enforcement. Their role is to carry out the agreed-upon penalty when a rule is broken. The sense that the threat—do X, or else Y will happen—is impersonal is important for the morale of those subject to it. Ideally, neither the rule nor its implicit threat varies with the person enforcing it or with the person subject to the coercion. Relying on rules is fairer than depending on the whim of each enforcer.

Once we recognize how coercion works through impersonal rules in nearly all organizations, we can also recognize how the market's effectiveness is also dependent on an extensive system of impersonal threat. Consider what happens when prices rise, for example when the price of steel increases because all the pure iron ore gets used up and less pure ores like taconite must be used instead. Manufacturers who use steel in their production processes will be worse off, since if they make no changes, they must raise the price of their products to cover the higher price of inputs and will lose some customers. Many users of steel, such as appliance manufacturers, will try to save money by finding ways to use less steel per unit produced, or by using materials other than steel that now look more attractively priced. And many will not find either option sensible and will continue to use steel as before. All these manufacturers, however, face a kind of threat: if you don't change your use of steel, you will be worse off due to the rise in price.

This function of market "allocation" is what produces economic efficiency. Each purchaser of steel has an incentive to use it more efficiently, and those who are able to switch to some other substitute material (instead of steel) have an incentive to do so. Thus steel is allocated to its most valuable uses, at least as measured by market prices.

Many on the far right politically, like libertarian philosopher Friedrich Hayek, see markets as largely natural systems, and so think of this threat character of markets as similar to the threat implicit in an approaching thunderstorm: if you don't find shelter, you will get wet and may be hit by lightning. From this perspective, you may not like the threat, but it's not unjust. Others farther to the left, like communitarian philosopher Michael Walzer, see markets as institutions created by humans, and thus think of this same threat character of markets as similar to the impersonal rules that embody the coercive power of organizations. Although there is no need to designate anyone as the enforcer of the rules, since in markets the enforcement of the threat is automatic, the coercive power of markets nonetheless relies on a decision of government and citizens to set the rules of the market in a particular way.

There are many important debates about the appropriate role of government in the economy, and many different answers given in those debates based on both different moral assessments of what *should* happen and different empirical judgments about what *will be the results* of alternative government policies. It is, however, important to note that the possession of coercive power by government is neither unique nor uniquely objectionable. Governments can impose more severe penalties than parents, teachers, or employers can—and so there are dangers in governmental power—but the structure of coercion in human relationship is the same. Every occasion of coercive power—whether by individuals, organizations, or government—needs to be evaluated by a moral judgment.

Conclusion

In this chapter, we have seen four important frameworks that will prepare the reader for the chapters to come. The first is the notion that every economy must solve four particular problems of economic life: allocation, distribution, scale, and the quality of human relationships. Different positions on structuring economic life will stress one or the other of these more than the rest, but no position is acceptable unless it addresses all four adequately.

The second is the analysis of the moral ecology of markets, which identifies four characteristics of economic life on which various political philosophies differ. Every position from left to right on the political spectrum has a list of abusive practices that are sufficiently objectionable that they must be made illegal in order for the economic system to be just. Similarly, each has an idea of what goods or services are so "essential" that they must be provided, particularly to citizens unable to pay for them. Third, each has an idea of the appropriate standards of morality that must exist among individuals and within organizations in order that the economic system operate morally. Lastly, each has a view of the character of civil society, each considering a vibrant civil society essential for a vibrant economy. Deciding any of these four issues requires both a moral judgment about what *should* happen and an empirical judgment about what *will* happen if morally motivated action is taken. Both ethics and science must always be involved.

The third is the understanding within sociology of the relation between, on the one hand, the freedom and agency of individual persons and, on the other, the causal effects of social structures. Social structures, like the market, "emerge" from the past interaction of individuals and generate both enablements and restrictions that have causal effect in the lives of individual agents. Any moral assessment of economic life must take into account the fact that different people experience different enablements and restrictions in daily economic life.

The fourth is the character of coercion, noting that it is not only governments that exercise coercive power but also parents, teachers, employers, and the leaders of just about every organization that has a goal to accomplish. Any role that government might play in the economy requires a careful assessment of both the moral arguments for or against it and an empirical analysis of all that such government action will accomplish, including both intended and unintended consequences. However, the fact that government uses coercive power does not set it off as somehow unique in human interaction. Any use of coercion should be subject to moral judgment.

These four general frameworks for thinking through the morality of economic life today will prove helpful as we review in the coming chapters what Christian social thought has taught regarding this interplay of moral judgment and empirical analysis. But before we can move to that task, it is important to examine the contributions of economics today.

Notes

1. See, for example, Linda S. Cordell, *Ancient Pueblo Peoples* (Washington, DC: Smithsonian Books, 1994).

2. This framework is outlined in greater detail in chapters 6 and 7, in Daniel K. Finn, *The Moral Ecology of Markets: Assessing Claims about Markets and Justice* (New York: Cambridge University Press, 2006).

3. Luigino Bruni and Stefano Zamagni, *Civil Economy: Efficiency, Equity, Public Happiness* (Oxford: Oxford University Press, 2007).

4. Margaret Archer, *Being Human: The Problem of Agency* (Cambridge: Cambridge University Press, 2000).

5. Christian Smith, *What Is a Person?: Rethinking Humanity, Social Life, and the Moral Good from the Person Up* (Chicago: University of Chicago Press, 2010), 25–26.

6. See, for example, Margaret S. Archer, *Structure, Agency and the Internal Conversation* (Cambridge: Cambridge University Press, 2003), 4–5.

7. Friedrich A. Hayek, *Law, Legislation and Liberty*, vol. 2, *The Mirage of Social Justice* (Chicago: University of Chicago Press, 1976), 69.

8. John Rawls, *A Theory of Justice* (Cambridge, MA: Harvard University Press, 1971), 65–75.

9. Thomas Wartenberg, *The Forms of Power: From Domination to Transformation* (Philadelphia: Temple University Press, 1990).

10. Servais Pinckaers, O.P., *The Sources of Christian Ethics* (Washington, DC: Catholic University of America Press, 1995), 360–61.

13

What We Should and Should Not Learn from Economics

Economics is the discipline that sets out to understand economic life. Thus, this social science should play a critical part in any attempt to answer questions about morality in economic life today. It is essential to understand what is occurring in economic life and what will change if we try to improve it. Moral values and religious vision are necessary for any Christian approach to economic life, but they are not sufficient. Good intentions do not guarantee good outcomes.

Economic science is a complex discipline both because of the intricacies of its concepts and because there are several different groups or schools of economic thought. To simplify the first, this chapter will present only a handful of ideas—those most basic to "the economic view" of the world. To simplify the second, the chapter will focus on the insights of "mainstream" economics, the majority position within professional economics in the United States. Other schools of economics—such as Institutionalism, Marxism, social economics, and others—have important things to say. Some of that will appear in the second half of this chapter in a critique of the mainstream approach, but throughout this chapter, "economics" and "economist" will refer to the mainstream. The constraints of space are the reason behind this restriction.

THE CONTRIBUTIONS OF ECONOMICS TO CHRISTIAN MORAL DISCERNMENT

The following six insights are fundamental to economics and helpful to moral reflection.[1] Economics says much more, of course, but these are most basic.

SCARCITY IS PERVASIVE.

The first insight is that scarcity is pervasive and fundamental. Scarcity names the condition that exists when our goals lie unachieved because of the limited resources we have at our disposal. Scarcity is most dramatic among the desperately poor of the world, but scarcity is also a characteristic of even the wealthiest nations and families.

Implicit in this notion of scarcity is the economist's definition of the true cost of anything as its "opportunity cost." That is, the cost of any goal is the next most attractive alternative that is foregone to achieve it. Thus, the true cost of buying a new car is not best described by its price but by what else you could have done had you used the money differently. Similarly, most college students think that the cost of education is the monetary cost of tuition, room, board, books, and fees. However, this is a dramatic *understatement*, since in most cases, the largest single cost of going to college is the employment income that the student foregoes by taking time to be educated. We should also note that the inclusion of food and lodging in the cost of college actually *overstates* its real opportunity cost because everyone needs to eat and sleep, whether they are in school or in the labor force.

Economists attend to two of the most fundamental means to resist scarcity: production and exchange. Humans have been "producing" economic goods since the era of our hunter-gatherer ancestors. Exchange is nearly as ancient: an attempt to improve our economic well-being by trading that which we have in abundance for something we don't have enough of, interacting with another whose own abundance and shortfall is the inverse of ours. This insight into the role of exchange and its impact on production is at the heart of the fundamental answer that Adam Smith gave to the question implicit in the title of his best-known work, *An Inquiry into the Nature and Causes of the Wealth of Nations*.[2] Smith argued there, and economists since have largely agreed, that this interest in improving one's economic well-being through exchange leads to a greater specialization of labor (which he called the "division of labor"), where more and more persons each produce a narrower range of products or services because they can increase their economic well-being by producing what they're most efficient at and entering into exchange with others. Without specialization, there would be neither schools nor cars, neither cellphones nor books, since we'd all be subsistence farmers.

One of the most important insights arising from this analysis is that, even today, scarcity is the most fundamental reason why there are poor nations. Although many who are cheerleaders for "free" markets rarely admit it, wealthy nations—as well as individuals and corporations from wealthy nations—have unleashed horrific injustices on poor nations and their peoples. But contrary to the views of many critics of markets, rich nations do not require the poverty of poor nations to sustain their prosperity. Putting it more concretely, the main reason that the carpenter in Ohio has a higher standard of living than the carpenter in Guatemala is that the U.S. carpenter produces more per day. This is no insult to the Guatemalan, who may typically work "harder" than his American counterpart, since the American has both better tools and a far more sophisticated economic infrastructure that provides timely delivery of quality processed materials.

Consider one bit of evidence against the "our wealth requires their poverty" thesis as applied to South and Central America. Each year, total production in United States is about $15 trillion worth of goods and services. An additional 15 percent over that amount is imported from abroad. But most U.S. imports come from other wealthy nations, with only 6 percent of total imports coming from South and Central America. Six percent of 15 percent is less than 1 percent. Even if those imports were the result of pure theft and exploitation, could the vast prosperity of the U.S. *require* that small 1 percent addition? And, of course, the imports are not simply the results of exploitation. A roughly equivalent value of U.S. goods and services is transferred to South and Central America in exchange for the imports.

What about profits made in poorer nations that are "repatriated" back to the U.S. by multinational firms? Isn't this evidence of exploitation? Not usually. Simply ask yourself how your city council would think about a large, financially stable firm from out of state that wanted to build a factory in your area. Would anyone worry that the profits would be sent back to corporate headquarters? Hardly. What the city seeks is investment that creates jobs and increases economic activity. One of the most important facts about debates on world poverty is that partisans on both left and right agree on the basic solution: that all able-bodied people should have the skills and opportunity to support their own families through productive daily work. Often, the main ingredient missing is investment.

Once again, however, it's important to stress that U.S. citizens, corporations, and the U.S. government have had an immense influence in poorer nations, both good and bad, with U.S. interests all too frequently aligning with local elites to establish policies and practices that have undermined the life prospects of untold millions. Applying the best insights of economics can help to undo some of that damage.

The same is true here in the global North, where a proper understanding of environmental scarcity can, for example, help us avoid what environmental economist Herman Daly has called "uneconomic growth."[3] Because the ecological capabilities of our planet to provide natural resources and absorb our wastes are limited, we face the critical problem of scale identified in the previous chapter.

One final comment on the relation of scarcity and morality is needed. Economist Benjamin Friedman has found that in democratic societies, governments and citizens almost always become less generous toward those "on the margins"—the poor, the sick, immigrants, etc.—when average incomes have been dropping for several years. Thus he argues that steady economic growth not only helps those gainfully employed but has the added benefit of making assistance to those who need it most more likely.[4]

Scarcity is pervasive and fundamental.

SELF-INTEREST CAN BE MORALLY CONSTRUCTIVE.

The second insight that economists would offer is that self-interest is a powerful and often positive motive in people's lives. This idea is frequently overstated, typically by proponents of so-called "free" markets who irresponsibly inflate the limited notion of Adam Smith's "invisible hand" to the quite fallacious assertion that all we need to do is look out for our own interests and the interests of everyone will be served.

But if we confine ourselves to the more circumspect view, we conclude that there are indeed conditions under which individuals should be left free in markets to pursue their interests in accord with their own vision—namely, if the moral ecology of markets described in the previous chapter is working well. That is, if the laws that structure markets are properly defined, if essential goods and services are provided to those who cannot provide them for themselves, if most people and organizations live out a lively morality that readily goes beyond the minimum requirements specified by law, and if civil society is vibrant, we can typically count on self-interest in markets to be constructive and not morally offensive. Of course, as we also saw in the last chapter, defining what is proper in each of these four areas requires both empirical assessment and moral judgment. The point is that whatever your view of economic life, under the proper conditions self-interest can be helpful.

PRICES MATTER.

The third insight is that prices matter. On the face of it, of course, few would object. The primary advantage of a price "system" occurs because changes in price convey important information quickly over great distances. To take but one example, there are a variety of ways to produce electricity, and as the price of carbon-based fuels rises due either to scarcity or a charge for emitting carbon dioxide, and as "green" energy prices fall due to technological advance and economies of scale, electric utilities will find it more and more in their interest to switch from fossil fuels to renewable energy.

Here it is worth noting, of course, that although prices are often paid in dollars and cents, they need not be. An increase in nonmonetary costs, such as a rise in the psychological discomfort attached to a certain behaviors, will tend to reduce the occurrence of such behavior, just as a rise in the price of automobiles will tend to reduce the purchase of them. This would be the economist's interpretation of the role of public challenges to racist or sexist language, to give but one example. Prices matter.

PERFECTION ISN'T OPTIMAL.

The fourth insight is that perfection is not best, at least not under conditions of scarcity. While perfection would be nice, it usually costs far too much to be a prudent goal. This principle sometimes appears in conversations about environmental policy, where economists raise hackles by their assertion that the optimal amount of pollution is not zero. The point is that the first, say, 20 percent reduction in pollution from current levels does far more good for public health and costs far less than does a second 20 percent reduction. At some point, the benefit of further reducing pollution is not worth the extra expense. As one wag has phrased this thesis about perfection, "Not everything worth doing is worth doing well." Everything is, however, worth doing optimally.

One important application of this insight is implicit in the economist's rejection of the ethical claim that "human life is infinitely valuable." While this claim is intelligible within the Christian tradition, one would have to admit that if human life were indeed infinitely valuable, then even the slightest risk of loss of life would be an unacceptable price to pay. But because the claim is not literally true, the optimal expected annual number of highway deaths is not zero. Each year in the U.S. some 40,000 people are killed and another 2.5 million injured in traffic accidents. Why don't we reduce the speed limit on freeways to forty or thirty miles an hour? While this would undoubtedly save many lives, the lost time that we would impose on ourselves would be substantial. It is not immoral to drive at higher speeds or for governments to allow this. In general, the moral relevance of this fourth insight to much of individual life and most of institutional life is that the complete elimination of evil is not morally optimal under conditions of scarcity.

EVEN GENEROSITY IS AFFECTED BY PRICE.

The fifth insight is that even altruistic behavior is responsive to prices. Although other-regarding behavior is in important ways morally different from narrowly self-interested action, in some economically (and morally) important ways the two are quite similar.

Economists focus on incremental (or "marginal") change. At any one time, people have already allocated their time, money, and resources to some combination of narrowly self-interested and other-regarding efforts. A change in the cost of altruistic behavior will, on average, change its frequency. For example, studies have shown that a change in the rate of deductibility of charitable contributions on our income tax returns changes the national total of such contributions.[5] When terrorists arrange for a second bomb to kill emergency responders ten minutes after a car bomb explosion, they too employ this principle, though viciously. More positively, the Peace Corps, VISTA, and Teach for America have engaged more than 300,000 Americans in generous voluntary service by reducing the upfront time, effort, and anxiety required to do so; reducing the cost makes the service more likely. Even altruistic behavior is responsive to prices.

PUBLIC POLICY SHOULD RELY ON ECONOMIC INCENTIVES.

The sixth insight economists would propose is that public policy should depend on narrowly self-interested incentives and not on appeals to altruism. This is the more fruitful form of the specious claim that people are by and large narrowly self-interested. It does not deny that our public figures can effectively appeal to altruism, as President Richard Nixon did in 1973 when, in the face of an unprecedented rise in the price of petroleum and looming shortages, he urged citizens to turn their thermostats down to 68 degrees. One implication of the economist's advice today is that we will better address global warming by raising the monetary price of carbon emissions than by encouraging people to live more simply. Of course, Christians know we can and should do both.

The economist's awareness of the importance of narrowly self-interested behavior has generated three ancillary constructs helpful far beyond economics: the free rider problem, the special interest effect, and the notion of regulatory capture. A free rider is someone who chooses not to get involved with others who are joining forces to address a problem because he will benefit from any solution the others generate, whether or not he pitches in to help. He "rides" free. Examples include how the dishes stacked in the kitchen sink get washed when one of the four students living in the apartment never seems to get around to washing them—or how the local Chamber of Commerce makes civic improvements in town while some businesses refuse to join in. When voluntary morality proves insufficient, this sort of "collective choice" problem requires enforceable rules.

The special interest effect occurs when a small group has much to gain from a decision of a governing body (whether of a nation, a city, a university, etc.) and will invest much time and effort to bring that decision about, while the others in the organization are so numerous that no one person has much to lose—and thus no one has much incentive to work to prevent that decision. The special interest effect is why the Congress heavily subsidizes U.S. cotton production (with most benefits going to wealthy U.S. cotton farmers) even though this causes a drop in world cotton prices that further impoverishes small African cotton farmers. This continues today even though such subsidies are clearly illegal under the rules of the World Trade Organization. Examples of the special interest effect are legion.

But while the unjust outcomes generated by the special interest effect can stoke the prophetic ire of those who press for greater justice in society, it also provides a sobering slap in the face, because one frequent result of the special interest effect is "regulatory capture." When policies are approved, including those aiming for greater justice, they typically must be administered by some board or regulatory agency. The special interest effect makes it quite likely that those with the most at stake will invest much money, time, and effort in shaping the agenda and even populating this board, while the many citizens, who would each lose very little from bad implementation of the new policy, have far less incentive to get involved and prevent this regulatory capture. For example, most citizens cannot name even a single member of their city's planning commission, while most property developers in town are on a first-name basis with them. And that's just one of a thousand boards, agencies, commissions, and committees whose decisions structure our daily lives at the local, state, and national level.

The complexities involved in counteracting the free rider problem, the special interest effect, and regulatory capture do not mean we shouldn't bother to adopt more just policies; they simply call us to be more realistic about the challenges of creating a more just society.

SHORTCOMINGS OF THE ECONOMIC PERSPECTIVE

In addition to the insights that mainstream economics today has to offer to improve our moral reflection on economic life, there are definite shortcomings and biases built into the approach of mainstream economics that stand in the way of a clear understanding of economic life and thus of any adequate moral judgment about it. As Charles Wilber has put it, "The world view of mainstream neoclassical economics is closely associated with the notion of the good embedded in its particular scientific paradigm."[6]

THE ECONOMIC VIEW OF THE HUMAN PERSON

Economics as an independent discipline matured greatly in the early nineteenth century in England, simultaneously with the dominant philosophical perspective of the day, utilitarianism. Major figures such as Jeremy Bentham and John Stuart Mill developed the implications of the utilitarian perspective for philosophy, economics, and morality. Through this process, Anglo-American economics inherited a very particular—and even peculiar—view of how persons make decisions. The story is a long one and we need not go into detail here, but put briefly, economics took from this philosophical perspective a view of the human person as possessing certain goals in life and a rational capacity to accomplish those goals (to maximize their "utility" or happiness). Employing this view, economists adopted the model of "rational maximization," simultaneously reaping the added benefits of applying the mathematical calculus to the economics involved. The shorthand name for this perspective is *homo economicus*, economic man. Economists, as economists, claimed no expertise in understanding how people make decisions, but instead depended on the best "psychology" of the day, even though all this occurred before the rise of the discipline of modern psychology in the late nineteenth century.

In the twentieth century, economists became more sensitive to charges that they were using an outdated psychology.[7] In accord with the official method of the discipline to be more empirical, they left behind the psychological model of "marginal utility theory" (describing *how* people make decisions), at least officially, and replaced it with "revealed preference theory" (which requires only that people be able to decide which of two bundles of goods they prefer). The main problem, however, has been that most economists have maintained an instinctive conviction that they actually *do* understand how people make decisions—rationally striving to accomplish as many of their goals as possible—even though their official empiricist methods have rejected such naïve presumptions about what occurs within the human psyche. Thus, today we have a peculiar situation where economists think through real-world problems employing an understanding of how people make decisions even though such assumptions are technically illegitimate within their science.

There are five concerns with this overly simplified model.

PSYCHOLOGICAL EGOISM

The economist understands human decision making as a process of trying to maximize one's utility or happiness, regardless of what generates happiness for any particular person. In many parts of life—especially where tradeoffs are the main issue—the model makes good sense. When you decide which of two shirts to buy or where to invest your savings or even whether to accept a promotion at work that will require your family to move to a different city, you have competing goods at stake and yet somehow come to a decision.

The downside of all this is that in the economist's parlance, everyone is "self-interested" at all times, in the sense that they are pursuing the interests they hold. No judgment is made as to whether the interest is moral or immoral, since economists hope to avoid value judgments. But this means that both Mother Teresa and the felon in Calcutta are self-interested, even though she served the poor and he stole from them.

The economic model of human decision making is a form of "psychological egoism," an empirical claim that people act only to further their own interests. ("Ethical egoism" is the claim that people have the moral obligation to further their own interests.)[8] This leaves economic discourse unable to even talk about a distinction that is critically important for the economic (and other) choices of most market participants: the difference between good and evil. Choosing to ignore this distinction handicaps the ability of economic science to truly understand people's economic behavior.

THE SOURCE OF CONSUMERS' GOALS

The standard economic model presumes that each person's goals have been chosen by the individual person, whether consumer or producer, and thus entails the systematic denial of the impact of culture and advertising on the goals people have. If Madison Avenue advertisers are able to convince people to buy things that they would not otherwise want to buy, much of the economist's confidence that markets serve people's real interests would be undermined.

The grocery ads in the local paper list prices and sales; they provide the consumer with helpful information. But "Madison Avenue" ads aim primarily at changing tastes, aiming to raise the consumer's estimate of the value of what they are selling. Much more could be said about the subtle power of advertising, but it may be sufficient to note that no twenty-something male has ever been aware of wanting to drink this or that brand of beer because of the beautiful women in those TV beer ads. The major breweries, however, spend millions of dollars on advertising each year because they know better.

CONSUMER EFFICIENCY

The second problem with the economist's presumption of rationality is the question of whether consumers are actually efficient in achieving the ends they aim for. Mary Hirschfeld has argued persuasively that although economists talk insightfully about the efficiency of business firms in improving production, they pay no attention to whether or not consumers might improve their consumption.[9] We know from experience, and certainly from the history of Christian views of economic life, that we are sinners, or to put it in less religious terms, we frequently make choices that run counter to our real interests and even counter to our best judgment. As Andrew Yuengert has put it, the economist's view of rationality includes making tradeoffs but envisions no possibility of real internal conflict within the person's choices.[10] Yet as we saw in the testimony of St. Paul in Chapter 4, we can recognize every day a struggle in each of us, where we know what we should do and yet we do not do it. The oversimplification of such complex human experience leaves the discipline of economics unable to really understand what happens within human decision making.

A firm that is not efficient is presumed to be driven out of business by other firms that are, but this does not happen to individual consumers or families. They "stay in business" even though they may be very inefficient in how they turn their material resources into their own happiness. This, of course, is a secular version of Augustine's observation that people want happiness but so often live lives that don't in the end make them happy. This insight further undermines the economist's assumption that consumers rationally maximize their happiness.

ECONOMIC COMPULSION

We must also ask whether people are always as "free" as the economist's model presumes. Albino Barrera, in *Economic Compulsion and Christian Ethics*, has argued persuasively that not all choices made by people in markets can really be described as simply free.[11] There are circumstances, particularly for the poor, where a choice made to avoid a truly terrible situation by accepting a different but still terrible situation is made under compulsion. Barrera uses an example borrowed from Aristotle, who described the choice of the captain of a ship in the midst of a major storm at sea who decides to throw overboard all of the ship's cargo in hopes that at least he and the crew will survive. On the one hand, the captain has surely made this decision and no one forced him to. On the other hand, he clearly did something he did not want to do, making a decision under duress and "against his will" that Aristotle points out we cannot call fully free, but rather a mixed act. When the negative effects of markets are serious enough, economic compulsion does occur in the lives of the poor and it undermines real freedom. None of this appears in the economist's model of human decision making.

MEANS AND ENDS

Economists sometimes overlook—and the news media almost always forget—the difference between ends and means in economic life. Focusing on overall production, such as Gross Domestic Product (GDP), as a proxy for human well-being ignores two problems. The first is that many economic activities add to GDP but do not represent a rise in human welfare—such as buying an extra lock for the door because of rising crime or purchasing more gasoline due to more frequent traffic jams on the freeway. The second is that most of the other things in GDP are no more than "inanimate objects of convenience." As Amartya Sen has put it, "there are excellent reasons . . . for not seeing incomes and opulence as important in themselves, rather than valuing them conditionally for what they help people achieve, including good and worthwhile lives."[12] Thus, although mainstream economics has mathematically sophisticated ways to talk about tradeoffs in economic life, it can't deeply grasp the difference between means and ends—particularly ultimate ends—and so has a truncated view of human happiness.

To summarize these five shortcomings, the economist's understanding of human choice is reductionistic, in that it takes a very complex reality in actual economic life and reduces it to an oversimplified abstract model of how people make decisions. Economists such as Milton Friedman have defended this stance within economics, describing it simply as a scientific model with no claim to actually be describing reality.[13] But there are two main problems with this attempted defense of the economist's claim. The first, as we've already seen, is that most economists do in fact believe people make decisions this way. As James Boyd White has said, if we repeat something often enough, we come to believe it.[14]

The second is that if this were a truly unrealistic view of how people decide things, economists ought to have no confidence whatsoever that the results their models generate will be of any use to policymakers in deciding how to actually steer the economy. Economists often claim to be able to provide value-neutral advice to elected officials about what economic policies to enact. But beneath this claim is the assumption that economists really understand how policymakers make decisions—namely by a process of rational maximization. If economists admit they *do not* really know what goes on in the human mind, they have no grounds for claiming they can influence a legislator's decisions in a value-neutral way.

EFFICIENCY AND THE ULTIMATE GOAL OF ECONOMIC LIFE

Economists value efficiency, and in doing so endorse a prudent approach to economic life. Efficiency attempts to get the most from the inputs to some productive process or, to put it another way, given a particular goal, efficiency attempts to achieve the goal with the least expenditure of resources possible.

However, we must always ask: Efficiency with respect to what? Efficiency is never a value in itself but is only a measure of our service to other values. Think for example of a corn farmer in Iowa. One could argue that producing and running large tractors and harvesters and the heavy use of nitrogen fertilizers entails an immense expenditure of energy and thus farmers should return to plowing with horses and to fertilizing with manure because this would result in a far more efficient use of energy. All this is quite true, of course, but no Iowa farmer will turn the clock back a hundred years. Clearly the farmer's time is a major factor here and if the farmer is to have an income comparable to those of his cousins in the city, he will have to produce more per hour than is possible with horses. This is a matter of a conflict between labor-efficiency and energy-efficiency.

The question should always be: What goal is it that efficiency will serve? Given the limitations that economists have imposed on themselves, there is no way to answer within economics the question about the ultimate goal of economic life, as that requires insights from a number of disciplines and ways of thinking beyond economics. Within economics, efficiency is typically defined as improving production, conserving the economically measurable inputs to production. But as we have heard in the history of Christian views of economic life, for Christians—and for just about everyone else as well—the ultimate goal of economic life is far more complex than maximizing production, or even maximizing one's own income. These are only means to more important ends. Economists measure wealth, but in fact, it is more helpful to think of the goal of economic life as prosperity.

Prosperity does indeed require some degree of wealth, as those who are desperately poor cannot be said to be prosperous. But prosperity is far more complex than that. We can understand prosperity by considering Thomas Hobbes's description of what the state of nature (before any government is formed) would be like. As we saw earlier, he said it would be "solitary, poor, nasty, brutish, and short."[15] Real prosperity is not simply the opposite of the second of these but the opposite of all of these conditions.[16]

There are two important lessons to draw from this insight. The first is that societies have many goals beyond the ken of economic science: life in meaningful community, security of person and self, civility and morality, physical well-being, spiritual health, etc. This criticism of the mainstream economist's focus on wealth as measured in money terms is an old one, dating at least back to the mid-nineteenth-century economist Thomas Cliffe Leslie, who observed that, "No inconsiderable part of the present wealth of the United Kingdom consists of intoxicating drink."[17] Andrew Yuengert has outlined the elements that Catholic social thought identifies as the goals of economic life embodied in the notion of sustainable prosperity for all: "the virtues, personal initiative, social relations, and material goods."[18] Markets—and the myriad of discrete exchanges between individuals—can help us accomplish some of these goals. But neither markets nor economic science will ever tally up the full range of costs and benefits entailed.

Thus, the second lesson is, as Jon Gunnemann puts it, that "only government can count costs for society as a whole."[19] That is, we can trust markets in spite of their partial engagement with human value only if the society through its government can structure market relationships to prevent the worst abuses that would otherwise occur.

THE ABSENCE OF RECIPROCITY

In the standard economic story, there are only two kinds of economic interactions: the exchange of equivalents (contracts or market exchanges) and the giving of gifts. However, as Luigino Bruni and Stefano Zamagni have argued, reciprocity is equally critical.[20] In reciprocity, unlike economic exchange, the recipient of a benefit is under no strict obligation to return the favor, but, unlike receiving a pure gift, the recipient is under a general expectation that beneficent action will be forthcoming, whether to the original donor or to others. This occurs, for example, when one person does a favor for another, whether worker for the boss, a supplier for a purchasing agent, or someone holding open the door for a stranger whose arms are full. Reciprocity generates the oxygen of social trust that gives breath to daily communal life. Ignoring the role of reciprocity in the economy leaves the economist with an incomplete picture.

Economists do have an explanation for such behaviors, but it is too thin to be adequate. They describe each person as rationally estimating whether the cost of doing a favor will be offset by the expected benefits that may come later. However, from a purely empirical point of view, most people do favors for others because of their long-term character or virtue and not out of a calculation. They often act out of benevolence rather than self-interest.

THE ECLIPSE OF INSTITUTIONS

The economist's careful focus on rational adjustment to changing economic conditions ("marginal change") tends to eclipse the role of background institutions, both in facilitating human interaction and in shaping human perceptions and goals, as articulated in the sociologist's understanding of the social construction of reality and the sociology of knowledge that we saw in Chapter 1. Joseph Schumpeter cautioned that capitalism's drive toward more rationality and ever-greater profits undermines the foundations of morality that capitalism inherited from an earlier age, foundations it needs today but cannot itself generate.[21] For example, among the causal factors behind the financial crisis of 2008 was a willingness of many financial managers to put their personal profits ahead of the economic success of their clients.

Also entailed in the absence of an adequate treatment of institutions is the near invisibility of economic power in the economist's view of competitive markets. Careful attention to the role of power in economic life is needed not only for moral judgment but for empirical accuracy as well.[22]

THE OVEREMPHASIS ON SCARCITY

The emphasis of mainstream economics on scarcity as a ubiquitous constraint has merit, but it overstates the importance of scarcity in human life. Wants are not necessarily infinite, although economists often assume they are. As we have seen, Christianity has consistently advocated reducing our wants to increase our happiness. Yet interestingly, nearly everyone in our culture makes a mistake similar to the economist's. For just about everyone, including those who are severely critical of mainstream economics, the excuse most frequently employed in daily life is that time is scarce. When something isn't getting done, how often have you said, or heard others say, that "there just aren't enough hours in the day"? What kind of an explanation is this?

In truth, this is like complaining that we can't run up more flights of stairs because the earth's gravity is so strong. We'd feel a bit foolish to use this as an excuse. Gravity is what it is. But there are exactly twenty-four hours in each day. Complaining about either limit is both a waste of valuable time (since there's nothing to be done about it) and irresponsible (in the sense that the very articulation of the complaint takes us off the hook of personal responsibility for our situation). We might just as effectively speak about an abundance of time, in line with the abundance of God's provision and promise, as did Douglas Meeks in his book, *God the Economist*.[23] An attitude that "there's simply not enough to go around" can allow us to rationalize our neglect of the poor or our resistance to just taxation as "excessive."

Thus, economists are right to point out the role of scarcity and our consequent need to make tradeoffs, but their critics are also correct to object to the overextension of the notion of scarcity in a world where we the prosperous need to acknowledge our abundance.

THE MORAL DEFENSE OF MARKETS

Economists employ but rarely acknowledge a moral argument embedded deep in mainstream economics that defends the institutions of capitalism. Economists have developed mathematical models that describe both the decisions of producers in trying to make a profit (called marginal productivity theory) and the decisions of consumers in deciding how to spend their budget to buy a mix of goods and services that allow them to accomplish as many of their goals as possible (whether through marginal utility theory or revealed preference theory). Together these two "sides" of the economic transaction—supply and demand—are united in a "general equilibrium" that shows, in theory, how prices in a "perfectly competitive" market can ultimately be traced to the efforts and values of consumers and producers. This acts, then, as a very fundamental moral endorsement of markets, since by this analysis markets do serve these basic interests of all participants.

However, as we saw just above, there are a number of assumptions that simply do not hold in reality. Consumers' goals are not always chosen by them, but often influenced by advertising and the culture more broadly. Even with goals of their own, consumers are often not efficient in accomplishing those goals (recall the internal struggles we all have about buying things we know we ought not). We can recall again Augustine's wise observation that people want to be happy, even while living lives that will not make them so. In addition, of course, real markets never fulfill the various conditions of perfect competition and complete information that the idealized general equilibrium model assumes.

THE QUALITY OF ECONOMIC RELATIONSHIPS

In the previous chapter we examined the four problems that every economy must solve: allocation, distribution, scale, and the quality of relations. Economists focus intensely on the economic transactions of individual economic agents (whether individuals or firms). This is what happens in markets. But there are serious problems in relying on markets to solve all the problems of economic life, particularly the quality of relations in economic life.

Markets give strong incentives for some relationships to be attended to carefully, for example, between a firm and its customers. At the same time, if there are plenty of willing workers, markets can give the signal that employers can be harsh with their employees and that the pervasiveness of scarcity requires everyone to be less generous and more self-serving if they are to thrive in a competitive culture. Proper moral conviction can be a counterbalance to such unfortunate market incentives, but we need to be clear that markets simultaneously help and hinder morality.

CONCLUSION

Any attempt to ask what the history of Christian views of economic life should mean for us today will require not only a knowledge of that history but also a working knowledge of economics, both its strengths and its weaknesses. As a discipline, economics sets out to analyze what happens in economic life. Much of what the discipline has produced has been of immense help in understanding and ordering economic life in service to important human goals. At the same time, however, anyone employing those insights of economics—whether economists themselves or citizens thinking about economic life—must be aware of the shortcomings embedded by the assumptions employed in mainstream economics. In this chapter we have reviewed both contributions and shortcomings.

The contributions of economics to Christian moral discernment:

1. Scarcity is pervasive.
2. Self-interest can be morally constructive.
3. Prices matter.
4. Perfection isn't optimal.
5. Even generosity is affected by price.
6. Public policy should rely on economic incentives.

Shortcomings of the economic perspective:

1. The economic view of the human person
2. Efficiency and the ultimate goal of economic life
3. The absence of reciprocity
4. The eclipse of institutions
5. The overemphasis on scarcity

6.   The moral defense of markets
7.   The quality of economic relationships

The result of this complexity is that while Christians today need to be economically savvy in how they think about economic life, they must also be cautious in employing the insights of economics because of the limitations of the method and the inability of economics to grasp the larger goals implicit in the economic life that economists study.

The same challenge has been faced by the leaders of Christian churches, both Catholic and Protestant, in more recent times. As we shall see in the next four chapters, like their predecessors from the early church onward, they begin with the wisdom of the tradition and an assessment of the economic situation in their own day. In turn, their wisdom becomes part of the inheritance of each of their successors. Such are the dynamics of a living religious tradition.

Notes

1. Much of this chapter was earlier presented in my presidential address to the Society of Christian Ethics in January 2009 and subsequently published in the *Journal of the Society of Christian Ethics* 20 (2010) as "The Promise of Interdisciplinary Engagement: Christian Ethics and Economics as a Test Case." Used with permission.

2. Adam Smith, *An Inquiry into the Nature and Causes of the Wealth of Nations* (London: W. Strahan & T. Cadell, 1776); reprint ed. Edwin Cannan (New York: Modern Library, 1937).

3. See, for example, Herman E. Daly, *Ecological Economics and Sustainable Development: Selected Essays of Herman Daly* (Northampton, MA: Edward Elgar, 2007).

4. Benjamin M. Friedman, *The Moral Consequences of Economic Growth* (New York: Knopf, 2005).

5. See, for example, Martin Feldstein and Amy Taylor, "The Income Tax and Charitable Contributions," *Econometrica* 44, no. 6 (Nov. 1976): 1201–22.

6. Charles K. Wilber, "Ethics and Social Economics: Association for Social Economics Presidential Address," *Review of Social Economy* 62, no. 4 (Dec. 2004): 425–39.

7. For an insightful study of this issue by an economist and philosopher, see John B. Davis, *Individuals and Identity in Economics* (New York: Cambridge University Press, 2011).

8. See, for example, William K. Frankena, *Ethics*, 2nd edition (Englewood Cliffs, NJ: Prentice-Hall, 1973), 17–23.

9. Mary Hirschfeld, "From a Theological Frame to a Secular Frame: How Historical Context Shades Our Understanding of the Principles of Catholic Social Thought," in *True Wealth of Nations: Catholic Social Thought and Economic Life*, ed. Daniel K. Finn (New York: Oxford University Press, 2010), 165–97.

10. Andrew M. Yuengert, "Rational Choice with Passion: Virtue in a Model of Rational Addiction," *Review of Social Economy* 59, no. 1 (March 2001): 1–21. See also Geoffrey Brennan and Anthony M. C. Waterman, "Christian Theology and Economics: Convergence and Clashes,"

in *Christian Theology and Market Economics*, ed. Ian R. Harper and Samuel Gregg (Cheltenham, UK: Edward Elgar, 2008), 77–93.

11. Albino Barrera, *Economic Compulsion and Christian Ethics: New Studies in Christian Ethics* (Cambridge: Cambridge University Press, 2005).

12. Amartya Sen, *The Idea of Justice* (Cambridge, MA: Harvard University Press, 2009), 226.

13. Milton Friedman, *Essays in Positive Economics* (Chicago: University of Chicago Press, 1953), 3–46.

14. James Boyd White, "Economics and Law: Two Cultures in Tension," *Tennessee Law Review* 54, no. 2 (Winter 1987): 192–98.

15. Thomas Hobbes, *Leviathan*, chapter 13.

16. Churches Together in Britain and Ireland, *Prosperity with a Purpose* (London: Churches Together in Britain and Ireland, 2005), 20.

17. Thomas Edward Cliffe Leslie, *Essays in Political Economy*, 2nd edition (1888) (New York: Augustus M. Kelley, 1969), chapter 15, "On the Philosophical Method of Political Economy," 164.

18. Andrew M. Yuengert, "What Is Sustainable Prosperity for All," in *The True Wealth of Nations*, ed. Daniel K. Finn, 37–62.

19. Jon P. Gunnemann, "Christian Ethics in a Capitalist Society," *Word and World* 5, no. 1 (Winter 1985): 49–59, at 57.

20. See, for example, Stefano Zamagni and Luigino Bruni, *Civil Economy: Efficiency, Equity, Public Happiness* (Oxford: Oxford University Press, 2007), 41–43.

21. Joseph Alois Schumpeter, *Capitalism, Socialism, and Democracy* (New York: Harper & Bros., 1947).

22. Fernando Fuente Alcántara, "La Propiedad," in *Manual de Doctrina Social de la Iglesia*, (Madrid: Biblioteca de Autores Christianos Fundacion Pablo VI, 1993), 461–64.

23. M. Douglas Meeks, *God the Economist: The Doctrine of God and Political Economy* (Minneapolis: Fortress Press, 1989).

PART IV

Modern Church Teaching on Economic Life

14

Pope Leo XIII and Pope Pius XI

Something quite dramatic occurred in the eighteenth- and nineteenth-century economic life of Europe, and in 1891 it brought a pope—Leo XIII—to focus a formal encyclical on economic issues and "the social question" for the first time in the history of Christianity. That something was the Industrial Revolution.

The situation

Some remedy must be found, and quickly found, for the misery and wretchedness which press so heavily at this moment on the large majority of the very poor.

After the old trade guilds had been destroyed in the last century . . . it gradually came about that the present age handed over the workers, each alone and defenseless, to the inhumanity of employers and the unbridled greed of competitors.

Pope Leo XIII, *Rerum novarum* 2 & 6

Throughout human history, most people had been subsistence farmers. A few were craftsmen, but whether in ancient Rome or the Middle Ages, most people did not earn a wage. Most struggled to raise enough food so that their portion of the harvest would be sufficient to allow them to survive the winter. The Industrial Revolution changed things dramatically.

Pope Leo XIII

Born in 1810 to a family of nobility just thirty-five miles from Rome, Vincenzo Gioacchino Pecci was educated by the Jesuits both as a child and in university. He earned doctorates in theology and canon law by age twenty-six and he was ordained a priest of the diocese of Rome at age

---

twenty-seven. He was assigned as provincial administrator in one of the Papal states in central Italy and became widely known for his successful campaign against corruption and organized crime.

He was made an archbishop at age thirty-four, and oversaw the diocese of Perugia for more than thirty years, after which he was elected pope, taking the name of Leo. Known for his intellectual and diplomatic skills, he served as pope for twenty-five years, dying at age ninety-three.

The essence of the Industrial Revolution was the invention of new machinery and eventually a new source of power—steam—that altered traditional ways of producing the ordinary necessities of daily life. Factories became much more efficient at making those products, and those who traditionally made them at home were left without customers. Their products could not compete with the lower prices of manufactured goods. This increase in productivity caused similarly unprecedented shifts in living situations.

Multitudes left the villages and rural areas where their families had lived for centuries. Because of the lack of work there, they moved to the cities where in the new "manufactories" they might be able to find the only jobs available. The conditions within factories were terrible. Employers held the upper hand. Wages were pitifully low and the boss could simply fire a worker who became injured on the job or even complained about the conditions. He simply hired another unemployed applicant off the street. As Paul Misner put it in his survey of social Catholicism in this period, "The early factory workers had the worst of both the old agrarian and the new industrial order."[1] Living conditions in the cities for ordinary workers often were even worse. Several unrelated people typically shared the same small room. No heat, no running water; for some the only toilet was an open courtyard. Without the traditional support systems of the rural parish they had left, many were desperate.

Christian groups met all across Europe in an attempt to understand and counteract these changes.[2] One was the Fribourg Union, including various Catholic intellectuals and Fribourg's bishop, Gaspard Mermillod.[3] Trade unions of all kinds sprang up in attempts to organize workers to resist the harsh authority of factory owners. Governments were torn but typically sided with the wealthy, whose voices were far stronger in the halls of government than those of the working poor, who typically didn't even have the right to vote.

In this situation, Pope Leo wanted to speak out against the harsh conditions that threatened the livelihood—and the faith—of so many ordinary workers. He did this by means of an encyclical, literally a letter but in effect an extensive treatise, addressed in his day to all the Catholic bishops of the world (though addressed by more recent popes to all people of good will).

Eternal destiny

God has not created man for the fragile and transitory things of this world, but for Heaven and eternity. . . . Whether or not you have riches and all the other things which are called good is of no importance in relation to eternal happiness. But how you use them, that is truly of utmost importance.

Pope Leo XIII, *Rerum novarum* 33

Leo's encyclical, like *Quadragesimo anno* written forty years later by Pope Pius XI, addressed many economic issues in great detail. Nonetheless, he cautioned that improvements in the lives of the worker, like all things on earth, must be held in proper perspective by people of faith. Faith leads Christians—whether popes or uneducated laity—to be concerned about issues of justice in the world, but, as creatures redeemed in Christ, never in isolation from our ultimate destiny in God.

PROPERTY

God's intention

The church has always unanimously maintained that nature, rather the Creator Himself, has given man the right of private ownership, not only that individuals may be able to provide for themselves and their families but also that the goods which the Creator destined for the entire family of mankind may through this institution truly serve this purpose.

Pope Pius XI, *Quadragesimo anno* 45

Yet, however the earth may be apportioned among private owners, it does not cease to serve the common interest of all, inasmuch as no living being is sustained except by what the fields bring forth. Those who lack resources supply labor, . . . the compensation for which is drawn ultimately from no other source than from the varied products of the earth and is exchanged for them.

Pope Leo XIII, *Rerum novarum* 14

Leo's encyclical seemed to some in his day as a novel Christian confrontation with the economic life of the world. However, for anyone who understands the history of Christian views of economic life, as this volume has made clear, his arguments were deeply embedded in the tradition of the earliest Christians—a tradition that saw God's intentions in the creation of the earth as the definitive starting point for any understanding of how economic life should proceed.

At the same time, given the threat that Leo and Pius saw in the secular, even antireligious, labor unions of the day, these popes described private property in ways that were stronger than any of the previous understandings of private property in the history of Christian belief. As we saw in Chapter 7, Thomas Aquinas taught that private property was a wise "addition to natural law." Nature brought forth no private ownership; it was created by human prudence, with good reason. It is an indication of how Catholic social thought responds to the challenges of each era that Popes Leo and Pius increased the moral warrant for private property ownership by arguing, beyond Thomas, that personal ownership was not simply a human creation but rather an intention of "the Creator himself." In the language of Thomistic natural law, this would make private property part of the eternal law, a status that Thomas himself would not have endorsed. We can understand why these popes, in the face of an antireligious socialism, gave an unusually strong endorsement of private property—what one scholar called the church's "high water mark" of an individualist view of property.[4]

Thus Leo begins with the presumption, examined in earlier chapters, that God gave the earth to humanity to meet human needs and that although private ownership is good, it ought to be structured by law and lived out by individuals in accord with God's creative intention to meet the needs of all.

Socialists on property

The Socialists, exciting the envy of the poor toward the rich, contend that it is necessary to do away with private possession of goods and in its place to make the goods of individuals common to all, and that the men who preside over a municipality or who direct the entire State should act as administrators of these goods. They hold that, by such a transfer of private goods from private individuals to the community, they can cure the present evil through dividing wealth and benefits equally among the citizens.

Therefore, . . . they make the lot of all wage earners worse, because in abolishing the freedom to dispose of wages they take away from them by

> this very act the hope and the opportunity of increasing their property and of securing advantages for themselves.
>
> Pope Leo XIII, *Rerum novarum* 7 & 9

Pope Leo is eager to point out that the groups most involved in distorting the traditional Christian view of private property are socialists, who had been active throughout the nineteenth century in Europe in proposing alternatives to the harsh capitalism that held so many ordinary workers captive. It will help us to note, however, that Leo's concern about the socialists is not simply that their view of private property was wrong. The additional and more threatening difficulty he faced was that most socialists of the day were avidly antireligious. Thus added to the cultural dislocation of workers no longer living near the parish churches where their families had lived for generations, those same workers were now being actively recruited to become members of socialist—and antireligious—trade unions representing the workers against the power of the owners and managers of the factories. Many laborers simply walked away from their own religious traditions. This loss of so many traditional Catholics engendered in Leo a great urgency in addressing these issues.

This urgency may also explain to some degree an unfortunate error that Leo exhibits in his critique of the socialists. Very few of the socialists in nineteenth-century Europe actually called for the abolition of all private property. What was common to them all, however, was a strong condemnation of the private ownership of the "means of production": of the factories, machines, and tools that were used in the production of the goods now made so much cheaper by the Industrial Revolution.

> *Obligations of property*
>
> If the question be asked: How ought man to use his possessions? The Church replies without hesitation: man ought not regard external goods as his own, but as common so that, in fact, a person should readily share them when he sees others in need. . . . These are duties not of justice, except in cases of extreme need, but of Christian charity, which obviously cannot be enforced by legal action.
>
> Pope Leo XIII, *Rerum novarum* 36

> The Sacred Scriptures and the Fathers of the Church constantly declare in the most explicit language that the rich are bound by a very grave precept to practice almsgiving, beneficence, and munificence.
>
> Pope Pius XI, *Quadragesimo anno* 50

In spite of strong support for private property, Pope Leo was clear that those who own property had certain obligations that accompanied that ownership, even though many owners in the secular world refused to recognize them. In this, the popes followed the teachings from Scripture, the early church, and the Middle Ages. However, in another subtle shift that raised the importance of the rights of property ownership relative to its duties, Leo and Pius again differ from Aquinas. Thomas treated property ownership within the general theme of justice, so that the Thomistic obligation to share ("common use," as he termed it) is a duty of justice. These two popes saw largely a duty in charity—still an obligation, but not as serious as a duty of justice.

Pope Pius XI

Ambrogio Ratti was born in 1857, the son of a silk manufacturer. He studied in Milan and Rome, and was ordained a priest at age twenty-three. Famous for his work as a paleographer and librarian, he served in the Vatican Library and in the papal diplomatic corps, as nuncio (ambassador) to Poland.

Made Archbishop of Milan in 1921, Ratti was elected pope in 1922, taking the name Pius. He was known for his resistance to the fascism taking over Europe prior to World War II. He called for greater roles for the laity, modernized the Vatican Library, established Vatican radio, and reorganized the Pontifical Academy of Sciences. He died in 1939, at age eighty-one.

CAPITALISM AND SOCIALISM

The critique of capitalism

Just as the unity of human society cannot be founded on an opposition of classes, so also the right ordering of economic life cannot be left to a free competition of forces. For from this source, as from a poisoned spring, have originated and spread all the errors of individualist economic teaching. Destroying through forgetfulness or ignorance the social and moral character of economic life, it held that economic life must be considered and treated as altogether free from and independent of public authority, because in the market, i.e., in the free struggle of competitors, it would have a principle of self-direction which governs it much more perfectly than would the intervention of any created intellect.

Pope Pius XI, *Quadragesimo anno* 86

Leo and Pius were defenders of private property but were simultaneously harsh critics of the way in which the economic system in their day operated. Both were convinced that it was deeply wrong to maximize human freedom and minimize government control of the economy, and thus they rejected nineteenth-century "liberalism" (a philosophical perspective stressing the rights of individuals, a view associated today with what is called "conservatism" in the U.S.). The Catholic Church has traditionally had a deep appreciation of the role of civil authority in structuring human life, and it seemed clear that many of the problems facing Pope Leo in 1891 and Pope Pius in 1931 could be attributed to the rampant assertion of self-interest in economic life. The answer had to include not central planning, but a stronger governmental structuring of markets. Some conservative American Catholics have recently asserted that this critique of individualism was directed at its European, not American, versions, but Christine Firer Hinze argues persuasively that this is a misunderstanding.[5] Individualism in all its forms was the target. Here, the popes clearly reject the view that "free" markets are the answer and instead insist on a strong economic role for government in the legal definition of markets to prevent abuses that under-regulated markets would cause.

Investment and profit

Investing larger incomes to create abundant employment, provided that this work is applied to producing really useful goods, ought to be considered, as we deduce from the principles of the Angelic Doctor, an outstanding example of the virtue of munificence and one particularly suited to the needs of the times.

Pope Pius XI, *Quadragesimo anno* 46

For all the criticism that Leo and Pius launched against the dominant capitalist system, they nonetheless believed it could be reformed. As Joe Holland has argued, a fundamental opposition to nineteenth-century socialism led to an outreach to a new ally, "the moderate bourgeois," a reference to the rising commercial class whose success as business owners made them a powerful historical force.[6] Referring back to Thomas Aquinas, the "Angelic Doctor," Pope Pius recalled Thomas's statement that the merchant's economic activity might not be sinful if he put it to good use, including the creation of jobs for other people.[7] Thus we see that even in the midst of the terrible economic problems of the day, Pius was able to envision a more just economic system that maintained much of the freedom of the capitalist system of his day.

The critique of socialism

The fundamental principle of Socialism which would make all possessions public property is to be utterly rejected because it injures the very ones whom it seeks to help [workers], contravenes the natural rights of individual persons, and throws the functions of the State and public peace into confusion. . . . Private ownership must be preserved inviolate.

Pope Leo XIII, *Rerum novarum* 23

Pope Leo was clear that socialism was to be avoided because it rejected the notion of private property, as we have already seen, but by Pius's day, it was clear that socialism had broken into two parts. One, more strident and severe, was embodied in the ruthlessness of Joseph Stalin in the U.S.S.R. The other was represented in the socialist parties that competed in the democratic elections of nearly all nations of Western Europe. For these, Pius held out hope.

Changes in socialism

One might say that, terrified by its own principles and by the conclusions drawn therefrom by Communism, Socialism inclines toward and in a certain measure approaches the truths which the Christian tradition has always held sacred; for it cannot be denied that its demands at times come very near those that Christian reformers of society justly insist upon.

Pope Pius XI, *Quadragesimo anno* 113

However, in the end, Pius retained Leo's presumption that absolutely essential to socialism was a secular view of society and of the individual as unrelated to God. Although there were Christians who were also socialist, they were not a forceful enough presence in Europe to convince either pope that the two ideas might be brought together.

Collectivism and individualism

Accordingly, the twin rocks of shipwreck must be carefully avoided. For, as one is wrecked upon, or comes close to, what is known as "individualism" by denying or minimizing the social and public character of the right of property, so by rejecting or minimizing the private and individual character of this same right, one inevitably runs into "collectivism" or at least closely approaches its tenets.

Pope Pius XI, *Quadragesimo anno* 46

In sum, then, both Leo and Pius were openly critical of the two main structural alternatives for economic life: capitalist individualism and socialist collectivism. As we shall see later in this chapter, they maintained hope in a "third way" that might avoid the problems of both of these world historical systems.

WAGES

The just wage

We are told that free consent fixes the amount of a wage; that therefore the employer, after paying the wage agreed to, would seem to have discharged his obligation and not to owe anything more. . . . An impartial judge would not assent readily or without reservation to this reasoning.

A man's labor has two characteristics. First, it is truly personal, because work energy inheres in the person and belongs completely to him by whom it is expended, and for whose use it is destined by nature. Second, it is necessary, because man has need of the fruit of his labors to preserve his life, and nature itself, which must be most strictly obeyed, commands him to preserve it.

If labor should be considered only under the aspect that it is personal, there is no doubt that it would be entirely in the worker's right to agree to any wage . . . or even none at all. But . . . work is not only personal but necessary. . . . In fact, to preserve one's life is a duty common to all individuals, and to neglect this duty is a crime. Hence arises necessarily the right of securing things to sustain life, and only a wage earned by his labor gives a poor man the means to acquire these things.

> Let it be granted then that worker and employer may enter freely into agreements, in particular, concerning the amount of the wage; yet there is always underlying such agreements an element of natural justice, one more important and more ancient than the free consent of contracting parties, namely, that the wage shall not be less than enough to support a worker in reasonable and frugal comfort. If, compelled by necessity, or moved by fear of a worse evil, a worker accepts harsher conditions, which although against his will he must accept because an employer or contractor will offer no more, he is a victim of force and injustice.
>
> Pope Leo XIII, *Rerum novarum* 34

If Popes Leo and Pius could see hope for a more humane capitalism, that altered system would have to be one that did a much better job in providing a decent wage to ordinary workers. It was a fundamental tenet of the liberalism of his day, as it is for most advocates of "free" markets today, that the consent the worker gives in agreeing to a wage is sufficient to guarantee the justice of that wage. After all, the worker freely chooses to take the job; how could he be exploited? However, Leo makes clear that this presumption in liberalism is deeply wrong. Underlying his argument is the awareness of power relationships that exist in economic life, even though they tend to be ignored in liberal theory and are absent in the mainstream economic analysis of the business firm.

Leo articulates here an insight into freedom that is fundamental to the Christian point of view. We saw in Chapter 10 how John Calvin recognized oppression and robbery in situations where an employer could pay an inadequately low wage because the workers had no other options than to accept the job. In Chapter 13, we saw Albino Barrera's argument concerning how market forces can present such terrible choices to the poor that markets do indeed undermine their freedom as human persons.[8] We should recall that the price system in markets works so well precisely because a change in price signals to market participants that they should alter their behavior in the light of now higher or lower prices. If they don't, they will be worse off than they could be with a change. As we have seen, for example, this is why a higher price for petroleum pushes people to buy more fuel-efficient cars. This is one of the main reasons why markets are good for human flourishing. But when the poor are similarly pressed, they often have no options for change and simply suffer the severe impact of higher prices.

Pope Leo and all of his successors since have recognized that when workers are desperate to find employment in order to feed their family, they often have to agree to wages that are too low from a moral point of view. Catholic social thought recognizes that market compulsion can generate injustice in the workplace. This "force and injustice" not only requires more virtuous action by employers but, since this is not forthcoming from all employers voluntarily, it also calls for a different structuring of the economy by governmental decision.

Typically in the Western world this has taken the form of minimum-wage laws, which cover many but not all jobs in the economy. Recognizing that many workers make so low a wage as to be unable to support a family, many nations have instituted various government programs to supplement wages. The United States provides an "earned income tax credit" (EITC) to low-wage workers—meaning that workers receive a direct payment and not simply an income tax deduction (since many have incomes so low they don't pay income taxes). Many nations (including France, Austria, Switzerland, Germany, and Ireland) make payments to families with children, implicitly recognizing that a market wage may be sufficient for a single person but not for a family's provider. Similar to the U.S. child tax credit, in Germany a family receives the equivalent of about $250 per month for the first and second child under eighteen, about $260 for a third child, and $300 for the fourth and any additional children.[9] In Switzerland, payments per child are about the same.[10]

Limitations on implementing the just wage

Every effort must therefore be made that fathers of families receive a wage large enough to meet ordinary family needs adequately. But if this cannot always be done under existing circumstances, social justice demands that changes be introduced as soon as possible whereby such a wage will be assured to every adult workingman. . . .

In determining the amount of the wage, the condition of a business and of the one carrying it on must also be taken into account, for it would be unjust to demand excessive wages which a business cannot stand without its ruin and consequent calamity to the workers.

Pope Pius XI, *Quadragesimo anno* 71–72

At the same time that Pope Pius supports Leo's teaching on the just wage, he acknowledges that this may not always be feasible for a particular firm in the concrete situation. Pius recognizes that scarcity constrains even businesses, and he would not force the firm to self-destruct. However, this does not leave either the firm or the citizenry off the hook, as "social justice demands that changes be introduced" in the economic system that will eventually rectify the situation.

This once again would seem to imply some form of wage supplement such as a robust earned income tax credit.

Looking back, we can see that this is not a neat resolution of the issue of just wage, especially today when so many firms face competition from factories in parts of the world where people work for very low wages compared to those in the industrialized West. This problem of the just wage is the single most difficult one facing Catholic social thought on the economy today. A market system does not provide an adequate solution, as there are millions of people in the industrialized world making very low wages and unable to provide for a family what Leo called "reasonable and frugal comfort." The proper structuring of the moral ecology of markets to provide such income is an unresolved problem facing Christians even today. We who are prosperous are well treated by an economic system that treats many others with "force and injustice," to use Leo's words. Acknowledging that any particular firm may be unable to pay a just wage does not dissolve the indictment of our economic system. It presses us to do more to rectify the injustice.

WORKPLACE ORGANIZATIONS

Labor unions

The beneficent achievements of the guilds of artisans among our ancestors have long been well known. . . . In our present age . . . it is most clearly necessary that workers' associations be adapted to meet the present need.

Workers' associations ought to be so constituted and so governed . . . that the individual members of the association secure, so far as possible, an increase in the goods of body, of soul, and of prosperity.

Pope Leo XIII, *Rerum novarum* 69 & 76

In many nations, those at the helm of State, plainly imbued with Liberalism, were showing little favor to workers' associations of this type; nay, rather they openly opposed them. . . . There were even some Catholics who looked askance at the efforts of workers to form associations of this type as if they smacked of a socialistic or revolutionary spirit.

Pope Pius XI, *Quadragesimo anno* 30

Fundamental to the hopes of Leo and Pius for justice in the economic sphere is the role of labor unions. They referred to them as "workers' associations" and hoped at the time that they would be an adaptation of the traditional guilds that had for centuries structured the productive life of medieval Europe. In the guild, both master craftsman and young apprentices took part and resolved any problems that needed attention, from the quality of the work to the price to be charged. Leo and Pius were quite suspicious of most labor unions of the day, in large part because of the unionists' antireligious convictions, but the popes knew that the imbalance of coercive power between factory owners and workers might be offset if the workers could organize and negotiate with the owners on an equal level. Relying on the work of Catholic intellectuals such as Bishop Wilhelm Von Ketteler, they proposed a different kind of workplace organization. Thomas Shannon has described Pope Leo's focus on the need for the reform of economic institutions as "a critical turning point in Catholic thinking."[11]

Corporatism

The associations, or corporations, are composed of representatives of workers and employers of the same industry or profession and, as true and proper organs and institutions of the State, they direct the syndicates and coordinate their activities in matters of common interest toward one and the same end.

It is easily deduced from what has been said that the interests common to a whole industry or profession should hold first place in these guilds. The most important among these interests is to promote the cooperation in the highest degree of each industry and profession for the sake of the common good of the country.

Pope Pius XI, *Quadragesimo anno* 93 & 85

The primary hope, then, of Pope Pius XI was a kind of "third way" between liberalism and socialism that avoided both the autocratic coercive power of the factory owner over workers in capitalism as well as the class-warfare attitudes of so many socialist labor unions. The system they had in mind was known as "corporatism" and involved a modern version of the medieval guild. These associations (sometimes called "corporations" but not in the sense of our business corporations today) were made up of workers and managers and owners in any one industry or profession. The idea was that any problems that might arise, whether about wages or production processes or the setting of prices, should be addressed by all those involved in that industry, with all keeping the common good of the nation in mind.

There were clearly problems with this proposal. One challenge was that even though putting both owners and workers in the same organization might deal with their conflicting interests because they must talk with each other, it was quite likely that their common self-interest in one industry might lead them to take advantage of the nation as a whole. The second problem was historical. The actual development of institutions in the economy largely sidestepped this possible solution and instead moved to a different model altogether, one that the church itself eventually endorsed. That successful model was one where the national government plays the role of arbiter and sets the market rules for fair negotiations between unionized workers and factory owners in agreeing upon labor contracts.[12]

GOVERNANCE

The principle of subsidiarity

Just as it is gravely wrong to take from individuals what they can accomplish by their own initiative and industry and give it to the community, so also it is an injustice and at the same time a grave evil and disturbance of right order to assign to a greater and higher association what lesser and subordinate organizations can do. For every social activity ought of its very nature to furnish help to the members of the body social, and never destroy and absorb them.

Pope Pius XI, *Quadragesimo anno* 79

One of the facts of the world situation facing Pope Pius XI was the rise of European fascism, represented by Adolf Hitler in Germany and Benito Mussolini in Italy. Fascism is a political system quite different from socialism and communism but which also entailed strong governmental control of the economy. Thus in response to an urgent need, Pius proposed what has become a famous principle in international politics today: the principle of subsidiarity. As Christine Firer Hinze points out, this is a fundamental contribution of Pius XI to subsequent Catholic social thought.[13]

This principle concerns governance, addressing the "level" at which decisions ought to be made in a society. It says that preference should be given to the local level. That is, when a problem can be solved at a local or neighborhood level, that's where it should be addressed. Neighborhood cleanups are an example; individual neighborhood organizations can often organize them better than a citywide effort can. If the problem is too large or complex to be resolved there, then it ought to be addressed at the next higher level, perhaps city or county. Think of local school boards. If a problem cannot be resolved at that level, then the state or the nation will need to act. For example, in the civil rights movement in the United States, the rights of African Americans could only be assured by action at the national level. Clearly today, many problems require international coordination. Thus the principle of subsidiarity expresses a bias in favor of local resolution, even though the primary concern is that a problem be solved, not simply that it be dealt with locally. This also creates a bias in favor of market transactions over government control of economic life. Government must set the rules for market interactions but should not override the freedom of market participants unless the common good of the community requires it.

THE ROLE OF GOVERNMENT

The state

Since it would be quite absurd to look out for one portion of the citizens and to neglect another, it follows that public authority ought to exercise due care in safe-guarding the well-being and the interests of non-owning workers. Unless this is done, justice, which commands that everyone be given his own, will be violated.

Pope Leo XIII, *Rerum novarum* 49

This state of things was quite satisfactory to the wealthy, who looked upon it as the consequence of inevitable and natural economic laws, and who, therefore, were content to abandon to charity alone the full care of relieving the unfortunate, as though it were the task of charity to make amends for the open violation of justice, a violation not merely tolerated, but sanctioned at times by legislators.

Pope Pius XI, *Quadragesimo anno* 4

With regard to civil authority, Leo XIII, boldly breaking through the confines imposed by Liberalism, fearlessly taught that government must not be thought a mere guardian of law and of good order, but rather must put forth every effort so that "through the entire scheme of laws and institutions . . . both public and individual well-being may develop spontaneously out of the very structure and administration of the State."

Pope Pius XI, *Quadragesimo anno* 93

The purpose of the state in a democracy is self-government. It is clear in both Leo and Pius that the state plays a critically important role in economic life, primarily in two ways. The first is through the setting of the rules for what will be allowed within ordinary economic activity (what we called "defining markets by law" in Chapter 12), since the presence of sin means that a completely free and unrestricted interaction of persons in competitive markets leads to severe abuses (and an unproductive economy). But the second critically important function of government is to ensure care for those whose needs are unmet (called "the provision of essential goods and services" above). Much of this can be done by voluntary associations, and of course the Christian churches are among the most active in creating institutions such as hospitals, schools, and a variety of charitable agencies to meet human needs. Nonetheless, as the text above indicates, Pope Pius warned against the state ignoring its responsibilities to assist the needy, particularly those harmed in the economic system. It would be an injustice for a society to leave all assistance for the poor to private charity. This means that the prosperous must be willing to pay taxes sufficient to cover the public expenditure (whether the services are delivered by government agencies or by private service agencies funded by tax revenues).

CIVIL SOCIETY

Independent organizations

Let the State protect these lawfully associated bodies of citizens; let it not, however, interfere with their private concerns and order of life; for vital activity is set in motion by an inner principle, and it is very easily destroyed, as we know, by intrusion from without. . . .

If citizens have the free right to associate, as in fact they do, they must also have the right freely to adopt the organization and rules which they judge most appropriate to achieve their purpose.

Pope Leo XIII, *Rerum novarum* 75–76

An important distinction for Popes Leo and Pius, and for the Catholic tradition before and since, is the difference between society and the state. "The state" means the national government, and this is not the same thing as the society. The state is the governmental apparatus through which citizens in a democracy make decisions; it is an institution for self-government. At the same time, there is much that goes on in society, properly outside the reaches of government, largely in the many independent "voluntary associations" that people participate in, from the Chamber of Commerce and labor unions to elementary school PTAs and service organizations, from hobby clubs to political parties. Today we call this "civil society," and as we saw in Chapter 12, a vibrant civil society is critical to a well-functioning democracy and a humane economy. A concern for subsidiarity is based in this fundamental conviction that daily life should be lived by persons within various organizations with considerable freedom. Government has an important role to play, but it must respect the independence of the various organizations its citizens create.

WOMEN

Women

Certain occupations, likewise, are less fitted for women, who are intended by nature for work of the home—work indeed which especially protects modesty in women and accords by nature with the education of children and the well-being of the family.

Pope Leo XIII, *Rerum novarum* 60

Mothers, concentrating on household duties, should work primarily in the home or in its immediate vicinity. It is an intolerable abuse, and to be abolished at all cost, for mothers on account of the father's low wage to be forced to engage in gainful occupations outside the home to the neglect of their proper cares and duties, especially the training of children.

Pope Pius XI, *Quadragesimo anno* 71

The treatment of women by Leo and Pius looks to us in the twenty-first century as deeply sexist, as it presumes that a woman ought to stay at home raising children and would only have a job in the marketplace because of an unjust wage paid to her husband. Today we understand that both husband and wife may rightfully have careers in the marketplace—and that either might be a "stay-at-home" parent. But one can still find in this advice about women a culturally important lesson given in that earlier era: that the structure of markets must respect moral values rather than simply restructuring those moral values in order to achieve greater efficiency, profits, or general economic growth.

CATHOLIC SOCIAL THOUGHT

Both economic and moral analysis needed

Even though economics and moral science each employs its own principles in its own sphere, it is, nevertheless, an error to say that the economic and moral orders are so distinct from and alien to each other that the former depends in no way on the latter. Certainly the laws of economics, as they are termed, being based on the very nature of material things and on the capacities of the human body and mind, determine the limits of what productive human effort can and cannot attain in the economic field and by what means. Yet it is reason itself that clearly shows, on the basis of the individual and social nature of things and of men, the purpose which God ordained for all economic life.

Pope Pius XI, *Quadragesimo anno* 42

Looking back at how these two popes engaged the problems of their day, employing the insights of the Christian tradition this volume has reviewed, we can see thoughtful men attempting to sort out what we are challenged to sort out today. That is, they recognized that it was important to understand the economy as it exists, and in this they relied on the social scientific work of Jesuit scholars Heinrich Pesch and Oswald von Nell-Breuning.[14] They then correlated this knowledge of "what is" with the moral principles of the Christian tradition. They struggled, as we must today, with the difficulties created by the very real changes in "the world" when compared to the earlier eras of the Christian tradition. Holding on to what is essential and allowing for change in what is less important is the key, even though knowing precisely where to draw the line between them requires great knowledge and prudence.

CONCLUSION

Justice and charity

Admittedly, no vicarious charity can substitute for justice which is due as an obligation and is wrongfully denied. Yet even supposing that everyone should finally receive all that is due him, the widest field for charity will always remain open. For justice alone can, if faithfully observed, remove the causes of social conflict but can never bring about union of minds and hearts. Indeed all the institutions for the establishment of peace

> and the promotion of mutual help among men, however perfect these may seem, have the principal foundation of their stability in the mutual bond of minds and hearts whereby the members are united with one another.
>
> Pope Pius XI, *Quadragesimo anno* 137

For all the importance of justice, and its defense of the principles of right relationship among individuals and between individuals and society, Catholic social thought has always recognized that justice alone cannot suffice. As noted in Chapter 13, a deeper morality of individuals and groups is required. Pope Pius here reminds us that individuals, their organizations, and their societies must also be animated by charity, so that the severity which justice can sometimes generate is moderated by a deep personal concern of one for another. Jesus' teaching of the love of neighbor animates not only the Eucharist and daily personal life; it remains central to Christianity's response to "the social question."

Notes

1. Paul Misner, *Social Catholicism in Europe: From the Onset of Industrialization to the First World War* (New York: Crossroad, 1991), 27.

2. For a careful treatment of the development of Catholic thought in the decades prior to Pope Leo's 1891 encyclical, see Michael Joseph Schuck, *That They Be One: The Social Teaching of the Papal Encyclicals, 1740–1989* (Washington, DC: Georgetown University Press, 1991).

3. For more information on the Fribourg Union, see Normand Joseph Paulhus, *The Theological and Political Ideals of the Fribourg Union*, eScholarship, Boston College, 1983.

4. Ernest Fortin, "Sacred and Inviolable: Rerum Novarum and Natural Rights," *Theological Studies* 53, no. 2 (June 1992): 203–33.

5. Christine Firer Hinze, "Commentary on *Quadragesimo anno* (After Forty Years)," in *Modern Catholic Social Teaching*, ed. Kenneth R. Himes (Washington, DC: Georgetown University Press, 2005), 168.

6. Joe Holland, *Modern Catholic Social Teaching: The Popes Confront the Industrial Age, 1740–1958* (New York: Paulist, 2003), 289–99.

7. ST, II-II, q. 77, a. 4.

8. Albino Barrera, *Economic Compulsion and Christian Ethics* (New York: Cambridge University Press, 2005).

9. Similar to the U.S. child tax credit, this is the "Kindergeld" program of the Federal Republic of Germany, "Bundesministerium der Justiz." http://bundesrecht.juris.de/bkgg_1996/index.html. Accessed June 27, 2011.

10. Swiss Confederation, "Familienzulagen." http://www.bsv.admin.ch/themen/zulagen/00059/index.html?lang=de. Accessed June 27, 2011.

11. Thomas Shannon, "Commentary on *Rerum Novarum*," in *Modern Catholic Social Teaching*, ed. Kenneth R. Himes (Washington, DC: Georgetown University Press, 2005), 141.

12. For a description of this shift in church teaching from "a third way" proposal to a "meliorist" approach, see Franz Mueller, *The Church and the Social Question* (Washington, DC: American Enterprise Institute, 1984).

13. Christine Firer Hinze, "Commentary on *Quadragesimo anno*," 171.

14. For the use of Heinrich Pesch's work in *Rerum novarum*, see Thomas Shannon, "Commentary on *Rerum novarum*," in *Modern Catholic Social Teaching*, ed. Kenneth R. Himes. For the role of Oswald von Nell-Breuning in the writing of *Quadragesimo anno*, see Christine Firer Hinze, "Commentary on *Quadragesimo anno*," in *Modern Catholic Social Teaching*, ed. Kenneth R. Himes.

15

Pope John XXIII and Pope Paul VI

The mid-twentieth century saw further development in this tradition of Catholic social thought by means of the encyclicals *Mater et magistra* ("Christianity and Social Progress") and *Pacem in terris* ("Peace on Earth") by Pope John XXIII and *Populorum progressio* ("On the Development of Peoples") by Pope Paul VI. And it was in 1965 that the Second Vatican Council issued *Gaudium et spes* ("The Church in the Modern World"). All of these documents related the church's social principles to the problems of contemporary life.

The situation

We are filled with an overwhelming sadness when we contemplate the sorry spectacle of millions of workers in many lands and entire continents condemned through the inadequacy of their wages to live with their families in utterly sub-human conditions.

Pope John XXIII, *Mater et magistra* 68

While the fundamental moral commitments held steady, the world situation had changed in important ways since the time of Leo and Pius. Perhaps most important among those changes was the vivid awareness in the 1960s of the issues of poverty in "the third world," particularly in many newly independent nations emerging out of their colonial past. Dire poverty engulfed hundreds of millions of people all over the planet. Because the Catholic Church was present in all these nations, the popes felt a special responsibility to take a global view, rather than being locked into the concerns of Europe and North America only.

Pope John XXIII

Angelo Roncalli was born in 1881 to a farming family in northern Italy. He was ordained a priest at the age of twenty-six and served in World

---

War I as a medical corpsman and chaplain. He was made an archbishop at age forty-four, spending many years in various positions within the Vatican diplomatic corps.

He served as Archbishop of Venice for five years before his unexpected election as pope in 1958, at age seventy-seven, quite old by traditional standards. He chose the name John, more than six hundred years after the death of Pope John XXII. Down to earth and known for his personal visits to Rome's prison and to sick children, he was deeply loved by ordinary people, both Catholics and others.

John XXIII surprised the church and the world in calling the Second Vatican Council, a meeting of all Catholic bishops from around the world, which ushered in significant reforms in liturgy, ecumenism, and the mission of the church to the world. He did not live to see the end of the three-year Council, as he died in 1963 at age eighty-two.

INTEGRATING FAITH AND ECONOMIC CONCERN

Faith and economic life

The moral order has no existence except in God; cut off from God it must necessarily disintegrate. Moreover, man is not just a material organism. He consists also of spirit; he is endowed with reason and freedom. He demands, therefore, a moral and religious order.

Let men make all the technical and economic progress they can; there will be no peace nor justice in the world until they return to a sense of their dignity as creatures and sons of God, who is the first and final cause of all created being.

Pope John XXIII, *Mater et magistra* 208 & 215

Like the many voices we have heard earlier in this volume, Popes John and Paul were vividly aware of the importance of integrating economic life into the broader perspective of faith. This faith in God does two things simultaneously that look contradictory to many nonbelievers but in fact are complementary. First, faith requires that all of our actions on this earth should be ordered toward our ultimate destiny of eternal life with God. Second, faith commits Christians to an intense engagement with the world, in particular with a commitment to assisting those whose lives are most endangered by the excesses of our economic system. The same God who invites us to an eternal fulfillment provides a foretaste of that promise in this life, to the extent that human finitude and sin do not stand in the way.

DEVELOPMENT

The problem of development of nations

Probably the most difficult problem today concerns the relationship between political communities that are economically advanced and those in the process of development. Whereas the standard of living is high in the former, the latter are subject to extreme poverty.

Pope John XXIII, *Mater et magistra* 157

In the present day, however, individual and group effort within these countries is no longer enough. The world situation requires the concerted effort of everyone, a thorough examination of every facet of the problem—social, economic, cultural and spiritual.

Pope Paul VI, *Populorum progressio* 13

Giving technical and financial aid with a view to gaining control over the political situation in the poorer countries . . . A nation that acted from these motives would in fact be introducing a new form of colonialism—cleverly disguised, no doubt, but actually reflecting that older, outdated type from which many nations have recently emerged.

Pope John XXIII, *Mater et magistra* 171–72

The decades of the 1960s and '70s drew world attention to issues of the development of the poor nations of the global South. Many former colonies were now independent nations. They made their presence felt in the United Nations General Assembly, and their concerns animated much discussion within secular society and the church. Thus Popes John and Paul dealt at length with the needs of whole nations for assistance in recovering from the problems left over from colonialism and bringing themselves out of the poverty that has characterized so many peoples for centuries. And while the nations of the "first world" (the industrialized democratic nations of the West) and the "second world" (the nations of the communist bloc) had the potential to assist the poorer nations of the "third world," they often employed financial aid as a political tool. Both popes insisted it should serve first the recipient peoples.[1]

Integral human development

The development we speak of here cannot be restricted to economic growth alone. To be authentic, it must be well rounded; it must foster the development of each man and of the whole man. Neither individuals nor nations should regard the possession of more and more goods as the ultimate objective. Every kind of progress is a two-edged sword. It is necessary if man is to grow as a human being; yet it can also enslave him, if he comes to regard it as the supreme good and cannot look beyond it.It is not just a question of eliminating hunger and reducing poverty. It is not just a question of fighting wretched conditions, though this is an urgent and necessary task. It involves building a human community where men can live truly human lives, free from discrimination on account of race, religion or nationality, free from servitude to other men or to natural forces which they cannot yet control satisfactorily. It involves building a human community where liberty is not an idle word, where the needy Lazarus can sit down with the rich man at the same banquet table. On the part of the rich man, it calls for great generosity, willing sacrifice and diligent effort. Each man must examine his conscience. . . . Is he prepared to support, at his own expense, projects and undertakings designed to help the needy? Is he prepared to pay higher taxes so that public authorities may expand their efforts in the work of development? Is he prepared to pay more for imported goods, so that the foreign producer may make a fairer profit?

Pope Paul VI, *Populorum progressio* 14, 19, & 47

In continuity with the long history of Christian views of economic life, Pope Paul reminds his readers that the development they seek for poor nations is intimately related to the development that each of us needs as an individual person. That is, both kinds of development must be understood not simply as economic or even psychological but at a deeper level as an integral transformation of the person and the nation.

Pope Paul VI

Giovanni Battista Montini was born in 1897 in northern Italy to a father who was a lawyer and member of the Italian parliament and a mother with noble heritage. Although often ill as a child, he was a bright student and was ordained a priest at age twenty-two.

Montini spent most of his career in the papal civil service and was made Archbishop of Milan at age fifty-seven. Elected pope in 1963, he took the name Paul. Knowing the internal workings of the Vatican well, he reformed the Curia, established seventy-five as the mandatory retirement age for bishops, and changed the papal election procedures by restricting voting to Cardinals younger than eighty. He died in 1978.

The challenge that this sort of development presents to prosperous Christians is that proper personal development must entail a deep willingness to share one's resources not simply with those many in the world who need help in emergencies, but even more often, to fund the long-term development of essential systems for education and healthcare, for sewers, water, roads, and electricity around the globe. These are the social conditions—the enablements—within which the poor would have a chance to move themselves out of dire poverty and into a dignified life capable of supporting themselves and their families.

Potential solutions

We are all equally responsible for the undernourished peoples.

Pope John XXIII, *Mater et magistra* 158

We must repeat that the superfluous goods of wealthier nations ought to be placed at the disposal of poorer nations. The rule, by virtue of which in times past those nearest us were to be helped in time of need, applies today to all the needy throughout the world. And the prospering peoples will be the first to benefit from this.

Of itself, however, emergency aid will not go far in relieving want and famine when these are caused—as they so often are—by the primitive state of a nation's economy. The only permanent remedy for this is to make use of every possible means of providing these citizens with the scientific, technical and professional training they need, and to put at their disposal the necessary capital for speeding up their economic development with the help of modern methods.

Everything must be done to ensure that citizens of the less developed areas are treated as responsible human beings, and are allowed to play the major role in achieving their own economic, social and cultural advancement.

Pope John XXIII, *Mater et magistra* 163 & 151

While Popes John and Paul do not intend to construct a blueprint for what persons and nations should do in assisting economic development, they nonetheless outline the general framework that is necessary. They remind us that in a globalized world the traditional Christian principles commanding us to help needy neighbors must now be widened to include all people and all peoples of the earth. The best insights of science and technology need to be applied to solve the urgent problems of the poor of the world, and those very people must be engaged in the transformative process as active agents and not simply as passive recipients. The goal is that all able-bodied persons have the skills and opportunities to provide for self and family through gainful employment. Handouts are only a short-term solution.

JUSTICE

Commutative justice

In the meantime, justice must prevail in dealings between superiors and their subordinates. Legitimate contracts should govern these employment relations, spelling out the duties involved. And no one, whatever his status may be, should be unjustly subjected to the arbitrary whim of another.

Pope Paul VI, *Populorum progressio* 70

Social justice

Men, both as individuals and as intermediate groups, are required to make their own specific contributions to the general welfare.

Pope Paul VI, *Populorum progressio* 53

Every man has the duty of working faithfully and also the right to work. It is the duty of society, moreover, according to the circumstances prevailing in it, and in keeping with its role, to help the citizens to find sufficient employment.

Vatican II, *Gaudium et spes* 67

Distributive justice

Increase in production and productive efficiency is, of course, sound policy, and indeed a vital necessity. However, it is no less necessary—and justice itself demands—that the riches produced be distributed fairly among all members of the political community.

Pope John XXIII, *Mater et magistra* 168

In identifying the moral principles that pertain to economic life, the popes and the Christian tradition before them identified distinct aspects or dimensions of justice that must be attended to. The influential German scholar Josef Pieper summarized the elements of this tradition in identifying three essential dimensions to the Catholic view of justice.[2]

Commutative justice is that form of justice that should exist between two individuals. This is the kind of justice that most citizens of Western culture today recognize immediately. It is one-to-one justice. It is the justice of contracts and economic exchange. If I sign a contract, I should fulfill its terms. If I borrow something from you, I should return it. If I steal something from you, I have an obligation to make reparation.

Social justice, sometimes called "general justice," is part of the moral glue that holds societies together. In 1937 Pope Pius XI defined social justice: "It is of the very essence of social justice to demand for each individual all that is necessary for the common good. But . . . it is impossible . . . unless . . . each individual man in the dignity of his human personality is supplied with all that is necessary for the exercise of his social functions."[3] Each individual has a personal obligation to contribute to the general welfare, most typically through a person's gainful employment, but in less formal ways as well. At the same time, social justice requires that society *make possible* the contributions that individuals have an obligation to provide.[4]

Because daily employment is the most frequent way that people contribute to the good of others, society has an obligation to structure its economy in a way that will generate employment for all able to work. As we have seen, the Christian tradition has long taught that God gave the earth to humanity in order that the needs of all be met. Since the Industrial Revolution, the ordinary way for the vast majority of people to have access to the goods of the earth is spending wages earned in gainful employment. Thus the popes teach that employment is a right, founded in this ancient moral tradition, now interpreted in a new era. So a sufficient number of jobs are required if any economic system is to be judged to be just. But society must also cultivate other paths for the contributions of all, for example, through a vibrant civil society and democratic governments that listen and respond to their citizens.

Distributive justice is that dimension of justice that structures the relationship of the community to the individual. Here lies the ancient moral mandate of meeting the needs of those who cannot meet their own. In an earlier, nondemocratic age, distributive justice was understood simply as a virtue of the king or emperor. However, in a democracy every citizen is responsible for how the government and society are structured, and thus every citizen today has a role to play in ensuring that their community attends to this fundamental moral demand: that the needs of all be met.

RIGHTS AND DUTIES

Rights

We must speak of man's rights. Man has the right to live. He has the right to bodily integrity and to the means necessary for the proper development of life, particularly food, clothing, shelter, medical care, rest, and, finally, the necessary social services. In consequence, he has the right to be looked after in the event of ill health, disability stemming from his work, widowhood, old age, enforced unemployment, or whenever through no fault of his own he is deprived of the means of livelihood. . . .

Moreover, man has a natural right to be respected. He has a right to his good name. He has a right to freedom in investigating the truth, and—within the limits of the moral order and the common good—to freedom of speech and publication, and to freedom to pursue whatever profession he may choose. . . .

He has the natural right to share in the benefits of culture, and hence to receive a good general education, and a technical or professional training consistent with the degree of educational development in his own country.

Human beings have also the right to choose for themselves the kind of life which appeals to them: whether it is to found a family—in the founding of which both the man and the woman enjoy equal rights and duties—or to embrace the priesthood or the religious life.

In the economic sphere, it is evident that a man has the inherent right not only to be given the opportunity to work, but also to be allowed the exercise of personal initiative in the work he does.

The conditions in which a man works form a necessary corollary to these rights. They must not be such as to weaken his physical or moral fiber, or militate against the proper development of adolescents to manhood. Women must be accorded such conditions of work as are consistent with their needs and responsibilities as wives and mothers.

A further consequence of man's personal dignity is his right to engage in economic activities suited to his degree of responsibility. The worker is likewise entitled to a wage that is determined in accordance with the precepts of justice. This needs stressing. The amount a worker receives must be sufficient, in proportion to available funds, to allow him and his family a standard of living consistent with human dignity.

As a further consequence of man's nature, he has the right to the private ownership of property, including that of productive goods.

> As a human person he is entitled to the legal protection of his rights, and such protection must be effective, unbiased, and strictly just.
>
> Pope John XXIII, *Pacem in terris* 11–27

A right is a claim that one person has that other persons are under a moral obligation to respect. As we saw in Chapter 11, the dominance of the language of universal human rights is a modern development. This language about rights possessed by all humans does not appear in the Scriptures or the early church or in Aquinas's medieval reflections on justice. In its resistance to liberal individualism in the eighteenth and nineteenth centuries, the Roman Catholic Church had condemned the idea of human rights. Thus as Drew Christiansen, S.J., puts it, the emphasis on rights in *Pacem in terris* "constitutes a rapprochement with the Enlightenment and political liberalism."[5] The notion of human rights, then, stands as a helpful example of the development of moral doctrine, not only within the Christian tradition but the secular world as well. The rights enumerated here in Pope John's famous encyclical *Pacem in terris* identified various claims of every human being. A concern for these fundamental needs of all persons is quite vividly apparent in earlier centuries, but the stress at that time was on the obligations of the prosperous or the king to ensure that these needs would be met. With the development of a more democratic point of view within Western political philosophy, the language of rights arose to name the claim that the needy had to receive such help.

Not all interpretations of human rights are created equal. Many in the secular world today simply assert that humans have rights, without any real explanation as to why. The continuity of the Christian tradition in this regard is apparent: for Christians, humans have such rights precisely because of their human dignity rooted in their creation "in the image and likeness of God," as the first creation story in Genesis indicates. In this way, the natural law tradition of Aquinas is broadened to include "natural rights."

Duties

The natural rights of which we have so far been speaking are inextricably bound up with as many duties, all applying to one and the same person. These rights and duties derive their origin, their sustenance, and their indestructibility from the natural law, which in conferring the one imposes the other.

> Thus, for example, the right to live involves the duty to preserve one's life; the right to a decent standard of living, the duty to live in a becoming fashion; the right to be free to seek out the truth, the duty to devote oneself to an ever deeper and wider search for truth.
>
> The right to own private property entails a social obligation as well.
>
> It is useless to admit that a man has a right to the necessities of life, unless we also do all in our power to supply him with means sufficient for his livelihood.
>
> Pope John XXIII, *Pacem in terris* 28, 29, 22, & 32

Universal human rights arise from the dignity of each human person, rooted in creation in the image of God and in God's intention for the interaction of human persons. Because of these roots, every right entails duties borne by the person holding that right. Many of these duties refer to one's personal life, as when the heads of the family have an obligation to support and educate their children. Yet public duties exist as well, including the duty to share one's surplus in service to others. As Michael and Kenneth Himes have put it, "Human rights in Catholic teaching are moral claims which ought to have legal standing because they are claims to goods which are necessary for the person to participate with dignity in the communal life of a society."[6]

THE JUST WAGE

> The remuneration of work is not something that can be left to the laws of the marketplace; nor should it be a decision left to the will of the more powerful. It must be determined in accordance with justice and equity; which means that workers must be paid a wage which allows them to live a truly human life and to fulfill their family obligations in a worthy manner.
>
> Other factors too enter into the assessment of a just wage: namely, the effective contribution which each individual makes to the economic effort, the financial state of the company for which he works, the requirements of the general good of the particular country—having regard especially to the repercussions on the overall employment of the working force in the country as a whole—and finally the requirements of the common good of the universal family of nations of every kind, both large and small.
>
> Pope John XXIII, *Mater et magistra* 71

> Finally, remuneration for labor is to be such that man may be furnished the means to cultivate worthily his own material, social, cultural, and spiritual life and that of his dependents.
>
> Vatican II, *Gaudium et spes* 67

The popes of the mid-twentieth century did not shrink from maintaining the traditional teaching of Leo and Pius concerning the just wage. Once again, mere market consent does not guarantee the justice of a wage, which must be sufficient for a family to live its life "in a worthy manner." That worthiness entails not just material survival but also a cultural and spiritual thriving, which requires both personal and material resources. At the same time, the popes recognize that broader reforms in the nation are necessary, since some firms may be unable to provide a just wage without facing financial ruin in a competitive economy.

Property

> **The rights and duties of property owners**
>
> The right of private ownership of goods, including productive goods, has permanent validity. It is part of the natural order, which teaches that the individual is prior to society and society must be ordered to the good of the individual.
>
> Concerning the use of material goods, Our Predecessor [Pope Pius XII] declared that the right of every man to use these for his own sustenance is prior to every other economic right, even that of private property. The right to the private possession of material goods is admittedly a natural one; nevertheless, in the objective order established by God, the right to property cannot stand in the way of the axiomatic principle that the goods which were created by God for all men should flow to all alike, according to the principles of justice and charity.
>
> Pope John XXIII, *Mater et magistra* 109 & 43
>
> As St. Ambrose put it: "You are not making a gift of what is yours to the poor man, but you are giving him back what is his. You have been appropriating things that are meant to be for the common use of everyone. The earth belongs to everyone, not to the rich." These words indicate that the right to private property is not absolute and unconditional.
>
> Pope Paul VI, *Populorum progressio* 23

> But it is not enough to assert that the right to own private property and the means of production is inherent in human nature. We must also insist on the extension of this right in practice to all classes of citizens.
>
> Pope John XXIII, *Mater et magistra* 113

In *Mater et magistra*, Pope John distanced himself from the overly strong endorsements of private property by Popes Leo and Pius. In the words of Marvin Mich, he thereby "recovered the Thomistic tradition and carried it forward."[7] There is indeed a right of the owners of goods and it would be a violation of commutative justice for others to steal from them. However, such ownership bears the duty in justice to use one's surplus to come to the aid of others. Relying on the same history we have reviewed in this volume, Pope Paul quotes Ambrose of Milan: when we give to the poor we are actually giving them what they deserve in justice and not giving simply out of our charity.

Pope John proposes a new twist on these traditional discussions about the rights *of* the owners of property. He proposes that all classes of people should possess not just an abstract right of ownership *if* they own property. He says more and more people *should own* property, perhaps suggesting a right *to* own property.

THE ECONOMY AND THE STATE

> *The importance of individual initiative*
>
> It should be stated at the outset that in the economic order first place must be given to the personal initiative of private citizens working either as individuals or in association with each other in various ways for the furtherance of common interests.
>
> But however extensive and far-reaching the influence of the State on the economy may be, it must never be exerted to the extent of depriving the individual citizen of his freedom of action. It must rather augment his freedom while effectively guaranteeing the protection of his essential personal rights. Among these is a man's right and duty to be primarily responsible for his own upkeep and that of his family. Hence every economic system must permit and facilitate the free development of productive activity.
>
> Pope John XXIII, *Mater et magistra* 51 & 55

When discussing the economy, the church's teaching is clear in endorsing the importance of the individual initiative of private citizens; there is no call here for central planning or a communist state. The Christian view of the person envisions a society of strong individuals—active persons who take initiative and responsibility for their own lives. This speaks strongly in favor of markets and independent businesses.

The dangers of free markets

Certain concepts have somehow arisen out of these new conditions and insinuated themselves into the fabric of human society. These concepts present profit as the chief spur to economic progress, free competition as the guiding norm of economics, and private ownership of the means of production as an absolute right, having no limits or concomitant social obligations.

The economy is supposed to be in the service of man. But if it is true that a type of capitalism has given rise to hardships, unjust practices, and fratricidal conflicts that persist to this day, it would be a mistake to attribute these evils to the rise of industrialization itself, for they really derive from the pernicious economic concepts that grew up along with it.

The teaching set forth by our predecessor Leo XIII in *Rerum novarum* is still valid today: when two parties are in very unequal positions, their mutual consent alone does not guarantee a fair contract; the rule of free consent remains subservient to the demands of the natural law. In *Rerum novarum* this principle was set down with regard to a just wage for the individual worker, but it should be applied with equal force to contracts made between nations: trade relations can no longer be based solely on the principle of free, unchecked competition, for it very often creates an economic dictatorship. Free trade can be called just only when it conforms to the demands of social justice.

Pope Paul VI, *Populorum progressio* 26 & 59

In addition to endorsing the importance of individual initiative, the popes are quite clear in pointing out the shortcomings of inadequately structured markets, in particular the damage they cause to many people who lack sufficient assets, whether financial, physical, or psychological. In recognition of the wider, now global, concern of the modern world, Pope Paul argues that the standards for individual economic justice (for example that market consent does not guarantee justice) now apply in the relations between entire nations engaging in international trade. He challenges the nations of the industrialized world to restructure trade in a way that does not simply rely on market negotiations but is designed to give definite advantages to the poor nations of the world. There have been few success stories to report, but one of them is the decision by the World Trade Organization (WTO) to loosen pharmaceutical patents to allow for the cheaper production of AIDS drugs in developing nations.[8]

Technology

Certainly, the Church teaches . . . that scientific and technical progress and the resultant material well-being are good things and mark an important phase in human civilization. But the Church teaches, too, that goods of this kind must be valued according to their true nature: as instruments used by man for the better attainment of his end.

Similarly, Our Predecessor, Pius XII, rightly asserted that our age is marked by a clear contrast between the immense scientific and technical progress and the fearful human decline shown by "its monstrous masterpiece . . . transforming man into a giant of the physical world at the expense of his spirit, which is reduced to that of a pygmy in the supernatural and eternal world."

Pope John XXIII, *Mater et magistra* 246 & 243

As with so many other means that humans have to improve life, technology is understood by the church as both a true asset and a real danger. The advances of science and technology can make life better for many in the world whose lives are currently mired in poverty and neglect. At the same time, it is also quite possible for a kind of "spirit of technology" to take over human consciousness and make spiritual awareness far more difficult. As always, Catholic social thought insists on a balanced approach.

The state and the economy

Nevertheless, considerations of justice and equity can at times demand that those in power pay more attention to the weaker members of society, since these are at a disadvantage when it comes to defending their own rights and asserting their legitimate interests.

The government is also required to show no less energy and efficiency in the matter of providing opportunities for suitable employment, graded to the capacity of the workers. It must make sure that working men are paid

> a just and equitable wage, and are allowed a sense of responsibility in the industrial concerns for which they work.
>
> Pope John XXIII, *Pacem in terris* 56 & 64

Because the government has the obligation to attend to the common good, the modern popes have always insisted that the state play an active role in guaranteeing justice, including a just wage, and in structuring the economy properly.

THE COMMON GOOD

> We must add, therefore, that it is in the nature of the common good that every single citizen has the right to share in it—although in different ways, depending on his tasks, merits and circumstances.
>
> Pope John XXIII, *Pacem in terris* 56
>
> Every day human interdependence grows more tightly drawn and spreads by degrees over the whole world. As a result the common good, that is, the sum of those conditions of social life which allow social groups and their individual members relatively thorough and ready access to their own fulfillment, today takes on an increasingly universal complexion and consequently involves rights and duties with respect to the whole human race. Every social group must take account of the needs and legitimate aspirations of other groups, and even of the general welfare of the entire human family.
>
> Vatican II, *Gaudium et spes* 26
>
> We consider it altogether vital that the numerous intermediary bodies and corporate enterprises—which are, so to say, the main vehicle of this social growth—be really autonomous, and loyally collaborate in pursuit of their own specific interests and those of the common good.
>
> Pope John XXIII, *Mater et magistra* 65

One of the most fundamental of the concepts employed in Catholic social thought is the notion of the common good. The idea behind the common good comes from much earlier in the tradition,[9] but the popes here make clear that the common good simultaneously entails the good of each individual citizen as well as the good of the community, something that individual citizens contribute to. Virgil Michel, O.S.B., has helpfully described this notion of the common good as entailing two separate dimensions. The first he calls "the common conditions of social life." The second is "the attainment of the good life by all, at least to a minimum degree."[10]

The common conditions of social life are those parts of life that we all depend upon but that no one of us can provide by ourselves: "all the prerequisite conditions and established arrangements of a public or general social nature that are needed before individuals can attain their natural end here on earth."[11] Included here are peace and order in society, social organization, freedom, and opportunities for work, education, and self-development. The second dimension of the common good entails each person's attainment of a good life, at least minimally, in accord with the ancient requirement that the needs of all be met.

Yet while every person has an obligation to contribute to the building up of these common conditions of life—frequently through civil society organizations they belong to—the goal of the common conditions is that every individual thrive in his or her journey through life.

Conclusion

Popes John XXIII and Paul VI understood a life of faith as integrated—from personal prayer to public worship in the liturgy, from mutual support with the church community to public service to the poor, to a transformation of sinful social structures. In this they see the church's social teaching as addressing the concrete problems of each era in history. Basic principles, as Thomas Aquinas had earlier said, have validity across time and space. But the diversity of situations that occur in different nations and at different times in human history require that those principles be applied with prudence, discerning what is possible in the current situation, what should be affirmed and when, and what should be condemned, inviting Christians to act on these prudential judgments in both the public and private sectors.

This concreteness of religious thought that has developed over many centuries can be frustrating for those who look for a single answer to provide to every time and place, but it is the only adequate way to proceed. The past two chapters have examined Catholic thought on economic life, but we now turn to contemporary Protestant thought in striving to address the question undergirding this volume: What does the history of Christian teaching on economic life mean for us today?

Notes

1. John Sniegocki provides a more critical analysis of the position of the twentieth-century popes, calling Pope John XXIII an overly optimistic "modernization" theorist. See John Sniegocki, *Catholic Social Teaching and Economic Globalization: The Quest for Alternatives* (Milwaukee: Marquette University Press, 2009), 114–21.

2. Josef Pieper, *Justice* (London: Faber & Faber, 1957).

3. Pope Pius XI, *Divini redemptoris*, 51.

4. Charles Curran has sorted through debates about the meaning of "social justice" in the work of Pope Pius XI and afterwards. See Charles Curran, *Catholic Social Teaching, 1891–Present: A Historical, Theological, and Ethical Analysis* (Washington, DC: Georgetown University Press, 2002), 188–98.

5. Drew Christiansen, S.J., "Commentary on *Pacem in terris*," in *Modern Catholic Social Teaching*, ed. Kenneth R. Himes (Washington, DC: Georgetown University Press, 2005), 226.

6. Michael J. Himes and Kenneth R. Himes, *Fullness of Faith: The Public Significance of Theology* (New York: Paulist, 1993), 46.

7. Marvin Mich, "Commentary on *Mater et magistra*," in *Modern Catholic Social Teaching*, ed. Kenneth R. Himes, 200.

8. For a description of the decision and its particular effects in India, see www.medico.de/media/indische-generika-und-aids.pdf. Accessed January 31, 2012.

9. For a careful description of the Catholic notion of the common good—and its classical sources in ancient Greek thought—see David Hollenbach, *The Common Good and Christian Ethics* (New York: Cambridge University Press, 2002).

10. Virgil Michel, O.S.B., *Christian Social Reconstruction* (Milwaukee: Bruce, 1937), 126–32.

11. Ibid.

16

Contemporary Protestant Thought on Economic Life

The Protestant Reformation, as we saw in Chapter 10, was a challenge to Roman Catholicism on a wide range of fundamental issues, from sin and redemption to the character of the Christian church. Yet in spite of these differences, we also saw a remarkable similarity in the understanding of economic life in Protestant and Catholic traditions. Today that similarity endures: the Protestant and Catholic churches of our day continue to base their view of the economy on the fundamental commitments of the gospel. Thus it will be helpful to treat in this chapter contemporary Protestant views of economic life, prior to returning in the next chapter to the most recent of papal statements on these matters.

In 2004, the World Alliance of Reformed Churches met in Accra, the capital of Ghana and formerly a main shipping point for the Atlantic slave trade. The delegates—from 250 churches in 110 nations, including the Presbyterian Church and the United Church of Christ in the U.S.—visited two "slave castles" on the coast. There they reflected on the dominant role in the slave trade that was played by Dutch Reformed Christian merchants, soldiers, and political leaders who lived and worshiped God in the castles' quarters, just one floor above the dungeons where captured people were kept in waiting for the arrival of ships destined to take them to America. Over three centuries, more than fifteen million horrified Africans were taken from their homes, sold to traders, transported, and sold again in the Atlantic slave trade—and more than a million others died in this brutal process.

The delegates reported their angry bewilderment that committed Christians, their own spiritual ancestors, could lead so bifurcated a life: worshiping a loving God, being themselves committed to love of neighbor, but simultaneously condemning other humans to a life of pain and degradation in slavery. They asked, "How could these forbears of Reformed faith deny so blatantly what they believed so clearly?"

But after some time of "tears, silence, anger, and lamentation," the delegates came to ask that same question about themselves, so many of whom were comfortable citizens of prosperous nations in a world where hundreds of millions live without the most basic necessities of life. As they put it, "today's world is divided between those who worship in comfortable contentment and those enslaved by the world's economic injustice and ecological destruction who still suffer and die."[1]

Like Catholics, Protestant Christians have searched for the implications of Christian economic views as they pertain to life in an industrialized world. And they bring to this task a strong awareness of the power of sin in the lives of ordinary believers. Unlike Catholics, however, Protestant denominations lack the clear lines of denominational teaching authority and central authoritative figures represented by the bishops and pope in the Roman Catholic tradition. Of course, this looser understanding of teaching authority in Protestantism is no accident. It is rooted in the Reformation's view of church that rejects a central ecclesiastical office with as much power and authority as the pope possesses for Roman Catholics. As a result, it is not as easy to summarize Protestant thought on economic life.[2] In this chapter, we will focus on official texts of both mainstream Protestant denominations (Episcopalian, Lutheran, Methodist, Presbyterian, and United Church of Christ) and the National Evangelical Alliance (representing forty denominations and thousands of individual churches).

Two cautions are in order. The first is that no individual denominational statement would likely be endorsed in its entirety by all Protestants denominations. Still, many of the texts quoted in this chapter give an indication of what we might call a general consensus among Protestant churches about economic life. Some statements quoted here, however, indicate a diversity of perspective on a few issues.

The second is that, just as the official Catholic teaching of the popes is only a part of overall Catholic thought on economic ethics, denominational statements are far from the total of Protestant thought on economic life. In both traditions, many scholars write faithfully and creatively on Christian economic ethics independent of their church's leadership.[3] Of course, most of those Protestant scholars have been called upon for service in drafting the statements of their own denomination. This is a much wider and more public process than the consultations that occur prior to the publication of most papal statements, another result of the differences in ecclesiology in these two great streams of Christianity.

Faith engenders public action

The Church, the baptized people of God, is created by the Holy Spirit through the Gospel to proclaim and to follow God's crucified Messiah. . . . The Gospel liberates from sin, death, and evil and motivates the church to care for neighbor and the earth. . . . Faith is active in love; love calls for justice in the relationships and structures of society. It is in grateful response to God's grace in Jesus Christ that this church carries out its responsibility for the well-being of society and the environment.

Evangelical Lutheran Church in America, "The Church in Society"[4]

We also engage in public life because Jesus is Lord over every area of life. Through him all things were created (Col. 1:16-17), and by him all things will be brought to fullness (Rom. 8:19-21). To restrict our stewardship to the private sphere would be to deny an important part of his dominion and to functionally abandon it to the Evil One. To restrict our political concerns to matters that touch only on the private and the domestic spheres is to deny the all-encompassing Lordship of Jesus (Rev. 19:16).

National Association of Evangelicals, "For the Health of the Nation"[5]

Born out of protest, Protestant Christianity understands the importance of resisting evil and critiquing all areas of human life with the biblical witness. The many short- and long-term policy questions affecting economic life should be seen both in their immediate context and from the perspective of our relation to God and the ultimate nature of reality. As Philip Wogaman put it, "theological reflection on the meaning of Christ has given birth to insights which are profoundly relevant to the important economic problems of the age."[6]

THEOLOGICAL FOUNDATIONS

The reality of sin

As a church we confess that we are in bondage to sin and submit too readily to the idols and injustices of economic life. We often rely on wealth and material goods more than God and close ourselves off from the needs of others.

Evangelical Lutheran Church in America, "Economic Life"[7]

> Secure in God's love, we affirm the goodness of life and confess our many sins against God's will for us as we find it in Jesus Christ. We have not always been faithful stewards of all that has been committed to us by God the Creator. We have been reluctant followers of Jesus Christ in his mission to bring all persons into a community of love.
>
> United Methodist Church, "Social Principles"[8]

Fundamental to any Christian understanding of economic life in every age is an awareness of the reality of sin and its consequences in our lives, both personal and institutional.

> *Already but not yet*
> Through faith in the Gospel, the Church already takes part in the reign of God announced by and embodied in Jesus. Yet, it still awaits the resurrection of the dead and the fulfillment of the whole creation in God's promised future. In this time of "now . . . not yet," the Church lives in two ages—the present age and the age to come. The Church is "in" the world but not "from" the world.
>
> Evangelical Lutheran Church in America, "The Church in Society"

Aware, then, of the power of both sin and redemption in Christ, Christians experience a new reality often described as "already, but not yet." That is, Jesus promises that the reign of God is already breaking into the world and at the same time is not yet come to fulfillment, an impossibility given the reality of sinfulness in this world. As we saw in Chapter 4, the New Testament community understood this sense of living in two ages simultaneously. Many today have lost that awareness.

> *Scripture*
> Scripture is the normative source in this church's deliberation. Through the study of Scripture, Christians seek to know what God requires in the church and the world. Because of the diversity in Scripture, and because of the contemporary world's distance from the biblical world, it is necessary to scrutinize the texts carefully in their own setting and to interpret them faithfully in the context of today.
>
> Evangelical Lutheran Church in America, "The Church in Society"

Following in the footsteps of Martin Luther himself, Protestants begin with the Scriptures as providing the norm for our life and thought. Scripture plays an essential role in Catholic thought as well, but is not as central there simply because of a greater reliance both on the interpretation of biblical texts in later Christian history and on a virtue ethics arising out of the natural law.

Love and justice

The incarnation confers dignity not only on humanity but on everything with which humanity is united in biophysical interdependence. The incarnation opens the eye of faith to a new vision of the whole. . . .

Justice in the prophetic tradition is a spiritual discipline, an act of worship, without which the value of other spiritual disciplines—prayer, fasting, sacrifice—are negated (Isa. 58:1-10; Amos 5:21-24; Hos. 6:6).

Presbyterian Church USA, "Hope for a Global Future"[9]

God identifies with the poor (Ps. 146:5-9), and says that those who "are kind to the poor lend to the Lord" (Prov. 19:17), while those who oppress the poor "show contempt for their Maker" (Prov. 14:31). Jesus said that those who do not care for the needy and the imprisoned will depart eternally from the living God (Matt. 25:31-46). The vulnerable may include not only the poor, but women, children, the aged, persons with disabilities, immigrants, refugees, minorities, the persecuted, and prisoners. God measures societies by how they treat the people at the bottom.

National Association of Evangelicals, "For the Health of the Nation"

Moreover, in the church's experience of the Spirit, the world is filled with the glory of God (Isa. 6:3; Ps. 19:1; Eph. 4:6). God is not only beyond but in the creation as the vivifying, reconciling, liberating, and sanctifying presence of the Spirit. Indeed, God is intimate with the creation, experiencing the joys and agonies of all creatures (Rom. 8:19-25). The whole creation is thereby endowed with value and dignity by association with the sacred. It is to be valued as it is valued by God, who chose to be present within it.

Presbyterian Church USA, "Hope for a Global Future"

Central to the Christian vision are love and justice. Jesus calls us, his disciples, to love God and love our neighbor as ourselves. And central to that love of neighbor is attention to the injustices caused both by concrete decisions of sinful people and the unintended effects of social and economic structures. This awareness of the relation of love and justice allows Christians to draw implications for both face-to-face relationships and for the institutions within which we live out our daily lives.

Prophetic confrontation

As a prophetic presence, this church has the obligation to name and denounce the idols before which people bow, to identify the power of sin present in social structures, and to advocate in hope with poor and powerless people. When religious or secular structures, ideologies, or authorities claim to be absolute, this church says, "We must obey God rather than any human authority" (Acts 5:29). With Martin Luther, this church understands that "to rebuke" those in authority "through God's Word spoken publicly, boldly and honestly" is "not seditious" but "a praiseworthy, noble, and . . . particularly great service to God."

Evangelical Lutheran Church in America, "The Church in Society"

Because the Protestant tradition arose out of a protest against the abuse of the Christian tradition by the Church of Rome, Protestants have a special appreciation for a righteous prophecy modeled on the experience of the Hebrew prophets. Implicit here is a deep understanding that social structures, whether of the secular world or religious authorities, are subject to sin at times arising out of arrogance of those in authority and at times simply the unintended consequence of human interaction. Thus it is essential that Christians have the courage to speak up in the name of God as did Amos and Isaiah in the Hebrew Scriptures. Today, this instinct is called forth by multiple forms of injustice in economic and political life.

SOCIAL STRUCTURES AND INDIVIDUALS

Faith commitments employ science

Evangelical Christians seek in every area of life to submit to the authority of Scripture (2 Tim. 3:16-17; Rom. 15:4; 1 Cor. 10:11). Nevertheless, many contemporary political decisions—whether about environmental science, HIV/AIDS, or international trade—deal with complex sociological or technological issues not discussed explicitly in the Bible. As Christians engaged in public policy, we must do detailed social, economic, historical, jurisprudential, and political analysis if we are to understand our society and wisely apply our normative vision to political questions. Only if we deepen our Christian vision and also study our contemporary world can we engage in politics faithfully and wisely.

National Association of Evangelicals, "For the Health of the Nation"

For all the importance of theological reflection and prophetic denunciation of evil, Protestant thought also understands the importance of intellectual analysis and the use of good natural and social science in understanding the complex issues facing Christians today. While Protestantism has historically been critical of Catholicism's great confidence in reason, beginning with a critique of the philosophical dependence of Catholic thought on Aristotelian philosophy in the work of Thomas Aquinas, Protestants are neither anti-intellectual nor inexperienced in integrating the best of contemporary secular science with theological reflection.

Persons and systems

From the Bible, experience, and social analysis, we learn that social problems arise and can be substantially corrected by both personal decisions and structural changes. On the one hand, personal sinful choices contribute significantly to destructive social problems (Prov. 6:9-11), and personal conversion through faith in Christ can transform broken persons into wholesome, productive citizens. On the other hand, unjust systems also help create social problems (Amos 5:10-15; Isa. 10:1-2) and wise structural change (for example, legislation to strengthen marriage or increase economic opportunity for all) can improve society. . . . Lasting social change requires both personal conversion and institutional renewal and reform.

National Association of Evangelicals, "For the Health of the Nation"

After engaging issues of economic and social reform in the nineteenth century,[10] most evangelical churches during the twentieth century resisted paying attention to public institutions out of a concern that it would align them with the Social Gospel movement of liberal Protestantism and would undermine the ultimately important focus on a personal relationship with God. However, the National Evangelical Alliance has made clear that there has been an important turn toward institutional life among these Christian churches. The most public demonstration of this shift was seen in the role of the "Moral Majority" and other conservative Christian groups in American politics that tend to limit political concern to what the media call "social" issues. Nonetheless, the National Association of Evangelicals, the most important group of evangelical churches in the U.S., has extended these institutional concerns beyond family and sexual morality to poverty, unemployment, and "creation care."

ECONOMIC LIFE

Property ownership

Human need and the right to ownership often are in tension with each other. The biblical understanding of stewardship is that what we have does not ultimately belong to us. We are called to be stewards of what God has given for the sake of all. This stewardship includes holding economic, political, and social processes and institutions responsible for producing and distributing what is needed for sufficiency for all. Private property is affirmed insofar as it serves as a useful, yet imperfect means to meet the basic needs of individuals, households, and communities.

Evangelical Lutheran Church in America, "Economic Life"

It comes as no surprise, then, that contemporary Protestant churches would remain faithful to the teachings of Martin Luther and Augustine of Hippo on property ownership that we reviewed in Chapters 10 and 5. Christians are called to be stewards of the possessions they own. The institutions of private property, while affirmed, are "imperfect means" to meet the needs of all and thus stand under the judgment of God, who intends that none of his children live without the fundamental necessities of life. Articulating a goal quite similar to that of the popes in the previous chapter, Rebecca Todd Peters calls for "the creation of an economic system that self-consciously acknowledges its moral framework."[11]

Scarcity and abundance

God provides abundantly for the needs of the world. When we view life with this understanding, we live out of a theology of abundance. When we do not, we live out a theology of scarcity, and we hoard and care for our own needs at the exclusion of others' needs, in fear that we will not have enough in the future. Jesus teaches us the shortcomings of such an attitude (Lk 12:22-34).

United Church of Christ, "Faithful Response"[12]

> Because humans are reconciled through Christ, "enslaving poverty" is "an intolerable violation of God's good creation. . . . The church cannot condone poverty, whether it is the product of unjust social structures, exploitation of the defenseless, lack of natural resources, absence of technological understanding, or rapid expansion of populations."
>
> Presbyterian Church USA, "Hope for a Global Future" (quoting from the United Presbyterian Church's *Mission Responsibility through Investment Manual*, New York, May 1979)
>
> Restoring people to wholeness means that governmental social welfare must aim to provide opportunity and restore people to self-sufficiency. While basic standards of support must be put in place to provide for those who cannot care for their families and themselves, incentives and training in marketable skills must be part of any well-rounded program.
>
> National Association of Evangelicals, "For the Health of the Nation"

God's plan as revealed in the Scriptures is that the needs of all be met, whether they are currently unmet through physical disability, or age, or an inability to find a job in spite of efforts to do so. The concern here is not simply physiological or psychological but spiritual as well. As Philip Wogaman has put it, "Profound physical insecurity can undermine the overall sense of security on which our receptivity to God's grace often practically depends."[13]

Just as in the Hebrew Scriptures, the economic goal is not simply that people have enough food to live on today, but that they be restored to self-sufficiency. God's aim for economic life is a world where persons are able to support themselves and their families. Thus "welfare" programs for the poor need to be constructed so as not to create a dependency among the able-bodied but must be generous in assisting them to return to self-sufficiency. Many people, of course, will never be able to achieve self-sufficiency due to age or disability, and they deserve support in accord with both the teaching of Jesus and the tradition inherited from ancient Israel.

> *Inequality*
>
> Though the Bible does not call for economic equality, it condemns gross disparities in opportunity and outcome that cause suffering and perpetuate poverty, and it calls us to work toward equality of opportunity. God wants every person and family to have access to productive resources

> so that if they act responsibly they can care for their economic needs and be
> dignified members of their community.
>
> National Association of Evangelicals, "For the Health of the Nation"

As we have seen in earlier chapters, the premodern Christian world did not speak of economic inequality but rather focused on the meeting of needs of all. Issues of economic inequality are a modern concern. Nonetheless, Christians recognize that great disparities between people of different social status can be quite debilitating, not only with poverty leaving people unable to care for themselves but with gross inequality undermining the self-respect needed for participation in the broader community.

> *Participation*
>
> Economic justice includes both the mitigation of suffering and also the restoration of wholeness. Wholeness includes full participation in the life of the community. Health care, nutrition, and education are important ingredients in helping people transcend the stigma and agony of poverty and re-enter community.
>
> National Association of Evangelicals, "For the Health of the Nation"

As we have seen, the premodern world did not speak much about the participation of individuals in the life of the community. This concern has arisen with the rise of democracy in the West. Nonetheless, Protestant thought has come to recognize that an essential part of a life of meaning and well-being today requires that the individual have the opportunity to participate in social, political, and economic life. Thus participation is a basic need today and this has implications both for political life—for example, resisting policies that reduce voting by low-income groups—as well as in economic life—supporting policies that encourage job and business creation.

MARKETS

> We claim all economic systems to be under the judgment of God no less than other facets of the created order. Therefore, we recognize the responsibility of governments to develop and implement sound fiscal and monetary policies that provide for the economic life of individuals and

corporate entities and that ensure full employment and adequate incomes with a minimum of inflation. We believe private and public economic enterprises are responsible for the social costs of doing business, such as employment and environmental pollution, and that they should be held accountable for these costs. We support measures that would reduce the concentration of wealth in the hands of a few. We further support efforts to revise tax structures and to eliminate governmental support programs that now benefit the wealthy at the expense of other persons.

United Methodist Church, "Social Principles"

In countries in the global south or north, many people feel and actually are less in control of their economic destiny. Workers employed by multinational companies may experience this loss more than others. Nation-states have also ceded power. Especially in the global south, governments have less control over their own economic policy and may feel compelled to do what international institutions and multinational corporations dictate. As the nation-state loses power, the citizens of democratic nations also lose some of their capacity to direct their nation and their lives.

United Church of Christ, "Faithful Response"

Contemporary Protestant thought on economic life recognizes the productivity of market relationships, both for the capacity to create new investments and to provide employment.[14] As Rebecca Blank has put it, "there is no viable alternative to the market as an organizing principle for an economic system in a complex society."[15] There is no simplistic condemnation of competitiveness, but awareness that an excess of competitiveness can erode human relationships and undermine a life of faith. John Raines has described this problem as "the moral separation between capital and community," as a way of criticizing the choices of firms that take little or no notice of the problems left behind when production shuts down in an industrialized nation and moves halfway around the globe.[16]

Most fundamental here is the conviction that economic systems are like all human creations, subject to the judgment of God. As a part of God's created order, an economy should be judged by the fundamental requirements of human life established in the ancient relationship between God and Israel. This leads to an awareness that claims in favor of a "self-regulating" market cannot be sustained in the presence of those forms of poverty and suffering that tend to be generated as a by-product of market forces. The difficulty, as Thomas Ogletree puts it, is that "these harmful tendencies are difficult to contain . . . because they are directly linked to factors that render free-market economies effective in the first place."[17] Immediately relevant here, of course, are the structures of analysis—such as the four problems of economic life and the moral ecology of markets—treated in Chapter 12.

INTERNATIONAL TRADE

International economic relationships

Developing countries that have opened their economies to global markets have generally reduced poverty over time more than those that have not, but the terms of trade often work to the disadvantage of developing countries. Seeking more just exchanges "for all" through investment and trade is a significant challenge. The danger is that less developed parts of the world, or less powerful groups within a country, will be exploited or excluded from participation in global markets.

Evangelical Lutheran Church in America, "Economic Life"

Economic globalization has yielded some positive outcomes for society as a whole. But seen through the lens of faith, it has also produced great economic and social injustice. The rules and institutions that shape economic globalization must be fundamentally changed if God's creation and all God's children, in both the global south and north, are to benefit.

United Church of Christ, "Faithful Response"

International trade remains a controversial issue. On the one hand, there is general awareness in Protestant thought that participation in markets, both domestic and international, can provide more jobs and lower consumer prices in developing nations. At the same time, however, the rules of trade are typically structured by international negotiations in which the industrialized nations, and powerful corporations within them, are able to capture a disproportionate share of the advantages of trade. Trade is also criticized both for the environmental damage caused by long-range shipping and for the treatment of workers where poorly structured markets do not guarantee basic human rights.

Transnational corporations

The economic power of large transnational corporations continues to grow, making some of them larger than many national economies. Along with this financial strength comes an inordinate potential to influence political decisions, local and regional economies, and democratic processes in society. The power they wield, enhanced through mergers and buyouts, can have positive effects, but it can also hold others captive to transnational corporate interests. The global community must continue to seek effective ways to hold these and other powerful economic actors more accountable for the sake of sufficient, sustainable livelihood for all.

Evangelical Lutheran Church in America, "Economic Life"

Therefore, we reject the current world economic order imposed by global neoliberal capitalism and any other economic system, including absolute planned economies, which defy God's covenant by excluding the poor, the vulnerable and the whole of creation from the fullness of life.

World Alliance of Reformed Churches, "Accra Confession"

The mainline Protestant churches have been articulate in identifying the ways in which large transnational corporations have the financial strength and political clout to take advantage of local opportunities for profit anywhere in the world. Given the great psychic distance between a firm's board of directors and the local populations affected by corporate decisions, significant damage can and often does occur, a fact of economic life calling for stronger rules for international economic relationships, both within each nation and internationally. We see here an important difference between the mainline churches and the evangelical churches, with the latter less critical of the prevailing market system. As illustrated in the quote from Accra Confession above, mainline denominations with politically active churches in developing nations tend toward explicit denunciations of capitalism in their international statements.[18]

ADVERTISING

We consume goods and use services to meet our needs. To increase consumption and expand sales, businesses stimulate ever new wants. Rather than human need shaping consumption, advertising and media promotion both shape and expand wants. Our very being becomes expressed through what we have or desire to possess. When consuming to meet basic needs turns into consumerism as an end in itself, we face a serious crisis of faith.

Evangelical Lutheran Church in America, "Economic Life"

Economic life, of course, is most vivid in the daily experiences we have as persons in earning a living and in purchasing goods and services. The influence of advertising on consumption patterns is significant, in spite of the fact that very few of us are conscious of that influence in our own lives. As part of an ancient Christian tradition that calls for a focus on the truly important things in life, the Protestant churches have been careful to critique the excesses of consumerism that typify so much of modern economic life.[19]

WORK

Vocation

Our calling from God begins in the waters of Baptism and is lived out in a wide array of settings and relationships. Freed through the Gospel, we are to serve others through arenas of responsibility such as family, work, and community life. Although we continue to be ensnared in the ambiguities and sin of this world, our vocation is to seek what is good for people and the rest of creation in ways that glorify God and anticipate God's promised future. . . .

Employers have a responsibility to treat employees with dignity and respect. This should be reflected in employees' remuneration, benefits, work conditions, job security, and ongoing job training. Employees have a responsibility to work to the best of their potential in a reliable and responsible manner.

       Evangelical Lutheran Church in America, "Economic Life"

Aware of God's call—our "vocation," as we saw in the teaching of Martin Luther—Christians understand all of life to be a response to a generous God. Work, then, becomes an important part of one's religious response to the world, whether one is an employee or an employer. Both have important responsibilities. As John Raines and Donna Day-Lower have put it, "Work is not, fundamentally, about making a living or a profit but how we dwell together meaningfully and well."[20]

Unions

Power disparities and competing interests are present in most employment situations. . . . Because employees often are vulnerable and lack

> power in such negotiations, they may need to organize in their quest for
> human dignity and justice.
>
> Evangelical Lutheran Church in America, "Economic Life"

Contemporary Protestant thought also recognizes the significance of labor
unions in winning for working people both an adequate wage and the rights
that should be theirs. The Episcopal Church has supported passage of living-
wage legislation,[21] and the United Church of Christ has even argued that it is a
"responsibility of workers to organize for collective bargaining."[22]

GLOBALIZATION

> *A globalized world*
>
> God's world is one world. The unity now being thrust upon us by
> technological revolution has far outrun our moral and spiritual capacity
> to achieve a stable world. The enforced unity of humanity, increasingly
> evident on all levels of life, presents the Church as well as all people with
> problems that will not wait for answer.
>
> United Methodist Church, "Social Principles"
>
> We further believe that care for the vulnerable should extend beyond
> our national borders. American foreign policy and trade policies often have
> an impact on the poor. We should try to persuade our leaders to change
> patterns of trade that harm the poor and to make the reduction of global
> poverty a central concern of American foreign policy.
>
> National Association of Evangelicals, "For the Health of the Nation"

Recognizing that modern communication and transportation technologies have
made national borders quite porous, Christians are now met with new
challenges, including the difficult task of taking responsibility for effects of
markets that harm others at a great distance around the world. The lack of
international governance structures means that traditional national rules will
not suffice and that national leaders must be creative in addressing economic
problems, particularly for the poor of the world.

The 2000 General Convention of the Episcopal Church endorsed six
principles for responsible economic development, principles that would be
widely endorsed throughout Protestant Christianity: partnership, respect,
empowerment, oneness with creation, distributive justice, and people-centered

development.[23] Central here is the notion that providing the poor with food, clothing, and shelter is essential to development but cannot possibly suffice. The Christian vision of a full and fulfilling human life includes the notion of self-sufficiency that we saw in Chapter 5 in the patristic use of the Stoic notion of *autarkia*. That is, the poor of the world need assistance in coming to be able to support themselves and their families.

It is clear that some redistribution of wealth will be necessary, but the point of that is not simply the provision of needed goods and services directly—except in an emergency. The point is to provide the education and infrastructure necessary for the poor to become self-supporting.

THE ENVIRONMENT

The religious importance of creation

All creation is the Lord's, and we are responsible for the ways in which we use and abuse it. Water, air, soil, minerals, energy resources, plants, animal life, and space are to be valued and conserved because they are God's creation and not solely because they are useful to human beings.

United Methodist Church, "Social Principles"

We affirm that God-given dominion is a sacred responsibility to steward the earth and not a license to abuse the creation of which we are a part. We are not the owners of creation, but its stewards, summoned by God to "watch over and care for it" (Gen. 2:15). This implies the principle of sustainability: our uses of the Earth must be designed to conserve and renew the Earth rather than to deplete or destroy it.

National Association of Evangelicals, "For the Health of the Nation"

Arising out of the scriptural endorsement of the God-given dignity of creation independent of human life, Christians understand that the scale of our technology threatens the biosphere God has given us. The second creation story in Genesis identifies humanity's responsibility to care for the earth, and thus the notion of sustainability becomes critical for Christian faith and life today.

Obligations to future generations

The Sabbath and Jubilee laws of the Hebrew tradition remind us that we may not press creation relentlessly in an effort to maximize productivity (Exodus 20:8-11; Leviticus 25). The principle of sustainability means providing an acceptable quality of life for present generations without compromising that of future generations.

Evangelical Lutheran Church in America, "Caring for Creation"[24]

God has granted us stewardship of creation. . . . However, . . . [our] action jeopardizes the natural heritage that God has entrusted to all generations. Therefore, let us recognize the responsibility of the church and its members to place a high priority on changes in economic, political, social, and technological lifestyles to support a more ecologically equitable and sustainable world leading to a higher quality of life for all of God's creation.

United Methodist Church, "Social Principles"

Several of the mainline Protestant denominations have explicitly identified global warming as a critical threat to the sustainability of our planet. Few evangelical churches have taken on this issue so directly, where environmental concern is summed up under the notion of "creation care," without any explicit reference to concrete policy issues over which there is considerable political, though not scientific, debate.

Alongside the obligation of Christians to respect the integrity of creation out of God's own design for it, Christians are also aware that the damage done to the environment causes greater problems for the poor and marginalized than for the wealthy and middle class. Thus a second important theme in environmental commitment arises from the broader concern that Christians have for racial and ethnic minorities and the poor. Laura Stivers has suggested that cultivating a sense of "rootedness to particular places" can help Christians make this shift to greater awareness of such environmental problems.[25]

CIVIC LIFE

DEMOCRACY

Democracy

While our allegiance to God takes precedence over our allegiance to any state, we acknowledge the vital function of government as a principal vehicle for the ordering of society.

United Methodist Church, "Social Principles"

> God is the source of all true law and genuine liberty. He both legitimates and limits the state's authority. Thus, while we owe Caesar his due (Matt. 22:15-22; Mark 12:13-17; Luke 20:20-26), we regard only Jesus as Lord. As King of Kings, Jesus' authority extends over Caesar. As followers of Jesus, we obey government authorities when they act in accord with God's justice and his laws (Titus 3:1). But we also resist government when it exercises its power in an unjust manner (Acts 5:27-32) or tries to dominate other institutions in society.
>
> National Association of Evangelicals, "For the Health of the Nation"
>
> Government is intended to serve God's purposes by limiting or countering narrow economic interests and promoting the common good.
>
> Evangelical Lutheran Church in America, "Economic Life"

Within the Christian tradition, government is both a necessity for the structuring of life and a locus where God's expectations for human life can to some extent be embodied in civic order and the restraint of human sinfulness.

> *Human dignity and human rights*
>
> The concept of the image of God provides a basis for Christian affirmations of the dignity of individuals, human rights, and democratic procedures. It suggests that human beings have a God-given dignity and worth that unite humanity in a universal covenant of rights and responsibilities—the family of God. All humans are entitled to the essential conditions for expressing their human dignity and for participation in defining and shaping the common good.
>
> Presbyterian Church USA, "Hope for a Global Future"

Most Protestant denominations have endorsed the notion of human rights, which as we've seen has come to be an important part of public moral discourse in the world today. The fact that the nations of the world came to ethical agreement on the 1948 "Universal Declaration of Human Rights"[26] indicates that the idea of human rights offers an important way for integrating moral concerns into secular policy discussions at the national and international levels.

Yet, like the teaching of the popes we reviewed in the previous chapter, Protestants reject the individualistic interpretation of rights—rights without duties—that so many people embrace today. The inadequacy of the dominant notion of rights has led some like Alasdair MacIntyre to reject natural rights and human rights as mere fictions.[27] Yet, as Jon Gunnemann has argued, Christians would better understand the invention of rights language in the modern period as "a creative response of moral language to inevitable situations of moral conflict."[28]

Christians understand creation "in the image of God" as the source of human dignity and of rights—whether human, civil, or economic. As a result, rights make sense as claims on others only within a web of duties to others, within human relationships where all strive for the common good. Some denominational statements, particularly within the Evangelical Lutheran Church of America, largely avoid the language of rights, but this has been done to give preference to a biblical vocabulary and not out of any rejection of rights language.[29] Thus with the proper understanding of rights, Protestant churches endorse the notion of human rights as faithful to the biblical witness.

The role of government
Government must fulfill its responsibilities to provide for the general welfare and promote the common good.
National Association of Evangelicals, "For the Health of the Nation"
Paying taxes to enable government to carry out these and other purposes is an appropriate expression of our stewardship in society, rather than something to be avoided.
Evangelical Lutheran Church in America, "Economic Life"

Although many on the political right have come to identify taxes with injustice and exploitation, the Christian tradition has seen the obligation to pay taxes not as a burden but as an appropriate participation in the process of self-government. Robert Stivers has suggested an alternative image to counteract resistance to just taxation: "Taxes are not a 'taking away' but a 'withholding,' that is, a holding on by the community to the socially generated product for purposes of extending the common good."[30]

CIVIL SOCIETY

Civil society
An important way that Christians carry out their citizenship is through participation in voluntary associations and movements, both religious and secular. At times, these groups may serve a prophetic function as they protest particular evils, question unexamined assumptions, challenge unjust

---

> or immoral practices, and organize for structural changes in the work place, local community, and wider world.
>
> Evangelical Lutheran Church in America, "The Church in Society"

In spite of the importance of government and public participation in the political process, much of the organization of daily life occurs through the institutions of civil society. These groups, examined in earlier chapters, play a critical role in enabling people to accomplish their goals, both more narrowly self-interested and more broadly public spirited, in cooperation with others.

PUBLIC POLICY

> *Public policy*
>
> There are difficult and complex trade-offs and ambiguities in the dynamic processes of economic life. As believers, we are both impelled by God's promises and confronted with the practical realities of economic life. We often must choose among competing claims, conscious of our incomplete knowledge, of the sin that clouds all human judgments and actions, and of the grace and forgiveness given by Christ.
>
> Evangelical Lutheran Church in America, "Economic Life"
>
> Evangelicals may not always agree about policy, but we realize that we have many callings and commitments in common: commitments to the protection and well-being of families and children, of the poor, the sick, the disabled, and the unborn, of the persecuted and oppressed, and of the rest of the created order. While these issues do not exhaust the concerns of good government, they provide the platform for evangelicals to engage in common action.
>
> National Association of Evangelicals, "For the Health of the Nation"

Protestant thought recognizes public policy as a realm of the possible. Principles must be brought to bear, of course, but differences in how best to apply those principles—and uncertainties about the likely effects of alternative policies—lead to a respect for difference in public life. In fact, the disagreements within each church are significant, because as we have seen in earlier chapters in this volume, there is room for some disagreement even among well-intentioned and well-informed Christians when particular issues arise.

Personal responses

Lifestyle implications

Frugality denotes moderation, temperance, thrift, cost-consciousness, efficient use, and a satisfaction with material sufficiency. It means morally disciplined production and consumption for the common good, now and in the future. It reflects "the everlasting covenant between God and every living creature" (Gen. 9:16).

Presbyterian Church USA, "Hope for a Global Future"

We challenge ourselves, particularly the economically secure, to tithe environmentally. Tithers would reduce their burden on the earth's bounty by producing ten percent less in waste, consuming ten percent less in non-renewable resources, and contributing the savings to earthcare efforts. Environmental tithing also entails giving time to learn about environmental problems and to work with others toward solutions.

Evangelical Lutheran Church in America, "Caring for Creation"

Christian faith entails a relationship with God that ought to transform the personal life of each believer. Thus the Christian churches have universally called for changes in personal behavior to reject the consumerism of so much unnecessary expenditure and to endorse simpler ways of living that are less threatening to the environment. Some have gone so far as to propose an environmental tithe. Tithing, of course, is the ancient tradition of giving 10 percent of one's income back to the Lord, traditionally proposed simply in monetary terms in support of the budgets of churches and of nonprofit social service agencies. Environmental tithing takes this notion farther and proposes the significant reduction in the use of resources and the production of wastes.

This requires not only action but a faith-filled awareness, at times more vivid in the lives of Christians more directly in personal contact with suffering in the world. Regarding the global economic system as a whole, many Christians from the developing world have adopted what Karen Bloomquist has called "a spirituality of resistance, reflected in a suspicion of false promises of 'the system.'"[31]

Prayer

Above all, we commit ourselves to regular prayer for those who govern, that God may prosper their efforts to nurture life, justice, freedom, and peace.

National Association of Evangelicals, "For the Health of the Nation"

Perhaps most fundamental in the Christian view of a personal response to economic issues is the importance of prayer. All denominations would support the urging of the National Association of Evangelicals in calling for prayer not only for oneself but for elected officials at all levels of government so that economic life will be structured more in accord with God's plan.

THE CHURCH ITSELF

The church as actor

The Church as an employer, property owner, consumer, investor, and community of believers can be as caught up in the reigning economic assumptions as the rest of society. But despite the Church's failings, through the Word and the sacraments, we are forgiven, renewed, and nourished.

Evangelical Lutheran Church in America, "Economic Life"

Not only are individual Christians called to be active in personal and institutional transformations, but the churches themselves are called to be self-critical. At its General Convention, the Episcopal Church has called upon "each Province and Diocese to devise a program of study, reflection and action" to live out the moral commitments of faith in public life.[32] Quite naturally, every denomination understands the importance of study and reflection prior to action in the world. Thus churches engage in education for people of all age groups to help all believers better understand the relation of faith and contemporary problems.

At the same time, of course, the churches involved are also economic actors as owners of property, consumers of resources, employers, and investors (at least for those churches with an endowment). Here too, the Christian faith requires of the church a high standard of moral responsibility, one that all of its members should take responsibility for.

CONCLUSION

Summary of concerns

The Scriptures make it clear that a biblical agenda is broad and urgent. God's concern extends from the protection of marriage and the family to justice for the poor and the oppressed, from the sanctity of human life to care for creation, and the furtherance of peace and freedom. Political or policy prescriptions alone will not solve all of our problems, but we are called to action and the renewal of human structures as we wait for the fullness of God's kingdom.

National Association of Evangelicals, "For the Health of the Nation"

The Church has the "treasure" of the Gospel "in earthen vessels to show that the transcendent power belongs to God and not to us" (2 Cor. 4:7). We in the Evangelical Lutheran Church in America set forth these affirmations and commitments in society with the prayer that our words and deeds may be earthen vessels that witness to the power of the cross. We care for the earth and serve the neighbor in society with the joyful confidence that God's faithfulness alone sustains the church and renews our faith, hope, and love.

Evangelical Lutheran Church in America, "The Church in Society"

In summary, the contemporary Protestant churches have each in their own way made strong statements about the importance of economic life for Christian faith. Each has its own denominational tradition for incorporating the biblical witness and understanding the tradition of Christian witnesses who lived in earlier centuries. Universal across those denominations is the conviction that God's concern for the world and its people must be shared by all Christians.

Call to action

We call all Christians to a renewed political engagement that aims to protect the vulnerable and poor, to guard the sanctity of human life, to further racial reconciliation and justice, to renew the family, to care for creation, and to promote justice, freedom, and peace for all.

National Association of Evangelicals, "For the Health of the Nation"

All Christians are called to action, both personal and institutional. Evangelical churches share with their mainstream Protestant brothers and sisters the conviction that each Christian is called to take action in public life. Such action in a pluralistic society will not result in governments at local, state, or national level that do precisely what the gospel calls for. Yet Christians have a responsibility to press for the basic standards of care for the poor and the earth that are so fundamental to the Christian commitment.

God's final triumph

Based on this vantage point of faith, "sufficient, sustainable livelihood for all" is a benchmark for affirming, opposing, and seeking changes in economic life. Because of sin, we fall short of these obligations in this world, but we live in light of God's promised future that ultimately there will be no hunger and injustice.

Evangelical Lutheran Church in America, "Economic Life"

We believe in the present and final triumph of God's Word in human affairs and gladly accept our commission to manifest the life of the gospel in the world.

United Methodist Church, "Social Principles"

As people of faith, Protestant Christians understand that in the end it is God's work and not humanity's that brings these efforts to fruition. Standing in God's judgment, each Christian and each church looks forward to a day when beyond the limits imposed by the sin and finitude of our current life, there will be neither hunger nor injustice nor environmental decay.

Notes

1. World Alliance of Reformed Churches, "Letter from Accra," Introduction to "The Accra Confession: Covenanting for Justice in the Economy and the Earth," August 12, 2004. http://warc.jalb.de/warcajsp/side.jsp?news_id=157&part_id=0&navi=1. Assessed January 14, 2012.

2. For a promising proposal to develop an ecumenical Protestant social teaching, see Thomas W. Ogletree, "Renewing Ecumenical Protestant Social Teaching," in *The World Calling: The Church's Witness in Politics and Society* (Louisville: Westminster John Knox, 2004), 97–121.

3. Constraints of space make it impossible to address the work on economic ethics of many of these scholars. For example, Carol Robb articulates a helpful feminist critique of economics in her *Equal Value: An Ethical Approach to Economics and Sex* (Boston: Beacon, 1995).

4. Evangelical Lutheran Church in America, "Church in Society: A Lutheran Perspective," adopted at the second biennial Churchwide Assembly of the Evangelical Lutheran Church in America, August 28–September 4, 1991. http://www.elca.org/What-We-Believe/Social-Issues/Social-Statements/Church-in-Society.aspx. Accessed January 16, 2012. Reprinted with permission from the Evangelical Lutheran Church in America.

5. National Association of Evangelicals, "For the Health of the Nation: An Evangelical Call to Civic Responsibility," 2004. http://www.nae.net/images/content/For_The_Health_Of_The_Nation.pdf. Accessed January 6, 2012:

6. J. Philip Wogaman, *The Great Economic Debate: An Ethical Analysis* (Philadelphia: Westminster, 1977), 40.

7. Evangelical Lutheran Church in America, "Economic Life: Sufficient, Sustainable Livelihood for All," adopted at the sixth Churchwide Assembly on August 20, 1999, Denver, Colorado. http://www.elca.org/What-We-Believe/Social-Issues/Social-Statements/Economic-Life.aspx. Accessed January 16, 2012.

8. United Methodist Church, "Social Principles, Preamble," from *The Book of Discipline of the United Methodist Church*, 2008. http://www.umc.org/site/apps/nlnet/content.aspx?c=lwL4KnN1LtH&b=5065913&ct=6467355. Accessed January 16, 2012.

9. Presbyterian Church, "Hope for a Global Future: Toward Just and Sustainable Human Development," approved by the 208th General Assembly (1996) Presbyterian Church (USA). http://oga.pcusa.org/publications/hope-for-a-global-future.pdf. Accessed January 15, 2012. Reprinted by permission of the office of the General Assembly, Presbyterian Church (USA).

10. The 1973 6th General Conference of the Evangelical Alliance endorsed assistance to labor unions, an eight-hour day, and arbitration. Oral report of John Fea, "How Evangelicals Got to Today," Catholics and Evangelicals for the Common Good, September 30, 2011, Washington, DC.

11. Rebecca Todd Peters, "Economic Justice Requires More Than the Kindness of Strangers," in *Global Neighbors: Christian Faith and Moral Obligation in Today's Economy*, ed. Douglas A. Hicks and Mark R. Valeri (Grand Rapids, MI: Eerdmans, 2008): 91.

12. United Church of Christ, "Faithful Response: Calling for a More Just, Human Direction for Economic Globalization," July 2003.

13. J. Philip Wogaman, *Economics and Ethics*, 59.

14. For an articulate defense of democratic capitalism by a Lutheran ethicist, see Robert Benne, *The Ethic of Democratic Capitalism: A Moral Reassessment* (Philadelphia: Fortress Press, 1981).

15. Rebecca M. Blank, "Viewing the Market through the Lens of Faith," in *Is the Market Moral?: A Dialogue on Religion, Economics, and Justice*, ed. Rebecca M. Blank and William McGurn (Washington, DC: Brookings Institution, 2004), 12.

16. John C. Raines, "Conscience and the Economic Crisis," *The Christian Century* 99, no. 27 (Sept. 1, 1982): 883–87, at 886.

17. Ogletree, *The World Calling*, 71.

18. There are, of course, voices in the global North that are also highly critical. See, for example, Pamela K. Brubaker, "Reforming Global Economic Policies," in *Justice in a Global Economy: Strategies for Home, Community, and World*, ed. Pamela Brubaker, Rebecca Todd Peters, and Laura A. Stivers (Louisville: Westminster John Knox, 2006).

19. In an analogous vein, however, Protestant Christian ethicists have recognized the capacity for popular culture at times to "stretch the moral imagination" of people, as Bono has done. See Douglas A. Hicks, "Global Poverty and Bono's Celebrity Activism: An Analysis of Moral Imagination and Motivation," in Hicks and Valeri, *Global Neighbors*, 43–62.

20. John C. Raines and Donna C. Day-Lower, *Modern Work and Human Meaning* (Philadelphia: Westminster, 1986), 112.

21. General Convention, *Journal of the General Convention of the Episcopal Church*, Columbus, Resolution 2006-DO47 (New York: General Convention, 2007), 667–68.

22. United Church of Christ, "Affirming Democratic Principles in an Emerging Global Economy," resolution adopted by the Twenty-first General Synod, 1997, Columbus, Ohio. http://www.ucc.org/synod/resolutions/AFFIRMING-DEMOCRATIC-PRINCIPLES-IN-AN-EMERGING-GLOBAL-ECONOMY.pdf. Accessed January 15, 2012.

23. General Convention, *Journal of the General Convention of the Episcopal Church*, Denver, Resolution 2000-A002 (New York: General Convention, 2001): 438.

24. Evangelical Lutheran Church in America, "Caring for Creation: Vision, Hope, Justice," August 28, 1993, Kansas City, Missouri.

25. Laura A. Stivers, "Holding Corporations Accountable," in Brubaker et al., *Justice in a Global Economy*, 72–74.

26. United Nations, "Universal Declaration of Human Rights." http://www.un.org/en/documents/udhr/. Accessed February 1, 2012.

27. Alasdair C. MacIntyre, *After Virtue: A Study in Moral Theory* (Notre Dame: University of Notre Dame Press, 1984).

28. Jon P. Gunnemann, "Human Rights and Modernity: The Truth of the Fiction of Individual Rights," *Journal of Religious Ethics* 16, no. 1 (Spring 1988): 160–89 at 161.

29. Email exchange with Dr. Karen Bloomquist, former senior staff member of both the Evangelical Lutheran Church in America and the Lutheran World Federation. January 29, 2012.

30. Robert L. Stivers, "Tax Ethics: An Oxymoron?" in *Reformed Faith and Economics*, ed. Robert L. Stivers (Lanham, MD: University Press of America, 1989), 87–108, at 104. For a helpful review of Protestant thought on taxation, see Donald W. Shriver Jr. and E. Richard Knox, "Taxation in the History of Protestant Ethics," *Journal of Religious Ethics* 13, no. 1 (Spring 1985): 134–60.

31. Karen L. Bloomquist, "Engaging Economic Globalization as Churches," *Ecumenical Review* 53, no. 4 (Oct. 2001): 493–500 at 494.

32. General Convention, *Journal of the General Convention of the Episcopal Church*, Phoenix, Resolution 1991-D041 (New York: General Convention, 1992): 366.

17

Pope John Paul II and Pope Benedict XVI

As we have seen throughout history, church leaders in every century have asked themselves the same question: What does the history of Christian views of economic life mean in our time? *Their* best attempts at answering it became part of that same tradition, which other Christians then employed in answering the question in a later age. Thus it is helpful to look carefully at the reflections of Pope John Paul II and Pope Benedict XVI, as these represent very recent efforts to answer this question in the tradition of official Roman Catholic social teaching.

Pope John Paul II

Karol Wojtyła was born in 1920 in Poland, the youngest of three children. He began university studies at eighteen, but a year later became a manual laborer when the Nazi occupation of Poland closed the university. He resumed studies after the war and was ordained a priest at age twenty-six, and then went to Rome for a doctorate in theology. He taught ethics at the University of Lublin and earned a second doctorate in philosophy.

At thirty-eight, he was made the youngest bishop in Poland, and five years later he was appointed Archbishop of Krakow. At age fifty-eight, Archbishop Wojtyła was elected Pope, taking the name John Paul. He traveled the world far more than any previous pope, and had a special concern for young people, establishing World Youth Day. He died in 2005, at age eighty-four, having been pope for twenty-six years, the second-longest time in that office in church history.

Faith and economic life

> *The gospel as judge of our situation today*
>
> There can be no genuine solution of the "social question" apart from the Gospel, and "new things" can find in the Gospel the context for their correct understanding and the proper moral perspective for judgment on them.
>
> Many other people . . . live in situations in which . . . the rules of the earliest period of capitalism still flourish in conditions of "ruthlessness" in no way inferior to the darkest moments of the first phase of industrialization.
>
> Pope John Paul II, *Centesimus annus* 5 & 33

Like their predecessors, Popes John Paul and Benedict insist on both an accurate grasp of what is going on within the economy of their day and a vivid awareness that all thinking about our participation in that economy must be understood in the context of faith.

Pope John Paul II makes clear that, as in ages past, the church attends carefully to the desperate situations that so many people around the globe live in, and he reminds the reader that any discussion of recent developments in human history (those "new things," the literal translation of *rerum novarum*) needs to be rooted in the gospel and its concern for both the immanent and the transcendent dimensions of human life.

Work

> *Human work*
>
> It is always man who is the purpose of the work, whatever work it is that is done by man—even . . . the most monotonous, even the most alienating work.
>
> Through work, man not only transforms nature, adapting it to his own needs, but he also achieves fulfillment as a human being.
>
> Pope John Paul II, *Laborem exercens* 6 & 9
>
> At one time the natural fruitfulness of the earth appeared to be, and was in fact, the primary factor of wealth, while work was, as it were, the help and support for this fruitfulness. In our time, the role of human work

> is becoming increasingly important as the productive factor both of non-material and of material wealth.
>
> Pope John Paul II, *Centesimus annus* 20

Pope John Paul II insists that any analysis of the economy from a moral point of view must begin with the human person active in producing goods and services, that is, active in work. Through work the human person not only provides for the needs of self and family but for the needs of all, as the worker's products are distributed through a market system.

John Paul recognizes the major shift that has occurred in economic life, a shift to what some have called "the knowledge economy," where intelligence and creativity are more and more the sources of wealth.[1] In the ancient world, the wealthy were rich because of the land they owned, whether used for agriculture or mining. In our day, although some are wealthy due to owning natural resources, most of the wealthiest among us own very little land; their ownership of ideas makes them wealthy. Thus Bill Gates has a spectacular home, but he owns far less land than even a minor patrician in ancient Rome. This change in the character of wealth has important implications for both individual life and public policy, since education becomes more and more important and even postsecondary education qualifies as a fundamental need in industrialized nations.

THE JUST WAGE

> **Just wage based in common use**
>
> The justice of a socioeconomic system . . . deserves in the final analysis to be evaluated by the way in which man's work is properly remunerated in the system. Here we return once more to the first principle of the whole ethical and social order, namely, the principle of the common use of goods. . . . Wages . . . are still the practical means whereby the vast majority of people can have access to those goods which are intended for common use.
>
> Pope John Paul II, *Laborem exercens* 19

While some neoconservative Catholics have either ignored or dismissed the traditional Catholic teaching on just wage, Pope John Paul II insists that any just economic system must provide exactly that. With good reason, the church's magisterium has rejected any change in this teaching. This principle is extremely important because it arises out of the ancient notion of the "common use" of goods, which the Pope calls "the first principle" of the social order. This is the starting point for the Catholic view of just distribution and the key to the Catholic answer to the question in Chapter 12 as to what goods and services are so essential that they should be provided to all who are unable to provide for themselves. Throughout the Christian tradition, the meeting of the needs of all has been the gold standard by which the economic situation in every era has been measured.

As has been clear in earlier chapters, Jews and Christians have understood the material world as intended by God in creation to meet human needs. Throughout most of human history most people had access to basic necessities through farming. But since the Industrial Revolution, most people in economically advanced societies have access to the goods of the earth by spending wages earned in gainful employment. In our era, the requirement that the needs of all should be met can only be fulfilled, the Pope argues, if jobs are plentiful and wages are sufficient for workers to purchase what they need.

Like his predecessors, however, the Pope recognizes that there may be situations where market competition makes a just wage impossible at the level of an individual firm—threatening the firm's viability. To the extent this occurs, the market stands judged as unjust. Lutherans have a strong sense of living an indicted life, but all Christians know the experience of living in a sinful world—and all understand that further steps should be taken. In such cases the state may supplement the market wage, for example through grants to families or to mothers, as is done in some European nations, or, as in the United States, by the earned income tax credit we noted in Chapter 14. The justice of a wage cannot be decided independent of institutional context.

INDIRECT EMPLOYER

The concept of indirect employer includes both persons and institutions of various kinds, and also collective labor contracts and the principles of conduct which are laid down by these persons and institutions and which determine the whole socioeconomic system or are its result. . . . The indirect employer substantially determines one or other facet of the labor relationship, thus conditioning the conduct of the direct employer when the latter determines in concrete terms the actual work contract and labor relations. . . . The concept of indirect employer is applicable to every

> society, and in the first place to the State. For it is the State that must conduct a just labor policy.
>
> Pope John Paul II, *Laborem exercens* 17

To describe the social relationships and institutions that stand behind the relationship of employees and the employers who directly hire them, John Paul speaks of "the indirect employer." In doing so, he uses a personal term, "employer," to identify the systems that structure the context within which any individual business hires any individual employee. Cultural expectations (for example, that large firms will help alcoholic employees get treatment) and social pressure (for example, that the local hardware will contribute funds to support Little League baseball) are part of the indirect employer but so is the government, whether at the local, state, or national level. Government sets the rules for markets, thereby identifying what is legally acceptable behavior in the employment situation. Labor law, for example, is critical in limiting the power of large firms (the "direct employer") over their employees, an important part of which is the presence of labor unions.

UNIONS

> All these rights . . . give rise to yet another right: the right . . . to form associations for the purpose of defending the vital interests of those employed in the various professions.
>
> Pope John Paul II, *Laborem exercens* 20
>
> The role of trade unions in negotiating minimum salaries and working conditions is decisive in this area.
>
> Pope John Paul II, *Centesimus annus* 15
>
> Union demands should not be turned into a kind of group or class "egoism," although they can and should also aim at correcting . . . everything defective in the system of ownership of the means of production or in the way these are managed.
>
> Pope John Paul II, *Laborem exercens* 20

Like his predecessors, Pope John Paul stresses the importance of labor unions in assisting ordinary workers to offset the immense advantages in power that corporations have today even more than in the past. A large and wealthy corporation can survive hardship for quite a long period; the average worker is often dependent upon the next paycheck for the ordinary necessities of life, and has little leverage when negotiating with employers as an individual. Thus unions are extremely important to prevent unjust coercion by firms. Nonetheless, like all persons and organizations, unions too can exhibit a sinful egoism that looks out only for their members and not for the common good. John Paul cautions them to attend to both aims.

OWNERSHIP

Property

God gave the earth to the whole human race for the sustenance of all its members, without excluding or favoring anyone. This is the foundation of the universal destination of the earth's goods. . . . But the earth does not yield its fruits . . . without work. . . . In this way, man makes part of the earth his own, precisely the part which he has acquired through work; this is the origin of individual property.

Pope John Paul II, *Centesimus annus* 31

The above principle . . . diverges radically from the program of collectivism as proclaimed by Marxism and . . . differs from the program of capitalism practiced by liberalism. . . . In the latter case, the difference consists in the way the right to ownership of property is understood. The Christian tradition has never upheld this right as absolute and untouchable. On the contrary, it has always understood this right within the broader context of the right common to all to use the goods of the whole of creation: the right to private property is subordinated to the right to common use, to the fact that goods are meant for everyone.

Pope John Paul II, *Laborem exercens* 14

The pope reiterates the traditional Christian endorsement of the personal ownership of goods, including the ownership of business and factories ("the means of production"). Although he does not quote Thomas Aquinas directly, the pope uses the phrase "the universal destination of the earth's goods" as a twentieth-century translation of Thomas's statement that "inferior things are ordained for the purpose of meeting man's needs."[2] This leads the pope to insist on "common use," part of Thomas's argument that private ownership is a wise economic institution but goods ought to be used as if they were held in common, in the sense that if I have more than I need, my property ownership rights include the duty in justice to share my surplus with another who has less than he or she needs. Elsewhere, John Paul also talks about private property existing "under a social mortgage,"[3] as another way of identifying the obligations that owners of property have, even though many today who are influenced by the dominant liberal individualism of our culture regularly deny that such obligations exist.

Owning the means of production

Ownership of the means of production . . . is just and legitimate if it serves useful work. It becomes illegitimate, however, when it is not utilized or when it serves to impede the work of others, in an effort to gain a profit which is not the result of the overall expansion of work and the wealth of society. . . .

The obligation to earn one's bread by the sweat of one's brow also presumes the right to do so. A society in which this right is systematically denied, in which economic policies do not allow workers to reach satisfactory levels of employment, cannot be justified from an ethical point of view.

Pope John Paul II, *Centesimus annus* 43

The outcome of this analysis is deeply rooted in the Christian tradition and represents an important development of Christian doctrine on economic life. It is quite legitimate for individuals to own the means of production, but only if they understand the role that factories, businesses, and other productive assets play in the economy today. Because work is the only way for most people to have access to the goods of the earth, those who own the means of production can have a legitimate claim to that property only if those productive assets actually support and expand the opportunities for work in society.

This is a strong position and might be a shock to many Catholics in the business world, but we can see that it is a natural outgrowth of three thousand years of religious reflection on economic life. Corporations are not free simply to look at the bottom line to decide whether to create or eliminate jobs, whether to close factories now or later. This fundamental reality is why Pope John Paul often spoke of "the priority of labor over capital."[4] Humans and their work have far more importance than do the machines they use and buildings within which they toil.

This teaching does not require the bankruptcy of a firm under extreme competitive pressure. But those who own those machines and buildings—corporations and their stockholders, usually—must recognize the injustice of putting increased profits over employment or of "following the principle of maximum profit, trying to establish the lowest possible wages."[5] Thus it is a serious injustice that U.S. law directs firms to serve first and foremost the interest of their stockholders. Corporate law could instead allow or even encourage firms to attend to the welfare of workers and the community. We will return to this issue in Chapter 19.

THE ECONOMIC SYSTEM

THE VIEW OF MARKETS

Markets

There is certainly a legitimate sphere of autonomy in economic life which the State should not enter. The State, however, has the task of determining the juridical framework within which economic affairs are to be conducted, and thus of safeguarding the prerequisites of a free economy, which presumes a certain equality between the parties, such that one party would not be so powerful as practically to reduce the other to subservience.

It would appear that, on the level of individual nations and of international relations, the free market is the most efficient instrument for utilizing resources and effectively responding to needs. But this is true only for those needs which are "solvent"—insofar as they are endowed with purchasing power—and for those resources which are "marketable"—insofar as they are capable of obtaining a satisfactory price. But there are many human needs which find no place on the market.

Pope John Paul II, *Centesimus annus* 15 & 34

The Church's social doctrine holds that authentically human social relationships of friendship, solidarity and reciprocity can also be conducted within economic activity, and not only outside it or "after" it.

Benedict XVI, *Caritas in veritate* 36

While Pope John Paul II was writing *Centesimus annus* in 1990, he was vividly conscious of the transformations going on in Eastern Europe, particularly in his homeland of Poland, where a labor union, Solidarity, had successfully pushed the Communist Party of Poland out of office without bloodshed. The new government was choosing a structure for the economy of Poland, as were several other eastern European nations. To prepare himself to write the encyclical, John Paul invited to his private residence some two dozen world-renowned economists, only some of whom were Catholic, to solicit their advice as to what he should say about economic life.[6] The pope's increased economic sophistication shows in the encyclical.

Thus as we see in the quotations above, the pope endorses markets as a sphere of independence for individuals and firms, whose autonomy the state must respect. At the same time, the government must structure markets through "the juridical framework" in order that the worst abuses that might otherwise occur are eliminated by law. This we saw earlier in Chapter 12 as the necessary definition of markets through law, the first element in the moral ecology of markets. In deciding on this juridical framework, many technical judgments must be made but also many moral decisions, as to which activities are so morally abusive that they should be outlawed.

John Paul also recognizes that while markets are immensely efficient in the allocation of resources to their most highly valued uses, there are other important problems of economic life that the market is very inefficient at solving. The two most important examples are the needs of those who do not have money to participate in the market, and those resources, like the environment, that are not bought and sold in the marketplace but must be respected nonetheless. This is a clear recognition of something else we saw in Chapter 12: that every economy must solve four problems, not simply one or two. While markets do fairly well in solving the problem of allocation, its principle of distribution (you get what others are willing to pay you for whatever you have to sell) ignores those with nothing to sell. Markets are also unable to solve the problem of scale since they encourage the parties to an economic transaction to ignore externalities, like the damage inflicted on the biosphere. In addition, as Pope Benedict makes clear, the moral character of human relationships (the fourth problem every economy must solve) must be understood to involve not just personal friendships but also the market-structured relationships of employment.

CHOOSING AN ECONOMIC SYSTEM

Capitalism and socialism

The fundamental error of socialism is anthropological in nature. . . . The good of the individual is completely subordinated to the functioning of the socioeconomic mechanism.

The human inadequacies of capitalism and the resulting domination of things over people are far from disappearing. . . . Indeed, there is a risk that a radical capitalistic ideology could spread which refuses even to consider these problems, in the a priori belief that any attempt to solve them is doomed to failure, and which blindly entrusts their solution to the free development of market forces.

Can it perhaps be said that, after the failure of Communism, capitalism is the victorious social system, and that capitalism should be the goal of the countries now making efforts to rebuild their economy and society? . . . The answer is obviously complex.

If by "capitalism" is meant an economic system which recognizes the fundamental and positive role of business, the market, private property and the resulting responsibility for the means of production, as well as free human creativity in the economic sector, then the answer is certainly in the affirmative, even though it would perhaps be more appropriate to speak of a "business economy," "market economy" or simply "free economy."

But if by "capitalism" is meant a system in which freedom in the economic sector is not circumscribed within a strong juridical framework which places it at the service of human freedom in its totality, and which sees it as a particular aspect of that freedom, the core of which is ethical and religious, then the reply is certainly negative.

Pope John Paul II, *Centesimus annus* 13, 33, & 42

Written in 1991, *Centesimus annus* includes Pope John Paul's reflections on the choices that Poland and other Eastern European nations were then making about how to structure the economy, choosing among various forms of capitalism and socialism. He asks directly the question whether such nations should choose to be capitalist. His answer appears to some as a bit cryptic, since he simply gives conditions under which one might judge capitalism favorably or unfavorably. In this, the pope is aware of his role as a religious leader of Catholics throughout the world, who live in vastly different economic situations, and for whom different economic structures might be appropriate. While some on the political right have interpreted these words as a simple endorsement of capitalism, it is clear that his awareness of the abuses capitalism generates in so many parts of the world prevents him from any kind of blanket endorsement of the capitalist system. At the same time, however, he understands that a moral market system is possible if the four elements of the moral ecology of markets are in proper order.[7]

BUSINESS

Business and profit

A business cannot be considered only as a "society of capital goods"; it is also a "society of persons."

The Church acknowledges the legitimate role of profit as an indication that a business is functioning well. . . . But . . . it is possible for the financial accounts to be in order, and yet for the people . . . to be humiliated and their dignity offended.

Pope John Paul II, *Centesimus annus* 43 & 35

Once profit becomes the exclusive goal, if it is produced by improper means and without the common good as its ultimate end, it risks destroying wealth and creating poverty.

Benedict XVI, *Caritas in veritate* 21

Although many in our culture think of business corporations as simply organizations of the owners of business—stockholders—who get to make the rules of the firm in their own favor, Catholic social teaching insists that a business is a society of persons, including owners, managers, and workers, and closely related to suppliers and those in the communities who are influenced by the firm's decisions, popularly known as "stakeholders." He insists that profit ought not be the only goal of the firm, flatly rejecting a famous statement of economist Milton Friedman who asserted that the social role of business is to make a profit.[8]

As Michael Naughton has argued, "The theological insight of Benedict's 'logic of gift' should serve as a basis to understand business as a 'community of persons.' Rather than being an imposition from outside, it provides an important source for understanding the nature and purpose of business."[9]

THE DANGERS OF EXTREME INEQUALITY

Inequality and trust

Through the systemic increase of social inequality, both within a single country and between the populations of different countries (i.e. the massive increase in relative poverty), not only does social cohesion suffer, thereby placing democracy at risk, but so too does the economy, through the progressive erosion of "social capital": the network of relationships of trust,

> dependability, and respect for rules, all of which are indispensable for any form of civil coexistence.
>
> Pope Benedict XVI, *Caritas in veritate* 32

The Christian tradition has insisted on the equality of all persons in the eyes of God, but has not had much to say about income inequality. The emphasis has been on the meeting of the needs of all. In fact, Catholic social teaching has recognized morally appropriate differences in income in response to longer hours or harder work, or for occupations requiring longer periods of education, or for businesses bearing greater risk.[10]

Nonetheless, Pope Benedict warns of the dangers of our very unequal distribution of income and wealth. In this, he echoes significant recent research showing that nations with higher levels of income inequality seem to be less well off than equally wealthy nations with lower levels of income inequality. Richard Wilkinson and Kate Pickett reviewed scores of studies in the area of health and social problems and argue not only that the poor are worse off in more unequal nations but that even the wealthy in wealthy societies with high income inequality are worse off than their wealthy peers in similarly wealthy societies where the income inequality is lower.[11]

The fundamental claim of Wilkinson and Pickett is that nations with high income inequality have a more harshly competitive and even resentful culture of relationship—both between rich and poor and within each income group—that has significant negative effects both physiologically (higher levels of hypertension, heart problems, etc.) and psychologically (greater stress among the well-to-do and social alienation among the poor, more crime, higher rates of teen pregnancy, etc.).

Much more empirical study needs to be done before this research can bear fruit in public policy, but it does resonate with Catholic social thought. The inclusion of economic inequality as a serious moral problem may become an important development of Christian economic ethics in the twenty-first century.

How unequal is the distribution of income and wealth in the U.S.? Economist Dan Ariely conducted studies to compare three things: how unequal Americans think the distribution of wealth is, the extent of inequality Americans themselves would prefer, and the facts of wealth inequality in the U.S. He found that Americans of all sorts—whether Republicans or Democrats, rich or poor—thought there was far less wealth inequality in the U.S. than there actually is. The average estimate for the percentage of all wealth owned by the wealthiest 20 percent of Americans was between 55 and 60 percent, whereas the actual number is about 83 percent. And all groups said they preferred a level of inequality that was even less than what they (erroneously) thought existed. The preferred percentages ranged from about 30 to 40 percent.[12]

And what does an 83 percent share of wealth amount to? One way to picture this is to recall the various properties on the board in the game, Monopoly. If the game were being played by five players, the wealthiest player (the top 20 percent) would own all the colored properties. The second wealthiest player would own the four railroads, and the third would own Water Works and the Electric Company. The two poorest players would own nothing. Inequality of income and wealth in the U.S. is quite dramatic; it is higher than in other advanced nations and much greater today than thirty years ago. Thus income inequality itself, and not simply unmet needs, ought to increase in importance in any moral evaluation of economic life.

JUSTICE

Justice

Even prior to the logic of a fair exchange of goods and the forms of justice appropriate to it, there exists something which is due to man because he is man, by reason of his lofty dignity.

Pope John Paul II, *Centesimus annus* 34

The market is subject to the principles of so-called commutative justice. . . . But the social doctrine of the Church has unceasingly highlighted the importance of distributive justice and social justice for the market economy.

Benedict XVI, *Caritas in veritate* 35

Justice is inseparable from charity, and intrinsic to it. Justice is the primary way of charity or, in Paul VI's words, "the minimum measure" of it. . . . On the one hand, charity demands justice: recognition and respect for the legitimate rights of individuals and peoples. It strives to build the earthly city according to law and justice. On the other hand, charity transcends justice and completes it . . . by relationships of gratuitousness, mercy and communion.

Benedict XVI, *Caritas in veritate* 6

Popes Benedict and John Paul are clear that the economy must be characterized by all three forms of justice reviewed in Chapter 15—commutative, distributive, and social justice—and not simply by the first.

Benedict XVI

Born in 1927, Joseph Aloisius Ratzinger grew up in Bavaria, in southern Germany. A bright student in the seminary at age seventeen, he was conscripted into the German army during World War II. He concluded seminary studies after the war and was ordained a priest in 1951. Following graduate school, he taught at the universities of Bonn, Tübingen, and Regensburg, and was a theological consultant at the Second Vatican Council. At age forty-nine, he was made Archbishop of Munich and Freising, where he remained for four years, until Pope John Paul II appointed him Prefect of the Sacred Congregation for the Doctrine of the Faith, formerly known as the "Holy Office."

Upon the death of Pope John Paul II in 2005, Cardinal Ratzinger was elected pope, taking the name Benedict, in honor, he said, of both Pope Benedict XV and St. Benedict of Nursia. He retired in 2013.

Justice is not in any way contradictory to charity, but the two are different. Justice represents a sort of moral minimum of charity that every society requires of all its citizens. Charity endorses justice but also goes beyond it in a deep concern for persons that becomes clear in the gift-character of those relationships, as we will soon see.

The common good

To take a stand for the common good is on the one hand to be solicitous for, and on the other hand to avail oneself of, that complex of institutions that give structure to the life of society, juridically, civilly, politically and culturally, making it the *pólis*, or "city." The more we strive to secure a common good corresponding to the real needs of our neighbors, the more effectively we love them.

Every Christian is called to practice this charity, in a manner corresponding to his vocation and according to the degree of influence he wields in the *pólis*. This is the institutional path—we might also call it the political path—of charity, no less excellent and effective than the kind of

> charity which encounters the neighbor directly, outside the institutional mediation of the *pólis*.
>
> Benedict XVI, *Caritas in veritate* 7

Like their predecessors, Benedict and John Paul insist on the common good. Benedict points out that this common good includes not just individual actions in service of others but also the creation and maintenance of institutions that structure life, some governmental and some societal, which are the prerequisites for the "common conditions of social life" that we saw in Chapter 12. No one of us individually can provide the security that allows us to travel about our neighborhoods without fearing theft or bodily harm. No one of us can provide the system of police and the courts or of education or of culture, even though all of these are critically important for any one of us having a full and fulfilling life. Benedict makes clear that this kind of attention to building up the structures of our society is just as important as the face-to-face personal service that we are also called to provide to those in need around us.

CARITAS IN ECONOMIC LIFE

> *Gratuity and reciprocity*
>
> In commercial relationships, the principle of gratuitousness and the logic of gift as an expression of fraternity can and must find their place within normal economic activity.
>
> Benedict XVI, *Caritas in veritate* 36
>
> Through his work he enters into two inheritances: the inheritance of what is given to the whole of humanity in the resources of nature, and the inheritance of what others have already developed on the basis of those resources, primarily by developing technology.
>
> Pope John Paul II, *Laborem exercens* 13
>
> In fact, if the market is governed solely by the principle of the equivalence in value of exchanged goods, it cannot produce the social cohesion that it requires in order to function well. Without internal forms of solidarity and mutual trust, the market cannot completely fulfill its proper economic function.
>
> Benedict XVI, *Caritas in veritate* 35

Beginning with the fundamental gift of salvation through the life, death, and resurrection of Jesus Christ, both popes insist that the economy will only operate well if all involved in it have a lively sense of gratitude for the gifts that we are given. Although some think of the economy as all about one-to-one deals made to transfer goods, Catholic social thought insists that even such contractual relations must be founded on a more basic awareness of the gift of one person to another. Benedict talks explicitly about "reciprocity," a kind of relationship that stands between a pure gift (where nothing is expected in return) and a contract (where what is to be given in return is carefully specified and legally enforceable). As Stefano Zamagni and Luigino Bruni have argued, the market requires reciprocity frequently in daily economic life.[13]

As we saw in Chapter 12, social scientists have developed the notion of "social capital," which Benedict calls "the network of relationships of trust, dependability, and respect for rules."[14] Societies with more social capital have greater trust in their economic relationships and operate more efficiently than societies that must spend more resources on surveillance and enforcement of rules. People in such societies lead more fulfilling lives. In a very real sense, social capital is the stock of trust in a society, and trust is built up by relations of reciprocity, within which people, quite realistically, learn to trust more when prior acts of trust have proven successful. It is clear that Pope Benedict values efficient allocation, the first of the four problems of economic life we reviewed in Chapter 12, but he recognizes that addressing the fourth problem, the quality of relations, is essential to solving the first.

Hybrid firms

Alongside profit-oriented private enterprise and the various types of public enterprise, there must be room for commercial entities based on mutualist principles and pursuing social ends to take root.

The diversified world of the so-called "civil economy" and the "economy of communion" . . . does not exclude profit, but instead considers it a means for achieving human and social ends.

Benedict XVI, *Caritas in veritate* 38 & 46

One way that gratuity and reciprocity in economic life become institutionally structured occurs in what Pope Benedict calls "hybrid firms." These are business firms that make a profit but are committed to spending a sizable portion of that profit for the common good. Examples include banks whose profits go to a foundation that gives the money back to the community and firms that are part of the Focolare Movement's "economy of communion," where one third of the profit of the firm is spent to meet the needs of the poor and one third for education, with one third reinvested in the firm for further growth.[15] Gratuitousness and reciprocity regularly occur in the daily life of ordinary for-profit firms as well. The owner of a small manufacturing firm asks his shop foreman if he and the workers will work three upcoming Saturdays to get a rush order out the door on time. The foreman may agree as a favor to his boss—a gift—but both understand that the foreman or workers may later ask a favor of the boss (perhaps to have an afternoon off to watch a son's soccer game), when the boss, too, is likely to grant the favor. Such examples of mutual trust built up through relationships of reciprocity are essential to a good work situation. They give reality to Pope Benedict's "logic of gift" even in "ordinary" profit-making firms.[16]

STATE AND SOCIETY

Structures of sin

The decisions which create a human environment can give rise to specific structures of sin which impede the full realization of those who are in any way oppressed by them. To destroy such structures and replace them with more authentic forms of living in community is a task which demands courage and patience.

Pope John Paul II, *Centesimus annus* 38

Both John Paul and Benedict are clear that sin is ultimately a personal decision of individuals in defiance of God's will, in contradiction to a choice that would have led the sinner to a more flourishing and fulfilling life. Nonetheless, both are aware that our actions as individuals both help to create and sustain the institutions within which we live and are deeply shaped by them. When those institutions provide incentives for individuals to undertake destructive behaviors, they are rightly called "structures of sin." As Eduardo Bonnín has pointed out, these typically come into being not out of sheer evil but when "one fundamental interest, in itself justified, is transformed into an absolute, dominating over all countervailing interests."[17]

The popes are aware of the sociologist's understanding—reviewed in Chapters 1 and 12 of this volume—that our world is to a large extent socially constructed, and that both our perceptions and our feasible options are deeply dependent upon social structures that have emerged over time. These structures act as causal forces through the enablements and restrictions that emerge in the lives of individuals. A responsible Christian economic ethic requires each one of us then to be active in transforming sinful social structures.[18]

The subjectivity of society

The social nature of man is not completely fulfilled in the State, but is realized in various intermediary groups, beginning with the family and including economic, social, political and cultural groups which stem from human nature itself and have their own autonomy, always with a view to the common good. This is what I have called the "subjectivity" of society.

Authentic democracy . . . requires . . . the "subjectivity" of society through the creation of structures of participation and shared responsibility.

Pope John Paul II, *Centesimus annus* 13 & 46

Because government is not the same thing as society, Catholic social thought has long recognized that economic life will not be just without a vibrant civil society. John Paul went so far as to talk about society having a "subjectivity," made up of both a vibrant life inside each of these organizations and particularly in the lively interaction among them in society. More individualistic views of civil society see individuals joining such organizations simply to accomplish their own interests. The Catholic view is far more organic and understands that our individual participation in civil society organizations must include concern for the common good. This conscious effort to serve both the organization's members and the common good of the larger community is part of the subjectivity of society, society's way of understanding and improving itself. While this is not the language of the discipline of sociology we saw in Chapter 1, it does name within Christian morality the ways social structures emerge from and are sustained by the actions of individuals. These structures have a reality rooted in individual interaction but exert a causal force independent of those individuals.

State and employment

The State could not directly ensure the right to work for all its citizens unless it controlled every aspect of economic life and restricted the free initiative of individuals. This does not mean, however, that the State has no competence in this domain, as was claimed by those who argued against any rules in the economic sphere. Rather, the State has a duty to sustain business activities by creating conditions which will ensure job

> opportunities, by stimulating those activities where they are lacking or by supporting them in moments of crisis.
>
> Pope John Paul II, *Centesimus annus* 48

All that has been said above about employment and business firms means that government has a fundamental responsibility to structure the economy to give proper incentives so that sufficient job opportunities will be created, particularly during recessions when employment lags. This is not a matter of some sort of preference for big government in itself, but rather recognition that the state must do what is necessary for the common good. At the same time, John Paul recognizes that firms, not governments, should be the direct source of those jobs, an indication of the value he places on both subsidiarity and efficiency.

> *Solidarity and subsidiarity*
>
> Solidarity . . . is not a feeling of vague compassion or shallow distress at the misfortunes of so many people, both near and far. On the contrary, it is a firm and persevering determination to commit oneself to the common good; that is to say to the good of all and of each individual, because we are all really responsible for all.
>
> Pope John Paul II, *Solicitudo rei socialis* 38
>
> The State must contribute to the achievement of these goals both directly and indirectly. Indirectly and according to the principle of subsidiarity, by creating favorable conditions for the free exercise of economic activity, which will lead to abundant opportunities for employment and sources of wealth. Directly and according to the principle of solidarity, by defending the weakest, by placing certain limits on the autonomy of the parties who determine working conditions, and by ensuring in every case the necessary minimum support for the unemployed worker.
>
> Pope John Paul II, *Centesimus annus* 15
>
> The principle of subsidiarity must remain closely linked to the principle of solidarity and vice versa, since the former without the latter gives way to social privatism, while the latter without the former gives way to paternalist social assistance that is demeaning to those in need.
>
> Benedict XVI, *Caritas in veritate* 58

The popes employ the principles of solidarity and subsidiarity to understand and shape public life. Solidarity is a relationship among individuals in society but is also an important goal of government at every level, looking out in particular for those who are least able to look out for themselves. Subsidiarity, the principle we saw in Chapter 14 introduced by Pope Pius XI in the 1930s, now takes on an important economic meaning in addition to its original political sense. Subsidiarity endorses the individual interaction of persons in markets as opposed to any sort of government central planning of the economy.

There is a real tension between solidarity and subsidiarity, a very Catholic tension that requires individuals and government to respect both principles, because overdoing either one will threaten the other. A prudent balance is needed, emphasizing now one, then the other, depending on the context.

Systems of social welfare

By intervening directly and depriving society of its responsibility, the Social Assistance State leads to a loss of human energies and an inordinate increase of public agencies which are dominated more by bureaucratic ways of thinking than by concern for serving their clients, and which are accompanied by an enormous increase in spending. In fact, it would appear that needs are best understood and satisfied by people who are closest to them and who act as neighbors to those in need.

Pope John Paul II, *Centesimus annus* 48

The market has prompted new forms of competition between States as they seek to attract foreign businesses. . . . These processes have led to a downsizing of social security systems as the price to be paid . . . with consequent grave danger for the rights of workers, for fundamental human rights and for the solidarity associated with the traditional forms of the social State.

Benedict XVI, *Caritas in veritate* 25

A number of conservative commentators have pointed to paragraph 48 in *Centesimus annus* as a basis to call for a sharp reduction in government support for the poor and unemployed. As Kenneth Himes has argued, John Paul did indeed criticize one form of government support: bureaucratic and impersonal "help."[19] Nonetheless, other things John Paul said before and since—and the clear statement of Pope Benedict in *Caritas in veritate*—indicate that John Paul intended no condemnation of government welfare programs in general but only those too bureaucratic to respect the human dignity of recipients, so badly structured that able-bodied citizens are tempted to dependency instead of independence. Most people receiving government "welfare" assistance, of course, are too young, too old, or too sick to support themselves; for these people, fear of "government-induced dependency" is a red herring.

DEVELOPMENT

Economic development

Hunger is not so much dependent on lack of material things as on shortage of social resources, the most important of which are institutional.

It should also be remembered that, in the economic sphere, the principal form of assistance needed by developing countries is that of allowing and encouraging the gradual penetration of their products into international markets, thus making it possible for these countries to participate fully in international economic life.

Benedict XVI, *Caritas in veritate* 27 & 58

Popes John Paul and Benedict have reiterated the concern of Paul VI that the economic development of poor nations is critically important to the church. The "social resources" needed are institutions that will guarantee that basic needs will be met—for example, food and water as human rights—and a real participation by the poor in markets—so all can support self and family by gainful employment. Markets are critically important in the process. Those on the left who condemn international trade as nothing but damaging to poorer nations will find little support in Catholic social teaching.

Integral Human Development

Authentic human development concerns the whole of the person in every single dimension. Without the perspective of eternal life, human progress in this world is denied breathing-space. Enclosed within history, it runs the risk of being reduced to the mere accumulation of wealth; humanity thus loses the courage to be at the service of higher goods.

Benedict XVI, *Caritas in veritate* 11

There are some people, the few who possess much, who do not really succeed in "being" because, through a reversal of the hierarchy of values, they are hindered by the cult of "having"; and there are others, the many who have little or nothing, who do not succeed in realizing their basic

---

human vocation because they are deprived of essential goods. The evil does not consist in "having" as such, but in possessing without regard for the quality and the ordered hierarchy of the goods one has.

Super development . . . easily makes people slaves of "possession." . . . An object already owned but now superseded by something better is discarded, with no thought of its possible lasting value in itself, nor of some other human being who is poorer.

Pope John Paul II, *Solicitudo rei socialis* 28

Like Paul VI before them, these two popes insist upon integral human development, that is, the development of a whole person in all dimensions. While this requires a preoccupation with the well-being of huge numbers of people on the planet living in desperate poverty, it also entails a deep concern for the spiritual poverty of so many of us in the prosperous regions of the world as well. How often do we feel the need to trade in our cellphone for the latest version, even when the old phone works quite well for us? Each of us is challenged to ask the question whether we have become slaves to our possessions. We can hear in this question the challenge presented by the Fathers of the early church to the wealthy of their day: those who are possessed by their possessions are unable to live without them. Those who are the masters of their possessions can prove this by giving them away to help those in need. Material goods are good but must be kept properly ordered within a proper hierarchy of goods.

The environment

Attitudes toward nature

At the root of the senseless destruction of the natural environment lies an anthropological error: . . . Man . . . forgets that this is always based on God's prior and original gift of the things that are.

Pope John Paul II, *Centesimus annus* 37

Nature is at our disposal not as "a heap of scattered refuse." . . . It is a wondrous work of the Creator containing a "grammar" which sets forth ends and criteria for its wise use.

Benedict XVI, *Caritas in veritate* 48

Both Benedict and John Paul make clear the concern of the church for the environment. At root, the world is a gift from God, and embedded in that gift are certain structures for the flourishing of the natural world. Thomistic thought speaks of the structures of the natural law, but Benedict here employs the analogy of grammar. To learn a language, we must respect its grammar, how that language works. The natural world has certain natural structures—which in natural evolution do change, as a language may change over time. This does not tell us exactly where to draw the line between acceptable and unacceptable uses of the natural world—which requires a judgment of prudence in the local situation—but it does remind us that drawing that line is a religious necessity.

Global governance

The global common good

In this respect I wish to mention specifically: the reform of the international trade system, . . . the world monetary and financial system, . . . an international juridical order.

Pope John Paul II, *Solicitudo rei socialis* 43

In order not to produce a dangerous universal power of a tyrannical nature, the governance of globalization must be marked by subsidiarity, articulated into several layers and involving different levels that can work together. Globalization certainly requires authority, insofar as it poses the problem of a global common good that needs to be pursued. This authority, however, must be organized in a subsidiary and stratified way, if it is not to infringe upon freedom and if it is to yield effective results in practice.

Benedict XVI, *Caritas in veritate* 57

Because the world economy is now so integrated, so globalized, it only makes sense that the popes insist on some sort of international juridical order to structure international markets, just as every national or local market needs an appropriate legal structure. However, Benedict is careful to remind us that a simple top-down government would violate the principle of subsidiarity, and thus the structures of international governance are not likely to be based on any confederation of all national governments. Far more likely is a polyarchic system of governance, a further development of a large number of international agreements structuring this or that part of the economy, each attuned to the common good. Thus both those on the left who condemn international trade and those on the right who condemn efforts to better structure international trade to make it more just will be challenged here by Catholic social teaching.

CONCLUSION

Catholic social thought

Open to the truth, from whichever branch of knowledge it comes, the Church's social doctrine receives it, assembles into a unity the fragments in which it is often found, and mediates it within the constantly changing life-patterns of the society of peoples and nations.

Benedict XVI, *Caritas in veritate* 9

The Church has no models to present; models that are real and truly effective can only arise within the framework of different historical situations, through the efforts of all those who responsibly confront concrete problems in all their social, economic, political and cultural aspects, as these interact with one another.

Pope John Paul II, *Centesimus annus* 43

These popes, like others before them, are vividly aware of the challenges faced by the church in addressing economic life. On the one hand, Catholic social thought provides insight and analysis that individuals can then employ in thinking through the economic problems they face. On the other hand, the church has always argued that it does not present a particular model of how to structure the economy or the polity. Different nations have different histories and are in different stages of economic development. Both cultural and economic differences mean that there may be need for different models in different places. Nonetheless Catholic social thought provides principles for thinking about these issues that will, if employed, keep a balance among all the concerns for a flourishing human life. As Kristin Heyer has put it, the Catholic stance is "institutionally depoliticized yet socially and politically active in service of protecting human life and dignity and pursuing the common good."[20]

Progress and the Kingdom

The Church well knows that no temporal achievement is to be identified with the Kingdom of God, but that all such achievements simply reflect and in a sense anticipate the glory of the Kingdom, the Kingdom which we await at the end of history, when the Lord will come again.

> Pope John Paul II, *Solicitudo rei socialis* 48
> Man's earthly activity, when inspired and sustained by charity, contributes to the building of the universal city of God, which is the goal of the history of the human family. In an increasingly globalized society, the common good and the effort to obtain it cannot fail to assume the dimensions of the whole human family . . . to shape the earthly city in unity and peace, rendering it to some degree an anticipation and a prefiguration of the undivided city of God.
>
> Benedict XVI, *Caritas in veritate* 7

As we finish this review of the 3000-year history of Christian views of economic life, we are reminded of the integrity of an authentic life of faith, with prayer and Eucharistic worship flowing naturally into service and the work of justice. Our work to improve the world we live in is intimately related to our ultimate destiny. There should be no mistake: we cannot create the kingdom of God on earth. The Christian tradition has taught us that only God can bring forth this ultimate reign of peace and justice. Nonetheless we know that the God who intends our ultimate and eternal fulfillment intends as well a foretaste of that fulfillment—as much as is possible amidst the sin and finitude of our daily lives. Thus action today is not cut off from our ultimate destiny with God after our deaths. It is, as Pope Benedict puts it, both an anticipation and a prefiguration of that ultimate joy.

Notes

1. For further discussion of the knowledge economy and Christian ethics, see Albino Barrera, *Modern Catholic Social Documents and Political Economy* (Washington, DC: Georgetown University Press, 2001), 205–17.

2. ST, II-II, q. 66, a. 7.

3. Pope John Paul II, *Solicitudo rei socialis*, 42.

4. Pope John Paul II, *Laborem exercens*, 12. http://www.vatican.va/holy_father/john_paul_ii/encyclicals/documents/hf_jp-ii_enc_14091981_laborem-exercens_en.html. Accessed May 10, 2012.

5. Ibid., 11.

6. The record of that meeting has been published in Pontifical Council for Justice and Peace, *Social and Ethical Aspects of Economics: A Colloquium in the Vatican* (Vatican City, 1992).

7. For a more detailed treatment of the conditions under which Pope John Paul would endorse a market system, see Daniel K. Finn, "John Paul II and the Moral Ecology of Markets," *Theological Studies* 59, no. 4 (Dec. 1998): 662–79.

8. Milton Friedman, *Capitalism and Freedom* (Chicago: University of Chicago Press, 1962), 133.

9. Michael Naughton, "The Business Enterprise," in chapter 6 of *The Moral Dynamics of Economic Life: An Extension and Critique of Caritas in veritate*, ed. Daniel K. Finn (New York: Oxford University Press, 2012).

10. See, for example, U.S. Conference of Catholic Bishops, *Economic Justice for All: Pastoral Letter on Catholic Social Teaching and the U.S. Economy* (Washington, DC: National Conference of Catholic Bishops, 1986), para. 74 and 185.

11. Richard G. Wilkinson and Kate Pickett, *The Spirit Level: Why Greater Equality Makes Societies Stronger* (New York: Bloomsbury, 2010).

12. "Building a Better America—One Wealth Quintile at a Time," Michael I. Norton and Dan Ariely, http://www.people.hbs.edu/mnorton/norton%20ariely%20in%20press.pdf. Accessed January 31, 2013.

13. Stefano Zamagni and Luigino Bruni, *Civil Economy: Efficiency, Equity, Public Happiness* (Oxford: Oxford University Press, 2007).

14. Pope Benedict XVI, *Caritas in veritate*, 32. http://www.vatican.va/holy_father/benedict_xvi/encyclicals/documents/hf_ben-xvi_enc_20090629_caritas-in-veritate_en.html. Accessed May 9, 2012.

15. For further discussion of the economy of communion, see Lorna Gold, *New Financial Horizons: The Emergence of an Economy of Communion* (Hyde Park, NY: New City, 2010).

16. Daniel K. Finn, "Charity and Truth in Business: Profit, Gift and Social Capital," in *Origins* 41, no. 10 (July 21, 2011): 149–54.

17. Eduardo Bonnín Barceló, Sch.P., *Estructuras de pecado y pecado social: Elementos para una síntesis teológica* (México, D.F.: Instituto Mexicano de Doctrina Social Cristiana, 2007), 28–29.

18. John Paul consistently tied the transformation of "unjust structures" to "the liberation of man from every slavery that threatens him." See "La Evangelización de la Cultura," address given to intellectuals, scientists, and artists in Quito, Ecuador, January 30, 1985. *Mensajes Sociales de Juan Pablo II en America Latina* (Santiago, Chile: Consejo Episcopal Latinoamericano, CELAM, 1986), para. 405.

19. Kenneth Himes, "The New Social Encyclical's Communitarian Vision," *Origins* 21, no. 10 (Aug. 1, 1991): 166–68.

20. Kristin E. Heyer, *Prophetic & Public: The Social Witness of U.S. Catholicism* (Washington, DC: Georgetown University Press, 2006), 47.

PART V

Coming to Conclusions

18

Principles for an Economic Ethic Today

The fundamental question raised in this volume is simply stated: What are the implications of the history of Christian views of economic life for our economic life today? We have now completed the historical survey that began with ancient Israel and concluded with the work of Pope Benedict XVI. In this chapter, we will review eight basic convictions and thirteen essential elements for an economic ethic today that arise from that tradition.

It is an unfortunate fact of contemporary life that Christians on left and right politically have frequently proposed particular economic implications of Christian belief, making very selective use of this tradition. That is, too many Christians today—including many scholars—have prior ideological commitments about the optimal shape of economic life that lead them to be selective in their use of the tradition, citing those portions that support their point of view but ignoring those that do not.

For example, the primary Christian perspective on the political left today is frequently described as "liberationist," a reference to liberation theology and related schools of thought. From the liberationist perspective, most people in the poor nations of the world and many within the wealthy nations have been exploited by a capitalist system driven by greedy self-interest and a willingness to use people in the pursuit of maximum profit. These Christian voices point to the strong defense of the poor in the Christian tradition and its insistence on the meeting of human needs. Similarly, they appropriately stress the obligations of property owners to share their surplus with the needy. Catholic voices among them stress papal support for labor unions, and papal criticisms of "liberalism" and its overly individualistic view of the world. However, these same liberationist voices tend to ignore those parts of the tradition that find a moral justification for business and markets and they too often ignore the many positive evaluations of markets and individual initiative in recent papal teaching.

On the political right, an even greater distortion occurs. Economically conservative Catholics, usually referred to as "neoconservatives" in the United

States, stress those portions of the tradition that defend the ownership of private property, and they cite the many positive things said by recent popes in praising markets and in recognizing the benefit to the poor nations of the world provided by access to international markets. Yet neoconservatives largely ignore arguments in the tradition that run counter to their own views. Thus there is almost no discussion of the justice obligations of the owners of private property to share their surplus with the needy and no mention of the just wage or the critique of capitalism and individualism that all the modern popes have included along with their appreciation for the good things that markets can do.

One helpful way to engage these debates over the structure of the economy and the role of morality within it is to consider the framework of the moral ecology of markets described in Chapter 12. There, we saw that all perspectives on the morality of markets, across the political spectrum, provide an answer to the same basic questions about economic life. Those four questions concern the definition of markets by law, the provision of essential goods and services, the morality of individuals and groups, and a vibrant civil society.

Thus our question about what the tradition of Christian thinking about economic life should mean for us today can be reinterpreted to ask how that tradition would answer these four questions. More precisely, what would be the range of acceptable answers along the political spectrum that the Christian tradition could approve of? This approach recognizes that there is room for some disagreement on practical solutions but that the tradition dismisses some possible answers as unacceptable.

In the remainder of this chapter, we will consider two clusters of ideas that will be helpful in answering our basic question. The first is a list of eight basic convictions, and the second will identify thirteen elements fundamental to the relation of faith and economic life. The following two chapters will make these insights more concrete.

To understand "what the tradition means today," it will be helpful to recall the question that began Chapter 2: How does a living tradition mean? We have seen the answer to this question of "how" embodied in the religious reflection on economic life from the Hebrew Scriptures to the statements of Pope Benedict XVI today. Leaders in each era employed the wisdom they inherited to address the particular economic situation faced by the believers of their day. Both church leaders and ordinary believers today are called to do the same.

Up to this point, this volume has attended to arguments from various strands of the Christian tradition, both Catholic and Protestant. However, to come to more concrete implications of that tradition, this chapter and the next two will focus on the Roman Catholic tradition, employing its categories and logic. Many Protestants will hopefully find the analysis congenial, but it will focus on and arise from the categories of Catholic social thought.

FUNDAMENTAL CONVICTIONS ABOUT ECONOMIC LIFE

It would be convenient if we could summarize what the Catholic tradition means today in a single short list of principles, or even in one brief chapter. But life is rich and the problems we face are complex. (If they were simple, they would have been solved long ago!) And this Catholic heritage, as we have seen earlier, is symphonic: its comprehensive vision relies on many interdependent and mutually enriching ideas. Listening carefully for their harmony, counterpoint, and texture will allow the reader to be better able to make his or her own assessment of what this tradition means for economic life today. In doing so, it is helpful to acknowledge eight fundamental convictions arising out of that tradition.

THE RELIGIOUS FOUNDATION

BOTH CREATION AND REDEMPTION CALL US TO A MORE RESPONSIBLE LIFE.

Christians understand that they have been created in the image of God and redeemed in Jesus Christ. These two realities of creation and redemption generate a host of crucial implications for humanity, extending far beyond the economic dimensions of life on which this volume focuses. We are a grateful, "Eucharistic" people, deeply aware in both personal prayer and public liturgy of our dependence on a loving God. The sense of ourselves as created and redeemed shapes our commitment to participate in economic life in a more just and charitable way.

The Fathers of the early church were insistent that the created character of the world imposed important obligations on those who by human law have come to own a part of that world. Thomas Aquinas built his system of natural law ethics on the fact of God's creation. He expanded on Aristotle's notion of human virtue as a "habit" that leads us to choose to fulfill ourselves in accord with God's vision for human flourishing.

The tradition has been equally insistent on the centrality of our redemption in Christ, and on salvation freely given by God. Martin Luther taught powerfully—and the Catholic church today reaffirms—that we do not earn salvation by our good works, but that anyone redeemed in Christ should indeed be active in service to others, especially to those "least of my brothers and sisters," following the example of Jesus himself.

Thus it is because we are both created and redeemed that Christians take economic life so seriously, dedicated to contributing to God's plan. Humanity's eschatological destiny extends beyond this life but, in the words of Pope Benedict XVI, it is critical that we work "to shape the earthly city in unity and peace, rendering it to some degree an anticipation and a prefiguration of the undivided city of God."[1]

ECONOMIC LIFE IS RELIGIOUSLY SIGNIFICANT.

We saw in Chapter 3 that the Christian tradition has derived from the Genesis creation story two fundamental insights related to the doctrine of creation: that the material world is good and that it is a gift. This is the scriptural basis for the sacramental character of the material world, that it is translucent to the divine. Unlike some religions where truly religious people attempt to escape the world, Christianity has understood the material world to be good. Out of this goodness comes the conviction that what we do in daily life, our ordinary job that contributes to the production of goods and services for the people of our Earth, is not evil or even neutral but is genuinely positive in its contribution to humanity and in God's plan for its well-being. This tradition has recognized the religious importance of economic life from its scriptural praise for the savvy managerial prudence of Joseph working for the Pharaoh in Egypt, all the way up to modern papal appreciation for the entrepreneur's contributions in the creation of wealth. The challenge, of course, is to live out that economic life in a morally virtuous manner.

SETTING PROPER GOALS

FAITH IN GOD REQUIRES THE PROPER ORDERING OF GOODS.

Fundamental to one's relation with God is a proper understanding of the ordering of the many "goods" that humans regularly seek, whether autos or iPods, friendship or love, meaningful work or interesting recreation. As we saw in Chapter 4, Augustine of Hippo distinguished between using and enjoying goods, arguing that we will only be happy if we understand that the goods of our daily life must never become so important as to disturb our deeper relationship with God, the ultimate good of our lives. As he put it, people want to be happy but so often live lives that will not make them so. Thomas Aquinas made a similar argument when he insisted on the proper ordering of earthly goods to our ultimate end in God. Vincent Miller has helpfully investigated the dual problem caused by contemporary consumerism: that consumption replaces religious practices in people's search for fulfillment and that religion itself comes to be seen as just another commodity.[2] The distortion of priorities plays an equally important role in our current environmental problems.

HUMAN DEVELOPMENT MUST BE INTEGRAL.

The Catholic tradition insists that the development each individual person goes through in life—and the development every nation should experience—must be "integral." This development must attend to both the individuality of each person and to every person's communal character. Development must not be limited to increasing material or even psychological and social well-being but should include an integrated personal, communal, cultural, and religious well-being. As Aquinas saw it, our goal is indeed happiness, but that happiness must be the most authentic kind and not the ephemeral enjoyment that so often is mistaken for true happiness. In the words of Jesus, "what good is it for someone to gain the whole world yet forget their soul?" (Mark 8:36).

LIFE AS INDIVIDUAL AND SOCIAL

FAITH REQUIRES ATTENTION TO BOTH INDIVIDUAL AND INSTITUTIONAL LIFE.

The history of religious views of economic life that we have reviewed in this volume makes clear that in every age both individual virtue and proper institutional arrangements have been seen as essential for a moral economic life. The tradition has been most attentive to this relationship of person and institution during eras when people of faith were in control of their own political destiny. In ancient Israel, it was strongest when the Israelites were not under the control of a foreign power. In the Christian tradition, it was clearest when Christians were in control of government, as in the Roman Empire after Constantine, in medieval Europe, and in much of Protestant Europe in the seventeenth century.[3]

Today we live in pluralist democracies where religious leaders typically do not have political authority. Nonetheless, the principles of justice regarding the economy can be articulated in secular as well as religious language, which means that Christians can have a direct impact on national debates about how institutions are shaped, whether those be governmental or private institutions, whether business firms or voluntary associations.

Thus it is religiously important to attend to issues we reviewed in Chapters 12 and 13, such as the relation of personal decision and social structures, the character of coercion, the four problems of economic life, and the moral ecology of markets. To live in the midst of social institutions and not attend to their causal influence on our moral life is like trying to play table tennis while ignoring a strong crosswind.

BOTH PERSONS AND INSTITUTIONS CAN BE SINFUL.

The Christian doctrine of Original Sin reminds us that we are all sinful. Sin characterizes our actions—not always or in every way but often and pervasively enough to convince an attentive person that, as the apostle Paul put it, "I do not do the good I want to do, but the evil I do not want to do, this I keep on doing" (Rom. 7:19). As individual persons, we are sinful.

Starting in Chapters 1 and 2, we reviewed the importance of social institutions in human life. Sociology teaches us that only persons are agents in social life. Therefore only persons can "commit sins"; only persons can be "sinful" in this most literal sense. But as we saw in Chapter 12, social structures "emerge" out of human interactions and have causal impact on people—through restrictions and enablements. Persons who possess authority (and thus coercive power) or who simply enjoy advantages (enablements) within those structures can and often do make conscious and sinful use of institutional restrictions on others. Yet restrictions can also unjustly limit the life possibilities of millions without anyone's conscious decision. All that is required to sustain those structures is the ongoing support of leaders and ordinary citizens.

The teaching of Pope John Paul II resonates with this sociological insight when he warns of "structures of sin."[4] Pope Benedict has pointed to "the presence of Original Sin in social conditions and in the structure of society."[5] Mark O'Keefe, O.S.B., describes this situation: "Human persons—free moral agents—are not only at the root of social sin (though perhaps remotely), they also perpetuate it. Structures of sin continue to exist because individual people continue to operate freely within them."[6] As Eduardo Bonnín has argued, such an analysis often requires a change of laws, for example, those governing the employment contract "so the means of production will be at the service of work."[7] In all matters relating to social structures, personal morality is essential but it cannot suffice.

APPLYING PRINCIPLES TO PARTICULAR SITUATIONS

BOTH THEOLOGY AND SCIENCE ARE NEEDED.

Although we have spent most of this volume reviewing religious texts about economic life, it is clear from them and from our contemporary intellectual situation that the tradition requires an integration of religious principles with a firm grasp of the factual situation at any one place and time. Every concrete decision about how to act as an individual or about how an organization should be structured requires two judgments: one empirical and another normative. The empirical judgment assesses what is going on around us and how various potential actions of ours will change things. Such predictions are never certain, but it would be naïve to take action hoping that we will have a particular effect when we should have known we will not. As we saw in Chapters 12 and 13, the disciplines of economics and sociology are especially helpful.

Yet any empirical judgment would lack direction if it were not combined with a normative judgment about what ought to occur. Combining these empirical and normative judgments in a decision to take a particular action requires prudence, a virtue described in Chapter 8 and that we will encounter again later in this chapter.

CHRISTIAN SOCIAL THOUGHT IS A STOREHOUSE OF WISDOM.

Pope John Paul II has described Catholic social thought as a storehouse of wisdom, "which being ever living and vital, builds upon the foundation laid by our Fathers in the faith."[8] That storehouse ought not be thought of as a file cabinet whose drawers we pull out to extract preprinted recipes for what we should do today. The tradition provides no timeless economic blueprint. As we have seen continually throughout this volume, Christian leaders in each century have understood that storehouse of wisdom as a source of principles for how to proceed but in each era have had to bring those principles to bear, often in new ways in the context of their own time.

We have seen a number of developments in moral teaching concerning economic life within the Christian tradition: on slavery, usury, human rights, and the moral respectability of a life of commerce. In each case, the conditions in the world changed and the Christian tradition needed to decide whether to retain a particular teaching in its original form or whether a more fundamental principle of Christian life required a change in that earlier teaching in the new situation. After centuries of endorsing slavery in some instances, in the modern world Christians came to condemn it in all its forms. The reason for a change in the teaching on slavery, of course, was the more fundamental insight that every human being is a child of God and has a fundamental human dignity which slavery violates.

On the other hand, many other fundamental teachings have not changed. Consider for example the teaching on property ownership as entailing obligations to the needy, which church authorities today have maintained in accordance with the Scriptures and the Fathers of the early church.

The decision about what should and should not change in the teaching on economic life is a difficult but necessary one.[9] Some naïvely cling to a fundamentalism that ignores previous changes in teaching in hopes of avoiding similar decisions today. Others, often driven by prior ideological commitments to baptize or demonize the market system, uncritically ignore portions of the tradition without providing a reasoned explanation arising from within the tradition itself.

ELEMENTS FOR AN ECONOMIC ETHIC

The eight basic convictions entailed by living out faith in Christ within economic life have important implications that can be expressed in thirteen basic elements critically important for a Catholic economic ethic today. Some of these—like human dignity—are fundamental moral realities; others such as love and justice are basic virtues. Still others—like solidarity or sustainability—are characteristics of a vibrant social life.

THE FOUNDATION

HUMAN DIGNITY

The most basic principle of Catholic social thought is that human life is sacred and every human person is endowed with a fundamental human dignity, arising from creation in the image of God and from the redemptive suffering, death, and rising of Jesus Christ. This means that individual initiative and creativity should be part of every person's life and that gainful employment should not simply be an economic necessity but also a means for the full development of human personhood. It also means that everyone has an obligation to protect the human dignity of others. Recall Basil the Great reflecting on the fate of the father trying to decide whether to sell one of his sons into slavery to prevent the starvation of his family. Situations of dire need, human trafficking, racism, and the abusive, demeaning treatment of women, immigrants, or members of ethnic minorities all stand as violations of this fundamental principle.[10]

THE COMMON GOOD

The Christian tradition is neither individualist nor collectivist; it balances the two dimensions of human life, individual and social. Thus the common good entails, as we saw in Chapter 15, two aspects. The first comprises those common conditions of social life that are necessary for each individual to thrive but that no one individual can provide. These include peace, security, order, and opportunity in society and a healthy community and natural environment, and they require concerted public efforts—by society, individuals, and government. The second dimension of the common good is the attainment of the good life by all, at least to a minimum degree. This requires a special focus on the poor and marginalized, not because God loves them more than others but because God's attention has been most focused on those whose human flourishing is most threatened.

THE MOST BASIC VIRTUES

LOVE

The most fundamental moral directive Jesus gave his disciples was to love. In fact, he said, "By this everyone will know that you are my disciples, if you love one another" (John 13:35). Most often in Christian history, love has been identified with interpersonal relationships, and it is indeed essential there, whether those one-to-one relationships are deeply personal or more casual.

But love—"charity" in the more classical expression—is equally essential in institutional relationships. As Pope Benedict XVI has put it,

> Charity is at the heart of the Church's social doctrine. Every responsibility and every commitment spelled out by that doctrine is derived from charity which, according to the teaching of Jesus, is the synthesis of the entire Law (cf. Mt 22:36- 40). It gives real substance to the personal relationship with God and with neighbor; it is the principle not only of micro-relationships (with friends, with family members or within small groups) but also of macro-relationships (social, economic and political ones).[11]

Of course, love in institutional relationships has different contours and expressions than in personal relations. It is the other principles of Catholic social thought that spell out what love entails in public life.

JUSTICE

Justice consists of our obligations toward others and theirs toward us, and it directs all our actions toward the common good. In the Christian tradition justice is an integrated notion, but there are three distinct dimensions that have traditionally been distinguished, each of which plays a role in resolving the question, "Who gets what?"—one of the four problems of economic life reviewed in Chapter 12.

Commutative justice

The Judeo-Christian tradition has always insisted on honesty in one-to-one economic transactions: "Do not use dishonest standards when measuring length, weight, or quantity. Use honest scales and honest weights" (Lev. 19:35-36). I must return what I borrow and must make reparation if I steal. If I hire you to work for me, I have an obligation to pay a fair wage. We saw in Chapter 12 the four problems that every economy has to address: allocation, distribution, scale, and the quality of human relations. Commutative justice is most closely identified with the critical economic need for an efficient allocation of resources to their most highly valued use. Commutative justice is essential in that process because it constitutes the basic rules of marketplace ethics—fulfilling agreements, not stealing, not stooping to fraud, etc. Without a strong sense of commutative justice, markets cannot function.

Commutative justice is also essential for a just distribution—for example in fair wages—and in supporting proper human relations in economic life. Jon Gunnemann has argued persuasively that critical to commutative justice is the existence of mutual competence of those entering into an exchange and a world of shared meanings between them, conditions that become less frequently present as the economy becomes more globalized.[12] Thus commutative justice requires action by both civil society organizations and government (which Pope John Paul II identified as a critical "indirect employer" of each worker).

Distributive justice

This tradition has consistently identified obligations of those who have responsibility for the whole community, whether a king or emperor in an earlier age or a democratically elected government today. As Pope John Paul II put it, "Even prior to the logic of a fair exchange of goods and the forms of justice appropriate to it, there exists something which is due man because he is man, by reason of his lofty dignity."[13] Distributive justice is that form of justice that requires us to organize economic life so that the needs of all are met. Those unable to meet their own needs have a rightful claim on those of us who are prosperous, though it is critical to provide such assistance in a way that respects human dignity and minimizes the risk of dependency in the able-bodied. In the by-gone age of monarchies, it was kings and princes who bore the primary responsibility for distributive justice. Today, in a democracy, not only elected officials but all citizens share that duty.

Social justice

Social (or "general") justice is what Thomas Aquinas called a general virtue. As Normand Paulhus has made clear, it directs other more particular virtues (including the particular virtues of commutative and distributive justice) to the common good.[14] In doing so, social justice articulates obligations of the individual to contribute to the community's good, and obligations of the community to enable each individual to contribute.

The apostle Paul wrote that those who don't work should not eat (2 Thess. 3:10-11). Scholars tell us he was most concerned about those Christians who were so certain of a quick second coming of Christ that they gave up their ordinary work. But the Judeo-Christian tradition has always taught that all able-bodied persons have an obligation to work, a duty to support themselves and their families and to contribute to the community. This obligation to contribute to the community includes not just a productive job, but in our age, when there are so many threats to ecological balance, it also includes obligations to respect the integrity of creation. In this way, the problem of finding the proper scale of the economy in the biosphere—ensuring that our human "footprint" is not too large—is a part of the obligation of social (or "general") justice.

Because everyone has an obligation to contribute, there is the reciprocal obligation on the part of society as a whole to structure itself so that all persons have the opportunity to contribute. Politically, this means that all citizens must have the opportunity to participate in public deliberations and elections. Economically, this means that the private sector and government together have an obligation to ensure a sufficient numbers of jobs so that all those who are able to work can find employment to support themselves and their families.

Rights and duties

As we have seen, the Catholic tradition is quite at home in articulating many of the standards of justice in terms of rights. For example, due to the requirements of distributive justice, the orphan has a right to sustenance and the unemployed worker a right to assistance. But as we saw in Chapters 11 and 16, rights also entail duties.

Everyone's idea of rights entails duties in one sense: that the holder of a human right has the duty to respect that same right in others. But the Catholic understanding goes far beyond this. The unemployed worker who has a right to assistance also has the duty to seek work and to get a job to support self and family. Some neoconservative Catholics have objected to such economic rights because, they say, rights must apply equally to all, in which case even a lazy lout could insist on receiving financial assistance from the community.[15] But this misunderstands the Catholic view: every right entails duties.

EMBODYING VIRTUE IN DAILY LIFE AND STRUCTURES

POWER

Power is the ability to act or significantly affect something, including the capacity to direct or influence the behavior of others. The ability to act and influence others at a personal level is part of the ordinary, integral development that the Christian tradition has endorsed for all people. Powerless people are incomplete, even when this happens through no fault of their own.

In institutional life, power is ubiquitous; it is essential for the creative life of businesses, the vibrancy of churches, the proper structuring of markets by government, the daily life of families, and a host of other activities. Particularly important, in part because of its frequent invisibility, is coercive power: the use of an effective threat to bring about compliance. Person A says to Person B: "You must do X, or Y will happen," and Person B complies.

Parents, coaches, employers, teachers, and the highway patrol all employ coercion, as do dictators and tyrants. Citizens pressing their elected officials rightly attempt to use coercion when they threaten to withhold their votes in the next election. As we saw in Chapter 12, when an organization is functioning well—whether a family, a business firm, or a nation—subordinates understand why the rules exist and how they work, and they craft a rich and meaningful daily life without resentment of the coercive power of authorities. As we will see in greater detail later in this chapter, those exercising power in such organizations should act with transparency and accountability (which varies depending on the governance structure of the organization). A lack of transparency in a democratic culture can create the perception of a self-serving exercise of power, even when power is exercised virtuously, generating suspicion, resistance, and potentially outright rebellion.

Official papal teaching has yet to provide a substantive analysis of power, but at its best, coercion is an ordinary part of life. It is part of the software that allows daily life to boot up each morning. When exercised morally, it is as valuable as friendship or service. The challenge is to understand coercion and ensure that it is exercised with justice and prudence, serving the common good.

SOLIDARITY

The reality of solidarity among people dates back to the Hebrew Scriptures, but the word "solidarity" came to a central theoretical place in the teaching of

Pope John Paul II, who employed the principles of solidarity and subsidiarity to understand and shape public life. As we said in the previous chapter, solidarity is "a firm and persevering determination to commit oneself to the common good; that is to say to the good of all and of each individual, because we are all really responsible for all."[16] It is a relationship among individuals in society and in different societies, and between nations in a globalized world. And, according to the pope, solidarity is a particularly important goal of government at every level, looking out in particular for those who are least able to look out for themselves. Solidarity and its companion, subsidiarity, are critically important in addressing the fourth problem that every economic system must face: the quality of human relationships.

SUBSIDIARITY

Pope Pius XI brought the notion of subsidiarity into worldwide conversation, and it now stands as a fundamental principle, often appealed to by world leaders today. The *Compendium of the Social Doctrine of the Church* describes subsidiarity as having both positive and negative aspects. The positive means that "societies [i.e., organizations] of a superior order must adopt attitudes of help ('subsidium')—therefore support, promotion, development—with respect to lower-order societies."[17] The negative sense of subsidiarity "limits such intervention from usurping the power and agency of lower level governments, communities and institutions, including the family"[18] by insisting that higher-order groups shouldn't impose a solution on more local groups if the latter are able to solve a problem on their own. Subsidiarity is founded on the insight that each person is called to flourish and to take responsibility for that flourishing for themselves and their dependents—and that this frequently requires assistance from society or government. This preference for the local is also a strong endorsement for markets, where cooperation among individuals, and not government central planning, solves many economic problems.

Unfortunately, some Catholics on the political right have misrepresented subsidiarity as referring only to its negative aspect: saying simplistically that private groups and not government should address all problems. The principle, however, begins with the assumption that problems need to be solved. Its negative dimension gives a preference for the more local setting when solutions are available at several levels.

SUSTAINABILITY

A widespread public awareness of environmental problems is a very recent development in human history, for the simple reason that such environmental problems have become a global threat only in the past century, due to the rapidly growing scale of human technology in the biosphere. Nonetheless, we know from the tradition that the nonhuman world has always been held in respect and in fact has been recognized as having a relationship with the Creator independent of us humans. As the psalmist said: "Praise the LORD from the earth, you great sea creatures and all ocean depths, lightning and hail, snow and clouds, stormy winds that do his bidding" (Ps. 148:7-8). This requires, then, that we use creation with respect for its integrity, in accord with our responsibilities as stewards for the natural world. Tremendous ecological challenges face the world, threatening severe hardship for many, particularly the poorest and those with few options in life.

RECIPROCITY — Social Capital .

Trust is fundamental to the proper quality of human relationships in any economy, one of the four problems every economy faces. Suspicion and mistrust are economically inefficient—because we need to spend so many extra resources making rules, checking up on others, and punishing rule-breakers. Mistrust is also dehumanizing, since human flourishing occurs only when we can trust others and they us. As we saw in Chapter 12, social scientists have developed the notion of "social capital" of an organization or society as a sort of stock of trust that is available, recognizing that some groups or societies have more of this social capital than others. Thus trust can be understood as a "flow": social capital grows when trust expands in a group and shrinks when people trust less.

As Pope Benedict XVI indicated in *Caritas in veritate*, it is reciprocity that helps build trust.[19] Reciprocity occurs in a relationship that is neither purely contractual (where one's obligation is enforceable by law) nor solely based in gift (where with a pure gift there is no expectation of any reciprocal action). In reciprocity, there is a general expectation that the other will respond, whether to the initial actor or to a third party. The uncertainty of a response to the initial gift and the vulnerability of the initial actor is what builds trust once that response actually occurs—and this process of reciprocity is an ordinary part of daily economic life. Thus reciprocity, in both personal and economic life, builds trust, which builds social capital. Social capital, then, is a crucial feature of moral life and an essential economic asset, both for any individual business or family and for society as a whole.

HOSPITALITY

Hospitality is the warm and generous reception of guests or strangers, and it needs to be recognized as a fundamental part of Catholic social thought. We saw in Chapter 3 how the Hebrew Scriptures directed the Israelites to welcome resident aliens as members of their family. As we saw in Chapter 7, the Rule of Benedict stressed the importance of hospitality: "All guests who present themselves are to be welcomed as Christ."[20] But it is not only monks who should be hospitable. Nearly everyone values hospitality extended to guests in their home. In this sense, hospitality represents a specific embodiment of love extended to "outsiders."

Hospitality is also an important principle for institutions far larger than families or even monasteries. It can and should characterize the way any organization—whether a business, university, hospital, or government office—interacts with those "outsiders" who come to them—whether customers, students, the sick, or just ordinary citizens. Hospitality plays a large part in the resolution of that fourth problem of economic life: the quality of relations. Whether it is a county clerk answering a citizen's question about a property tax statement or an electronics store employee dealing with an irate customer, these relationships with "others," at their best, are characterized by hospitality.

The dictionary also gives a second definition of hospitality: "the ready receptivity especially to new ideas and interests."[21] This constitutes an extension of the notion of hospitality into intellectual life that is equally important for Christians who are called to embody love of neighbor in all areas of life. People with different views on public policy or on fundamental issues of life ought to demonstrate a kind of hospitality in engaging those "others" with whom they disagree, even if those disagreements are severe. Political life today—even discussions of public policy within the Christian churches—is too often uncivil or downright nasty. Opponents too often demonize each other and engage the other's arguments only to find fault.

Civility is needed, and civility is better than mere tolerance of the other, but both are thin compared to a theological sense of hospitality that recognizes the presence of God in every other human being. Civility is the oil in the engine of social life that keeps the gears of interaction from overheating and locking up. Hospitality goes farther and requires even more: meeting the other with deep respect, real attention, and generous listening. It is both spiritual discipline for individuals and a humanizing policy for organizations.

PARTICIPATION

Scripture scholars tell us that the point behind so many of the laws of the Hebrew Scriptures—such as the sabbatical, Jubilee, and gleaning laws—was to ensure that all Israelites had access to the resources necessary to be full and respected participants in Israelite society.[22] Thus today, particularly in democratic nations, we understand the right to participate in political and economic life as essential to what a good life entails, and in that sense participation is one of those necessities of life to which all persons have a right.

But participation is also a duty. As we have seen, social justice obliges everyone to contribute to society through daily work and through participation in public discourse directed toward the common good. Society has the obligation to facilitate that participation. No longer focused on the agricultural world of the Hebrew Scriptures, the needs related to participation in the twenty-first-century "knowledge economy" include education and employment with just wages.

Participation is so fundamental to human dignity that, as Meghan Clark has put it, "Civil, political, economic, social and cultural rights are all grounded . . . in the right of the human person to participation."[23]

TRANSPARENCY

Transparency in physics is the characteristic of a substance (such as glass) that allows light to pass through it, and, in turn, allows an observer to see through the substance. Applied analogically in the social world, transparency is that characteristic of an organization which allows "outsiders" to see what's happening inside. The moral importance of transparency today represents another development in the tradition of Christian social ethics, one entailed by the importance of participation in social and economic life.

Democratic governments owe a strict accountability to their citizens, who, as we've just seen, have both a right and a duty to participate. Transparency is the first step: allowing citizens to attend meetings where decisions are made or at least learn about the substance of those decisions soon afterwards. In a democratic culture, members of most nongovernmental organizations—whether service clubs, labor unions, chambers of commerce, or churches—have come to expect access to the results and rationales of decisions taken by their leaders. Authentic participation is impossible without this access to information. Because all such organizations rely on rules—and the coercive power described in Chapter 12—effective leaders understand that the only way to ensure members that coercion is not being used for the selfish purposes of the leadership is to engage in transparent practices of governance. Even parents can in most cases more effectively guide and discipline their teenage children if they are clear about their reasons and are open to questions about them.

Of course, some issues need to be kept confidential, for good reason. In nearly all cases, the details of the evaluation of a subordinate by a manager, or of a president by a governing board, should be kept confidential to protect the right to a good reputation of the one being evaluated. And proprietary information such as trade secrets ought to be protected. Yet the more frequent reason those exercising power want to avoid transparency is to avoid accountability. A Christian economic ethic calls for taking a higher road.

PRUDENCE

As we saw in Chapter 8, prudence is the virtue that enables us to apply general principles in resolving particular practical issues. Prudence doesn't decide on those principles but, as Thomas Aquinas puts it, prudence decides "in what manner and by what means" those principles will be implemented in concrete situations.[24]

Putting principles into action is complicated, largely because life is complex and there are often several important values at stake in any situation, and accomplishing some of those values to a greater extent often means accomplishing others less well. And, of course, even if we know how to properly order the values at stake, things are further complicated by the fact that what this or that proposed action will accomplish is itself usually unclear and often in dispute even among social scientists. Prudence is what makes for wise decisions concerning which action to take.

Because of this complexity, principles that are put into action through prudence typically allow for a range of alternatives. Some Catholic commentators, however, have distorted this aspect of prudence, refusing, for example, to acknowledge the injustices caused by markets and instead claiming that prudence allows them to disagree with the popes by rejecting the fundamental criticisms of capitalism in Catholic social thought.

Others have tried to argue that since prudence is involved in applying Catholic principles to economic issues, actions that are "intrinsically evil" (i.e., always wrong) should trump economic issues in the public life of Catholic citizens.[25] But this is oversimplified in two ways. First, any decision about what strategy to use in restricting intrinsically evil actions (e.g., abortion) itself requires prudence (for example, should it be approached at the state or national level? should one press for a law or a Constitutional amendment?, etc.). Second, in Catholic moral theology, the simple fact that some actions are always wrong doesn't guarantee that they are the most important. As Pope John

Paul II put it, "The fact that only the negative commandments oblige always and under all circumstances does not mean that in the moral life prohibitions are more important than the obligation to do good indicated by the positive commandments."[26] Prudence is ubiquitous and its presence does not diminish the moral importance of the efforts prudence guides.

CONCLUSION

In this chapter we have begun the process of answering the question: What does the history of Christian views of economic life mean for the twenty-first century? We began with eight fundamental convictions of Christian faith engaging economic life.

1. The religious foundation

- Both creation and redemption call us to a more responsible economic life.
- Economic life is religiously significant.

2. Setting proper goals

- Faith in God requires the proper ordering of goods.
- Human development must be integral.

3. Life is individual and social.

- Faith requires attention to both individual and institutional life.
- Both persons and institutions can be sinful.

4. Applying principles to particular situations

- Both theology and science are needed.
- Christian social thought is a storehouse of wisdom.

We then identified thirteen basic elements of Catholic social thought critical for economic life.

1. The Foundation

- Human dignity
- The common good

2. The most basic virtues

- Love
- Justice

3. Embodying virtue in daily life and structures

- Power
- Solidarity
- Subsidiarity
- Sustainability
- Reciprocity
- Hospitality
- Participation
- Transparency
- Prudence

These ideas arise from the biblical witness and the long tradition of reflecting upon it in every age. They help to focus and concretize our attention in addressing the fundamental question of this book, but further implications flow from them. And to those we now turn.

Notes

1. Benedict XVI, *Caritas in veritate* 7.
2. Vincent J. Miller, *Consuming Religion: Christian Faith and Practice in a Consumer Culture* (New York: Continuum, 2004).
3. Gustavo Gutiérrez and Richard Shaull, *Freedom and Salvation: A Political Problem* (Atlanta: Knox, 1977), 6–15.
4. Pope John Paul II, *Centesimus annus* 38.
5. Pope Benedict XVI, *Caritas in veritate* 34.
6. Mark O'Keefe, O.S.B., *What Are They Saying About Social Sin?* (Mahwah, NJ: Paulist, 1990), 61.
7. Eduardo Bonnín Barceló, *Estructuras de pecado y pecado social: Elementos para una síntesis teológica* (México, D.F.: Instituto Mexicano de Doctrina Social, 2007), 37. Bonnín here builds on the insight of Pope John Paul II that the ownership of capital depends on its facilitating meaningful, gainful employment.
8. Pope John Paul II, *Centesimus annus* 3.
9. See, for example, John Thomas Noonan, *A Church That Can and Cannot Change: The Development of Catholic Moral Teaching* (Notre Dame: University of Notre Dame Press, 2005).
10. Maarten Biermans articulates the meaning of human dignity for the international labor markets in his *Decency and the Market: The ILO's Decent Work Agenda as a Moral Market Boundary*, PhD dissertation, University of Amsterdam, 2012.
11. Pope Benedict XVI, *Caritas in veritate* 2.
12. Jon Gunnemann, "Capitalism and Commutative Justice," *Annual of the Society of Christian Ethics* (1985): 101–22.

13. Pope John Paul II, *Centesimus annus* 34.

14. Normand J. Paulhus, "Uses and Misuses of the Term 'Social Justice' in the Roman Catholic Tradition," *Journal of Religious Ethics* 15, no. 2 (Fall 1987): 261–82.

15. See, for example, Michael Novak, "The Rights and Wrongs of 'Economic Rights': A Debate Continued," *This World* (Spring 1987): 43–52.

16. Pope John Paul II, *Solicitudo rei socialis* 38.

17. *Compendium of the Social Doctrine of the Church* (Washington, DC: U.S. Conference of Catholic Bishops, 2004), para. 186.

18. Vincent J. Miller, "Santorum and the Lobotomization of Subsidiarity," *America* (Jan. 8, 2012). http://americamagazine.org/blog/entry.cfm?blog_id=2&entry_id=4852. Accessed January 30, 2012.

19. Benedict XVI, *Caritas in veritate* 57.

20. *The Rule of St. Benedict*, chapter 53.

21. Merriam-Webster Unabridged Dictionary, online.

22. See, for example, Leslie J. Hoppe, O.F.M., "The Torah Responds to the Poor," *The Bible Today* 32 (Sept. 1994): 277–82.

23. Meghan J. Clark, "Integrating Human Rights: Participation in John Paul II, Catholic Social Thought and Amartya Sen," *Political Theology* 8, no. 3 (July 2007): 299–317, at 300.

24. ST, II-II, q. 47, a. 6.

25. For a helpful and accessible discussion of intrinsic evil within the political application of Catholic moral theology, see M. Cathleen Kaveny, "Intrinsic Evil and Political Responsibility: Is the Concept of Intrinsic Evil Helpful to the Catholic Voter?" *America* 199, no. 13 (Oct. 27, 2008): 15–19.

26. John Paul II, *Veritatis splendor*, para. 52.

19

Implications for an Economic Ethic Today

The basic convictions and elements for an economic ethic identified in the previous chapter can now be applied more directly to economic life. We can identify with some confidence a number of important implications about what the history of Christian views of economic life means for us today. These would still require a more concrete application in particular places and times. Nonetheless, these seventeen implications will give endorsement to some particular positions for personal life and for public policy and will lead to the rejection of others, creating a range of acceptable options within Catholic social thought.

Morality and Law

PERSONAL MORALITY IS FUNDAMENTAL TO ECONOMIC LIFE.

The relation between a believer, a believing community, and God is central to Christianity. Thus individual Christians have an obligation in their own personal choices to embody the values required for a moral life. Living a moral life will never earn salvation—as that is a gift of God—but believers should indeed be active in living life as God intends. The same is true for economic life, as an employee or employer, consumer or merchant. All talk of institutional transformation is empty when there is no embodiment in our personal lives of the goods we aim to achieve institutionally.

Two central concerns about personal lifestyles are consumerism and the environment. Today we, the prosperous, so often buy things that we don't need, things that in many ways can keep us from a fuller life. Recalling Augustine's assertion that people want to be happy but live lives that will not make them so, we each can review our purchases to ask whether in fact these are truly deepening our relationship with others and God or whether they amount to a fixation on temporal pleasures that leave us less able to attend to the more important things in life. Similarly, it is helpful to learn more about the treatment of workers who produce what we buy. "Fair trade" vendors can assist in making more just consumption decisions.

A similar set of concerns surrounds our choices as they affect the environment. We can so easily choose damaging patterns of transportation—the kind of car we drive and the kind of travel we do—and in our home life—our patterns of consumption and recycling in daily life. The Christian tradition's concern for respecting the integrity of creation calls all to a careful appraisal of how our personal lifestyles affect ecological problems we face as a human community.

And yet, for all the importance of personal morality in economic life, we must not make the mistake that Michael and Kenneth Himes call "the ideology of intimacy," judging public life by the moral standards of interpersonal care. They quote Parker Palmer to make this point: "We must learn to accept and appreciate the fact that public life is fundamentally impersonal. Relations in public are the relations of strangers who do not, and need not, know each other in depth."[1] Morally inappropriate expectations of intimacy can lead to escapism and a rejection of the Christian obligation to improve sinful social structures.

LAW SUPPORTS MORALITY.

An individualistic view of human life tends to see the law as simply a restriction on human freedom. This is not, however, the view of law within the Christian tradition. Recognizing the sinfulness of all humans, the tradition has understood law as performing an important civic function in service to morality. The threat of penalty keeps many people from doing evil. But we are all sinners and are tempted to cut moral corners. The possibility of a government tax audit helps even generally virtuous people pay the taxes they owe. We all strive to live a virtuous life, without the need for the civil law, but few of us can say we've never broken a speed limit or that the threat of a speeding ticket has never led us to drive more slowly than we'd like when we are late for an appointment. As we saw in Chapter 12, the coercive power of law, properly employed, supports morality.

In general, the law represents a sort of floor of moral standards that are required of all people in justice, what Pope Benedict called "the minimum of charity."[2] Thus the law assigns penalties to violations of those most basic standards of morality. Christians, of course, are called to a higher moral standard in addition.

There are some basic standards of morality that ought not be translated into civil law. We recall Aquinas's argument that since humans cannot see the thoughts of others, there is no practical way for human law to forbid destructive thinking, even though a higher moral standard makes the coveting of goods and persons immoral. Similarly, Aquinas argued that forbidding all evil deeds causes more harm than good, as a law against lying would both tie up the courts with petty disputes and would destroy the spontaneity that enriches everyday speech. But even more importantly, Christians hold themselves to the moral standard of love—a personal concern for others—that in its richness and voluntary spontaneity is not conceivably encapsulated in civil law.

GOVERNMENT MUST BE STRONG BUT NOT TOO STRONG.

Because government plays such an important role in the moral ecology of markets, the morality of the market requires a government that is strong enough to design and enforce the proper rules for markets (in the face of pushback from vested economic interests that inevitably resist those rules). And the provision of essential goods and services involves various levels of government—from local school boards providing education to the national government providing courts and funding various services necessary to the well-being of citizens who cannot provide for themselves. The morality of persons and organizations is, as we have seen, greatly supported by laws forbidding the worst abuses (such as laws against racial segregation and sexual harassment). Even civil society organizations are aided by preferential tax treatment by local and national authorities. As we saw in Chapter 15, the common good entails various common conditions of social life that individuals cannot provide for themselves but that the community as a whole can establish, with a critical role played by the government. All this requires a strong and active government.

At the same time, however, there are many reasons why governments should be kept from being too strong. Governments can overreach and try to micro-manage economic and personal affairs that should, in accord with the principle of subsidiarity, be left to individuals and private organizations. Government office holders can use their offices to line their own pockets if there is not an active oversight by citizens' groups insisting on transparency and accountability. And governments can usurp activities better accomplished by civil society organizations. Thus for example, it is often better for governments to pay private charities to provide services to the needy rather than provide them directly.

As with so many things in life, the powers of government can be a problem if they are either too great or too small.

MARKETS

WEALTH CREATION IS GOOD.

The first creation story in Genesis tells us that God saw the natural world as good. Out of that fundamental presumption, the Fathers of the early church insisted that "goods are called good because they do good."[3] God intends thriving for all humans, both eternally and, to the extent possible, even now. For this reason, wealth itself is good, understanding "wealth" here not as the abundance of possessions that makes a person "rich," but as the sum total of goods and services produced in a nation or the world. Similarly good are the work, creativity, invention, and entrepreneurship that generate wealth. As we saw in Chapter 13, economists are especially attuned to the challenges of scarcity and the means available to generate greater wealth.

Yet we must recall that material wealth itself is not the same as well-being but only a rough proxy for it. Gross domestic product (GDP), which measures all the economic activity in the nation, cannot be identified with our ultimate earthly goal, which is the integral well-being of all persons. While the creation of wealth is critically important—in particular for the 1.4 billion people around the globe in extreme poverty living on less than $1.25 per day[4]—we should recall that wealth must be a servant and not the master of our decisions. Those who own wealth in the form of businesses (the means of production) need to recognize the truth of Pope John Paul II's teaching that the moral justification of this particular form of wealth depends on its part in God's plan—creating jobs by means of which ordinary workers can have access to the goods of the earth.

PRIVATE PROPERTY CONTRIBUTES TO A MORAL ECONOMIC LIFE.

As we saw in Chapter 9, Thomas Aquinas taught that nature on its own does not know property ownership, but that human wisdom created it for the benefit of human life. It is morally important that persons and families can own things—whether the bare necessities of food, clothing, and shelter—or the means necessary for the higher things in life—such as education, a comfortable home, or recreation. Although incomes vary greatly, having ownership over things provides an important dimension of human fulfillment, in that the person can undertake life projects, can take on goals and accomplish them. This sense of personal initiative is an important part of human agency and a reflection of human dignity, sharing in God's creative plan for humanity.

At the same time, however, Aquinas and the whole tradition from the Hebrew Scriptures to the present have recognized that there are definite limits on the rights of those who own property. God's intention that the material world should meet the needs of all stands as a limit internal to the proper definition of property ownership. Thus "private" property does not mean that I can do what I want with the things I own. As Pope John Paul II indicated, there is a "social mortgage" on such property, a set of obligations that are typically fulfilled both through personal action—direct sharing with the poor—and through governmental action—the only way to ensure that everyone in a large and pluralistic society will have access to the necessities of life.

MARKETS ARE HUMAN CREATIONS SUBJECT TO MORAL ASSESSMENT.

Albino Barrera has outlined a number of important benefits that markets provide.[5] They allocate resources to productive uses, and allocate products and services to valued ends. Markets offer an important sphere of human freedom, and encourage innovation and investment. They increase our efficiency in the use of resources, and market forces are often helpful tools within government policies (e.g., a carbon tax or a cap-and-trade system) aimed at securing values that markets by themselves ignore. In addition, markets facilitate interpersonal and intergenerational lending, so that young families can borrow money to buy a home and retirees can live off the assets they saved during their working years.

Markets have both positive and negative effects. Markets encourage a number of important virtues. As Adam Smith argued, when properly structured, markets press business firms to be considerate of their customers and creative in becoming more efficient. On the other hand, markets also encourage certain vices such as cutting corners or treating employees or suppliers poorly if those behaviors will increase profits. Markets generate new products and production processes, at times leading to the demise of whole industries, as when the automobile replaced the horse-drawn wagon and the airplane the oceangoing passenger ship. Joseph Schumpeter called this the process of "creative destruction."[6] Consumers typically benefit from this process, but it also leaves behind large numbers of persons who have no resources to sell and at times causes terrible harm in the lives of persons when longstanding livelihoods disappear. This is the downside of creative destruction—hard but not terrible when the people harmed have skills and opportunities to find other employment but devastating for those less well situated, like literally hundreds of millions of people around the world.

In an age of globalization, with increased psychic distance between corporate boards and the persons who may be harmed by their decisions, it is all the more important for a moral stance to characterize both the mindset of decision makers and the rules by which the economic game is played.

ECONOMIC EFFICIENCY IS AN IMPORTANT MORAL VALUE.

As we saw in Chapter 13, efficiency means getting the most out of the resources at hand—or, equivalently, accomplishing a goal with the least expenditure of resources possible. Those resources are most often goods or services that are denominated in monetary terms, such as iron ore in making steel or a teacher's time in educating six-year-olds. However, resources also include things we don't typically buy and sell in the market, such as the psychological stress in drivers caught in heavy traffic or the discomfort of eyes and lungs caused by air pollution. A concern for efficiency tries to reduce the costs of doing whatever it is we do.

The connection to morality is easiest to recognize when the costs we're trying to reduce are clearly obstacles to human flourishing. Here we can think of pain, disease, and death. And we can recognize that conserving nonrenewable natural resources will leave more of them for our great-grandchildren. But even the ordinary productive efficiency of a local business—or of a multinational corporation—is morally important. Producing goods or services using more natural resources than necessary is wasteful and raises prices to the consumer. Of course, striving for such efficiencies can at times endanger other moral values, and so economic efficiency is not an absolute value and profit-seeking can go too far, as we have seen.

Yet even the much-maligned practice of speculation is not without its moral merits. Speculation entails buying more of a product, for example, fuel oil, today in the expectation of selling it in the future at a higher price. The extra demand today does indeed raise today's prices, harming those who need fuel oil now, especially the poor. However, when the speculator eventually sells that product, today's speculation will generate a greater supply of fuel oil in the future than there would have been, and thus prices at that future date will be lower than they would have been—which will help the poor. Speculation creates higher prices now but lower prices later, regularly rendering markets more efficient in providing products with smaller swings in price. Thus speculation is like taking interest when lending money. Because it is economically helpful, it is allowed, even though its harsh effects in the lives of the poor must be offset by independent societal or governmental guarantees assuring that the needs of all will be met.

When citizens call for stronger regulations to reduce economic injustice, they must be very careful to keep in mind the moral importance of efficiency and the economic productivity it can engender. As happens so often in life, too much of either is counterproductive. The same modern insights into how social structures operate that lead us to press for greater justice in markets should lead us to value economic efficiency as well. Both represent important developments of doctrine generated by the interplay of social science and Christian moral commitment.

A CONDITIONAL MORAL APPROVAL OF SELF-INTEREST IN MARKETS IS POSSIBLE.

There is much heated debate about the morality of markets, but this is often focused too narrowly on how markets should be legally structured. Equally important are the three other elements of the moral ecology of markets reviewed in Chapter 12. Catholic social thought does not attempt to tell people exactly how to structure their economic lives. Yet it does hold out a conditional moral endorsement of self-interest in markets, and of markets more generally—if the four elements of the moral ecology of markets are properly established.

The market itself must be properly structured by law. Essential goods and services must be provided to those unable to provide them for themselves. Individuals and organizations must embody basic principles of morality that go beyond the minimum norms required by law. And civil society organizations must elicit a vibrant engagement of persons aiming for both their own personal interests and for the common good. Although Catholic social thought does not specify in detail all four of these elements, Chapters 18, 19, and 20 provide a concrete indication of what range of choices is morally acceptable. The laws that define markets by prohibiting the worst abuses leave economic actors free to make choices in their own interests—often in competition with the interests of others. Within a properly structured moral ecology of markets, Christians can justly seek their interests in economic life—even while we recognize that the moral life calls us to go beyond the requirements of justice. As Michael and Kenneth Himes have observed, "Catholicism's optimism regarding the person's ability to act on motives other than self-interest means that in creating a social order institutions can rely upon human dispositions toward cooperation and self-giving, not just competition."[7]

Although self-interest in markets can in the proper situation have a conditional moral defense, without the proper definition of markets and their context, self-interest within markets is frequently nothing but sinful selfishness.

And since none of us lives in a world or a nation where the moral ecology of markets is already justly structured, we understand there is much work to be done in transforming, as Pope Benedict put it, "that complex of institutions that give structure to the life of society, juridically, civilly, politically and culturally."[8] To the extent that the moral ecology of markets falls short of its proper contours, we the prosperous stand complicit in the injustices thus created. There are many reasons why the market economy today deserves praise, but many as well why it must be criticized and changed.

BENEFICIARIES OF THE MARKET SYSTEM ARE COMPLICIT IN THE HARMS MARKETS CAUSE TO DISTANT OTHERS.

Understanding how markets operate, we the prosperous, who benefit so much from the efficiency and productivity of markets, must admit that we are complicit in the harms markets so frequently cause for distant others. Those harms might be explicit, as when poor workers in North Carolina or Mexico lose their jobs when the manufacturing plants are moved to China, or they might be even more indirectly caused as when the poor farmers in Bolivia are left behind by economic processes that occur, as Pope John Paul said, "over their heads."[9]

More needs to be said about the manner of our causal effect on markets. On the one hand, no one of us has a perceptible influence on the harms caused to unfortunate people around the world, since if any one of us simply stopped buying and selling altogether, the harms would continue unabated. Yet as our brief survey of the sociology of institutions in Chapter 12 indicated, because all of us together do indeed create and sustain this social structure we call the market, we do have a causal responsibility for the harms markets generate.

Thus our obligation to offset that complicity may need to result in various changes in both personal action and public policy. Consumers today can become far better informed about the production processes generating the products they purchase. Fair trade coffee and college campus decisions to buy sweatshirts from responsible textile suppliers are important examples. The decision of the nation to reduce trade barriers will generate lower prices for consumers but can have the effect of putting significant numbers of people out of work. Thus trade adjustment assistance is a morally important response, providing funds to dislocated workers for retraining and relocation to find a decent job.

A similar issue of national complicity surrounds immigration policy in the United States, where approximately eleven million people, mostly Mexicans, live in the United States without proper documentation. Some on the political right have self-righteously called for them all to be deported, but it is an economic fact that many industries in the U.S. depend upon the work of these undocumented workers. The Christian tradition recalls the biblical charge that the "stranger in the land"—the undocumented worker of the time—should be treated with the respect of a family member,[10] even if they do not possess all the same rights as citizens. The U.S. Bishops, for example, have proposed comprehensive immigration reform that would both treat undocumented workers better and invest in economic development in Mexico, so fewer Mexican workers would feel the need to travel to the U.S. simply to feed their families back at home.[11]

INTERNATIONAL TRADE IS GOOD BUT MUST BE SUBJECT TO RULES.

Commercial activity that crosses national borders provides opportunities for exchange quite similar to those within a nation, though the likelihood of hardships created by the process is greater. Just as the building of the railroads in the nineteenth century allowed bakers in Boston to buy less expensive wheat grown in the Midwest and sell bread for a lower price, so international trade today allows consumers to pay lower prices for a wide range of agricultural and manufactured products. The downside to such trade is that local producers are left without a job—whether that is nineteenth-century farmers who used to grow wheat in New England or twenty-first-century workers who used to make televisions in Chicago.

Many people have opposed international trade on the grounds that it undermines traditional communities, which it certainly does. The problem, of course, is that growing wheat in Kansas and shipping it to Boston did the same. Christians are committed to living a communal life, but the character of our communities has changed dramatically over the centuries. We saw earlier in this chapter the importance of avoiding "the ideology of intimacy" in public life. What is needed for contemporary communitarian theory is a social and political—but not a sentimental—concept of community.[12]

In addition, others, especially labor unions, have objected to the loss of jobs that trade generates, forgetting two important things. The first is that when a nation imports goods of one kind, it typically "pays for" those goods by exporting goods or services of another kind. Lower employment in one sector is typically accompanied by higher employment in another. The second is that while Christians should recognize the loss of a job at home as a moral loss, the creation of a job for an unemployed worker in another nation is a moral gain.

Because the pain of dislocation from trade and the difficulty of finding another job are the result of a conscious decision by government to reduce trade barriers, the nation should be willing to take some of the benefits created by trade and spend them to relieve some of the pain. Thus as we have seen, justice would require the raising of taxes sufficient to fund "trade adjustment assistance" to pay for retraining and/or relocation expenses of those unemployed because of increased trade.

Serious injustice to workers can accompany trade, particularly when the firms involved in international commerce benefit from lax labor and environmental laws in developing nations, or from lax enforcement when appropriate laws do exist. Serious violations of workers' rights occur regularly—from peremptory firings and denial of bathroom breaks to unsafe working conditions and sexual harassment. Similarly, some nations are attractive sites for "dirty" industries because of environmental laws that are weak or unenforced. Even more egregious are the restrictions (tariffs and/or quotas) nearly all wealthy nations have put on the importation of textiles and agricultural products from poor nations—even while those same prosperous countries press developing nations to open their own markets to import industrial products and professional services. The playing field is anything but level. All such conditions violate fundamental principles of Christian economic ethics we have seen in the previous chapter.

For these reasons, international trade agreements should include stipulations for labor and environmental safeguards. Historically, the World Trade Organization has avoided such "nontrade" issues out of a realistic fear that protectionist forces opposed to trade will invent labor or environmental issues simply to restrict trade in order to protect their narrow vested interests. Although it is difficult to achieve a balance between these competing values, the answer cannot be a focus on only one value to the neglect of others.

THE CONDITIONAL MORAL ENDORSEMENT OF MARKETS DOES NOT JUSTIFY SELF-INTEREST IN LOBBYING.

As we have seen, Catholic social thought can provide a conditional moral approval of self-interested action in markets. If the four elements of the moral ecology of markets outlined in Chapter 12 are properly structured, the exercise of self-interest can be justified (though, of course, self-interest is not the only goal that individuals and organizations should be pursuing). As we saw in Chapter 13, Adam Smith, too, had a number of conditions in mind when he endorsed "the invisible hand" of the market.

Only after the rules and moral context of the game are properly defined is the exercise of one's own interests—attempts to win the game—justifiable. But when we move to a different context, such as governmental debates about what the rules of the game should be, we must leave behind this "economic" justification for self-interest.

Thus lobbying by business corporations cannot enjoy any moral approbation from the potential moral endorsement just described for the market-based actions of those same corporations. Lobbying is typically an attempt to change a law to benefit the firms involved. It would be wrong for the hockey-playing universities in colder regions of the U.S. to petition the NCAA to require that all hockey practices occur outdoors on natural ice rinks, because this would unfairly doom hockey at schools in warmer climates. This sort of exercise of self-interest in changing the rules of the game is quite different from that exercised by the hockey teams themselves, who exert their self-interest in trying to win the game within the rules.

Similarly, when business firms turn to Congress to shape the rules of the game, arguments based on the common good are required. The same is true, of course, for the lobbyists of labor unions and other organizations. The fact that all lobbyists actually do appeal to the common good in making their argument to lawmakers is an indication of the validity of this insight, even though such appeals are all too often an insincere cover for narrow self-interest.

BUSINESS AND LABOR

A MORAL ECONOMY MUST PROVIDE SUFFICIENT EMPLOYMENT AT JUST WAGES.

We have seen time and again that Catholic social thought understands gainful employment as essential for fulfilling the ancient Judeo-Christian commitment to the meeting of needs. Whereas in most of human history most people were subsistence farmers and met their needs by keeping a share of the food they grew, in the advanced nations today the vast majority of us attain our rightful access to the goods of the earth through the wages we earn in employment. Thus we saw the popes conclude that employment is a human right and wages must be sufficient to provide "reasonable and frugal comfort." The discrepancy within our current capitalist system between these obligations and the reality of morally inadequate wages and high unemployment stands as an ongoing indictment of the economic system.

Some on the political right have argued that given the new institutional framework of the global market system, Christianity should give up its concerns about just wages and a right to employment, since these simply "do not work" in a modern capitalist system. However, as we have seen, the popes have resolutely refused to drop these concerns and have instead held them as central to the Christian message about economic life. Pope John Paul II went so far as to claim that proprietors and stockholders of businesses can justify their ownership only by the creation of jobs and the payment of just wages. We saw in Chapter 11 how Christian teaching on usury, slavery, and human rights changed in order to remain faithful to more fundamental moral commitments. However, the teaching on the just wage has *not* changed, precisely out of faithfulness to the traditional conviction that God intends all people to meet their needs.

In the light of unemployment and low wages, most industrialized nations have developed laws and programs to assist workers, ranging from European rules making it hard to lay off workers to American reliance on unemployment insurance during a recession. Similarly, as we saw earlier, wages are often supplemented by payments to families or, in the U.S., by the Earned Income Tax Credit.

From the perspective of critics of markets on the left, immoral firms mistreat their workers through low wages and layoff notices during recession—and government is then simply making up for these grave injustices. A more positive perspective is possible in Catholic social thought: that firms and all individuals involved in the market system should openly acknowledge these moral failures in the way markets deal with employment and wages and then become strong advocates of those very government programs that supplement low wages (particularly for workers with families) and provide protection for the unemployed.

What cannot be defended within this tradition is either ignoring the systemic obligations entailed in the just wage doctrine or refusing to raise sufficient government revenues through taxation to structure appropriate supplements to low wages and for periods of temporary unemployment. Such assistance must be provided in ways that minimize the risk of creating dependency, but wage supplements create much less of this risk than do welfare payments to the long-term able-bodied unemployed. Catholic social teaching requires more than this (recall Pope Benedict's teaching on the logic of gift), but these are minimum standards of justice.

THE BUSINESS FIRM IS A COMMUNITY OF PERSONS, NOT ONLY OF INVESTORS.

The modern popes insist that the business firm be understood as a community of all persons that make up that organization—owners, managers, and workers—and not simply as a group of owners who get to make all the decisions. This is a stronger claim than the frequent advice in management literature that firms should consider the interest of all stakeholders, not simply all stockholders. A Catholic view of the firm recognizes the obligations that owners of capital have in the economy-wide process of providing employment for workers. And while no single firm has an obligation to offer a job to any single job applicant, the firm is under a moral obligation to recognize its part in that process and, at a minimum, to support societal and governmental efforts to respect the rights of workers.[13]

As we saw in the previous chapter, institutions are understood in the Catholic tradition as human creations and thus subject to moral evaluation. Some people today talk as if the character of the corporation in U.S. law is simply natural rather than created. But it was law that created the limited liability corporation, and the courts that declared corporations to have the status of legal persons. Thus there is nothing improper about citizens calling for more participative forms of governance.[14] One structural solution employed in parts of Europe is "co-determination," a law requiring that up to half of the members of corporate governing boards in large firms be elected by the firm's employees. Many highly successful firms in Germany and elsewhere are run in this way.[15]

Michael Naughton has pointed out that the attention to relation and gratuitousness that Pope Benedict calls for within the firm has been echoed by a number of business leaders and academics. As early as the 1970s, Robert Greenleaf called for the development of a "theology of institutions" that attends to "the category of relation."[16]

Beyond what law might require of all firms, Catholic social thought proposes a way to understand a firm at its best, with a structure and mission that some firms today already adopt and others could. Naughton describes a small but successful manufacturing firm in St. Paul, Minnesota, Reell Precision Manufacturing. Its founders explicitly set out to form an organization where workers are respected, where even top managers have time for a full family life, and where suppliers and customers are treated well. They need to make a profit, of course, and they do. But the firm's leadership compares profit to how a person might look at food: "It is essential in order to maintain your health and strength so you can realize your real purpose."[17] Profit is a means to an end, not the end itself.

LABOR UNIONS ARE A MORALLY IMPORTANT PART OF A JUST ECONOMY.

From Leo XIII's *Rerum novarum* onward, the popes of recent centuries have uniformly supported the creation of labor unions by working people. As we saw in Chapter 14, Leo argued that the power of employers easily exceeded that of workers, particularly without "workmen's organizations." He recognized that employers can frequently impose harsh working conditions and an unjustly low wage on workers, who consent to them because of a lack of options.

The preferred approach of Leo and Pius XI—the "corporatist" organization of workers, managers, and owners in each industry—did not prove viable, and labor unions as we know them appeared instead. These aim to be a countervailing power to allow workers to stand up to the greater power of well-endowed firms. Workers seek to join unions for a number of other reasons: a living wage, greater safety in the workplace, retirement and health benefits, security against being fired without good reason, and a fair administration of workplace rules. Unionized workers fare better than other workers in all these categories.[18]

Union membership in the U.S. as a percentage of all workers has been dropping for decades. There are several causes: international trade, the shift of employment from manufacturing to service industries, the slanting of U.S. labor law in favor of employers, and a growing employer militancy against unions, including the hiring of "union busting" firms to help businesses stop efforts to unionize the workplace.

Of course, unions can become as sinful and oblivious of the common good as businesses can. They must aim for the good of all and not simply their members. Yet the existence of a few irresponsible labor unions no more condemns all unions than the existence of some irresponsible firms condemns all businesses. Because of the connection between a wage and the meeting of needs (including healthcare and retirement savings), Catholic social thought has consistently supported the right of workers to organize unions.

CARE FOR PERSONS AND THE EARTH

THE NEEDS OF ALL MUST BE MET.

Throughout the history of Jewish and Christian views of economic life, there has been an unwavering insistence that a moral economic system must meet the needs of all. This is, in a sense, the gold standard for morality in economic life. From the gleaning laws of the Hebrew Scriptures that require the farmer to leave the corners of the field of wheat unharvested, to Thomas Aquinas's explanation of private property ownership as requiring the prosperous to use their surplus to meet the needs of others, to modern papal teaching about the social mortgage on all property, the tradition has understood God's relationship with humans as requiring that the natural world be employed to meet the needs of all. This is not some quaint and irrelevant belief of ages past. It has been the bedrock of Christian teaching on economic life and remains vividly true today. This is the theological foundation for the preferential option for the poor, and it is the central concern in the Christian answer to the question, "What goods and services are essential?"—a query posed in Chapter 12 as part of the moral ecology of markets. This insight is why the common good makes no sense unless it includes at least a minimum of frugal comfort for everyone.

Needs, of course, are culturally contextual. They are not absolute, not the same in all places. Thus the tradition does not insist on some sort of daily minimum number of calories or minimum shelter from the weather through clothing and home. Needs are, as the philosopher Michael Walzer has explained, "expansive."[19] They do tend to grow as the average material wealth of a society rises. In part this is because of an appropriate rise in the general expectation for normal human comfort as people move out of abject poverty, but also this is in part due to the change in economic and cultural context that greater wealth brings on for even the prosperous.

Thus in many parts of the United States today, an automobile is a necessity; without a car one cannot get to work or to the grocery where there is not adequate public transit. At the same time, of course, in our sinfulness we can easily come to think of something as a need when it isn't. So, for example, while a case might be made that twenty-somethings today need a cellphone in order to participate in daily cultural life, there would seem to be little reason that special ring tones for a cellphone are a necessity. When we look at the world market for ring tones, more than two billion dollars per year, there is little warrant for considering such extras anything but luxuries. Other examples of luxuries appearing to be necessities are plentiful. One very promising approach to "what people need" is Amartya Sen's "capability" approach: focusing on people's capacities to accomplish basic goals, such as the ability to age with economic security or to participate in political processes. Here the stress is not on having economic resources (since in some situations money cannot bring about the goal) but on each person's ability to accomplish fundamental goals.[20]

SEVERE ECONOMIC INEQUALITY UNDERMINES HUMAN WELL-BEING.

As we have seen, the history of Christian thinking on economic life has emphasized the meeting of needs and has not historically addressed itself to economic inequality, even though there has been a consistent assertion that rich and poor are fundamentally equal in the eyes of God. The Christian tradition has simply never argued that everyone should have the same income or wealth. In fact, it has recognized a number of morally important reasons for differences in income—for example, compensation for harder work or longer hours, or more years of educational preparation or for taking on greater risk.[21]

In Chapter 16 we saw Pope Benedict's warning that increasing inequality leads to "the progressive erosion of 'social capital': the network of relationships of trust, dependability, and respect for rules, all of which are indispensable for any form of civil coexistence."[22] Much recent research has supported this conclusion, ascribing the negative effects of inequality to a more harshly competitive atmosphere that inequality can generate, even for the wealthy in a society with high income or wealth inequality.[23] Thus although the meeting of needs remains fundamental to Catholic social thought, the tradition has developed an awareness of the importance of reducing extreme levels of inequality in order to protect human dignity.[24]

THE SUSTAINABILITY OF THE EARTH IS A RELIGIOUS AND ECONOMIC REQUIREMENT.

Our ecological problems on a global scale are quite recent in human history and thus the reflections on economic life in earlier eras of the Christian story do not explicitly address many of problems that we face today: global warming, threats to the ozone layer, the depletion of groundwater, the pollution of rivers, lakes, oceans, and atmosphere. Nonetheless, we have seen that there are theological resources in the Christian tradition for this analysis, in particular the understanding of the material world as having its own independent dignity and even a relation to the Creator independent of humanity.

We saw in Chapter 12 how the market system is incapable of determining the proper scale of the economy in the biosphere, because individual market agents have a strong incentive to ignore their third-party effects—externalities—if they are not constrained by law to account for them in their calculation of business profitability or consumer self-interest. As a result, mainstream economists recognize that there is an important role for government in regulating economic life so as to incorporate a concern for ecological responsibility through law. A secondary question concerns the policy instruments to be employed, and here economics is correct in advocating market-based solutions (for example, a carbon tax or a cap-and-trade system to reduce CO_2 emissions) rather than government mandates of particular technologies (which often become technologically outdated soon after being required).

CONCLUSION

In this chapter, we have briefly reviewed a number of important implications for economic life deriving from the analysis outlined in the previous chapter.

1. Morality and law

- Personal morality is fundamental to economic life.
- Law supports morality.
- Government must be strong but not too strong.

2. Markets

- Wealth creation is good.
- Private property contributes to a moral economic life.
- Markets are human creations subject to moral assessment.
- Economic efficiency is an important moral value.
- A conditional moral approval of self-interest in markets is possible.
- Beneficiaries of the market system are complicit in the harms markets cause to distant others.
- International trade is good but must be subject to rules.
- The conditional moral endorsement of markets does not justify self-interest in lobbying.

3. Business and labor

- A moral economy must provide sufficient employment at just wages.
- The business firm is a community of persons, not only of investors.
- Labor unions are a morally important part of a just economy.

4. Care for persons and the Earth

- The needs of all must be met.
- Severe economic inequality undermines human well-being.
- The sustainability of the earth is a religious and economic requirement.

This framework for approaching economic life in a morally responsible way may seem complicated. Yet it is the complexity of human life that requires us to reject simplistic analyses—whether from the political left or right—that pretend that one or two simple convictions will resolve all problems. The subtlety of the Christian tradition in addressing different economic situations over the centuries requires a similarly careful approach to economic issues today.

One more step is yet to be taken: what these views based in the Christian tradition mean for the proper relation among society, government, and the market. To that task we now turn.

Notes

1. Parker Palmer, *The Company of Strangers* (New York: Crossroad, 1986), cited in Michael J. Himes and Kenneth R. Himes, O.F.M., *Fullness of Faith: The Public Significance of Theology* (New York: Paulist, 1993), 146.

2. Benedict XVI, *Caritas in veritate* 35.

3. Clement of Alexandria, *Quis Dives Salvetur?*, 14, in Charles Avila, *Ownership: Early Christian Teaching* (Maryknoll, NY: Orbis, 1983), 43.

4. 2005 World Bank data. http://web.worldbank.org/WBSITE/EXTERNAL/EXTDEC/EXTRESEARCH/0,,contentMDK:21882162~page-PK:64165401~piPK:64165026~theSitePK:469382,00.html. Accessed January 31, 2012.

5. Albino Barrera, "Theological Foundations of the Market," in *The Moral Dynamics of Economic Life: An Extension and Critique of Caritas in Veritate*, ed. Daniel K. Finn (New York: Oxford University Press, 2012).

6. Joseph Schumpeter, *Capitalism, Socialism, and Democracy* (New York: Harper, 1975), 82–85.

7. Himes and Himes, *Fullness of Faith*, 38.

8. Benedict XVI, *Caritas in veritate* 7.

9. John Paul II, *Centesimus annus* 33.

10. Pontifical Biblical Commission, *Bible and Morality*, 132.

11. See U.S. Conference of Catholic Bishops, "Comprehensive Immigration Reform." http://www.usccb.org/issues-and-action/human-life-and-dignity/immigration/churchteachingonimmigrationreform.cfm. Accessed May 1, 2012.

12. Himes and Himes, *Fullness of Faith*, 35.

13. For a treatment of moral business practice in the Catholic tradition, see Pontifical Council for Justice and Peace, "Vocation of the Business Leader: A Reflection," Pamphlet published by the Council, 2012.

14. For a brief survey of German industrial standards for worker participation in governance, see Thomas Geoghegan, "Notebook: Consider the Germans," *Harper's*, March 2010, 7–9.

15. See M. Roth, "Employee Participation, Corporate Governance and the Firm: A Transatlantic View Focused on Occupational Pensions and Co-determination," *European Business Organization Law Review* 11, no. 1 (March 1, 2010): 51–85. See also Abraham Shuchman, *Codetermination: Labor's Middle Way in Germany* (Washington, DC: Public Affairs Press 1957).

16. Michael Naughton, "The Business Enterprise," chapter 2 in Finn, ed., *The Moral Dynamics of Economic Life*.

17. Quoted in Michael J. Naughton, "The Corporation as a Community of Work: Understanding the Firm within the Catholic Social Tradition," *Ave Maria Law Journal* (Winter 2006): 33–75, at 57.

18. For further treatment of the relation of labor unions and religion, see *A Worker Justice Reader: Essential Writings on Religion and Labor*, ed. Joy Heine and Cynthia Brooke (Maryknoll, NY: Orbis, 2010).

19. Michael Walzer, *Spheres of Justice: A Defense of Pluralism and Equality* (New York: Basic Books, 1983), 67.

20. See, for example, Amartya K. Sen, *Commodities and Capabilities* (Oxford: Oxford University Press, 1985).

21. See, for example, U.S. Conference of Catholic Bishops, *Economic Justice for All: Pastoral Letter on Catholic Social Teaching and the U.S. Economy* (Washington, DC: National Conference of Catholic Bishops, 1986), para. 74 and 185.

22. Benedict XVI, *Caritas in veritate* 32.

23. Richard G. Wilkinson and Kate Pickett, *The Spirit Level: Why Greater Equality Makes Societies Stronger* (New York: Bloomsbury, 2010). For a discussion of measuring economic inequality more accurately than a simple dependence on measuring income, see Douglas A. Hicks, *Inequality and Christian Ethics* (Cambridge/New York: Cambridge University Press, 2000).

24. Drew Christiansen, S.J., "On Relative Equality: Catholic Egalitarianism after Vatican II," *Theological Studies* 45, no. 4 (Dec. 1984): 651–75.

20

Society, Government, and Market: Getting the Relationships Right

Over the past two chapters we have seen an outline of an economic ethic for our day arising from the history of Christian views of economic life as understood within Catholic social thought. It will now be helpful to stand back and look at the basic contours of social, economic, and political life.

There is a strong tendency in contemporary life to engage this conversation as if it were simply about the relationship between markets and government. Important as that relationship is, however, the Catholic tradition has long held that it will not be understood properly unless we also include society in the picture. As Pope Benedict XVI put it, "the exclusively binary model of market-plus-state is corrosive of society, while economic forms based on solidarity, which find their natural home in civil society without being restricted to it, build up society."[1] Thus the Catholic view is that society, government, and market must be in proper relation for a moral economic life.

To achieve this, we need to attend to ten critical issues, discerning what the tradition of Catholic social thought implies.

THE RELATION OF SOCIETY, GOVERNMENT, AND MARKET

SOCIETY AS MORE BASIC THAN GOVERNMENT OR MARKET

Catholic social thought has insisted on the difference between government and society, and while many social goals must be achieved through governmental decision, the organizations of civil society are equally essential for a full human life. We saw that Pope John Paul II argued that this vibrancy of civil society represents a kind of subjectivity of society as a whole, a way that society thinks through its problems and addresses them.[2] This appreciation for society as an organic whole is often rejected by more individualistic perspectives, but it is an empirically more accurate way to understand social life and provides the basis for a solution to many of the problems we currently face. And as we saw in the previous chapter, it is reciprocity—actions based neither in contract nor pure gift—that generates the social trust that provides the oxygen of daily interpersonal and institutional relationships.

This appreciation for civil society organizations is particularly important in an age of globalization, where we need to develop a stronger juridical framework for international commerce in a world without a world government. The plethora of nongovernmental organizations that are involved in addressing the various aspects of international relationships is proof of the vibrancy of the conversation. Nation-states must come to better appreciate the role of such organizations, even those within each nation that may be highly critical of the party in power. Only through a process whereby people's organizations and the governments of nations can interact with transparency and accountability can a truly democratic and polyarchic governance be established.

The dignity of the human person is the starting point for thinking about society, government, and market. Because the Christian tradition has consistently seen the person as simultaneously individual and social, society is more fundamental than market and government, institutions that emerge from the interaction of persons in their daily lives. The family, of course, is the most basic institution within society.

DEMOCRATIC GOVERNMENT AS SELF-GOVERNMENT

One of the most peculiar and destructive changes in political life in the United States and a number of other nations in recent years has been the depiction of government as an oppressive force rather than as the institution that we the people have created for self-government. The driving force behind this shift seems to be an unfortunate fact of electoral politics: those who run for office "against government" have tapped into a resentment that humans are tempted to have against paying taxes and against anyone having power over them.

But such rhetoric plays with fire in a straw house. Or, as Lutheran bishop Peter Rogness described acidic political critique, "When in a democracy it is twisted to rally people against their own government, it is like an immune system run amuck that eats the very body in which it resides."[3] From the Christian perspective, democratic governments and the moral use of coercive power are essential in carrying out various duties, even when there is a disagreement among the citizenry as to how that is to be done. So often missing today is the traditional notion of the "loyal opposition," those opposed to what the majority party is doing but still respectful of the system, acting as they would want the other side to act when the government changes hands. Unfortunately, all too many politicians and their supporters endorse the view that their opponents are simply selfish and insincere.

Christians on the right too often ignore the necessary functions of government as understood in the tradition. Simply calling for "smaller government" without starting with government's necessary functions is like going into the shoe store and asking for smaller shoes without inquiring how large is the foot to be shod. Meanwhile, Christians on the left often naïvely overstate the role of government in the economy, presuming that governments will achieve whatever they intend. At the same time, the free-rider problem, the special interest effect, and regulatory capture reviewed in Chapter 13 caution us not to rely excessively on government.

We need lively substantive arguments within and between civil society organizations about what functions should be carried out through government and which not. This is an essential dimension of "the subjectivity of society," as Pope John Paul II described it. The Catholic tradition stresses that government must provide a strong juridical structure for the market to prevent abuses, must ensure that the needs of all are met, must respect the rights of individuals, and must allow and encourage civil society organizations to thrive. Government is how society governs its life together. It is not an alien force, even when "the other side" is in power.

RELIGIOUS PARTICIPATION IN PUBLIC DEBATE IN PLURALISTIC SOCIETIES

We saw in the previous chapter why economic life is religiously significant for Christians and how the defense of human dignity and the common good requires both personal morality and well-structured public institutions. Yet some secular critics have argued that Christians—and the faith-based organizations of civil society—ought not participate in public debate and should not try to influence government policy. One of those arguments is founded on a misunderstanding of the U.S. Constitution and "the wall between church and state." However, the Constitution's prohibition is not intended to prevent religious people from influencing government, but to prevent the government from formally endorsing ("establishing") any particular religion or Christian denomination as the official religion of the nation.

The other major objection is that because Christians base their arguments in religious claims about God or Jesus or the Bible, and because many people in the nation do not share that faith, Christians ought to remain outside of public discourse. But this objection misunderstands the character of all intellectual argument, as everyone across the political spectrum has their own experts on whom they rely. Marxists study Karl Marx, and libertarians John Locke, but when members of either group make an argument at city hall or in Congress we will hear no quotations from Marx or Locke. Instead they, just like Christians, will articulate their arguments in more widely accessible ways.

In this, Catholics have an advantage over Protestants, because of the historic appreciation within the Catholic tradition for philosophy and the use of human reason to sort out problems. Recall Thomas Aquinas's argument that because the natural world was structured by God in creation, human rationality, without the aid of biblical revelation, is able to discern a moral order through natural law ethics. Thus the Catholic tradition has historically been at ease in speaking in a vocabulary that is not specifically religious. Today it talks, for example, of human dignity and human rights, knowing that these are based on human nature, which is ultimately founded in God. Secular interpretations of these notions often fall short (e.g., many understand rights without complementary duties), but such language is nonetheless helpful in presenting the insights of the Christian tradition in a pluralistic culture.

One further misunderstanding of the role of religious conviction in the economy is created by a simple view of public life as entailing three "systems" in any society: a political system, an economic system, and a "moral-cultural" system. Michael Novak has proposed this typology for understanding the relationship of faith and economic life, but it can implicitly reduce faith (and values and science) to one of three co-equal sets of institutions, procedures, and meanings.[4] Novak no doubt introduces this idea to remind well-intentioned Christians that they shouldn't naïvely try to pass laws to force the economy to match all their high ideals.[5] Yet while he concedes that "public authority properly forbids some practices, regulates others, commands others," the themes he appeals to in the Christian tradition all seem to be chosen to support a smaller role for government in the marketplace.

Lacking in this typology is a balanced argument for how the insights of the moral-cultural system—and in particular, the Christian tradition—lead to endorsing some rules to structure markets but not others. Novak's call for personal virtue and corporate responsibility arising from the three-systems approach is needed but insufficient for an adequate Christian economic ethic. We must also take responsibility for shaping a moral ecology of markets that encourages spontaneity and creativity as a part of the integral human development of each person and generates wealth with far less harm to the vulnerable than occurs now, both domestically and around the world. Law supports morality, so it is essential that all citizens work for a well-structured system of laws.

POLITICAL DECISIONS ABOUT ECONOMIC STRUCTURES

MARKET-STRUCTURED SPONTANEITY

As we saw in Chapter 12, a market is an institution that embodies subsidiarity, allowing individuals to interact spontaneously with each other to accomplish their goals within the rules that forbid certain abusive activities. In this sense, markets are a peculiar mixture of spontaneity and design.

As we saw in the previous chapter, wealth creation and economic efficiency are morally important. Thus Christian social thought appreciates markets and even offers the possibility of a conditional moral defense of the exercise of self-interest in markets because of the many beneficial outcomes that markets make possible in the lives of ordinary people. From an economic point of view, we can say that markets have a kind of economic efficiency that a government can never attain. Economic conditions vary from hour to hour and from place to place, and individuals—locally situated and ready to act on knowledge they have personally obtained—can make better use of information and resources than can any government planning agency, which by nature must establish general procedures to be applied over time and space. The great libertarian philosopher/economist Friedrich Hayek correctly stressed this knowledge-based argument for markets.[6] It was indeed the inefficiency of the central planning system of the Soviet Union that led to its collapse in the late twentieth century.

In earlier ages, the Christian tradition was quite skeptical of commerce and "the merchant." The reason, of course, was that business greed undermines other values. This was part of what economist Joseph Schumpeter warned of when he argued that capitalism undermines its own moral foundations.[7] Thus Catholic social thought has consistently said that the logic and spontaneity of profit-seeking must be constrained, both by the personal morality of individuals in the market (who decide they will not seek a maximum of profit when this conflicts with basic moral values), by laws that forbid certain activities considered too abusive, and by the normative expectations of society's many organizations. Properly constrained, spontaneous self-interested action within markets can merit a (conditional) moral approbation.

One of the principal ways that societies appropriately limit the spontaneity of markets is to make certain types of economic exchanges illegal. These are referred to as "blocked exchanges." A wide variety of human values otherwise would face a quick end or a slow erosion. Thus we forbid the sale of babies to childless couples. Neither justice in the court system nor political power is to be bought or sold, nor citizens' votes in elections. And of course, the sale of a host of other goods and services is blocked, including heroin, state secrets, autos without seatbelts, surface-to-air missiles, and medical services from persons not certified as physicians. Perhaps most important here is the prevention of exchanges of desperation: the sale of self or a child into slavery, loans of money at exorbitant interest rates, or, in many sectors of the economy, accepting a job at less than the legal minimum wage. A completely spontaneous, literally "free" market would be a moral and economic disaster.

UNANTICIPATED AND UNINTENDED EFFECTS OF HUMAN DECISIONS

Any time we make a decision, there may well be effects that we do not anticipate and do not intend. This is true for institutions as well. Both government rule-making and market deal-making create unanticipated effects that decision makers should in many cases take responsibility for. Those who look to reduce the scope of government sometimes make reference to "the law of unintended effects," as if this phenomenon applies only to government action.[8] Of course, it does indeed apply to government action and thus elected officials must actively search for otherwise unforeseen effects. But such critics of government rarely apply the same standard to markets, even though its unanticipated effects often threaten justice and sustainability. This double standard exonerates harmful market decisions while indicting similarly detrimental decisions by governments.

In part, there is good reason for this asymmetry. On the one hand, markets work as well as they do because of the function of prices, and prices have the effects they do because they change the economic incentives of people far afield from the original causes of the change in price. Most of the time, this is a beneficial process. For example, a hard freeze in the coffee-growing regions of Colombia has an immediate effect on the price of coffee around the world, in anticipation of a shortage in future months. These higher prices lead people to conserve coffee now so that current supplies will stretch longer into the future and help compensate for shortages later. But similar dynamics lead to seriously damaging effects when market decisions are taken with little regard for the damage, whether that entails endangered species, environmental racism, communities eviscerated by plant relocation, or wealthy elites kept in power in developing nations by sweetheart deals with multinational firms. Markets are human creations and must be subject to moral assessment.

As we saw in the discussion of the four problems of economic life in Chapter 12, markets generate both good and bad unanticipated and unintended effects. The good is why markets deserve the conditional moral endorsement reviewed in the previous chapter. The bad effects, however, particularly damage done to the well-being of the poor and the environment, stand as indictments of markets and often require communal action through government. As we have seen, the beneficiaries of markets—both consumers and investors—are complicit in the harms that markets cause to distant others.

TAXATION

Since government—from local to national—is created to fulfill many needed functions, it should collect taxes to pay for them. Understanding democratic government as self-government is essential to understanding taxation. It is how we pay for the things we decide to do through government, many of which assist in solving the four problems every economy must face, as we saw in Chapter 12. Concerning taxation, there are two basic questions: how much money to raise from the citizenry, and how to raise it. Each entails important moral considerations.

First, the "how much" question requires an assessment of what things government should do. As we have seen, Catholic social thought has articulated a wide range of functions for government and thus endorses raising sufficient taxes to fund those activities. Some neoconservative Catholics have argued against government expenditures to help the poor on the grounds that this does not fulfill Christ's call to love the neighbor. Robert Sirico has said that "if we are required to do anything by law, and thereby forced by public authority to undertake some action, we comply because we must. That we go along with the demand is no great credit to our sense of humanitarianism or charity. The impulse here is essentially one of fear."[9] Given the mandate for Christians to care for the poor, Sirico's position entails our relying on private charity alone to take care of this. However, the major religious charities in the nation, such as Catholic Charities USA and Lutheran Social Services, receive more than 50 percent of their annual revenue from government, which counts on these organizations to provide services.[10] It is a rightwing illusion to think that government could simply withdraw from relief of the poor and that private sources would take care of the problem.

But at the more basic level, this view misunderstands the Catholic view of the relation of law and morality reviewed in the previous chapter in two ways. First, recognizing government as our self-governance, we together opt to tax ourselves in the interest of solidarity to assist the poor and unemployed.

This is an exercise of communal responsibility and distributive justice. On the other hand, it is a serious error to believe that the presence of a law constraining our actions means we can no longer act out of virtue simply because we'd be penalized for not doing so. This would lead to the nonsensical view that a male employer might conscientiously avoid the sexual harassment of female employees up until the day the state legislature makes such harassment illegal—at which point the employer begins avoiding this abuse only out of fear of punishment.

We are all called to personal service and charitable contributions to assist the needy, but we also, in part, fulfill our duty to care for others through the taxes we pay. If it weren't for government assistance, many needy people would receive no help. We saw in Chapter 14 how Pope Pius XI criticized the wealthy who were "content to abandon to charity alone the full care of relieving the unfortunate, as though it were the task of charity to make amends for the open violation of justice, a violation not merely tolerated, but sanctioned at times by legislators."[11]

A further argument often heard against raising taxes on the wealthy is that this will "kill jobs" because the wealthy would have otherwise invested the funds. There are two problems with this line of thinking. First, this would imply we'd be better off as a nation if only the middle class were taxed and the wealthy paid no taxes—so the wealthy would have even more money to invest. This clearly cannot be good public policy. The second is that it misunderstands how investors think. They don't invest because they are rich but rather because they want to become richer. It's not the wealth of the investor but the profitability of the investment that makes the difference. The wealthy may not like paying higher taxes, but consider the effects caused when those government revenues are spent, particularly during an economic slump when the wealthy shift many of their resources into gold or other "safe" investments that create few jobs. Whether caused by direct expenditures—on food by the poor, medical services for the sick, or road repair by state highway departments—or by the secondary expenditures—by the workers hired in other industries as a result of the higher incomes caused by the direct expenditures—the increased demand for goods and services will lead the wealthy to invest in job-creating businesses.

In addition to the "how much" question, there is the "how" question, which raises fairness as a fundamental moral question. What is the fairest way to raise taxes from a population of citizens of unequal income and wealth? Historically, there have been three general proposals for how taxes might be raised: equal amounts, equal proportion, or equal sacrifice. With either equal amount or equal proportion, it's clear that a family making, say, $20,000 per year will suffer real deprivation while a family making $200,000 a year could pay the same amount or the same proportion of their income with very little effect on consumption in their daily lives. Thus the third proposal—equal sacrifice—is the answer that corresponds to our requirement in social justice to contribute to the community. The rich should pay a higher proportion of their income in taxes than the middle class or the poor.

In the United States, the richest 1 percent of the population earn about 23 percent of the nation's income while the richest 20 percent earn more than 80 percent of all income.[12] Because they earn so much of the income, the wealthy also pay the vast majority of the income taxes collected. This leads some opponents of taxation to argue that it's unfair that any group should have to pay so much of the total income tax. However, nonpartisan studies have found that the richest 20 percent of the nation paid somewhere in the range of 16 percent of their income in federal income taxes, a number far below the highest tax rate in the nation but a number actually achieved because of the many tax breaks written into the law.

While prudence allows for a range of acceptable Christian views on taxation, the two fundamental principles of the Christian tradition most important here are the social justice obligation to contribute to the common good and the duty of the prosperous to share their surplus to ensure that the needs of all are met. It is deceitful for elected legislators to argue that government "cannot afford" to assist the poor or the elderly or unemployed; the taxation decisions of those very legislators determine what the government can afford to do, and those decisions should aim to raise revenues sufficient to fulfill government's proper role.

STRUCTURING INTERNATIONAL ECONOMIC RELATIONSHIPS

As we have seen, Catholic social thought has taken as a fundamental presumption that institutions should serve persons, a responsibility that falls to both society and government, typically within each nation. As the globalization of the economy has increased over the last century, international economic relationships have become far more important. Yet there is no world government to which people around the planet could turn to make the decisions concerning the rules structuring markets that are necessary if international markets are to receive the conditional moral approval that Christian ethics could provide. As a consequence, popes over the last century have explicitly identified the need for stronger global governance in economic life.

While the United Nations might seem ideally suited for this to happen, its structures are cumbersome and prudence indicates that at this point very few people would have sufficient confidence in its democratic capacities to trust it to become a true world government. In this situation, Pope John XXIII recommended "a true world political authority," and Pope Benedict XVI called for a reform of the UN and of the institutions of international finance "so that the concept of the family of nations can acquire real teeth."[13] This will need to arise from the mutual agreement of sovereign nations. Both justice and environmental sustainability will remain threatened until more effective international governance is developed. As with all levels of oversight, international governance structures must be strong enough to do what is needed but not so strong that they violate the rights or well-being of persons. The spontaneously democratic organizations of civil society or the integrity of creation are critical for achieving this balance.

GOVERNMENT'S ROLE IN THE KNOWLEDGE ECONOMY

Economists have long argued that one of the proper functions of government arises when markets do not achieve efficiency on their own. One important example of this concerns activities that have "positive externalities," meaning that a market transaction generates benefits for third parties—for which the participants to the exchange are not compensated. Examples here range from the corporate headquarters, whose beautifully manicured lawn improves the aesthetics of nearby homes, to a family's decision to inoculate their children against various diseases, which not only protects them but also makes it less likely that other children in school will get sick. In such situations, economics predicts that people will typically purchase an amount of goods based on the return to themselves (and not based on the benefits to others). Yet, the society as a whole would be better off if the overall demand for these products increased in light of the extra benefits that accrue to third parties. This is one of the fundamental reasons why governments subsidize both the inoculation of children and public education (since a well-educated populace has positive effects beyond the lives of the individuals involved).

Now that advanced economies are more dependent than ever before upon knowledge in the production of wealth, including intellectual property, there are newly important roles for government arising from the positive externalities that knowledge acquisition generates. It will be helpful to consider two cases. The first is the more ordinary subsidy to education, including K through 12, college education, and preschool programs like Head Start for the poor.

Society as a whole benefits when such unusually important social institutions are publically funded (whether the schools themselves are public or private).

However, a second area requires attention because of a change in market conditions in recent decades. Vernon Ruttan has pointed out that much of the most fundamental scientific research behind technological change in the past two hundred years has been financed by the U.S. government and other governments around the world.[14] Consider the precision machining of tools (developed by the U.S. government to create more accurate rifles during the Civil War), airplane technology (developed by the military from propeller-driven aircraft to jet fighters) and other fundamental technologies like electricity, computing, and the Internet. In all these cases government, often out of military interest, invested great amounts of money to develop new technologies that then became available to private firms for uses far beyond their intended military applications. Private firms typically find it unprofitable to invest in such fundamental research; it may in the end not result in a marketable product, or even if does, so many years may have elapsed by the time a marketable product is available that other investments are more attractive. Thus it is especially unfortunate that at a time when fewer firms are judging it economically profitable to invest in fundamental scientific research, governments are also cutting back on it.

As Albino Barrera has argued, knowledge is different from most other "goods" of economic life.[15] The cost of providing one more person with a car or a pair of shoes (what economists call the "marginal" cost) is quite high. But this is not true about knowledge. Once created, a new idea can assist one or a million people, limited only by the cost of spreading the idea, now made much cheaper by Internet access. Because of the positive externalities of new knowledge, there is a strong economic argument for government to play an active role in both the creation and dissemination of knowledge. Economic success in "the knowledge economy" requires workers with greater education and skills, and as a result the moral argument for such policies is rooted in the teaching on the importance of employment, itself rooted in God's intention to meet the needs of all.

Living love and justice

Prophecy without contempt

The prophetic tradition is an essential part of the Jewish and Christian heritage, and represents an important corrective to the abuses of the powerful. Prophecy is always uncomfortable for the prosperous since prophets are at times quite forceful in their ringing condemnation of injustice in the nation. Perhaps the most important twentieth-century example of this in the United States was Martin Luther King Jr., who fearlessly named the many faces of injustice embedded in the racism of American society. Mahatma Gandhi played a similarly prophetic role in India.

However, many today who launch criticisms of what they see as injustice and immorality in society do so with a kind of arrogance and contempt for those they attack, which is foreign to the tradition of authentic biblical prophecy. This corrupts relationships within society and undermines its subjectivity. The prophet, in the midst of harsh criticism of evildoers, is to remain a humble spirit, one aware of his or her shortcomings and sinfulness. Too much of contemporary criticism of the evils of life is embodied in a contemptuous dismissal of opponents. A true Christian prophecy stands against injustice but does so with deep respect for each person, embodying an awareness of human dignity rooted in our creation in the image of God.

The Poor as the Test of Morality of Any Economic System

We have seen throughout this history of Christian views of economic life that the gold standard for economic morality is the treatment of the poor in any society. The moral goal of economic life must not be measured by the heights of prosperity achieved by the prosperous, but rather by the depths of the poverty of the poor. Far more is involved in a full life than economic wealth, but having economic resources—both income and wealth—is critical for ordinary family life.[16]

This is the source of the principle of God's preferential option for the poor. Christians know that God loves all equally, but to repeat Jack Jezreel's example from Chapter 3, just as a parent will focus on the child whose life is in danger, so God focuses on the plight of the poor. We are challenged by our God's example and are called to share that preference. It is critical that we structure public life to be hospitable to those whose needs are unmet, embodying love not simply in personal relations but in the institutional framework for our life together.

Conclusion

In this chapter, we have reviewed ten issues critical for establishing the proper relationship among society, government, and market.

1. The relation of society, government, and market

   • Society as more basic than government or market

- Democratic government as self-government
- Religious participation in public debate in pluralistic societies

2. Political decisions about economic structures

- Market-structured spontaneity
- Unanticipated and unintended effects of human decision
- Taxation
- Structuring international economic relationships
- Government's role in the knowledge economy

3. Living love and justice

- Prophecy without contempt
- The poor as the test of morality of any economic system

Over these past three chapters we have examined from the perspective of Catholic social thought the framework and implications of the Christian tradition for economic life today, and what this means for the proper relationship among society, government, and market. Together, these various elements of a contemporary Christian economic ethic are indeed "symphonic," producing an integrity characterized by counterpoint—to achieve, as its best, a harmonic result. Hopefully, Protestant Christians may find that much of what has been presented here is helpful and faithful to the biblical witness as understood within the theology and tradition of their own denomination.

Notes

1. Benedict XVI, *Caritas in veritate* 39.

2. John Paul II, *Centesimus annus* 13, 36.

3. Peter Rogness, "Government Is Not the Enemy," *Minneapolis StarTribune*, February 6, 2011. http://www.startribune.com/opinion/115328634.html. Accessed January 31, 2012.

4. For example, Novak argues that "all institutions become sentinels and guardians against the excesses of other institutions." Thus rather than arguing that Christian ethics should, of its own theological resources and economists' empirical assessments, be cautious in proposing restrictions on markets, Novak implies that the economic system acts as a check on the moral-cultural system. Catholic social thought has always respected the empirical reality of economic life—which as we saw in the case of usury can lead to a change in moral teaching when the empirical reality changes. Nonetheless, structuring the economy must be a decision arising out of the moral, cultural, and political life, and not the facticity of the economic sphere. See Michael Novak, "Challenge to Benedict's Vision: Sin," in *The Moral Dynamics of Economic Life: An Extension and Critique of Caritas in veritate*, ed. Daniel K. Finn (New York: Oxford University Press, 2012).

5. Michael Novak, *The Spirit of Democratic Capitalism* (New York: Simon & Schuster, 1982), 351.

6. Friedrich A. Hayek, "The Use of Knowledge in Society," in *Individualism and Economic Order* (Chicago: University of Chicago Press, 1948), 77–91.

7. Joseph Alois Schumpeter, *Capitalism, Socialism, and Democracy* (New York: Harper & Bros., 1947).

8. For a fuller description of this debate, see Albert O. Hirschman, *The Rhetoric of Reaction: Perversity, Futility, Jeopardy* (Cambridge, MA: Belknap Press of Harvard University Press, 1991).

9. Robert Sirico, "Mandated Giving Doesn't Come from the Heart," *Religion and Liberty* 17, no. 4 (Fall 2007).

10. In 2009, Catholic Charities USA received 67 percent of its total revenues from government (http://www.catholiccharitiesusa.org/NetCommunity/Document.Doc?id=1924). Lutheran Social Services of Minnesota, for example, reports that in 2010 government funds represented 80 percent of total revenues (http://www.lssmn.org/About-Us/Financials/).

11. Pope Pius XI, *Quadragesimo anno* 4.

12. For details, see Economic Policy Institute, http://www.stateofworkingamerica.org/. Accessed January 16, 2012.

13. Benedict XVI, *Caritas in veritate* 67. For a series of recommendations on reforming the financial system, see Observatoire de la Finance, "For Finance That Serves the Common Good: Manifesto of the Observatoire de la Finance," available from 24 rue de l'Athénée, 1206 Genève, Suisse. See also the Pontifical Council for Justice and Peace, "Toward Reforming the International Financial and Monetary Systems in the Context of Global Public Authority," Pontifical Council for Justice and Peace (Rome: Libreria Editrice Vaticana, 2011).

14. Vernon W. Ruttan, *Is War Necessary for Economic Growth? Military Procurement and Technology Development* (New York: Oxford University Press, 2006).

15. Albino Barrera, O.P., *Modern Catholic Social Documents and Political Economy* (Washington, DC: Georgetown University Press, 2001), 205–17.

16. See James Bailey's argument for the importance of wealth in a path from poverty to self-sufficiency, *Rethinking Poverty: Income, Assets, and the Catholic Social Justice Tradition* (Notre Dame: University of Notre Dame Press, 2010).

21

Conclusion

The aim of this volume has been to investigate the history of Christian views of economic life so the reader can better decide how to apply the insights of that tradition to economic life in the twenty-first century. An unfortunate by-product of this focus is that many other important moral problems remain in the background, from biomedical and life issues, to sexism, racism, immigration, and many others.[1] The solutions considered have most frequently been those available to public policy and personal economic lifestyle, largely ignoring the important role of regular prayer and an active worship life in the church, both essential for adequate engagement with contemporary issues.

HOW THE CHRISTIAN TRADITION MEANS

Most of the chapters have focused on what that tradition has actually said. However, just as important has been attention to the question of method: How is it that one should decide what this tradition means today? As we phrased it in Chapter 2, we need to be attentive to *how* a living tradition means.

There are two methods that will not work. The first assumes that the teachings of the Christian tradition on economic life have been unchanging and exist independent of the contexts in which they were first articulated. We have seen ample evidence that several teachings have changed, particularly concerning usury, slavery, and the use of the language of human rights.

But a second method is also unacceptable: that Christians today can simply reject any part of the tradition they find inconvenient. Such an approach grants the tradition little or no authority in our lives and thinks of tradition simply as a museum where we might choose a piece to put on display—or not—depending on whether our preexisting view of what should occur in life is helped or hindered by it. All too many scholars writing on Christian economic ethics engage in this sort of irresponsible "cherry picking" of the tradition.

An authentic Christian understanding of our faith is rooted in the same living tradition that our spiritual ancestors in every age inherited, a tradition that both constrained and enriched their lives. They in turn passed on an even richer tradition to their spiritual descendants in later centuries. Instead of those two counterproductive methods, we must rely on the insights depicted by the hermeneutic circle we first saw in Chapter 2.

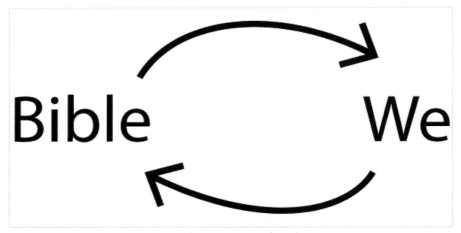

Figure 4. Today's Situation for Christians

We recognize that these ancient texts have authority over us and yet simultaneously we understand that we must be critical in our appropriation of them. We are thus left with difficult but promising conversations: between Christians today and the economic world in which we live and between Christians today and their predecessor communities throughout earlier history. Consider, for example, the plight of the poor today. We recognize that we should not attempt to replicate the Israelite Jubilee and return land to its original owners after forty-nine years, something that makes no sense in an industrialized world. At the same time, however, we are not simply free to ignore the ancient Hebrew concern to establish structures designed to ensure that everyone has the means to participate in normal economic life, in order to guarantee that the needs of all are met. The ancient gleaning laws no longer apply, and even the notion of a just wage is difficult to implement in a globalized market economy. But the implication of the tradition is that we must find structures that will accomplish the same underlying goals, both to assist those whom the market leaves with unmet needs and to enable each able-bodied worker to support self and family through gainful employment.

To complicate matters further, we must be attentive to the difference between morality and causality. While a moral critique might seem to require some particular change in economic life today, Christians must exhibit what theologian Paul Tillich once called "humility before the fact." That is, although science bears its own biases that we must be attentive to, it provides insights into how the world operates, both the natural and the social worlds. We must be attentive to what science has to say about the likely results of our attempt to make the world a better place.

The conclusions articulated in these final chapters will be contested by some commentators: on the left, for being too supportive of the market system, and, on the right, for being too skeptical of it. Some of those on the right will likely repeat the well-worn accusation that such conclusions are nothing more than "the politics of the Democratic Party," or are simply "warmed-over New Deal ideas." Yet such charges are flabby substitutes for an argument. They typify the "culture wars" attitude of many commentators on ethics and economics and most frequently arise from those with a long history of "cherry picking" from the Christian tradition only those themes supportive of a preexisting neoconservative bias in favor of markets while blatantly ignoring other equally fundamental themes that critique capitalist markets. A real argument—much needed—would return to the sources of Christian views of economic life, attending to their complexity and internal development.[2]

WHAT CAN ONE PERSON DO?

Closely related to the analysis of the market has to be the question of what each of us as individuals might do within it, since each must still work out a life, earning an adequate income. Important here, of course, are choices we make about our patterns of consumption, in recognition that all of us together generate the effect that markets have—many good and some quite negative for people and the environment. Similarly, what and how we consume is part of what shapes who we are. Thus we are reminded of Jesus' teaching on simplicity in talking of the lilies of the field in Chapter 4, and Clement of Alexandria's discussion of self-sufficiency in Chapter 5. David Cloutier has written insightfully about the importance of recovering the long-neglected idea of luxury in an effort to critique the overspending that characterizes so much of contemporary life.[3] As we saw in Chapter 18, faith requires the proper ordering of goods.

In addition, our tradition's stress on our obligations toward the poor requires each of us to engage in some form of service to others, often simply "helping out" in an institution serving those whose needs are unmet, whether a soup kitchen, food shelf, a nursing home, or some other service to the needy. A small proportion of us may find full-time work in such service, but all are called to engage in some way, both in direct action and by the pattern of our consumption and investment decisions.

However, there is a problem if this is all that we do. One of the classic stories illustrating this problem tells of a town on a river populated by citizens who were highly ethical and spent a good proportion of their time helping people who were drowning in the river, pulling them out and giving them the help they needed to survive and thrive. This life of generous service went on year after year until someone stopped to ask why it was that there were so many people coming down the river in danger of losing their lives.

Action for justice entails hiking upstream to find out why people are ending up in the river and taking steps to stop the process that puts them in the water in the first place. A multitude of organizations are committed to such works of justice, transforming institutions of daily life that harm one group or another. Recalling the language of sociologists that we reviewed in Chapter 12, there are many people—for example, members of racial or ethnic minorities, citizens of poor nations—who enjoy fewer "enablements" than the prosperous do, and who face far more "restrictions," and who, in spite of their efforts, have been unable to meet their own needs. Action for justice can be understood as trying to reduce those restrictions and to provide more enablements. Practically speaking, that may be work by a local faith-based community organization to alter the character of neighborhoods in low-income parts of the city. Or it might be work of the Catholic Relief Services around the world in "capacity building" efforts, noted in Chapter 1, to help people like Sharmila Marandi become active agents able to support themselves and transform their nation toward greater justice.

No one of us can attend to all the responsibilities that we all together have in life. Each of us rolls up our sleeves in focusing the majority of our time on one or two problems. Nonetheless, it is quite important that we stay aware of a wider range of issues and be prepared periodically to help out as needed in other arenas beyond our primary commitments. Our willingness to show up at City Hall, a meeting at our workplace, or a corporation's shareholders meeting at a critical time can make a difference when there are already others who are organizing to push for a change required in justice. Being willing to write that letter or email to an elected official at a critical point in legislative deliberations or to a business being pressed toward more just policies by a consumer group is another form of our willingness to implement greater justice in the world.

THE IMPORTANCE OF BEING SELF-CRITICAL

One of the main lessons to be learned from this volume is that without careful work to overcome the distortions in our own view of life, we will continue to see life largely as our culture does and will be unable to understand its shortcomings or our own complicity in the way the ordinary institutions of daily life harm others. It is critically important that we recognize the limitations of our own perspective.

In addition, while moral arguments are absolutely critical in thinking through our daily lives, it is important for us to be quite cautious when our moral arguments legitimate our own advantages in life. It is possible that our arguments seem perfectly correct, but even in such cases we should be especially careful—even suspicious—since history has so often shown how the wealthy and powerful have had a "good" moral defense of their privilege. This is true of the tribal leaders in primitive culture, of Greek land owners in ancient Athens, of wealthy patricians in classic Rome, of medieval lords and ladies in the age of Aquinas, and of King Louis XIV's claim to a divine right in seventeenth-century France. It has been true of Adolf Hitler and drug kingpins and Cambodian radical Pol Pot. The lesson here is that it is very easy for each of us to buy into arguments that defend our own enablements in life. We need to be unusually self-critical of those arguments.

In addition, it is quite important for us to listen with an open heart to those who challenge our point of view. We should respond as best we can to criticism—even when it seems irresponsible—and to do so with charity, not cynicism. In fact, we should seek out personal contact with those who would challenge our point of view and we ought to read more broadly than most of us do, since most of us tend to read only those websites and editorials with which we already agree.

Finally, we should combine generous reading with critical judgment. It's been said that there are two ways to read a book. The first is to read until something doesn't make sense and from then on to keep track of all the mistakes that the author makes. The second method, far superior, is to read until we come up against something that doesn't make sense and at that point give the author the benefit of the doubt. We should presume that it *does* make sense to the author but that we have not yet come to understand the sense it makes. We then need to work to discover *how* it makes sense to the author. Later, of course, we must make a judgment as to whether we think the author is right or wrong, but making that judgment too early in the process usually prevents us from understanding the arguments the author is actually making.

The same applies, of course, in face-to-face conversation. One test for generous listening is to ask whether we can describe the other's position in a way that would lead the other to say "Yes, that *is* what I believe." Truly understanding the other's arguments is not sufficient to guarantee a fair and accurate judgment of them, but it is necessary.

FAITH, HOPE, AND LOVE

As has been noted many times in this volume, Augustine of Hippo pointed out sixteen centuries ago that we are people wanting to be happy but so often living lives that won't make us so. In the end, we Christians today must do what Christians in every age have done: rely on the fundamental theological virtues of faith, hope, and love.

Our faith is in God, the God of Abraham and Sarah, of Moses and Miriam, who brought people out of ignorance and slavery into a covenant relationship. It is faith in the God of Jesus Christ, who sent his only son, who in turn was willing to suffer humiliation, torture, and death in commitment to God and in love of humanity. This is faith in the spirit of God, in whom twenty centuries of Christian believers have, in spite of their own sinfulness, attempted to live out a responsible life of Christian commitment.

We Christians live lives of hope, hope for the future, both earthly and eternal. Christian hope is not an optimism that things will turn out better tomorrow than today, nor a calculation that if we do X today, Y is likely to happen tomorrow. Rather, the theological virtue of hope is a vision guided by God's promise, which ties together present and future. Christians face the horizon of a realized eschatology, where, anticipating an eternal destiny, we strive to live out God's reign—however imperfectly—even now.

We Christians are called to love God and to love our neighbors as ourselves. These are demanding expectations, particularly in a world where so many not only have trouble loving their enemies but even find it hard to respect those with whom they disagree. The love shown in the life of Jesus calls all of us his followers and entails an obligation to live as he lived, extending a loving hand to sinners, the poor, and marginalized. The task is daunting, but with the presence of the Holy Spirit, all is possible.

The tradition of Christian social thought is like well water deep down. Most Christians are largely ignorant of it. It sits in the depths of history, waiting to be drawn up into the light of awareness by people now thirsting for a more meaningful life. These insights have, century after century, been pulled up from the depths of the tradition by an act of faith in God's revelation in Jesus Christ, in the wrestling of the people of God with the perennial questions of economic morality in every age.

There remain great intellectual challenges today in uniting a Christian moral perspective with the various competing accounts of economic causality. Yet this process of relating the moral vision of the tradition with the best of science, done thoughtfully and well, holds out three important promises: quenching humanity's thirst for meaning, bringing into some measure of prosperity those uncounted multitudes who today live in degrading poverty, and preserving for future generations the natural world whose integrity we have been charged to protect.

In striving toward these goals, the resources of Christian tradition that can irrigate economic life are accessible but for most Christians lie out of sight, like well water deep down. Employing those insights, we would water our hopes for that true flourishing which God intends for each of us and for all humanity—both in this life, to the extent our finitude and sinfulness allow— and eternally.

Notes

1. And to complicate things more, these problems are often interwoven. Barbara Hilkert Andolsen, for example, examines the relation of racism and sexism in her *"Daughters of Jefferson, Daughters of Bootblacks": Racism and American Feminism* (Macon, GA: Mercer University Press, 1986).

2. Even the distinguished British economist P. T. Bauer demonstrates his ignorance of the tradition when he objects to the popes using the phrase "the earth belongs to all," since, he asserts, this "is bound to provoke envy." He adds that "the spirit of these [papal] documents is contrary to the most durable and best elements in the Catholic tradition. They are indeed even unchristian." P. T. Bauer, *Reality and Rhetoric: Studies in the Economics of Development* (Cambridge, MA: Harvard University Press, 1984), 84 and 88. Bauer seems unaware that the popes borrow the phrase from widespread use by the Fathers of the early church.

3. David Cloutier, "The Problem of Luxury in the Christian Life," *Journal of the Society of Christian Ethics*, forthcoming.

Bibliography

Alcántara, Fernando Fuente. "La Propiedad." In *Manual de Doctrina Social de la Iglesia*. Madrid: Biblioteca de Autores Christianos, Fundacion Pablo VI, 1993.

Andolsen, Barbara Hilkert. *"Daughters of Jefferson, Daughters of Bootblacks": Racism and American Feminism*. Macon, GA: Mercer University Press, 1986.

Archer, Margaret. *Being Human: The Problem of Agency*. Cambridge: Cambridge University Press, 2000.

———. *Structure, Agency and the Internal Conversation*. Cambridge: Cambridge University Press. 2003.

Aquinas, Thomas. *Summa Theologica*. Translated by Fathers of the English Dominican Province. New York: Benziger Brothers, 1995.

———. *The Political Ideas of St. Thomas Aquinas*, edited by Dino Bigongiari. New York: Hafner, 1974.

———. *On the Psalms*. Ancient Christian Writers 29. New York: Newman Press, 1960, 272.

Augustine of Hippo. *The City of God*, XIV, 4. New York: Modern Library, 1950.

Avila, Charles. *Ownership: Early Christian Teaching*. Maryknoll, NY: Orbis, 1983.

Bailey, James. *Rethinking Poverty: Income, Assets, and the Catholic Social Justice Tradition*. Notre Dame: University of Notre Dame Press, 2010.

Barceló, Sch.P., Eduardo Bonnín. *Estructuras de pecado y pecado social: Elementos para una síntesis teológica*. México, D.F.: Instituto Mexicano de Doctrina Social Cristiana, 2007.

Barrera, Albino. *Economic Compulsion and Christian Ethics*. New York: Cambridge University Press, 2005.

———. *Modern Catholic Social Documents and Political Economy*. Washington, DC: Georgetown University Press, 2001.

———. "Theological Foundations of the Market." In *The Moral Dynamics of Economic Life: An Extension and Critique of Caritas in Veritate*, edited by Daniel K. Finn. New York: Oxford University Press, 2012.

Barry, Colman James. *Worship and Work: Saint John's Abbey and University, 1856–1956*. Collegeville, MN: Saint John's Abbey, 1956.

Bauer, P. T. *Reality and Rhetoric: Studies in the Economics of Development.* Cambridge, MA: Harvard University Press, 1984.

Benne, Robert. *The Ethic of Democratic Capitalism: A Moral Reassessment.* Philadelphia: Fortress Press, 1981.

Benedict XVI. *Caritas in Veritate.* http://www.vatican.va/holy_father/benedict_xvi/encyclicals/documents/hf_ben-xvi_enc_20090629_caritas-in-veritate_en.html. Accessed May 9, 2012.

Berger, Peter, and Thomas Luckmann. *The Social Construction of Reality: A Treatise in the Sociology of Knowledge.* Garden City, NY: Doubleday, 1966.

Biéler, André. *Calvin's Economic and Social Thought* (1961), edited by Edward Dommen. Translated by James Greig. Geneva: World Alliance of Reformed Churches, World Council of Churches, 2005.

Biermans, Maarten. *Decency and the Market: The ILO's Decent Work Agenda as a Moral Market Boundary.* PhD dissertation: University of Amsterdam, 2012.

Blank, Rebecca M. "Viewing the Market through the Lens of Faith." In *Is the Market Moral? A Dialogue on Religion, Economics, and Justice*, edited by Rebecca M. Blank and William McGurn. Washington, DC: Brookings Institution, 2004.

Bloomquist, Karen L. "Engaging Economic Globalization as Churches." *Ecumenical Review* 53 (Oct. 2001): 493–500.

Bloomquist, Karen L., and John R. Stumme. *The Promise of Lutheran Ethics.* Minneapolis: Fortress Press, 1998.

Bosrock, Mary Murray. *Put Your Best Foot Forward.* St. Paul, MN: International Educational Systems, 1997.

———. *Asian Business: Customs & Manners.* New York: Meadowbrook, 2007.

Brennan, Geoffrey, and Anthony M. C. Waterman. "Christian Theology and Economics: Convergence and Clashes." In *Christian Theology and Market Economics*, edited by Ian R. Harper and Samuel Gregg. Cheltenham, UK: Edward Elgar, 2008.

Brubaker, Pamela, Rebecca Todd Peters, and Laura A. Stivers, eds. *Justice in a Global Economy: Strategies for Home, Community, and World.* Louisville: Westminster John Knox, 2006.

Bruni, Luigino, and Stefano Zamagni. *Civil Economy: Efficiency, Equity, Public Happiness.* Oxford: Oxford University Press, 2007.

Camenisch, Paul. "Gift and Gratitude in Ethics." *Journal of Religious Ethics* 9 (1981): 1–34.

Casey, Thomas G. "Ave Atque Vale." *America* 200 (June 8, 2009): 16–18.

Chesterton, G. K. *Tremendous Trifles*. Salt Lake City: The Project Gutenberg Literary Archive Foundation, 2005. www.gutenberg.org/files/8092/8092-h/8092-h.htm. Accessed January 29, 2012.

Childs, James M., Jr. *Greed: Economics and Ethics in Conflict*. Minneapolis: Fortress Press, 2000.

———. "Ethics and the Promise of God: Moral Authority and the Church's Witness." In *The Promise of Lutheran Ethics*, edited by Karen L. Bloomquist and John R. Stumme. Minneapolis, MN: Fortress Press, 1998.

Christiansen, S.J., Drew. "Commentary on *Pacem in terris*." In *Modern Catholic Social Teaching*, edited by Kenneth R. Himes. Washington, DC: Georgetown University Press, 2005.

———. "On Relative Equality: Catholic Egalitarianism after Vatican II," *Theological Studies* 45 (Dec. 1984): 651–75.

Churches Together in Britain and Ireland. *Prosperity with a Purpose*. London: Churches Together in Britain and Ireland, 2005.

Ciardi, John. *How Does a Poem Mean?* Boston: Riverside, 1959.

Clark, Meghan J. "Integrating Human Rights: Participation in John Paul II, Catholic Social Thought and Amartya Sen." *Political Theology* 8 (July 2007): 299–317.

Cliffe Leslie, Thomas Edward. *Essays in Political Economy*, 2nd edition (1888). New York: Augustus M. Kelley, 1969.

Cloutier, David. "The Problem of Luxury in the Christian Life." *Journal of the Society of Christian Ethics* 32, no. 1 (2012): 3–20.

Compendium of the Social Doctrine of the Church. Washington, DC: U.S. Conference of Catholic Bishops, 2004.

Constantelos, Demetrios J. "The Hellenic Background and Nature of Patristic Philanthropy in the Early Byzantine Era." In *Wealth and Poverty in the Early Church and Society*, edited by Susan R. Holman. Grand Rapids, MI: Baker Academic, 2008.

Cordell, Linda S., *Ancient Pueblo Peoples*. Washington, DC: Smithsonian Books, 1994.

Curran, Charles. *Catholic Social Teaching, 1891–Present: A Historical, Theological, and Ethical Analysis*. Washington, DC: Georgetown University Press, 2002.

Daly, Herman E. *Ecological Economics and Sustainable Development: Selected Essays of Herman Daly*. Northampton, MA: Edward Elgar, 2007.

Dandamayev, Muhammad A. "Old Testament Slavery." In *The Anchor Bible Dictionary*, edited by David Noel Freedman et al. New York: Doubleday, 1992.

Davis, John B. *Individuals and Identity in Economics.* New York: Cambridge University Press, 2011.

Donahue, S.J., John R. "Biblical Perspectives on Justice." In *The Faith That Does Justice: Examining the Christian Sources for Social Change,* edited by John C. Haughey. New York: Paulist, 1977.

Eliade, Mircea. *The Myth of the Eternal Return, or Cosmos and History.* Translated by Willard R. Trask. Princeton: Princeton University Press, 1974.

Epiphanius of Salamis. "The Panarion of Epiphanius of Salamis, Books II and II," translated by Frank Williams. *Nag Hammadi and Manichaean Studies* 36 (Leiden: E. J. Brill, 1994), 116.

Evangelical Lutheran Church in America. "Caring for Creation: Vision, Hope, Justice," August 28, 1993, Kansas City, MO. http://www.elca.org/What-We-Believe/Social-Issues/Social-Statements/Environment.aspx. Accessed January 16, 2012.

———. "Church in Society: A Lutheran Perspective," adopted at the second biennial Churchwide Assembly of the Evangelical Lutheran Church in America, August 28–September 4, 1991. http://www.elca.org/What-We-Believe/Social-Issues/Social-Statements/Church-in-Society.aspx. Accessed January 16, 2012.

———. "Economic Life: Sufficient, Sustainable Livelihood for All," adopted at the sixth Churchwide Assembly on August 20, 1999, in Denver, Colorado. http://www.elca.org/What-We-Believe/Social-Issues/Social-Statements/Economic-Life.aspx. Accessed January 16, 2012.

Feldstein, Martin, and Amy Taylor. "The Income Tax and Charitable Contributions." *Econometrica* 44 (Nov. 1976).

Finn, Daniel K. "Charity and Truth in Business: Profit, Gift and Social Capital." *Origins* 41, no. 10 (July 21, 2011): 149–54.

———. "Economic Order." *The New Dictionary of Catholic Social Thought,* edited by Judith A. Dwyer. Collegeville, MN: Liturgical, 1994.

———. *The Moral Ecology of Markets: Assessing Claims about Markets and Justice.* New York: Cambridge University Press, 2006.

———. "John Paul II and the Moral Ecology of Markets." *Theological Studies* 59, no. 4 (Dec. 1998): 662–79.

———. *The True Wealth of Nations: Catholic Social Thought and Economic Life,* edited by Daniel K. Finn. New York: Oxford University Press, 2010.

———. *The Moral Dynamics of Economic Life: An Extension and Critique of Caritas in Veritate,* edited by Daniel K. Finn. New York: Oxford University Press, 2012.

Fisher, Eugene, and Leon Klenicki, eds. *Spiritual Pilgrimage: Texts on Jews and Judaism, 1979–1995*, New York: Crossroad, 1995.

Foreman, Mary. *Praying with the Desert Mothers*. Collegeville, MN: Liturgical Press, 2005.

Fortin, Ernest. "Sacred and Inviolable: Rerum Novarum and Natural Rights." *Theological Studies* 53 (June 1992): 203–33.

Frank, Robert H., Ben S. Bernanke, and Louis D. Johnston. *Principles of Economics: Brief Edition.* New York: McGraw-Hill Irwin, 2009.

Frankena, William K. *Ethics*, 2nd edition. Englewood Cliffs, NJ: Prentice-Hall, 1973.

Franzén, Torkel. *Gödel's Theorem: An Incomplete Guide to Its Use and Abuse.* Wellesley, MA: A. K. Peters, 2005.

Friedman, Benjamin M. *The Moral Consequences of Economic Growth.* New York: Knopf, 2005.

Friedman, Milton. *Capitalism and Freedom.* Chicago: University of Chicago Press, 1962.

———. *Essays in Positive Economics.* Chicago: Chicago University Press, 1953.

Friesen, Steven J. "Injustice or God's Will? Early Christian Explanations of Poverty." In *Wealth and Poverty in the Early Church and Society*, edited by Susan R. Holman. Grand Rapids MI: Baker Academic, 2008.

Fry, Timothy, O.S.B., translator. *The Rule of St. Benedict*. Collegeville, MN: Liturgical, 1982.

General Conference of the Evangelical Alliance. Oral report of John Fea, "How Evangelicals Got to Today," *Catholics and Evangelicals for the Common Good.* Sept 30, 2011, Washington, DC.

General Convention. *Journal of the General Convention of the Episcopal Church.* Columbus, Resolution 2006-DO47. New York: General Convention, 2007.

———. *Journal of the General Convention of the Episcopal Church.* Denver, Resolution 2000-A002. New York: General Convention, 2001.

———. *Journal of the General Convention of the Episcopal Church.* Indianapolis, Resolution 1994-D070. New York: General Convention, 1995.

———. *Journal of the General Convention of the Episcopal Church.* Phoenix, Resolution 1991-D041. New York: General Convention, 1992.

Gilder, George. "Where Capitalism and Christianity Meet." In *Border Regions of Faith: An Anthology of Religion and Social Change*, edited by Kenneth Aman. Maryknoll, NY: Orbis, 1987.

Gold, Lorna. *New Financial Horizons: The Emergence of an Economy of Communion.* Hyde Park, NY: New City Press, 2010.

Goosen, Gideon. *Spacetime and Theology in Dialogue*. Milwaukee: Marquette University Press, 2008.

Gordon, B. *The Economic Problem in Biblical and Patristic Thought*. Leiden: E. J. Brill, 1989.

Gunnemann, Jon. "Capital, Spirit, and Common Wealth." In *The True Wealth of Nations: Catholic Social Thought and Economic Life*, edited by Daniel K. Finn. New York: Oxford University Press, 2010.

———. "Capitalism and Commutative Justice." *Annual of the Society of Christian Ethics* (1985): 101–22.

———. "Christian Ethics in a Capitalist Society." *Word and World* 5 (Winter 1985): 49–59.

———. "Human Rights and Modernity: The Truth of the Fiction of Individual Rights." *Journal of Religious Ethics* 16 (Spring 1988): 160–89.

Gutiérrez, Gustavo, and Richard Shaull. *Freedom and Salvation: A Political Problem*. Atlanta: Knox, 1977.

Harrill, J. Albert. "Paul and Slavery." In *Paul in the Greco-Roman World: A Handbook*, edited by J. Paul Sampley. Harrisburg, PA: Trinity Press International, 2003.

Hayek, Friedrich A. *Law, Legislation and Liberty*, vol. 2, *The Mirage of Social Justice*. Chicago: University of Chicago Press, 1976.

———. "The Use of Knowledge in Society." In *Individualism and Economic Order*. Chicago: University of Chicago Press, 1948.

Heaney, Seamus. "Out of This World." *District and Circle*. New York: Farrar, Straus & Giroux, 2006.

Heine, Joy, and Cynthia Brook, eds. *A Worker Justice Reader: Essential Writings on Religion and Labor*. Maryknoll, NY: Orbis Books, 2010.

Heyer, Kristin E. *Prophetic & Public: The Social Witness of U.S. Catholicism*. Washington, DC: Georgetown University Press, 2006.

Hicks, Douglas A., and Mark R. Valeri, eds. *Global Neighbors: Christian Faith and Moral Obligation in Today's Economy*. Grand Rapids, MI: Eerdmans, 2008.

Hicks, Douglas A. "Global Poverty and Bono's Celebrity Activism: An Analysis of Moral Imagination and Motivation." In *Global Neighbors: Christian Faith and Moral Obligation in Today's Economy,* edited by Douglas A. Hicks and Mark R. Valeri. Grand Rapids, MI: Eerdmans, 2008.

———. *Inequality and Christian Ethics*. Cambridge and New York: Cambridge University Press, 2000.

Himes, Kenneth R. "The New Social Encyclical's Communitarian Vision." *Origins* 21 (Aug. 1, 1991): 166–68.

Himes, Kenneth R., Lisa Sowle Cahill, Charles E. Curran, David Hollenbach, and Thomas Shannon, eds. *Modern Catholic Social Teaching.* Washington, DC: Georgetown University Press, 2005.

Himes, Michael J., and Kenneth R. Himes. *Fullness of Faith: The Public Significance of Theology.* New York: Paulist, 1993.

Hinkelammert, Franz. "The Economic Roots of Idolatry: Entrepreneurial Metaphysics." In *The Idols of Death and the God of Life*, edited by Pablo Richard. Maryknoll, NY: Orbis, 1983.

Hinze, Christine Firer. "Commentary on *Quadragesimo anno* (After Forty Years)." In *Modern Catholic Social Teaching*, edited by Kenneth R. Himes. Washington, DC: Georgetown University Press, 2005.

Hirschfeld, Mary. "From a Theological Frame to a Secular Frame: How Historical Context Shades Our Understanding of the Principles of Catholic Social Thought." In *The True Wealth of Nations: Catholic Social Thought and Economic Life*, edited by Daniel K. Finn. New York: Oxford University Press, 2010.

Hirschman, Albert O. *The Rhetoric of Reaction: Perversity, Futility, Jeopardy.* Cambridge, MA: Belknap Press of Harvard University Press, 1991.

Hobbes, Thomas. *Leviathan; or, The Matter, Forme and Power of A Common Wealth Ecclesiasticall and Civil* (1651), edited by Michael Joseph Oakeshott. Oxford: Blackwell, 1960.

Holland, Joe. *Modern Catholic Social Teaching: The Popes Confront the Industrial Age, 1740–1958.* New York: Paulist, 2003.

Hollenbach, David. *Justice, Peace, and Human Rights: American Catholic Social Ethics in a Pluralistic World.* New York: Crossroad, 1988.

———. *The Common Good and Christian Ethics.* New York: Cambridge University Press, 2002.

Holman, Susan R., ed. *Wealth and Poverty in the Early Church and Society.* Grand Rapids, MI: Baker Academic, 2008.

———. *The Hungry Are Dying: Beggars and Bishops in Roman Cappadocia.* Oxford: Oxford University Press, 2011.

Hoppe, Leslie J. "The Torah Responds to the Poor." *Bible Today* 32 (Sept. 1994): 277–82.

John Paul II. "Address to the Jewish Community." At the Great Synagogue in Rome, April 13, 1986. *Spiritual Pilgrimage: Texts on Jews and Judaism, 1979–1995*, edited by Eugene Fisher and Leon Klenicki. New York: Crossroad, 1995.

———. "La Evangelización de la Cultura." Address given to intellectuals scientists and artists in Quito, Ecuador, January 30, 1985. *Mensajes Sociales de Juan Pablo II en America Latina.* Santiago, Chile: Consejo Episcopal Latinoamericano, CELAM, 1986.

John Paul II. *Centesimus annus.* http://www.vatican.va/holy_father/ john_paul_ii/encyclicals/documents/hf_jp-ii_enc_01051991_centesimus- annus_en.html. Accessed May 10, 2012.

———. *Laborem exercens.* http://www.vatican.va/holy_father/john_paul_ii/ encyclicals/documents/hf_jp-ii_enc_14091981_laborem-exercens_en.html. Accessed May 10, 2012.

———. *Solicitudo rei socialis.* http://www.vatican.va/holy_father/john_paul_ii/ encyclicals/documents/hf_jp-ii_enc_30121987_sollicitudo-rei- socialis_en.html. Accessed May 10, 2012.

———. *Veritatis splendor,* http://www.vatican.va/holy_father/john_paul_ii/ encyclicals/documents/hf_jp-ii_enc_06081993_veritatis-splendor_en.html. Accessed May 10, 2012.

Kaveny, M. Cathleen. "Intrinsic Evil and Political Responsibility: Is the Concept of Intrinsic Evil Helpful to the Catholic Voter?" *America* 199 (Oct. 27, 2008): 15–19.

Khalily, M. A. Baqui, Mahmood Osman Imam, and Salahuddin Ahmed Khan, "Efficiency and Sustainability of Formal and Quasi-formal Microfinance Programmes—An Analysis of Grameen Bank and ASA." *The Bangladesh Development Studies* 26 (June–Sept. 2000): 103–46.

Korgen, Jeffry Odell. *Solidarity Will Transform the World: Stories of Hope from Catholic Relief Services.* Maryknoll, NY: Orbis, 2010.

Lewis, Oscar. "The Culture of Poverty." *Society* 35 (Jan./Feb. 1998): 7–9.

Lull, Timothy F., ed. *Martin Luther's Basic Theological Writings.* Minneapolis: Fortress Press, 1989.

Luther, Martin. *Luther Werke, Kritische Gesamtausgabe, Briefwechsel.* Weimar: Hermann Böhlaus Nachfolger, 1930.

Martin Luther, *Luther's Works,* edited by Jaroslav Pelikan. Philadelphia: Muhlenberg, 1962.

MacIntyre, Alasdair C. *After Virtue: A Study in Moral Theory.* Notre Dame: University of Notre Dame Press, 1984.

Matin, Imran. "Rapid Credit Deepening and a Few Concerns: A Study of a Branch of Grameen Bank." *The Bangladesh Development Studies* 26 (June–Sept. 2000): 147–72.

Mattison, William C. *Introducing Moral Theology: True Happiness and the Virtues.* Grand Rapids, MI: Brazos, 2008.

Matz, Brian. "Alleviating Economic Injustice in Gregory of Nyssa's *Contra Usurarios.*" *Studia Patristica* 45 (2010): 549–53.

Maxwell, John. *Slavery and the Catholic Church.* Chichester and London: Barry Rose, 1975.

Meeks, M. Douglas. *God the Economist: The Doctrine of God and Political Economy.* Minneapolis: Fortress Press, 1989.

Mich, Marvin. "Commentary on Mater et magistra." In *Modern Catholic Social Teaching,* edited by Kenneth R. Himes. Washington, DC: Georgetown University Press, 2005.

Michel, O.S.B., Virgil. *Christian Social Reconstruction.* Milwaukee: Bruce, 1937.

Miller, Vincent J. *Consuming Religion: Christian Faith and Practice in a Consumer Culture.* New York: Continuum, 2004.

———. "Santorum and the Lobotomization of Subsidiarity." *America* (January 8, 2012), http://americamagazine.org/blog/entry.cfm?blog_id=2&entry_id=4852.

Misner, Paul. *Social Catholicism in Europe: From the Onset of Industrialization to the First World War.* New York: Crossroad, 1991.

Molina, S.J., Luis de. *La teoría del justo precio* (1593–1609). Madrid: Editora Nacional, 1981.

Mueller, Franz. *The Church and the Social Question.* Washington DC: American Enterprise Institute, 1984

National Association of Evangelicals. "For the Health of the Nation: An Evangelical Call to Civic Responsibility," 2004. http://www.nae.net/images/content/For_The_Health_Of_The_Nation.pdf. Accessed January 6, 2012.

Naughton, Michael. "The Business Enterprise." In *The Moral Dynamics of Economic Life: An Extension and Critique of Caritas in veritate,* edited by Daniel K. Finn. New York: Oxford University Press, 2012.

———. "The Corporation as a Community of Work: Understanding the Firm within the Catholic Social Tradition." *Ave Maria Law Journal* (Winter 2006): 33–75.

Niebuhr, Reinhold. *Moral Man and Immoral Society: A Study in Ethics and Politics (1932).* New York: Scribner, 1995.

Noonan, John Thomas. *A Church That Can and Cannot Change: The Development of Catholic Moral Teaching.* Notre Dame: University of Notre Dame Press, 2005.

Norris, Kathleen. *Amazing Grace.* New York: Riverhead Books, 1998.

Norton, Michael I. and Dan Ariely. "Building a Better America—One Wealth Quintile at a Time." http://www.people.hbs.edu/mnorton/norton%20ariely%20in%20press.pdf. Accessed January 31, 2013.

Novak, Michael. "Challenge to Benedict's Vision: Sin." In *The Moral Dynamics of Economic Life: An Extension and Critique of Caritas in veritate*, edited by Daniel K. Finn. New York: Oxford University Press, 2012.

———. *The Spirit of Democratic Capitalism*. New York: Simon & Schuster, 1982.

———. "The Rights and Wrongs of 'Economic Rights': A Debate Continued." *This World* (Spring 1987): 43–52.

Nozick, Robert. *Anarchy, State & Utopia*. Oxford: Blackwell, 1974.

Ogletree, Thomas W. *The World Calling: The Church's Witness in Politics and Society*. Louisville: Westminster John Knox, 2004.

O'Keefe, O.S.B., Mark. *What Are They Saying About Social Sin?* Mahwah, NJ: Paulist, 1990.

Panzer, Joel S. *The Popes and Slavery*. New York: Alba House, 1996.

Paulhus, Normand Joseph. *The Theological and Political Ideals of the Fribourg Union*. Scholarship at Boston College, 1983.

———. "Uses and Misuses of the Term 'Social Justice' in the Roman Catholic Tradition." *Journal of Religious Ethics* 15 (Fall 1987): 261–82.

Peifer, O.S.B., Claude J. *Monastic Spirituality*. New York: Sheed & Ward, 1966.

Pelikan, Jaroslav. *The Emergence of the Catholic Tradition: 100–600*. Vol. 1, *The Christian Tradition: A History of the Development of Doctrine*. Chicago: University of Chicago Press, 1973.

Peters, Rebecca Todd. "Economic Justice Requires More Than the Kindness of Strangers." In *Global Neighbors: Christian Faith and Moral Obligation in Today's Economy*, edited by Douglas A. Hicks and Mark R. Valeri. Grand Rapids, MI: Eerdmans, 2008.

Phan, Peter. *Social Thought*, vol. 20 of *Message of the Fathers of the Church*. Wilmington, DE: Glazier, 1984.

Pieper, Josef. *Justice*. London: Faber & Faber, 1957.

Pinckaers, O.P., Servais. *The Sources of Christian Ethics*. Washington, DC: Catholic University of America Press, 1995.

Pius XI. *Divini redemptoris*. http://www.vatican.va/holy_father/pius_xi/encyclicals/documents/hf_p-xi_enc_19031937_divini-redemptoris_en.html. Accessed May 10, 2012.

———. *Quadragesimo anno*. http://www.vatican.va/holy_father/pius_xi/encyclicals/documents/hf_p-xi_enc_19310515_quadragesimo-anno_en.html. Accessed May 10, 2012.

Pontifical Biblical Commission. *The Bible and Morality: Biblical Roots of Christian Conduct*. Libreria Editrice Vaticana, 2008.

Pontifical Council for Justice and Peace. *Social and Ethical Aspects of Economics: A Colloquium in the Vatican.* Vatican City: Pontifical Council for Justice and Peace, 1992.

———. "Toward Reforming the International Financial and Monetary Systems in the Context of Global Public Authority." Rome: Libreria Editrice Vaticana, 2011.

Presbyterian Church. "Hope for a Global Future: Toward Just and Sustainable Human Development," approved by the 208th General Assembly (1996) Presbyterian Church (USA). http://oga.pcusa.org/publications/hope-for-a-global-future.pdf. Accessed January 15, 2012.

Raines, John C. "Conscience and the Economic Crisis." *The Christian Century* 99 (Sept. 1, 1982): 883–87.

Raines, John C., and Donna C. Day-Lower. *Modern Work and Human Meaning*. Philadelphia: Westminster, 1986.

Rawls, John. *A Theory of Justice*. Cambridge, MA: Harvard University Press, 1971.

Robb, Carol. *Equal Value: An Ethical Approach to Economics and Sex*. Boston, MA: Beacon, 1995.

Rogness, Peter. "Government Is Not the Enemy." *Minneapolis StarTribune*, February 6, 2011.

Rousseau, Jean-Jacques. *The Social Contract*. New York: Hafner, 1947.

Roth, M. "Employee Participation, Corporate Governance and the Firm: A Transatlantic View Focused on Occupational Pensions and Co-determination," *European Business Organization Law Review* 11 (March 1, 2010): 51–85.

Ruttan, Vernon W. *Is War Necessary for Economic Growth? Military Procurement and Technology Development*. New York: Oxford University Press, 2006.

Schaefer, Jame. *Theological Foundations for Environmental Ethics: Reconstructing Patristic and Medieval Concepts*. Washington, DC: Georgetown University Press, 2009.

Schuck, Michael Joseph. *That They Be One: The Social Teaching of the Papal Encyclicals, 1740–1989*. Washington, DC: Georgetown University Press, 1991.

Schumpeter, Joseph Alois. *Capitalism, Socialism, and Democracy*. New York: Harper & Bros., 1947.

Schüssler Fiorenza, Elisabeth. *In Memory of Her: A Feminist Theological Reconstruction of Christian Origins.* New York: Crossroad, 1983.

Sen, Amartya. *The Idea of Justice.* Cambridge, MA: Harvard University Press, 2009.

———. *Commodities and Capabilities.* Oxford: Oxford University Press, 1985.

Shannon, Thomas. "Commentary on Rerum Novarum." In *Modern Catholic Social Teaching,* edited by Kenneth Himes. Washington, DC: Georgetown University Press, 2005.

Shriver Jr., Donald W., and E. Richard Knox. "Taxation in the History of Protestant Ethics." *Journal of Religious Ethics* 13 (Spring 1985): 134–60.

Sirico, Robert. "Mandated Giving Doesn't Come from the Heart." *Religion and Liberty* 17 (Fall 2007).

Shuchman, Abraham. *Codetermination: Labor's Middle Way in Germany.* Washington, DC: Public Affairs Press, 1957.

Smith, Adam. *An Inquiry into the Nature and Causes of the Wealth of Nations.* London: W. Strahan and T. Cadell, 1776. Reprint edited by Edwin Cannan. New York: Modern Library, 1937.

Smith, Christian. *What Is a Person?: Rethinking Humanity, Social Life, and the Moral Good from the Person Up.* Chicago: University of Chicago Press, 2010.

Sniegocki, John. *Catholic Social Teaching and Economic Globalization: The Quest for Alternatives.* Milwaukee: Marquette University Press, 2009.

Stern, Sasha. *Time and Process in Ancient Judaism.* Oxford: The Littman Library of Jewish Civilization, 2003.

Stivers, Laura A. "Holding Corporations Accountable." In *Justice in a Global Economy,* edited by Pamela Brubaker, Rebecca Todd Peters, and Laura A. Stivers. Louisville: Westminster John Knox, 2006.

Stivers, Robert L. "Tax Ethics: An Oxymoron?" In *Reformed Faith and Economics,* edited by Robert L. Stivers. Lanham, MD: University Press of America, 1989.

Swan, Laura, *The Forgotten Desert Mothers.* New York/Mahwah, NJ: Paulist Press, 2001.

Taylor, Charles. *A Secular Age.* Cambridge, MA: Harvard University Press, 2007.

Taylor, Charles R., Thomas A. Claus, and Susan L. Claus. *On-Premise Signs as Storefront Marketing Devices Systems.* Washington, DC: U.S. Small Business Administration, 2005: 9.12–9.13.

Tierney, Brian. *The Idea of Natural Rights.* Atlanta: Scholars, 1997.

Tolmie, D. Francois, ed. *Philemon in Perspective: Interpreting a Pauline Letter.* New York: De Gruyter, 2010.

Torvend, Samuel. *Luther and the Hungry Poor.* Minneapolis: Fortress Press, 2008.

Troeltsch, Ernst. *The Social Teaching of the Christian Churches.* Chicago: University of Chicago Press, 1976.

United Methodist Church. "Affirming Democratic Principles in an Emerging Global Economy," resolution adopted by the Twenty-first General Synod, 1997, Columbus, Ohio. http://www.ucc.org/synod/resolutions/AFFIRMING-DEMOCRATIC-PRINCIPLES-IN-AN-EMERGING-GLOBAL-ECONOMY.pdf. Accessed January 15, 2012.

———. "Faithful Response: Calling for a More Just, Human Direction for Economic Globalization," July 2003. http://www.ucc.org/justice/advocacy_resources/pdfs/economic-justice/callingfor-a-more-just-humane-direction-for-economic-globa.pdf. Accessed January 16, 2012.

———. "Social Principles, Preamble," *The Book of Discipline of the United Methodist Church,* 2008. http://www.umc.org/site/apps/nlnet/content.aspx?c=lwL4KnN1LtH&b=5065913&ct=6467355. Accessed January 16, 2012.

United Nations. "Universal Declaration of Human Rights. http://www.un.org/en/documents/udhr/. Accessed February 1, 2012.

U.S. Conference of Catholic Bishops. *Economic Justice for All: Pastoral Letter on Catholic Social Teaching and the U.S. Economy.* Washington, DC: National Conference of Catholic Bishops, 1986.

Walzer, Michael. *Spheres of Justice.* New York: Basic Books, 1983.

Wartenberg, Thomas. *The Forms of Power: From Domination to Transformation.* Philadelphia: Temple University Press, 1990.

Weidig, Dörte. "Three Myths about SME Finance," World Bank Publications. http://microfinance.cgap.org/2011/12/13/three-myths-about-sme-finance/. Accessed December 22, 2011.

Wesley, John. *The Works of John Wesley,* edited by Albert C. Outler. Nashville: Abingdon, 1984.

Wessels, Francois G. "The Letter to Philemon in the Context of Slavery in Early Christianity." In *Philemon in Perspective: Interpreting a Pauline Letter,* edited by Francois D. Tolmie. New York: De Gruyter, 2010.

White, James Boyd. "Economics and Law: Two Cultures in Tension." *Tennessee Law Review* 54 (Winter 1987): 192–98.

Wicks, Jared. *Luther and His Spiritual Legacy.* Theology and Life Series 7. Wilmington, DE: Glazier, 1983.

Wilber, Charles K. "Ethics and Social Economics: Association for Social Economics Presidential Address." *Review of Social Economy* 62 (Dec. 2004): 425–39.

Wilkinson, Richard G., and Kate Pickett. *The Spirit Level: Why Greater Equality Makes Societies Stronger*. New York: Bloomsbury, 2010.

Wogaman, J. Philip. *Economics and Ethics: A Christian Inquiry*. Philadelphia: Fortress Press, 1986.

———. *The Great Economic Debate: An Ethical Analysis*. Philadelphia: Westminster, 1977.

Worland, Stephen Theodore. *Scholasticism and Welfare Economics*. Notre Dame: University of Notre Dame Press, 1967.

World Alliance of Reformed Churches. "Letter from Accra," Introduction to "The Accra Confession: Covenanting for Justice in the Economy and the Earth." August 12, 2004. http://warc.jalb.de/warcajsp/side.jsp?news_id=157&navi=1. Accessed January 14, 2012.

Yuengert, Andrew M. "Rational Choice with Passion: Virtue in a Model of Rational Addiction." *Review of Social Economy* 59 (March 2001): 1–21.

———. "What Is Sustainable Prosperity for All." In *The True Wealth of Nations: Catholic Social Thought and Economic Life*, edited by Daniel K. Finn. New York: Oxford University Press, 2010.

Yunus, Muhammad, and Alan Jolis. *Banker to the Poor: Micro-lending and the Battle Against World Poverty*. New York: Public Affairs, 2003.

Index

Additional Praise for *Christian Economic Ethics*

"This is a much-needed and welcome addition to the scholarship on Christian economic ethics. Daniel K. Finn not only surveys the literature, but he also analyzes and applies it well to contemporary problems. His down-to-earth explanation of the tradition and its development makes this work accessible to a wide audience and ideal for course adoption."

Albino Barrera, O.P.
Providence College

"In this valuable book, Catholic ethicist and economist Daniel K. Finn provides readers with a learned, comprehensive, and remarkably lucid survey of the terrain of Christian economic ethics, its sources, history, interdisciplinary dimensions, and implications for contemporary practice. Intellectually rich yet accessible to a broad audience, the text incisively charts fundamental questions and basepoints marking Christian ethics and contemporary economics, drawing them into mutually-illuminating, critical dialogue."

Christine Firer Hinze
Fordham University

"*Christian Economic Ethics* by Daniel Finn provides a much-needed compendium of Christian thought about economic life across the ages. In addition to gathering the relevant texts, Finn offers a lucid discussion of the difficulties of bridging theological thought and modern economic understandings. The result is an invaluable introduction to theological reflection on economics."

Mary Hirschfeld
Villanova University

"It is hard to imagine a more ambitious topic or a more satisfying treatment of it. With consistently reliable and insightful analysis, this volume tackles the central issues that arise when Christians in any era address matters of economic justice. Taking seriously both theological texts and social scientific data, Finn offers a lively and informative survey that connects traditions of the past with realities of the present as well as directions for the future."

Thomas Massaro, S.J.
Jesuit School of Theology, Santa Clara University